EXCHANGE RATES, TRADE, AND THE U.S. ECONOMY

EXCHANGE RATES, TRADE, AND THE U.S. ECONOMY

Editors
SVEN W. ARNDT
RICHARD J. SWEENEY
THOMAS D. WILLETT

A Joint Publication of
American Enterprise Institute/Ballinger

BALLINGER PUBLISHING COMPANY
Cambridge, Massachusetts
A Subsidiary of Harper & Row, Publishers, Inc.

International Standard Book Number: 0-88410-948-8

Library of Congress Catalog Card Number: 84-28328

Printed in the United States of America

Library of Congress Cataloging in Publication Data

Main entry under title:

Exchange rates, trade, and the U.S. economy.

  Includes bibliographies and index.
  1. Foreign exchange problem – Addresses, essays, lectures.
2. Foreign exchange problem – United States – Addresses,
essays, lectures. I. Arndt, Sven W. II. Sweeney, Richard J.
III. Willett, Thomas D.
HG3851.E94 1985   332.4'560973   84-28328
ISBN 0-88410-948-8

CONTENTS

v

LIST OF FIGURES

LIST OF TABLES

xiiLIST OF TABLES

PREFACE

This volume, a joint project of the American Enterprise Institute for Public Policy Research and The Claremont Center for Economic Policy Studies, was conceived while the editors were associated with the Office of International Monetary Research of the U.S. Treasury. It was planned as a complement to the jointly sponsored Treasury–American Enterprise Institute Conference on exchange rate flexibility, the proceedings of which have been published in Jacob Dreyer, Gottfried Haberler, and Thomas D. Willett, eds., *Exchange-Rate Flexibility* (Washington, D.C.: American Enterprise Institute, 1978). The rapid speed of research developments and changing international monetary issues prompted delay of completion of the volume while a second generation of studies was completed after Professors Sweeney and Willett had moved to Claremont. All of the contributors were associated with the editors either as staff or consultants of the Office of International Monetary Research at the Treasury or as colleagues or graduate students at Claremont. In preparing this volume we have accumulated debts to far too many colleagues and staff at the American Enterprise Institute, Claremont, and the Treasury to thank individually here. However, we should like particularly to express our gratitude to Marc Bemer, D. B. Christenson, Massoud Darbandi, and Lori Harnack for their superb assistance in preparing the final version of the manuscript.

INTRODUCTION

We have now had over a decade of experience with the widespread usage of flexible exchange rates among the major industrial countries. While there is still considerable controversy over what this experience has shown, several major points are clear. One is that contrary to the fears of many critics, flexible exchange rates can form the basis for a viable international monetary system and need not lead to a breakdown of international cooperation and the crippling of world trade such as occurred during the 1930s. By the same token, however, the adoption of flexible rates has not proven to be a panacea for the problems that plagued the system of adjustable pegged rates that was established at Bretton Woods at the end of World War II.

Floating rates have displayed large fluctuations, and charges of over- and under-valued currencies have not ceased with the unpegging of exchange rates. Nor have concerns with international economic interdependence and the coordination of national monetary and fiscal policies been substantially diminished. While the switch from pegged to flexible exchange rates has had an important influence on the nature and relative quantitative significance of various channels of international economic interdependence, it does not allow countries to safely ignore the impacts of international developments on the domestic economy nor of domestic economic developments on other countries and the operation of the international system as a whole.

Even for a country as large and relatively self-sufficient as the United States, for example, many observers have expressed considerable concern about the size of our trade deficit in the early 1980s and its possible effects in depressing the domestic economy and stimulating protectionist pressures. On the positive side, the strength of the dollar over this period has been one of the major reasons for the decline in inflation. And, of course, developments in U.S. macroeconomic policies and the state of the economy continue to be a major focus of attention by our trading partners.

There are, perhaps, two major reasons why the change in our international monetary system has not changed the fundamental nature of international monetary relationships and debate as much as many (both advocates and critics) anticipated. First, as is now becoming increasingly but still far from universally recognized, the behavior of international financial flows and the exchange rate pressures that they generate are to a substantial degree a reflection of underlying economic and financial conditions, rather than an independent or autonomous influence. Thus, for example, studies of the magnitude of transactions costs in the foreign exchange market have concluded that what is important is not so much whether one has pegged or flexible exchange rates, but whether one is looking at tranquil or turbulent periods. And we have examples of both types of periods under both pegged and flexible rates. While international developments and the structure of the international monetary system can have important feedback effects on domestic economic and financial policies, these effects are typically not as dominant as advocates of various proposals for international monetary reform frequently assume. Changes in the international monetary system can be important—hence our interest in preparing this volume—but such changes will seldom, if ever, provide a quick fix for domestic economic disorders.

Second, under both pegged and flexible exchange rates, the central issue in evaluating the effects of the exchange-rate regime concerns judgments about the relationships between current and equilibrium exchange rates. At one extreme are the floating rate enthusiasts who assume that government pegging of exchange rates typically leads to the development of serious misalignments and disequilibrium that can be minimized simply by letting the private market work. Advocates of pegged rates, on the other hand, have frequently based their analysis on the assumption that the pegged rate is an approximately equilibrium one, while left to itself the private market will be inherently unstable, with destabilizing speculative bandwagon effects tending to alternatively push currencies up too high and down too low. Hence, their assumption that floating rates will provide an independent or autonomous source of uncertainty and instability.

The extent to which analysts are concerned about the strength of the dollar and the policies they prescribe will usually depend largely on their views of the causes of the strength of the dollar. For example, beliefs about whether the strong dollar of the 1980s and the weak dollar of the 1970s primarily reflected underlying economic and financial conditions and policies, or whether the dollar has been pushed up and down to disequilibrium levels by destabilizing speculative forces, are likely to have a major influence on one's view about the desirability of heavy official intervention in the foreign exchange market. Whether one is looking at the effects of exchange-rate behavior on international trade, on inflation, or on other important economic variables, the evaluation will usually depend on the cause of the exchange-rate behavior. In particular, are rates at equilibrium or disequilibrium levels?

For this reason, the first and longest section of this volume looks at what we have learned about exchange-rate determination and what we can say about the alleged tendency of floating rates to display excessive volatility or prolonged periods of over- or under-valuation. Part II considers the effects of flexible rates on international trade, while Part III looks at macroeconomic linkages under flexible exchange rates and the influence of international developments on the U.S. macro economy.

We shall not attempt a detailed summary of the contents of the volume in this introduction. Each major part of the volume begins with one or two broad survey papers that outline the major questions involved and summarize the broad conclusions of the major relevant theoretical and empirical research findings to date. These papers are designed to be accessible to those who are not technical experts in the field, and should convey to the interested reader an appreciation of the current state of the art in terms of both policy debate and the major results of technical analysis. (We hope and believe that experts in the field will also find these survey and perspective pieces of interest.) The remaining papers in each part are generally more technical and are aimed primarily at filling major theoretical and empirical gaps in our knowledge. We hope that this organization will make the volume useful to a broad range of readers, from those interested in a quick update on the current state of analysis in this area to those with major research or operational policy interests in one or more of the areas covered.

Part I deals with the recent theoretical analysis and empirical research on the causes of exchange rate fluctuations. The overview papers trace the development of important "new" theoretical paradigms of the past decade for viewing exchange rate behavior, the monetary approach and the more general asset approaches. These approaches stress particularly the importance of monetary conditions, international capital flows and expectations in the determination of exchange rates. Unfortunately, subsequent theoretical and empirical research presented here and elsewhere casts strong doubt on the empirical validity of the monetary approach, the most popular simple explanation of the causes of exchange rate variability.

Rising interest rates may be associated with either rising or falling exchange rates depending on the causes of the interest rate change. Likewise, while changes in relative money supplies and Purchasing Power Parity calculations do have a good deal of explanatory power for exchange rate developments over the long run, their predictive power in the short run is much more limited. Even over the long run, real factors can have important influences on equilibrium exchange rates.

We also find that the popular explanations of exchange rate volatility due to exchange rate overshooting caused either by destabilizing speculation or capital movements in response to interest rate changes appear to have only limited empirical applicability. To explain most of the observed exchange rate volatility we must look at other causes including expectations of both real and monetary developments. In many respects our conclusions about short-run exchange rate behavior is primarily negative, in the sense that we can explain why short run exchange rate analysis and prediction is much more difficult than implied by many popular views. Understanding these complexities is itself an important accomplishment, and should at least make us wary of the basis for many popular suggestions to promote exchange rate stability through interest rate manipulation or heavy official intervention in the foreign exchange market. Likewise, the available evidence strongly suggests that while the restoration of stability in underlying monetary and fiscal policies is not an entirely sufficient condition for exchange rate stability, it is certainly a necessary condition.

Part I also investigates the extent to which exchange rate behavior is "efficient" in the sense used in the finance literature, i.e., that the relative prices of currencies continuously embody all information that is economically available. As with a number of earlier studies, the empirical results are mixed. There does seem to be evidence of inefficiency across a number of exchange markets. One piece of evidence is that some mechanical buy-and-sell rules tend on average to outperform the market. However, we conjecture that a substantial part of this observed inefficiency is likely due to official intervention designed to halt or slow down exchange rate movements rather than to major deficiencies in the behavior of private speculation.

Parts II and III deal with the issues of whether the ups and downs of the dollar in the 1970s seriously damaged U.S. trade and investment, and whether they contributed significantly to the problems of domestic inflation and unemployment in the U.S. and world economy. One of the major points emphasized in these sections is the danger of looking at exchange rate changes in isolation. It is shown that the effects of exchange rate variations on both inflation and resource allocation will often depend crucially on the causes of variations. In analyzing the effects of exchange rate variability, particular attention is paid to clarifying the many ways in which exchange rate variability can increase the cost of international transactions and influence resource allocation, and in emphasizing that the alternatives to exchange rate flexibility will themselves often impose costs on those engaging in international activities. Analyses in this area have frequently suffered from considering too narrow a range of effects and from implicitly contrasting the costs of exchange rate variations with an ideal world where stable equilibrium rates are maintained at zero cost. In general, the studies in Part II suggest that flexible exchange rates have not placed as strong a burden on international trade as many had anticipated. They also survey recent developments in economic and financial analysis which may provide more efficient strategies for international risk management by looking at the extent to which exchange risk may be diversified away.

The studies concerned with inflation and macroeconomic stability in Part III show that flexible exchange rates do not eliminate all major channels of monetary and macroeconomic interdependence. They likewise show that in particular circumstances, the behavior of flexible exchange rates can create negative feedback effects on macroeconomies such as are emphasized in discussions of the so-called vicious circle of inflation and exchange rate depreciation. They stress that there are times when international coordination of monetary, fiscal, and exchange rate policies, if it could be effectively implemented, would improve global economic stability. These studies also show, however, that the likely magnitude of negative feedback, as well as the strengths of monetary and macroeconomic interdependence, are often greatly exaggerated in policy discussions. It does appear, however, that the strength of the dollar in the early 1980s did make an important contribution to the speed with which inflation was slowed in the United States.

The concluding paper in the volume considers the influence of the large U.S. budget deficits on the strength of the dollar and the consequent effects on international trade and on the U.S. and foreign macro economies. It highlights the differences in the types of exchange rate models that have been used to analyze the effects of the deficit and argues that while it is fairly safe to conclude that the budget deficits have been a major (although not the only) cause of the strong dollar, we have very little basis to offer confident predictions about how long the smooth international financing of such large budget deficits could be continued. Thus, over and above domestic considerations there are strong international reasons to bring the budget deficit under control in order to reduce the distortions in our international trade accounts caused by the international financing of the deficit and to reduce the possibility that such financing would be abruptly diminished in the midst of an international financial crisis. While real shocks and other considerations imply that the pursuit of stable domestic macroeconomic policies may not be a sufficient condition for avoiding exchange rate instability, there can be little question that this is a necessary condition.

EXCHANGE RATE BEHAVIOR

1 MODERN EXCHANGE RATE ANALYSIS

Thomas D. Willett

Exchange rate analysis has been a major growth industry over the past decade. The pressure of events—the growing recognition of the importance of international economic interdependence and the switch from pegged to flexible exchange rates for many countries—coincided with major changes in the theoretical paradigms used to analyze exchange rate issues. As is discussed in Chapter 2, the traditional emphasis on the central role of trade flows in the balance of payments and exchange rate determination as analyzed by the elasticities and Keynesian income approaches has given way to emphasis on the roles of international financial flows, expectations, and monetary conditions as highlighted in the new monetary and asset market approaches to exchange rate analysis.[1]

As is probably inevitable, these new approaches turned out to be not quite as new in many respects as some of their most enthusiastic supporters implied. Just as much of the older analysis had tended to underemphasize the role of capital flows and monetary conditions, the first generation of the new literature tended to neglect the continuing importance of the real side of international exchange.[2] Prodded in considerable part by the increased emphasis on empirical research, a second generation of analysis is well under way that combines the major insights of the older and newer approaches. We can still analyze the balance of payments in terms of the effects of economic fundamentals on the demand and supply of foreign exchange but must recognize that the foreign exchange market is like other forward-looking financial markets.

Changes in expectations about future developments in the economic fundamentals can have immediate impacts on exchange rates. Thus, for example, the current exchange rate changes are influenced not so much by whether the trade

3

balance is in surplus or deficit, but by whether the latest reported trade balance was larger or smaller than was expected. Recognition of this point has the important implication that large rapid movements in exchange rates are not necessarily evidence that the foreign exchange market is operating poorly. The economic fundamentals can shift and have shifted rapidly in many instances. Even when the current fundamentals themselves change only slowly, reasonable expectations about future developments in the fundamentals may show considerable variability. For example, fluctuations in the dollar are at times responses to the changing level of U.S. interest rates, which in turn may be caused by changes in the legislative outlook for scaling down the magnitude of the projected future U.S. budget deficits.

The behavior of forward and subsequent spot exchange rates suggests that much of our observed exchange rate movements under floating has been due to unanticipated developments. Given this major importance of news in explaining exchange rate fluctuations, it is not surprising that empirical attempts to model the short-term behavior of exchange rates have not tended to yield robust results. While some critics have pointed to the failures of empirical exchange-rate models to provide high levels of short-term explanatory power as evidence of market irrationality and the importance of destabilizing speculation, these results are, in fact, also quite consistent with the behavior of fully efficient foreign exchange markets that are being consistently bombarded with news from an unstable underlying environment.[3]

Another implication of modern exchange rate analysis is that there can be a very broad zone of disagreement among well-informed experts about their best estimates of what equilibrium levels of exchange rates should be. It is now widely recognized that, ceteris paribus, equilibrium exchange rates should be expected to change in line with differences in natural inflation rates. Thus, for many purposes analysis should focus on real rather than nominal exchange rates. However, real factors may cause sizable changes in long-run equilibrium real exchange rates. In such instances, the traditional elasticities analysis remains relevant. Furthermore, in the short-run, even monetary developments may have real effects which influence short-term equilibrium exchange rates.

Despite the considerable amount of empirical research that has been undertaken in recent years, there is still uncertainty about the precise magnitudes of the demand and supply elasticities of exports and imports for different countries. Thus, for example (as is illustrated in the appendix to this paper), a net shift of $5 billion a year in OPEC's investment allocation toward or away from the dollar could plausibly cause a change in the equilibrium exchange rate between the dollar and the German D-mark of anywhere from 3.5 to 22 percent, depending on whether the "true" export and import elasticities were on the higher or lower end of the range of econometric estimates and on whether the counterpart to the change in dollar holdings was concentrated on the mark or spread out over a number of currencies. Add to this uncertainties about the other key parameters in the structural determinant of the exchange rate and differences in expectations about future economic developments and the zone over which it becomes difficult to say that a currency is clearly over- or undervalued becomes wide indeed.

PRICES, INTEREST RATES, AND EXCHANGE RATES

While the prevalence of short-run deviations from purchasing power parity (PPP) has become widely recognized, it is still a common view that PPP calculations can give a reasonable guide to equilibrium exchange rates over the medium term. PPP calculations will be a good guide for such purposes, however, only for very small, highly open economies where the proportion of the economy not subject to competitive pressures from internationally traded goods and services is quite small or where the dominant disturbances are monetary shocks.[4] The popularity of medium term PPP assumptions has been due in considerable part to recognition that, in the short-run, changes in monetary policy can have real effects giving rise to the possibility of temporary exchange rate overshooting even if speculation in the foreign exchange market is efficient.

One of the most interesting developments in recent exchange rate analysis is the demonstration by Rudiger Dornbusch [1976] that in an open-economy Keynesian model with rational expectations and high capital mobility in the foreign exchange market, changes in monetary policy can cause the exchange rate to overshoot its medium-term equilibrium level. Thus, exchange rate overshooting need not be caused by destabilizing speculation. It can occur in speculatively efficient markets. The basic idea is that when changes in monetary policy cause short-term changes in real interest rates, then to equalize the incentives to move funds from one country to another the currency of a low interest rate country must be expected to depreciate and that of a high interest rate country to appreciate. Thus, if monetary expansion causes a temporary interest rate decline, the foreign value of the currency must fall below its medium-term equilibrium level so that there will be an expected appreciation gain from holding assets in that currency to offset the lower rate of interest. Likewise, tight money would cause the short-term equilibrium rate to appreciate above its medium-term equilibrium level. Thus, this type of model predicts that there will be short-run deviations from purchasing power parity but that such deviations will be self-reversing, thus maintaining purchasing power parity as a guideline for equilibrium exchange rates over the medium term. However, as is indicated by the following empirical studies by Pigott and Sweeney, despite some favorable initial indications, more systematic empirical testing shows that these models do not fit the data well. Differences in rates of inflation are probably the best single variable predictor of long-term trends in exchange rates, but deviations from particular PPP calculations (which themselves may vary considerably depending on the price measures and weighting schemes used) are not good predictors of future short-term exchange rate movements.

Nor do simple rules of thumb about interest rate-exchange rate relationships hold up well. According to a very common explanation, interest rate increases cause dollar appreciation and interest rate declines cause depreciation. This is based on traditional Keynesian reasoning. The new monetary approach models predict just the opposite relationship. High nominal interest rates are expected to be associated with a weakening of the dollar. As shown in Chapter 3, neither view turns out to predict well over substantial periods of time. One of the major practical contributions of the second generation synthesis of exchange rate analysis is that we should not expect strong systematic relationships between endogenous variables such as interest rates, trade balances, and exchange rates. The relationships over a particular period will depend crucially on the underlying causes of the movements in these variables.

Statements that trade surpluses should be associated with a strong currency and trade deficits with a weak currency assume that shifts in trade balances are the predominant autonomous developments. On the other hand, where shifts in capital flows are the major initial development we would find just the opposite relationship. Large capital inflows would cause the currency to appreciate and the trade balance to worsen. Similarly, if the cause of an increase in interest rates is a tightening of monetary policy, we would expect the currency to appreciate. On the other hand, if the interest rate rise is due to a worsening of inflationary expectations we would expect the currency to weaken in the foreign exchange market. Both types of causes of interest rate changes have been sufficiently important so that neither scenario provides accurate predictions over an extended period of time.

The need for deeper analysis applies as well to the effects of exchange rate movements. As is emphasized in Parts II and III of this volume, the effects of exchange rate fluctuations will often depend crucially on their causes. Where exchange rate volatility is caused by destabilizing speculation, such fluctuations can be appropriately deemed an independent cause of instability, and official intervention that reduces such fluctuations will reduce distortions and lead to more efficient resource allocation. On the other hand, where exchange rate movements reflect changes in underlying economic conditions, official attempts to suppress such movements may generate distortions and reduce the efficiency of resource allocation. Similarly, the effects of exchange rate changes on inflation-unemployment relations may vary tremendously depending on the cause of the change and expectations about policy responses.

SPECULATION, MARKET EFFICIENCY, AND OFFICIAL INTERVENTION

The fact that it is difficult to estimate equilibrium exchange rates with confidence within a narrow range and that large rapid changes in exchange rates are not by themselves clear evidence of market inefficiency does not imply that foreign exchange markets are fully efficient so that we can safely assume that whatever rate the market sets is an equilibrium rate. While it is difficult to devise any one single type of empirical test to evaluate unambiguously the efficiency of foreign exchange markets, the substantial amount of research that is discussed in this volume and the new empirical results presented by Sweeney do combine to suggest some important conclusions about how foreign exchange markets behave. The evidence does not offer much support for either of the popular extremes of views about the speculative behavior of exchange rates.

Exchange rate movements have not been dominated by the animal spirits or irrational whims of the Gnomes of Zurich as many critics still allege. It is true that swings in the degree of optimism or pessimism with which the market views the prospects of different currencies often contain subjective elements that deny rigorous quantification. However, as was indicated above, given the important role that expectations do and should play in exchange rate formation in efficient markets and the range of uncertainty about the empirical strength of various key relationships, it is not surprising that subjective judgments about how events will turn out or what the future courses of important policies will be will have an important influence on exchange rates. It is understandable that government officials would often be inclined to call irrational market expectations that do not conform to official projections. The inaccuracy of forward rates in predicting future spot rates clearly shows that the market is not always right ex post in its expectations, but systematic biases in the market's expectations appear relatively small when compared with the rather consistent optimistic biases of official projections.

Official views of appropriate exchange rates have frequently turned out to be substantially wide of the mark. There is enough evidence of official intervention by major industrial countries that was stabilizing to make a strategy of "betting against the central bank" far from risk free, but for a number of currencies the expected value of such a strategy may well be positive.[5]

The strongest enthusiasts of market efficiency can take little more comfort in the results of empirical research on flexible rates than can those who see strong official management of inherently unstable markets as the road to international monetary stability. In many of the efficient market models that have been popular in the economic and finance literature in recent years there is no scope for official intervention. The market will always make the best possible ex ante forecasts, and exchange rates will always be at equilibrium levels. Furthermore, because of the high degree of substitution among different types of assets, the private market would offset the effects of any unsterilized official intervention in the foreign exchange market so that official intervention could affect exchange rates only if it led to changes in monetary policy or market expectations. This is another of the theorems about the irrelevance of various government actions in the face of a farsighted efficient private market that have become so popular in recent years.

While this efficient market literature points to important truths about the limited scope for official intervention and the need to consider the important similarities between the foreign exchange markets and other financial markets, the various statistical tests for market efficiency do not typically show the positive results when applied to the performance of the foreign exchange markets (spot or forward) that they have for the major domestic U.S. financial markets. (See Chapters 6 and 11.)

A likely explanation is that, despite their large volume, the foreign exchange markets tend to be thinner than the major U.S. financial markets. On this view, "excessive" exchange rate volatility and more misalignments have been due more to an insufficiency of stabilizing private speculation than to actively destabilizing speculation. Thin markets characterized by insufficient stabilizing speculation do not appear to have been as persistent a problem and as major a cause of exchange rate volatility as some have conjectured.[6] Rather than being a normal state of affairs, thin markets seem to characterize particular periods of great instability and uncertainty. In thin markets, the weight of imbalances in current transactions can push exchange rates beyond the range most market participants believe to be justified by the fundamentals. However, because of limitations on the availability of funds for speculation and concerns about possible losses in a situation dominated by great uncertainty, market participants may believe that the exchange rate is much more likely to move in one direction than the other, without being able or willing to commit more funds to take advantage of this expected profit opportunity. In such circumstances the foreign exchange markets may appear disorderly, and official intervention may be able to exert an important stabilizing influence on exchange rates.

This may have been the case, for example, with the dollar at the bottom of its plunge in the late 1970s. A substantial decline in the dollar was clearly called for by changes in the economic fundamentals. There is some evidence that most participants in the market felt that the rate had fallen too far, yet lack of confidence in President Carter's economic policies and other uncertainties kept them from pushing the rate back up.[7] The speed with which a modest rebound of the dollar was engineered by announcements of a major change in monetary policy combined with a limited amount of official intervention is consistent with this interpretation. (At this level of analysis it is also, of course, consistent with the efficient market hypothesis that the changes in the rate were just rational market responses to changing expectations about economic policy).

However, such examples are not all that common and are at least equally matched by episodes of countries attempting to maintain their exchange rates at levels substantially different from market expectations. In such contexts, the industrial country governments have shown that they can usually successfully defend their currencies from "speculative attack" in the very short run, but when the horizon is lengthened from daily or weekly to a monthly or yearly time frame, the more typical outcome is that such official attempts at improving exchange rate stability are failures, both in the sense that they are forced by cumulating market pressures to abandon their efforts and in the sense that it became increasingly evident over time that the levels of the exchange rate that the government was seeking to maintain were not compatible with equilibrium.

In summary, the research completed to date does not support extreme efficient market hypotheses based on infinitely elastic speculative and asset substitution schedules; still less does it give comfort to views that heavier official management of exchange rates can promote more stable exchange rates in the absence of more stable underlying conditions and economic policies.

Efforts to develop time invariant estimates of the effectiveness of official intervention appear subject to major difficulties.[8] We should not expect a general answer to this question. A better approach would be to focus directly on studying the types of conditions under which official intervention may be effective and desirable and how well these conditions can be identified.

IS THE DOLLAR OVERVALUED?
DEFINITIONS AND ANALYSIS

This leaves the question of dollar overvaluation. Normally, terms such as over- or undervaluation imply disequilibrium. The classic case of disequilibrium prices are those that are not market clearing. From this perspective, official intervention to prop up a currency would cause overvaluation, and intervention to hold down a currency that was rising would cause undervaluation. With markets clearing and governments abstaining from intervention, we may still speak of over- or undervaluation in the sense that the current exchange rate may be viewed as temporary in relation to its trend. There could be two types of explanations for such a situation. One is that private speculation is not behaving in a stabilizing manner. Due to speculative inefficiencies such as destabilizing bandwagon effects or an insufficiency of stabilizing speculation, the current market clearing rate may not be the short-term equilibrium rate.

It is also possible to have expected movements in the exchange rate relative to its trend where markets are speculatively efficient. For example, it is well-known that the elasticities of demand and supply for many commodities are much lower in the short run than the long. Thus, where storage is very costly or there are insufficient initial stocks, a change in underlying conditions may cause greater changes in the short-term equilibrium price than in the medium-term equilibrium price. Storage costs and the like may keep profit maximizing speculation from fully eliminating expected changes in price. The seasonal factor in the room rate at resort hotels is an example. With free market exchange rates, the analog to storage costs for speculators is interest differentials. As was discussed above, temporary interest differentials caused by variations in monetary policy can cause short-term exchange rate overshooting so that the expected profits or losses from the new expected exchange rate path would compensate for the interest rate differential.

Exchange rate overshooting and short-term over- or undervaluation of a currency can occur in both speculatively efficient and inefficient markets. The welfare economics of the two types of cases differs substantially, however.[9] Where exchange rate overshooting is due to clearly identified speculative inefficiencies, offsetting official intervention would promote equilibrium rather than disequilibrium and would increase rather than reduce the efficiency of resource allocation. The case for official intervention to offset exchange rate overshooting in speculatively efficient markets is not so clear-cut, however. While it is possible to argue that such overshooting may generate policy relevant external effects on inflation–unemployment relationships and resource allocations that present a case for official intervention as a second-best policy, the analysis of this issue is still in its infancy. The first-best solution to concerns about exchange rate volatility from this source would be the adoption of greater stability in monetary and fiscal policies.

A fourth concept of over- or undervaluation is explicitly normative. The value of a currency is too high or too low relative to that needed to achieve some particular policy objective such as reducing inflation, stimulating economic growth, or promoting a stronger trade balance. Unfortunately, statements alleging over- or undervaluation quite frequently fail to indicate what concept is being used.

The dollar appreciated substantially in real as well as nominal terms in the early 1980s. Few would argue that the tightening of U.S. monetary policy and the increased confidence in the U.S. political and economic outlook relative to Europe should cause a substantial rise in the value of the dollar. But did the dollar become substantially overvalued as has been so frequently charged? It seems doubtful that much of the strengthening of the dollar came from foreign efforts to hold down currencies.

Likewise, arguments that the initial rise of the dollar contained a substantial element of overshooting in response to the tightening of monetary policy in the United States have not been borne out. The rapid rise of the dollar was not followed immediately by the weakening implied by efficient market overshooting models. While this might be explained by arguments that later developments have kept the dollar from falling, the initial pattern of forward exchange rates does not suggest that the market expected a sizable depreciation of the dollar over the short term. Nor does there appear to be strong evidence that the strength of the dollar in 1981–83 was due to destabilizing or insufficiently stabilizing private speculation. However, as is discussed in Chapters 2 and 18, the high long-term interest rates in the U.S. due in part to the huge current and projected future U.S. fiscal deficits appear to be one of the major causes of the strength of the dollar. Given this underlying budget situation and other factors generating large capital flows to the United States, the strength of the dollar in the early and mid-1980s does not seem unreasonable in a short-term market equilibrium sense.

A good case can nevertheless be made that the dollar became much too strong in a normative sense. Real exchange rate appreciation acts like a tax on exports and a subsidy to imports, thus reducing the international competitiveness of the U.S. economy. While the popular use of the trade balance as a measure of a country's economic health is a dangerously misleading oversimplification, neither should our international trade position be a matter of complete indifference to U.S. policymakers. Sensible arguments can be made that both U.S. and foreign economic welfare would be enhanced by a lower real value of the dollar and lower U.S. trade deficit. It is doubtful, however, that proposals to accomplish this objective through massive official intervention in the foreign exchange market would be effective.

A nontrivial portion of the strength of U.S. interest rates is the magnitude of current and expected future U.S. budget deficits. Suppose, for example, that, say, a quarter of the projected full employment budget deficits on the order of $200 billion is financed by capital flows from abroad. This reduction in the amount of domestic crowding out would be associated with a comparable trade deficit and appreciation of the dollar. Scaling up the simulation results presented in the appendix or applying the range of the commonly estimated sum of demand elasticities for U.S. exports and imports of between 2.0 and 4.0 suggest that the equilibrium change in the dollar needed to maintain the capital inflow-trade deficit combination of twenty to forty billion a year associated with high U.S. budget deficits could easily explain most of the real appreciation of the dollar.[10] The most effective way to improve U.S. trade competitiveness is to take decisive actions to bring the U.S. budget situation under control. A sizable portion of the current influence of the international sector on the economy is due itself to domestic U.S. economic policies.

NOTES TO CHAPTER 1

1. Other major characteristics of the recent literature include emphasis on the specification of stock-flow relationships and the implications of differential speeds of adjustment in different markets. The latter has been an important rediscovery by technical modelers of considerations emphasized by economists such as Gottfried Haberler and Fritz Machlup decades before. I have discussed the evolution of exchange rate analysis in more detail in Willett (1980; 1982), as does the following paper by Arndt and Pigott. These papers contain references to other surveys and primary literature.

2. This recent literature has also tended to overemphasize the assumption of perfect international capital mobility. This is discussed in Chapters 3 and 18.

3. On the poor performance of short-term exchange rate models, see Khan and Willett (1984) and Meese and Rogoff (1983) and on the interpretation of recent exchange rate volatility as news in efficient markets see Frenkel (1981), and Frenkel (1983). As might be expected, empirical exchange rate models appear to have a comparative advantage for analysis over longer time periods.
4. In the first case goods arbitrage would be sufficient to assure the approximation of PPP. Even for economies where traded goods are less dominant, however, PPP conditions could also be maintained as long as there were no changes in equilibrium relative prices. This condition would hold in turn under the assumption of monetary neutrality. While this is a questionable assumption for the short term, it generally appears to hold to a reasonable approximation over the longer term. This gives rise to the view that where monetary shocks are dominate, short run deviations from PPP will be self-reversing. For further discussions and references, see Chapters 2 and 4.
5. For references to the literature on the profitability and stabilizing versus destabilizing effects of official intervention, see Chapter 6.
6. For analysis and references, see Willett (1977), pp. 38–40.
7. See, for example, Willett (1979) and Kohlhagen (1982) and following discussions. This episode might alternatively be looked at as a possible example of a speculative bubble. See, for example, Woo (1984).
8. For recent surveys of studies on the effects of official intervention, see Solomon (1983) and Federal Reserve Board (1983).
9. See the discussions and references in Levich (1982) and in Chapter 9.
10. This type of analysis assumes high but less than infinite international capital mobility and neutral exchange rate expectations. An alternative approach based on the assumption of infinite capital mobility calculates the amount of expected exchange rate changes needed to offset real interest differentials. This approach has been used to estimate that high interest rates in the United States may be able to explain an appreciation of the dollar on the order of 30 percent. For further discussion see Chapter 3.

REFERENCES

Dornbusch, Rudiger. 1976. "Expectations and Exchange Rate Dynamics." *Journal of Political Economy* 84, no. 6 (December): 1161–76.

Frenkel, Jacob A. 1983. *Exchange Rates and International Macroeconomics* (Chicago: University of Chicago Press for the National Bureau of Economic Research).

Frenkel, Jacob A. 1981. "Flexible Exchange Rates, Prices, and the Role of "News": Lessons from the 1970s." *Journal of Political Economy* 89, no. 4 (August): 665–705. Reprinted in Jagdeep S. Bhandari and Bluford H. Putnam, eds. *Economic Interdependence and Flexible Exchange Rates* (Cambridge, Mass.: The M.I.T. Press): 3–41.

"Intervention in Foreign Exchange Markets: A Summary of Ten Staff Studies." 1983. *Federal Reserve Bulletin* 69, no. 11 (November): 830–36.

Kahn, Waseem, and Thomas D. Willett. 1984. "The Monetary Approach to Exchange Rates: A Review of Recent Empirical Studies." *Kredit und Kapital*, Heft 2 (17 Jahrgang): 199–220.

Kohlhagen, Steven W. 1982. "The Experience with Floating: The 1973–1979 Dollar." In Jacob S. Dreyer, Gottfried Haberler, and Thomas D. Willett, eds., *The International Monetary System: A Time of Turbulence* (Washington, D.C.: American Enterprise Institute for Public Policy Research): 142–79.

Levich, Richard M. 1982. "Overshooting in the Foreign Exchange Market." *Occasional Paper* #5 (New York: Group of 30).

Meese, Richard, and Kenneth Rogoff. 1983. "The Out-of-Sample Failure of Empirical Exchange Rate Models: Sampling Error or Misspecification?" In Jacob A. Frenkel, ed., *Exchange Rates and International Macroeconomics* (Chicago: University of Chicago Press for the National Bureau of Economic Research): 67–105.

Solomon, Robert. 1983. "Official Intervention in Foreign Exchange Markets: A Survey." *Brookings Discussion Papers in International Economics*, no. 1 (June).

Willett, Thomas D. 1982. "The Causes and Effects of Exchange Rate Volatility." In Jacob S. Dreyer, Gottfried Haberler, and Thomas D. Willett, eds., *The International Monetary System: A Time of Turbulence* (Washington, D.C.: American Enterprise Institute for Public Policy Research): 24–64.

Willett, Thomas D. 1980. "Policy Research Issues in a Floating Rate World." In *International Economic Policy Research* Conference Volume (Washington, D.C.: National Science Foundation): 124–58.

Willett, Thomas D. 1978. "The Fall and Rise of the Dollar." Testimony before the Subcommittee on International Economics of the Joint Economic Committee, U.S. Congress (December 14). Also available as Reprint No. 96, *The Fall and Rise of the Dollar* (Washington, D.C.: American Enterprise Institute for Public Policy Research, April 1979).

Willett, Thomas D. 1977. *Floating Exchange Rates and International Monetary Reform.* (Washington, D.C.: American Enterprise Institute for Public Policy Research).

Woo, Wing T. 1984. "Speculative Bubbles in the Foreign Exchange Markets." *Brookings Discussion Papers in International Economics*, no. 13 (March).

APPENDIX
EQUILIBRIUM EXCHANGE RATE ADJUSTMENTS
TO EXOGENOUS CHANGES IN INTERNATIONAL
CAPITAL FLOWS

Dean DeRosa

This appendix presents calculations of the likely range of exchange rate movements necessary to adjust trade flows to restore equilibrium in response to net changes in the flow demand for dollars such as might be caused by a change in international capital flows or oil import payments.

The simulation model used was developed at the Office of International Monetary Research at the U.S. Treasury. It is based on the multilateral exchange rate model developed by Armington.[1] It assumes that consumers in each country distinguish between traded goods produced at home and abroad according to a constant elasticity of substitution utility index. This allows the specification of own- and cross-price elasticities of demand for traded goods on a bilateral basis, given base period market shares, elasticities of substitution, and aggregate price elasticities of demand for traded goods in each country. It also assumes that total output of tradable goods in each country is less than perfectly elastic in response to price changes. The model, therefore, captures important dimensions of competition among domestic and foreign producers in different national markets and allows prices as well as production of traded goods to adjust in response to economic disturbances.

In the model, the elasticity of substitution provides a basic measure of the degree of competition among foreign and domestic producers in each national market. Cross-price elasticities then are determined in proportion to this basic competitiveness measure according to the market shares of competing exporters in each import market, while own-price elasticities are predominantly determined by the degree of competition in each market rather than by market shares. Net equilibrium changes of international capital flows are hypothesized to illustrate the multilateral exchange rate effects of nonmonetary disturbances to the international payments system. These capital flow changes depict a diversion of $5 billion (at annual rates) from the United States to one or more European countries. Two variants of the basic simulation exercise were carried out. In the first, the $5 billion are assumed diverted only to assets denominated in German marks. In the second, the same amount is assumed diverted in equal portions to assets denominated in the currencies of five different European countries – Germany, France, Belgium, the Netherlands, and Sweden.

In all cases the results were generated by assuming common values between 0.75 and 2.0 for substitution elasticities in the goods market of each different country in the simulation model. Elasticity of substitution estimates are not often reported in the literature. Therefore, for comparison, model-computed sums of export and import own-price elasticities of demand (in absolute value) for each country over the range of assumed substitution elasticity values are presented in Table 1A-1 alongside empirical estimates of price elasticities in international trade compiled by Robert Stern and his associates.[2] This comparison indicates that the range of assumed substitution elasticity values is largely consistent with recent empirical evidence on price elasticities in world trade. Finally, based on calculations made by the author using Stephen Magee's estimate of 10.0 for the price elasticity of U.S. export supply, the price elasticity of supply for tradable goods in each country was assumed equal to 1.73.[3]

The simulation results are set forth in Table 1A-2, which presents changes of equilibrium dollar exchange rates, both nominal and "real."[4] In the first scenario the net diversion of investment flows only to Germany causes the nominal and "real" dollar-mark rates to rise proportionally more than the other dollar exchange rates. By comparison, diversion of an equal volume of investments to the five European countries in the second scenario causes dollar prices of all five currencies to rise by similar proportions and by more than dollar exchanges for other world currencies.

Most importantly, the results in Table 1A-2 indicate that net shifts of international investment flows from the United States to major European countries

Table 1A-1. Own-Price Elasticities of Demand for Exports and Imports (*Sum of Absolute Values*).

Country	Model Values for Different Elasticity of Substitution Values				Estimates Compiled by Stern	
	0.75	*1.00*	*1.50*	*2.00*	*Range*	*"Best"*
United States	1.53	2.00	2.94	3.88	0.97 to 5.33	2.76
Canada	1.52	2.00	2.96	3.93	0.85 to 3.54	2.09
Japan	1.52	2.00	2.96	3.92	1.48 to 3.85	2.03
Austria	1.52	2.00	2.97	3.94	1.88 to 2.35	2.25
Belgium	1.53	2.00	2.95	3.90	1.27 to 2.30	1.85
France	1.52	2.00	2.96	3.92	1.45 to 3.80	2.39
Germany	1.54	2.00	2.92	3.84	0.89 to 3.36	1.99
Italy	1.52	2.00	2.96	3.93	0.16 to 3.39	1.96
Netherlands	1.53	2.00	2.95	3.89	0.61 to 3.52	1.63
Sweden	1.51	2.00	2.96	3.93	2.68 to 3.29	2.75
United Kingdom	1.52	2.00	2.95	3.91	0.46 to 3.32	1.13

Notes: Model values are averages of bilateral own-price elasticity values computed according to the Armington demand framework using different values of the elasticity of substitution in demand between traded goods and 1974 levels of trade between the major industrial countries and the rest of the world. In the last column, "best" estimates are approximate median values reported by Stern for each country.

Source: World trade model computations and Robert M. Stern, et al., *Price Elasticities in International Trade*.

Table 1A-2. Changes of U.S. Dollar Exchange Rates for World
Currencies (*Percent Change*).

Currency/Substitution Elasticity	Five Billion Dollars to Germany				One Billion Dollars to Each of Five European Countries			
	0.75	*1.00*	*1.50*	*2.00*	*0.75*	*1.00*	*1.50*	*2.00*
Canadian Dollar								
Nominal	2.81	2.06	1.44	1.18	2.83	2.07	1.45	1.18
Real	2.31	1.56	0.94	0.69	2.33	1.57	0.95	0.69
Japanese Yen								
Nominal	7.53	4.45	2.60	1.93	7.32	4.37	2.58	1.92
Real	6.97	3.92	2.09	1.43	6.76	3.84	2.07	1.42
Austrian Schilling								
Nominal	8.70	5.51	3.34	2.49	8.03	5.08	3.09	2.31
Real	8.66	5.31	3.03	2.13	7.96	4.86	2.76	1.94
Belgium Franc								
Nominal	12.66	7.13	3.94	2.81	16.80	10.57	6.60	5.08
Real	12.25	6.69	3.48	2.34	15.28	9.01	5.01	3.48
French Franc								
Nominal	10.49	6.20	3.56	2.59	13.02	8.01	4.78	3.56
Real	10.13	5.79	3.12	2.14	12.33	7.26	4.00	2.76
German Mark								
Nominal	22.27	13.18	7.79	5.85	15.85	8.84	4.90	3.53
Real	19.85	11.08	5.87	4.00	14.58	7.82	4.01	2.69
Italian Lira								
Nominal	8.63	5.34	3.19	2.36	8.12	5.09	3.07	2.29
Real	8.52	5.09	2.85	1.98	7.99	4.83	2.72	1.91
Dutch Guilder								
Nominal	14.30	7.93	4.31	3.04	17.19	10.53	6.41	4.87
Real	13.69	7.38	3.79	2.53	15.60	9.00	4.91	3.39
Swedish Kroner								
Nominal	11.00	6.32	3.56	2.57	20.07	12.96	8.22	6.38
Real	10.29	5.70	3.00	2.03	17.52	10.56	5.92	4.12
British Pound								
Nominal	6.63	4.26	2.64	1.99	7.05	4.53	2.79	2.10
Real	6.52	4.02	2.30	1.62	6.96	4.30	2.46	1.73

Notes: Exchange rate changes from diverting $5 billion in annual investment flows from the United States to Germany and, alternatively, to five European countries (Belgium, France, Germany, the Netherlands, and Sweden) simulated using a model of world trade and assuming different values for elasticities of substitution in demand between goods in world trade. Changes in "real" exchange rates are calculated from the model simulation results as the difference between the percent change in the nominal exchange rate and the percent change in the price ratio of traded goods produced by the United States and the given foreign country. Model results are based on 1974 levels of trade between the major industrial countries and the rest of the world.

of the magnitude hypothesized here can imply sizable dollar exchange rate adjustments, in both nominal and "real" terms. When elasticities of substitution are assumed in the low range of values, the "real" exchange rate adjustments are as great as 15 percent to 20 percent for the five currencies highlighted in the analysis, while for the other world currencies the increases are as great as 8 percent. Even when the upper range of substitution elasticity values is assumed, however, the "real" exchange rate changes are far from insignificant. For the five European currencies exchange rate changes are in the neighborhood of 4 percent, while for most other currencies they are about 2 percent.[5]

NOTES TO APPENDIX

1. See Paul A. Armington, "A Theory of Demand for Products Distinguished by Place of Production," *Staff Papers* (March 1969): 159–76; and Paul A. Armington, "A Many-Country Model of Equilibrating Adjustments in Prices and Spending," *Staff Papers* (March 1970): 23–26.
2. Robert M. Stern, Jonathan Francis, and Bruce Schumacher, *Price Elasticities in International Trade* (Toronto: Macmillan, 1976).
3. See Dean A. DeRosa, "A Survey of Recent World Trade Models With an Application to the 1971 World Currency Realignments" (Ph.D. dissertation, University of Oregon, 1975); and Stephen P. Magee, "A Theoretical and Empirical Examination of Supply and Demand Relationships in U.S. International Trade" (U.S. Council of Economic Advisors, October 1977). (Mimeo.)
4. The percent change in the "real" or "price-adjusted" exchange rate is computed as the difference between the percentage change in the nominal exchange rate and the percentage change in the price ratio for traded goods produced by the United States and the given foreign country. In other words, it is computed as the difference between percentage changes in the nominal exchange rate and a simple measure of the PPP exchange rate between two countries using export rather than domestic price indices as the basis of the PPP calculations.
5. These results would seem to be in accord with estimates made by the International Monetary Fund. Using a world trade model to gauge the magnitude of exchange rate changes necessary to produce trade balance changes for the major industrial countries, ranging from 1.5 to 3.5 percent of the level of 1977 trade flows, the Fund Staff found nominal exchange rate changes of the order of 5 to 15 percent necessary. See, International Monetary Funds, *Annual Report 1978* (Washington, D.C.: International Monetary Fund, 1978), p. 42.

2 EXCHANGE RATE MODELS
Evolution and Policy Implications
Sven W. Arndt and Charles Pigott

INTRODUCTION

Concern with exchange rates—their determination and their repercussions—has long been a major preoccupation of international economics. Theories of exchange rate determination can be traced to the bullionist debate of the late eighteenth century, which produced the earliest explicit theory, that of purchasing power parity. Policymakers have hardly been less concerned, as the use of exchange rates as policy instruments has an equally long tradition.

Nonetheless, the way in which economists think in formal terms about exchange rate determination has changed considerably in recent years. This partly reflects developments in macroeconomic theory, which has always provided the ultimate conceptual basis for international financial economics. However, it is no mere coincidence that this change has come with a major reordering of international monetary arrangements and the move to floating exchange rates. As is often the case in intellectual movements, the resulting changes in the objective environment have generated tensions between existing theories and observed behavior that have stimulated new approaches to exchange rate analysis. The switch to floating exchange rates has also significantly altered the practical concerns of policymakers, which have always been a major influence on exchange rate analyses and indeed on international economics generally.

In the following sections we critically examine the key features distinguishing the various conceptual frameworks used by economists to formulate and analyze international economic policy issues relating to exchange rate determination and to policy guidelines and responses over the postwar period. Our concern here is not with the formal technical aspects of these models (which have been extensively reviewed elsewhere)[1] but with the impression they convey to policymakers and other practical analysts about the fundamental determinants of exchange rates, the interpretation of their actual behavior, and the policy options available to deal with their consequences. We give particular attention to the similarities and contrast in policy outlooks provided by the traditional approaches used during the 1950s and 1960s and the new asset models of exchange rate determination that have largely replaced them. We then analyze perhaps the most thorny problem that has confronted the new models and exposed both their weaknesses and strengths—the causes and consequences of the extraordinarily high value of the dollar in recent years. We conclude with several important policy lessons that can be drawn from these models in light of the actual behavior of exchange rates since 1973.

As we argue throughout, the basic concerns and problems exchange rate theories are expected to answer have changed far less than the formal apparatuses used to express them. Newer theories continue to be preoccupied with three long-standing fundamental questions: What determines exchange rates in the long-run; how do the long-run determinants of exchange rates and other, temporary, factors influence short-run exchange rate dynamics; and what are the implications of exchange rate changes for domestic real and financial markets? Indeed, we will see that the most persistent problem that has faced exchange rate modeling attempts is also at the core of current controversies about the high dollar and its implications for U.S. competitiveness—namely, the reconciliation of the role of real and financial influences on exchange rates.

THE CONCEPTUAL SETTING

The evolution of exchange rate models over the postwar period represents a major shift in emphasis from the effects of *real* factors—those determining commodity supplies and demands and hence relative prices—to the influence of financial markets on exchange rates. This reflects in part the change in policy focus from the medium- to long-term impacts of discrete changes in exchange rate parities under an adjustable peg regime to the interpretation of short-term exchange rate fluctuations under floating.

The "Traditional" Models

During the 1950s and 1960s, models of exchange rate determination focused mainly on the real sector. Domestic commodity prices were generally (at least implicitly) assumed to be fixed—in this sense the models were Keynesian—so that exchange rate changes were unambiguously reflected in changes in the relative prices of traded goods. The principal problem addressed was the impact of exchange rate changes on trade and the current account.

In the simplest of these frameworks—the elasticities approach—the effects of exchange rate changes were confined to their influence on the relative prices of domestic versus foreign goods, and hence on their respective demands and supplies. Repercussions on nontraded sectors, aggregate income, prices, and wages were deemphasized, often leaving the impression that influences on the trade balance were confined to the "tradables" sectors alone.[2] This approach came to be challenged by "absorption" models in which the trade-balance effects of devaluation were seen to depend on conditions in the economy as a whole. Reflecting their Keynesian roots, these models focused on the interplay between domestic production and absorption, with the trade balance determined as the difference between them.

Thus, a country's trade balance (T) was seen as the difference between its total output (Y) and domestic absorption (A), with the latter generally divided into private consumption and investment and public expenditure, or

$$T = Y - A. \qquad (2.1)$$

It is clear from expression (2.1) that the trade balance rises and falls as output rises or falls relative to absorption.

In the first-generation absorption models, income effects were dominant, with marginal propensities to save and to spend assuming the central role played by tradables demand and supply elasticities in the earlier framework.[3] But, as these models were developed further, relative price and income effects were integrated, and wealth was given a role in determining the response of aggregate demand—as well as the demand and supply of tradables—to exchange rate changes.[4]

Absorption models improved the analytical rigor of exchange rate analysis, yet their policy outlook was very similar to that conveyed by the simpler elasticities approaches. The major reason is that both frameworks viewed exchange rates as largely determined in the real sector, and this view in turn influenced prevailing policy concerns and presumptions about the self-correcting features of the international mechanism.

In particular, when the exchange rate is presumed to be determined in the real sector, the magnitudes of supply and demand elasticities and of marginal propensities take on fundamental importance for policymakers. Low price elasticities in goods markets, for example, imply low elasticities in the markets for foreign exchange and thus suggest that large changes in exchange rates will be required to correct given imbalances in trade and payments. Doubts about the adequacy of elasticities—known in the forties and fifties as elasticity pessimism—gave rise to doubts about the efficacy of flexible exchange rates and thus influenced the choice of exchange rate regime. Subsequent empirical research generally found such elasticity pessimism to have been unjustified.[5]

The real-sector approach also critically influenced views about the sources and effects of exchange rate volatility. Since commodity demand and supply schedules generally shift more slowly and less abruptly than their financial sector counterparts, equilibrium exchange rates were presumed to change slowly as well. Accordingly, in policy discussions of the period high exchange rate volatility tended to be attributed to "destabilizing" speculation. Conversely, exchange rate volatility was generally viewed as undesirable since the uncertainty it engendered might well inhibit international trade. On the whole, the early approaches tended to take a rather negative view of exchange market speculation, an attitude sharply in contrast with more modern interpretations according to which speculative activity plays an important role in equilibrating asset markets and in facilitating adjustment to economic change.[6] Not surprisingly, this negativism was reflected in the policy advice proffered by analysts, so that policymakers on the whole tended to regard exchange market speculation as unwholesome and requiring official intervention to counteract it.

Finally, the focus on "real" causes and consequences of exchange rate movements substantially influenced views about the transmission of economic disturbances, and hence about the effects of one country's macroeconomic and exchange rate policies on others. Movements in one country's exchange rate were seen to have serious consequences for employment, income, and the trade balances of others. The possibility that exchange rates might insulate a nation from at least some external disturbances was only dimly perceived at best. When combined with the unhappy experiences with competitive currency depreciations during the 1930s, these perceptions tended to reinforce suspicions that exchange rate movements and the policies associated with them could be sources of considerable disorder unless they were substantially constrained by international cooperation.

Still, despite their serious limitations, the absorption models represented an important advance toward a general equilibrium view of exchange rates and their effects. At the least, they foreshadowed the monetary and other asset approaches in recognizing that financial markets had a role in determining exchange rates, even if this role was not fully understood and articulated. Yet because they assigned exchange rates a very limited role in affecting the demands for money and other assets—and hence in determining capital flows—they generally had little to say about the impact of monetary and debt management policies on exchange rates and the balance of payments, a weakness that became ever more apparent as such policies increasingly became the focus of controversy in domestic macroeconomic analysis.[7]

The Mundell-Fleming Model

It remained for Fleming and Mundell to provide an integrated general equilibrium description of the determination of exchange rates, in both asset and commodity markets.[8] Taking the Keynesian IS–LM framework as its basis, the Mundell–Fleming (MF) model viewed the exchange rate as adjusting to maintain equilibrium in the balance of payments—rather than simply the trade balance as in earlier models—giving trade and capital flows a coequal role in their determination. Because capital flows were viewed as responding to interest rates, money and debt-management policies were at last given a clear and important influence on exchange rates and the balance of payments. Furthermore, expectations about the future value of the exchange rate were seen to affect the relative yield of domestic versus foreign assets, and hence capital flows, giving them a central role in the determination of spot exchange rates.

Indeed, the MF model represented a substantial advance in thinking about the effects of macroeconomic policies. This is particularly evident in its treatment of the potential conflict, identified by earlier writers, between policies to attain "external" (balance of payments) versus "internal" (full employment) equilibrium.[9] The MF model recognized that macro policies had distinct, and generally varying, real income and interest rate effects. Hence, in principle, a "mix" of monetary and fiscal policies could be designed to achieve both internal and external balance. More generally, the framework provided an integrated description of the role of exchange rate, interest rate, and income adjustments in laying the basis for an analysis of the influences of capital mobility, expectations, and exchange rate flexibility on the relative effectiveness of monetary and fiscal policies.

The power of MF is attested to by the fact that it shaped most empirical balance of payments models developed during the late 1960s and 1970s, and indeed several quite recent models of exchange rate determination have retained its basic structure while modifying some of its specific relations.[10] A major attraction was the greatly augmented array of policies to affect employment and income, and the balance of payments and exchange rates, that the approach seemed to offer to policymakers. Interest rates, it appeared, could be manipulated to maintain balance of payments equilibrium while fiscal policy stabilized employment. The possibilities for fine tuning suggested by closed-economy models popular during the 1960s seemed nearly as great, in the MF approach, for open economies. MF also altered views about the interdependence of economic policies, by emphasizing that financial as well as commodity markets affected the transmission of economic disturbances and by suggesting that there were enough policy instruments to alleviate, if not resolve, many of the conflicts engendered by the relatively rigid linkages among economies implied by earlier models.

Still, in many respects MF went only partway in correcting the limitations of the earlier approaches. Since it retained the Keynesian assumption of fixed money wages, its relevance tended to diminish as concern with inflation mounted. Although it made an important advance in pointing out the critical role of expectations, it had little to say about how expectations were formed and in practice tended to assume they were static. This strictly limited its insights into the sources of exchange rate variability. More generally, the preoccupation with static expectations and short-run outcomes, which the approach shared with most macroeconomic models of the period, became a serious handicap as it became apparent that given short-run outcomes depended critically upon (anticipated) long-run consequences. Moreover, even MF's innovative analysis of policy mixes was later seen to be flawed by its failure to distinguish between stock and flow adjustment in financial markets, so that shifts in portfolio composition were erroneously treated as ongoing capital flows. The portfolio models developed in the late 1960s, in which this distinction was introduced, suggested that the scope for fine-tuning the external sector via interest rate manipulation was significantly less than appeared possible in the MF framework.[11]

The New Asset Models

The speculative crises precipitating the demise of the Bretton Woods regime and the subsequent move to floating shifted the focus of modeling efforts to the dynamics of market-determined exchange rates. In part this change represented an attempt to explain apparent contradictions between the predictions of existing theory and actual exchange rate behavior. Indeed, floating exchange rates partly disappointed the hopes of many of its advocates as exchange rates did not vary closely with national inflation rates and current account imbalances did not disappear or even narrow appreciably. More generally, exchange rates seemed to vary much more than many, perhaps most, observers were prepared to believe was true of their long-run determinants.[12] This gave rise to a widespread presumption (if only implicit) that has been an important influence on subsequent modeling efforts, namely, that exchange rate movements under floating largely reflect variations *around* their long-run values rather than changes in the long-run values themselves.

The framework that has developed from these experiences has come to be known as the asset approach to exchange rate determination. Its foundation is the proposition that exchange rates can be viewed as adjusting to keep asset markets continuously in equilibrium; hence, exchange rates are proximately determined by the stock demands and supplies for financial and real assets.

The asset approach does *not* contradict (in any practically essential way) the assumption of prior models that exchange rates vary to maintain balance of payments equilibria. Indeed, this is no less true of asset models than of the Mundell–Fleming framework. The appeal of the asset approach lies in the fact that, given the large size of asset stocks relative to commodity market flows *and* the rapid speed of adjustment in financial markets, the *potential* flows on capital account arising from exchange rate movements are apt to dominate those on the current accounts provided there are no substantial barriers to international capital mobility. Thus, in bringing financial markets into equilibrium the exchange rate also ensures balance of payments equilibrium. Viewed in this way, the asset approach is appropriate for the analysis of exchange rate variations of industrial countries with reasonably open financial systems. It certainly would be much less useful in describing exchange rate determination in cases where cross-border financial transactions were severely circumscribed.

While a completely satisfactory and workable explanation of modern-day exchange rate dynamics has yet to be developed, asset models have led to important new insights into the relative roles of asset and commodity markets in exchange rate determination. As the price of homogeneous assets traded in highly organized markets where information is widely and quickly dispersed, exchange rates are free to vary virtually instantaneously as present and prospective economic conditions change. Exchange rates affect the relative prices of foreign versus domestic goods and, in the process, critically determine trade flows and the current account. Thus, in the long run exchange rates must be compatible with equilibrium in commodity as well as financial markets. Ultimately, then, financial and real factors together determine exchange rates—and in much the same way as was earlier thought to be the case. However, by clarifying the mechanism of short-run exchange rate determination, the new view raises more insistently a question usually blurred by older analyses—namely, that of how long-run influences on exchange rates influence short-run behavior. More concretely, how does the exchange rate get to its long-run equilibrium as determined (in part) by real factors if at every moment it is determined by conditions in asset markets only?

The answer to this question lies largely with another theme embedded in the new view, that of expectations. Because assets are durable, their prices are very sensitive to anticipations about conditions affecting their value in the future. Thus, if the financial sector perceives a change in commodity market conditions that it judges will alter the exchange rate in the long run, that rate is apt to change immediately. In this way, asset markets serve as the channel through which long-term influences on the exchange rate affect its short-run behavior. In this view, expectations play an essential role in linking the long-run with the short-run, as well as real and financial sector influences, or stock and flow phenomena. If information flows properly and is efficiently used, current exchange rate behavior will not only be consistent with asset market equilibrium but with equilibrium in the economy at large.

Furthermore, the precise way in which expectations are formed becomes a critical issue under this view because it affects the dynamic adjustment of the exchange rate toward its long-run value. If expectations change only slowly when the economic environment is altered and are based on fairly limited information (as in adaptive expectations), changes in the long-run determinants of exchange rates are likely to lead to gradual and protracted adjustment. If expectations are more rational—in the sense of being based on all available information and adapted quickly to changes in policy regimes—the adjustment is likely to be more abrupt and rapid and the distinction between the short and the long run accordingly blurred.

Of course, the critical importance of expectations was recognized by earlier analysts.[13] However, the traditional approaches, when modeling exchange rates formally, nearly always assumed that expectations were static and thus did *not* change when policies were altered. The new approach adds considerably to the power and realism of exchange rate models by recognizing that expectations are endogenous—that is, dependent upon the policy environment in which they are formed. The implication is that expectations must be modeled as systematically as other behavioral mechanisms and that the way anticipations are formed is likely to depend upon perceptions about the direction of government policies. Although the precise way in which anticipations are actually formed remains to be discovered, the new approach has at least laid the basis for a more realistic and rigorous analysis of the consequences of economic disturbances and of government policies.

Exchange Rate Determinants in the Asset Approach

The way in which the asset approach links the long-run determinants of exchange rates to their short-run behavior can be seen from the relations among interest rates and current and expected future exchange rates that are its fundamental building-block. In particular, over any horizon the risk-adjusted domestic foreign nominal interest differential equals the expected (annual) depreciation of the home currency:

$$e_t = \bar{e}_{t,n} + n\left[i_{t,n} + s_{t,n} - i^*_{t,n}\right] \tag{2.2}$$

where e_t and $\bar{e}_{t,n}$ are the current and expected (n-year) future values of the home currency (measured in logarithms) and i and i^* are the home and foreign (n-year) nominal interest rates. The $s_{t,n}$ is a premium on home financial assets demanded by the market to compensate for risks associated with unexpected exchange rate changes and/or political risks from actual or potential barriers to repatriation of funds invested by foreigners.[14] Thus $i_{t,n} + s_{t,n}$ is effectively the risk-adjusted home interest rate.

As this illustrates, interest rates effectively link the current exchange rate to its expected future value in the asset approach. Variations in current exchange rates then reflect changes in interest rates and changes in their expected future values. Furthermore, the same relation holds for current and expected future real exchange rates (x_t and $\bar{x}_{t,n}$)—the nominal rates deflated by the ratio of domestic to foreign price indices—and the home and foreign real interest rates ($r_{t,n}$ and $r^*_{t,n}$):

$$x_t = \bar{x}_{t,n} + n\left[r_{t,n} + s_{t,n} - r^*_{t,n}\right] . \tag{2.3}$$

Breaking the current real exchange rate into its nominal exchange rate and relative price-level components gives a classification of influences on exchange rates first introduced by Isard.[15]

$$e_t = (p_t - p_t^*) + n [r_{t,n} + s_{t,n} - r_{t,n}^*] + \bar{x}_{t,n} . \qquad (2.4)$$

Viewed in this way, there are three basic influences on exchange rates: *inflation*, which determines the home versus foreign price level; *"real" factors* determining long-run commodity supply and demands and hence the long-run real exchange rate; and real (risk-adjusted) interest rates. Only the first two can have permanent effects on exchange rates—and hence are determinants of their long-run values—because (in the absence of capital controls) the risk-adjusted home and foreign real interest rates must ultimately be the same.[16] Clearly then the asset approach in principle allows real as well as financial factors to affect exchange rates, no less in fact than the eclectic earlier frameworks of Haberler, Yeager, and others.[17]

However, the asset approach does require that influences on current exchange rates be mediated by financial markets, helping to define more precisely than earlier approaches the way in which the long-run determinants of these rates affect their current values. For example, expected future inflation can, according to this approach, affect the current exchange rate only to the extent that it changes current prices or current real interest rates. Real factors affecting the demands for traded goods can have an immediate impact on the exchange rate to the extent that they alter perceptions about the long-run real exchange rate.

Contending Models

Despite the great potential generality of the asset approach, the models it has spawned have tended to be narrower in focus. Most of these new models concentrate on the price-level (inflation) and interest rate influences on exchange rates and largely neglect "real factors" affecting the real exchange rate in the long run. Nearly all, in fact, assume that purchasing power parity holds in the long run—that is, that the long-run real exchange rate is fixed. Differences among the models largely center about the influence of alternative types of assets on interest rates and hence on exchange rates.

The earliest formal asset approaches were the monetary models stemming from Johnson's "Monetary Approach to the Balance of Payments."[18] These were the first open-economy models to be based on the notion that exchange rate changes result from alterations in supply relative to demand for stocks of financial assets—in this case, money.

All subsequent monetary models rest on two foundations: monetary determination of national price levels; and purchasing power parity or equivalently money neutrality, at least in the long run. The distinguishing feature of these models is *not* their implication that home money supply increases induce currency depreciation (this is implied by alternative models as well) but their assumption that other variables affect exchange rates only through their influence on money demand. Thus, for example, an increase in home real income is predicted to lead to currency appreciation because it raises the amount of money demanded—a result in striking contrast to elasticities and related trade-balance explanations of exchange rates.[19]

The earliest and simplest monetary models explained exchange rate movements entirely in terms of money-induced variations in price levels, essentially presuming that purchasing power parity held continuously. These models have proved of significant value in describing long-term trends (or average rates of change) in exchange rates, mainly because these generally have been dominated by inflation differentials. However, their applicability to short-run exchange rate movements has been severely restricted by the fact that deviations from purchasing power parity have been both persistent and highly variable under floating. Indeed, monthly real exchange rate changes have been as volatile as their nominal counterparts and considerably more variable than money growth or inflation.[20]

This realization helped spur a clever and highly influential attempt by Dornbusch to rescue the main conclusions of the monetary approach while exploiting the interest rate implications of the empirically well-established lag between money and prices to explain observed deviations from purchasing power parity.[21] Dornbusch's model remains a purely monetary explanation of long-run exchange rates based on purchasing power parity but one in which money fluctuations have short-run impacts on real interest rates, and hence on the dynamics of both real and nominal exchange rates. Because prices respond only with a considerable lag, increases or decreases in nominal money initially change real money balances and hence real interest rates, with immediate impacts on real (and nominal) exchange rates. Indeed, since the liquidity preference theory implies that increases in money lower interest rates, the model's most controversial implication is that nominal exchange rates will overshoot their long-run equilibria—that is, change *more* than proportionately—in response to money disturbances. Thus, at one stroke, the model appears to explain in terms of the money-price lag both the observed departures from PPP and (given overshooting) the greater variability of exchange rate changes compared to fluctuations in money growth and inflation.

Money models, particularly the Dornbusch versions, have provided several very useful and practical insights into exchange rate behavior. At the least they have refocused attention on the role of monetary forces in determining exchange rates. For policymakers, they have underscored the critical role monetary policy, particularly expectations about its future course, can play in exchange rate stability. Indeed, to monetarists the lesson of these models is that fluctuations in money growth are likely to be a major source of exchange rate variability, suggesting that adherence to steady money growth is good for exchange markets no less than for the domestic economy. This latter conclusion does not necessarily follow from these models, however, if, as many believe, observed fluctuations of money growth reflect variations in money demand. In that case, bringing money back on target (rather than accommodating the money demand shifts) can increase the variability of both domestic interest rates and exchange rates.

These models have also provided new insights into the relations between interest rates and exchange rates. In particular, they have underscored that the conventional wisdom associating rising domestic interest rates with currency appreciation is strictly valid for *real* interest rate increases only. This can be seen from equation (2.4), which indicates that an increase in the home relative to the foreign real interest rate must, ceteris paribus (no change in domestic versus foreign price level or the expected future real exchange rate), raise the value of the domestic currency. Increases in domestic interest rates that simply reflect inflation, however, will generally be associated with currency depreciation, as the 'purchasing power parity' component of (2.4) (p^* - p) declines over time.

This analysis also implies that a given increase in the (annualized) long-term real interest rate is likely to have a much larger impact on the current real exchange rate than an equal increase in the short-term real interest rate. Suppose, for example, that capital mobility is 'perfect', so that there is no risk premium on home securities at any maturity. A one percentage point increase in the real interest rate on a 10-year home security (on an annualized discount basis) will raise the current real exchange rate by 10 percent, assuming no change in the expected 'long-run' real exchange rate for ten years from now; but an increase of the same amount in the one-year real interest rate *itself* raises the current real exchange rate by only one percent.[22] Thus, unless capital mobility is markedly lower for longer-term than for shorter-term instruments, increases in longer-term real interest rates will have much larger impacts on real exchange rates than changes in shorter-term real interest rates. Since longer-term interest rates are critically dependent on expectations of future short-term rates, this means in effect that the impact of real interest rate increases on exchange rates depends not only on their magnitude but their expected *duration.*[23] As we will argue in the next section, the potentially great 'leverage' longer-term real interest rates have on exchange rates may explain why the protracted shifts in monetary and fiscal policies experienced in the last several years have apparently had such great impact on currency values.

Still, while these models have led to important insights, actual experience suggests that their description of exchange rate behavior is unsatisfactory in several important ways. As Brittain originally noted, the overshooting explanation of greater variability in exchange rates than money implies that spot exchange rates vary more than forward rates; it also predicts that fluctuations in spot relative to forward rates (reflected in interest rate changes) should account for much of the observed variability in actual exchange rates. Neither implication, though, is supported by the evidence.[24] Likewise, the Dornbusch model implies that all variations in real exchange rates reflect fluctuations in real interest rates, because the long-run real exchange rate is assumed fixed. But this implies that real interest rates have varied markedly under floating, a conclusion that is *not* generally supported by studies of U.S. interest rates over the 1970s; these studies generally suggest that variations in (short-term) nominal U.S. interest rates during this period mainly reflected changes in expected inflation, with relatively little variability of the real interest rate.[25] As this suggests, many of this model's apparent conflicts with the data might recede if its long-run purchasing power parity assumptions were relaxed.[26] These problems do not necessarily invalidate these models (indeed we will argue later that they supply important insights about the impact of changes in *longer-term trends* in money growth) but they do suggest strongly that they will need to be significantly modified to account for other potential exchange rate determinants if they are to give a satisfactory explanation of observed behavior.

Portfolio Models

Another source of dissatisfaction with monetary models stems from their presumption that only money among the entire array of assets directly affects exchange rates. These models presume that domestic and foreign interest-bearing assets are perfect substitutes. The implication is that neither domestic debt management nor sterilized foreign exchange market intervention, both of which alter the supplies of domestic and/or foreign bonds, have any impact on currency values. This assumption, and monetary models' exclusion of real-sector influences, has left them with little to say about the exchange rate implications of fiscal policies or the monetary-fiscal policy mix.

Accordingly, considerable effort in recent years has been devoted to developing generalized asset or portfolio models of exchange rate determination that would account for these factors. While there is now a wide variety of such models,[27] most are distinguished from their monetary competitors by the assumption that domestic and foreign securities identical in maturity, taxability, and default risk are, because of their differing currency compositions, *imperfect* substitutes; that is, the portfolio approach rests on the existence of a foreign exchange "risk" premium—$s_{t,n}$ in expression (2.4)—reflecting the difference in ex ante returns on identical foreign and domestic assets and dependent upon the relative supplies of these assets. In this way, the mix of available assets—the proportions of outstanding money and bonds and the relative amounts of domestic and foreign bonds—exerts a potentially important influence on the short-run behavior of the exchange rate. This suggests that a wide variety of government policies affecting national debt composition—such as fiscal policy or intervention policy, whether sterilized or not—can affect exchange rates, in large part through (real) interest rates but possibly through other channels as well.

More surprisingly perhaps, these models allow the current account balance to exert a two-faceted influence. First, to the extent that asset preferences vary across nations, the world distribution of wealth will affect asset demands and hence may affect exchange rates. Because current account imbalances can lead to changes in the distribution of wealth, they may affect exchange rates through this channel. Furthermore, if, as is normally assumed, domestic residents do not hold foreign money and vice versa, net financial claims on foreigners can be increased (in the absence of official intervention) only by running a current account surplus—that is, by selling domestic commodities for foreign financial assets. This gives the current account another potential role in facilitating the portfolio adjustments of foreign and domestic nationals, the resulting capital flows again affecting exchange rates.

But perhaps the greatest potential use of asset models lies in their ability to depict the complex interactions among national financial markets and the relations of these to foreign exchange markets. In such models, credit conditions in one country may affect interest rates in another, via exchange rate changes, capital flows, or both. In a fashion largely precluded in monetary approaches, these frameworks can thus depict the interdependencies among national financial policies.

Still, recent work has raised increasing doubts about key features of the portfolio approaches. Empirical work on the foundation of these models—the risk premium—suggests that it may not be very large, or at least may not vary much in comparison with other exchange rate determinants; this work, moreover, has failed to relate that premium in any predictable and significant way to the supplies of interest-bearing assets.[28] Similarly, there is reason to doubt that the wealth transfers normally effected through current account imbalances are large enough to account for more than a small fraction of exchange rate changes.[29]

Back to Real Factors?

More fundamentally, portfolio models share with monetary approaches the neglect of permanent real influences on exchange rates that experience increasingly suggests may be of major importance. Evidence continues to accumulate that a substantial portion of the observed deviations from PPP persist indefinitely and that a major element of uncertainty about future exchange rates, even over long-term horizons, concerns their real components.[30] This suggests that exchange markets may closely resemble stock markets, where changing assessments of future real conditions, as well as inflation prospects, largely dominate current price movements. Thus, there is growing awareness that real influences on exchange rates must be modeled more explicitly if their current movements are to be understood and their evolution over time predicted. Work by researchers at the Federal Reserve Board of Governors and elsewhere not only suggests that such factors have had substantial influences on exchange rates but represents a serious attempt to model those influences as well.[31] Most of these efforts, though, have used proxies, such as current account variations, to explain shifts in long-run real exchange rates, leaving to future work the important task of uncovering their ultimate causes.

The experience of the last thirty years indicates clearly that the value of exchange rate models depends critically upon the quality of the macroeconomic ideas underlying them. Many of the advances in understanding exchange rates have, and continue to, come from improvements in analyzing fundamental domestic macroeconomic issues. Accordingly, given the great advances in macroeconomic theory in recent years, it is not unreasonable to expect a substantial improvement in the realism and relevance of exchange rate models in the near future.

EXCHANGE RATE THEORY AND THE HIGH DOLLAR

The spectacular rise of the dollar in recent years has posed an especially stern test of the policy-utility of exchange rate models. Between 1980 and the end of 1983, the dollar's nominal trade-weighted value (as measured by Morgan Guaranty Bank) rose by nearly 25 percent, bringing it to its highest level in nearly a decade vis-à-vis such strong currencies as the German mark and Swiss franc. More remarkably, the dollar has risen as much in real terms, resulting in a significant decline in the competitiveness of U.S. products on world markets. This decline in competitiveness has been a major factor in the precipitous deterioration of the U.S. current account balance from a surplus of $4.4 billion in 1981 to the record $40 billion deficit recorded for 1983.

Neither conventional wisdom nor the sophisticated economic models developed over the last decade seem to have adequately explained, much less predicted, the dollar's remarkable strength. Conventional wisdom, as well as most of the models discussed earlier, strongly suggest that relative inflation rates will dominate exchange rates over periods of several years or longer and that deviations from purchasing power parity disappear in the long run. Yet the dollar soared over 1980-81 even though U.S. inflation generally remained above the average abroad. The dollar has deviated further and longer from purchasing power parity (relative to the late 1970s) than at any time since the beginning of general floating, yet few if any analysts venture to predict when, or even if, this deviation will end. Nor has the widespread view that growing current account deficits lead to currency depreciation fared any better, since the dollar has continued to rise even as the U.S. current account balance fell by nearly $45 billion over 1981-83.

These apparent paradoxes are no doubt substantially responsible for the increasingly widespread perception that the dollar is grossly "overvalued"—by as much as 25 percent according to some estimates.[32] Several analysts have called for large-scale foreign exchange market intervention or other dramatic measures to bring the dollar down.[33] To a large extent these prescriptions stem from understandable concerns that the dollar's high value, whether justified by economic fundamentals or not, is harmful to U.S. and foreign welfare and also threatens to undermine the relatively liberal environment for international trade and investment evolved over the postwar era. However, these concerns also reflect a fairly widespread belief that the dollar's behavior in recent years is, if not actually inconsistent with the predictions of economic theory, at least not easily comprehended by that theory.

Below we analyze what economic theory can in fact say about the causes of the dollar's high value and whether, and in what sense, it can be termed overvalued. This analysis also illustrates the basic strengths and weaknesses of the exchange rate models developed over the last ten years in helping to understand actual movements in exchange rates. As we argue in more detail later, these models provide a fairly good description of the linkages between financial, particularly monetary, forces and exchange rates. They provide a much less satisfactory description of the real factors that help determine exchange rates in the long run, and of their influence on short-run exchange rate determination.

What Does Overvaluation Mean

Although many observers believe the dollar is overvalued, there is much less agreement about what this means precisely, in theoretical much less operational terms. Some commentaries suggest that market inefficiency, or misperceptions of market participants, have led to a dollar that is too high in relation to its fundamental determinants—that is, higher than the level that would presumably prevail in an efficient and rational market setting. For example, a dollar that was artificially elevated by capital controls, or by overly optimistic assessments of its long-run determinants, might be thought of as overvalued in this sense. Determining operationally whether a currency is too high or low in relation to its fundamentals is widely acknowledged to be very difficult, if not impossible, since it entails specification of the "right" model of exchange rate determination and measurement of fundamental determinants, several of which (e.g., expected future inflation) are not directly observable. Furthermore, studies of exchange rate determination have not uncovered any convincing evidence of market inefficiencies that are (for major industrial countries at least) massive enough to account for the remarkable extent and persistence of the dollar's rise.

In any case, those who have argued most persuasively that the dollar is overvalued generally do not assert that it is necessarily greatly out-of-line with *current* fundamentals. Rather, it is argued that market forces, particularly those emanating from financial markets, have pushed the dollar to a level well above that which can be sustained in the long run. Often underlying such contentions is the premise that the U.S. current account deficit cannot be sustained at its present level, so that the real value of the dollar ultimately must fall to bring the current account back toward balance.[34] It has also been argued that the dollar's value, even if sustainable in the long run, is nonetheless too high in a *normative* sense—that is, above the level consistent with an optimal allocation of resources, current and future.

Neither of these contentions can be dismissed out-of-hand: As argued below, the real value of the dollar almost certainly is above its long-run level, and there can be little doubt that the high real dollar is adversely affecting certain sectors of the U.S. economy. These arguments do reflect the continuing controversy over the role of financial and real factors in determining exchange rates in the short run and long run. Measures of the dollar's overvaluation are generally based on the presumption that purchasing power parity will hold in the long run, leaving little if any room for real factors to alter exchange rates permanently. This is also the view conveyed by most of the exchange rate models developed over the last decade—but only because they have focused nearly exclusively on financial market influences. Likewise, calls for drastic policy measures to bring the dollar down have sometimes suggested that any substantial deviation of exchange rates from the level consistent with long-run equilibrium in goods markets represents economic inefficiency in some sense. This in effect subordinates financial to real influences, which are presumed to be the main determinant of the "proper" or welfare-maximizing level of exchange rates. These arguments again serve to emphasize that much of the controversy about exchange rates is really about the relative roles of their financial and real determinants.

The Macroeconomic Policy Mix

As several analysts have pointed out, the broad features of the dollar's behavior in recent years are fairly consistent with theoretical predictions of the consequences of the relatively stringent monetary policy and stimulative fiscal policy followed by the U.S. since 1980. In particular, much of the dollar's strength can be attributed to the extraordinarily high level of U.S. real interest rates over this period, themselves presumably the consequences of this macroeconomic policy mix. This does not mean, of course, that macro policy provides a complete explanation of all of the dollar's movements over this entire period, but we would argue that it can largely explain why the dollar rose so sharply over 1980–82, and why it has remained so strong since then.

The dollar's rise began with the slowing of U.S. money growth in late 1979, a policy aimed at bringing inflation down gradually from the double-digit levels then prevailing. The subsequent results were broadly consistent with the predictions of conventional theory and macroeconomic models. Given the substantial lag between changes in money growth and inflation, the slowing of nominal growth led to a substantial and protracted decline in real money balances lasting for over two years; real M1 declined by nearly 2 percent annually over 1980–81. This decline in real liquidity put increasing upward pressure on nominal interest rates leading to even greater increases in real interest rates, as actual, and almost certainly expected, inflation was declining.[35] Short-term real interest rates, approximated by the difference between the nominal rate and the previous year's consumer price inflation, increased by nearly 3 percent between the end of 1979 and the end of 1981. More important for exchange rate determination, long-term nominal interest rates increased by nearly 4 percent over the same period, although by somewhat less in relation to abroad. Surveys suggest that short-term *and* medium-term inflation expectations fell substantially over 1980–82, implying that U.S. real long-term interest rates probably rose by several percentage points in relation to abroad. Such increases could account for much, if not most, of the dollar's rise, given any reasonable degree of capital mobility and the more than proportionate impact of longer term real interest rate changes on exchange rates described in the last section.

This process is, of course, consistent with the predictions of Dornbusch and analogous exchange rate models that rest on the lagged adjustment of prices to money. Nor was the dollar's rise over 1980–81 the only recent illustration of this process. The 'reverse' sequence of events occurred over 1976–78, as U.S. money growth, and subsequently inflation, rose sharply: real money balances rose, real interest rates fell to negative levels for shorter term maturities, and the nominal and real values of the dollar dropped sharply. And, as Niehans[36] has persuasively argued, the sharp rise in the British pound over 1979–81 was largely, although not entirely, due to the Thatcher government's slowing of M1 growth to reduce its domestic inflation. These episodes suggest, in fact, that Dornbusch and similar models can have substantial empirical relevance for situations in which the basic *trend* in money growth is changing, even though evidence suggests that they are much less useful in relating exchange rates and money on a shorter-term (e.g. monthly) basis.

But while the shift in U.S. monetary policy towards restraint provides a plausible explanation of the dollar's strength over 1980–81, it is much less successful in accounting for its continued rise since then. Shifts in money growth (to a first approximation) have no permanent impact on real interest rates or real exchange rates. Eventually inflation must respond to lower money growth, and indeed must fall below money growth to allow real liquidity to be reconstituted. This process began in 1982 – inflation fell nearly 2 percent below M1 growth in that year – and continued into 1983. This should have allowed real interest rates, and the dollar, to have declined, *eventually* by as much in real terms as it had initially risen.

The fact that the dollar is now actually stronger than in 1981 can largely be traced to the failure of real interest rates to fall after 1982, despite the abatement of pressures from monetary policy. As indicated earlier, short and long-term nominal interest rates are now nearly as high as their average 1981 levels, while surveys and the actual behavior of inflation suggest that real interest rates are, if anything, higher than in that year.

The most plausible and widely accepted explanation for the continued high level of U.S. interest rates, and hence the dollar's strength, is the large and growing U.S. budget deficit. In addition, the reduction in taxes on certain types of business investment has probably reinforced the deficit's impact on interest rates. This view has been disputed by those who point out that, historically, high budget deficits have not been associated with high real interest rates in the United States.[37] However, U.S. budget deficits in the past have typically occurred during recessions, when private credit demand is normally relatively weak, or during war periods. The present situation, with deficits on a *full-employment* basis exceeding 4 percent of our GNP for possibly many years, is nearly unprecedented in modern U.S. experience.[38] Such deficits could well be exerting very considerable upward pressure on real interest rates, particularly longer-term rates given the strong possibility that they will be a major source of pressure on credit markets for some years.[39]

Viewed in this way, the high U.S. budget deficits, high interest rates and the dollar, and the growing U.S. current account deficits are naturally related. Indeed, the growing current account deficits stemming from the dollar's strength can be viewed as 'effecting' a transfer of foreign savings to the U.S. to augment the domestic funds available to finance our budget deficits. That is, given the relatively high international mobility of capital among major industrial nations, it is natural that foreigners would, directly or indirectly, supply a substantial portion of the funds to finance our deficit. In effect, the United States is likely to be able to draw on the pool of foreign savings nearly as easily as it can draw on domestic savings. This transfer of funds can be effected, however, only if the United States runs an equal current account deficit, which in turn requires (initially at least) an increase in the real value of the dollar to produce the requisite reduction of our exports relative to imports.[40] Indeed, given that the U.S. accounts for less than one-third the total pool of (gross) savings generated by the industrial countries, it is not inconceivable that foreigners could ultimately supply one-half or more of the funds required to finance our budget deficits. This would entail current account deficits substantially greater than those now being recorded if, as many observers expect, U.S. budget deficits remain in the $150–200 billion range indefinitely.

Most exchange rate models have provided little, if any, guidance about the ultimate consequences of budget deficits, particularly their real impact.[41] These models do suggest—as does the earlier Mundell–Fleming framework—that U.S. real interest rates probably cannot permanently remain substantially higher than those abroad, given the relatively high mobility of capital that now seems to prevail among the major industrial nations.[42] The large inflows of foreign capital the U.S. is now receiving should eventually reduce pressures on domestic real interest rates, allowing them to fall over time. As real interest rates here fall, the dollar can also be expected to decline. However, very large (by historical standards) net inflows of foreign capital, and hence large current budget deficits, are apt to prevail so long as U.S. budget deficits remain high. And, depending on how the policies underlying the deficits affect the demand relative to the supply of U.S. products versus foreign products, the real value of the dollar needed to bring about such flows is likely to be different from—and may well be higher than the level that has prevailed historically.[43]

In short, the high U.S. real interest rates of recent years, and their impact on the dollar, can be regarded as the *temporary* consequences of U.S. monetary and fiscal policies. In a world of perfect capital mobility, even permanent fiscal deficits can and may well raise the long-run real value of the dollar. Thus the real value of the dollar can be expected to fall over time from present levels, but it cannot fall to a level that restores either U.S. competitiveness or our current account to historically 'normal' levels unless the budget deficits are substantially reduced.

Despite the fact that the dollar is probably substantially above its ultimate real level, it is at least questionable whether the term 'overvaluation' appropriately characterizes its present state. Slowing money growth temporarily reduces liquidity available to the private sector, requiring adjustments in the spending plans of businesses and households; similar adjustments are entailed by the increased demands on limited savings from higher budget deficits. In a closed economy, higher real interest rates serve as the main price signal that induces these adjustments. In an open economy, the resulting increase in the real exchange rate spreads the burden of adjustment to traded goods sectors. Thus the effective incidence of monetary and fiscal policies is different in an open economy than in a closed economy, with interest rate sensitive sectors affected less and tradeable goods sectors affected more. In any case, both the interest and exchange rate changes resulting from these policies, even where temporary, are natural and necessary consequences of the real sector adjustments they reflect. Thus the dollar is no more or less 'overvalued' than are U.S. interest rates, and the term is probably not appropriately applied to either.

This same argument implies that the high dollar and high U.S. real interest rates are leading to an allocation of real resources that is efficient *given the constraints imposed by the monetary and fiscal policies that are their ultimate cause.* Increased U.S. budget deficits can only be financed with an increase in U.S. private savings, reduction in domestic investment, and/or increase in borrowing from the pool of foreign savings. The higher dollar, by reducing our exports and increasing our imports, allows more of the deficit to be financed from abroad, reducing the 'burden' on domestic savings and investment. Preventing the dollar from rising, via foreign exchange market intervention or capital controls, would (assuming that this would even be possible) merely shift the sectoral adjustment. The resulting revised allocation of resources could easily be more costly than the present pattern.

Accordingly, while the high value of the dollar has unquestionably adversely affected U.S. competitiveness, just as high real interest rates have retarded investment in certain sectors, the blame properly rests with the policies that are the ultimate cause. These adverse impacts effectively represent the costs of reducing inflation and maintaining the tax and spending policies that have produced large and growing budget deficits. These costs must be weighed against the benefits of these policies. If the costs are found to exceed these benefits, only changes of the fundamental policies, and not short-term palliatives applied to the financial markets, can be expected to alleviate the adverse consequences *associated* with, but not properly attributed to, the high value of the dollar.

Lessons for Exchange Rate Modelers

Finally, the recent experience with budget and current account deficits and the high dollar again underscores the fact that *real* factors determining the supply and demand for commodities and the allocation of resources play an important role in determining exchange rates in practice, not only in theory, and influence exchange rates, primarily through expectations, in the short run and not only the long run. This experience, coupled with the history of oil price changes, suggests strongly that there can be significant changes in real exchange rates in the long run *and* that variations in current exchange rates often cannot be properly interpreted without taking these shifts into account. To say, that is, that exchange rates are determined in a *proximate* sense in financial markets is *not* to say that exchange rates are unaffected by real factors; real factors are, in fact, critical determinants of conditions in financial markets.

Given prospects that present economic policies will persist for a considerable time, policy debate is focusing increasingly on such questions relating to their *real* impacts as: what will be their ultimate consequences for the competitiveness of various U.S. goods; and what will be their impact on the level and sectoral distribution of U.S. investment? More generally, what is their ultimate real impact in an open economy with high international mobility of capital—that is, what sectors, domestic and foreign, are ultimately "crowded out," and to what extent? Despite their great contributions to understanding exchange rate dynamics, models developed over the last decade are generally not well suited to answer such questions. Such models will have to go beyond their present focus on exchange rate dynamics shaped by financial market forces to consider the real sectors much more explicitly, in order to illuminate the interactions between financial and real sectors in determining exchange rates and interest rates *and* the allocation of real resources in both the short and the long run.

POLICY LESSONS

From a policy perspective, the technical merits of alternative exchange rate models are not nearly as important as their larger implications about the basic forces influencing exchange rates and their interactions with the domestic economy. Policymakers and those advising them must be mainly concerned with

interpreting observed exchange rate movements and gauging their implications—
for the domestic economy and for their own policies, including the public's
perceptions about them. What policy lessons, then, can be drawn from exchange
rate models in view of the actual experience with floating exchange rates over
the last ten years?

Certainly one basic lesson is that no single mechanism or factor is likely to be
the sole determinant of exchange rates in practice. The foreign exchange market
repercussions of shifts in monetary and fiscal policies and fluctuating oil prices
over the last decade have repeatedly demonstrated that inflation rates, real interest rates, and "real" factors—those determining relative commodity prices in the
long-run—all can be important influences on observed exchange rate movements.
Moreover, these proximate determinants of exchange rates are themselves influenced by a wide variety of more 'fundamental' or 'exogenous' conditions.

The experience with floating exchange rates has also shown that the relative
importance of alternative determinants can vary substantially across countries
and change dramatically from period to period. Real interest rates have been a
major influence on the dollar since 1980, but they were probably much less important a force prior to then.[44] Inflation rates clearly will play a much more
prominent role in determining exchange rates during hyperinflations than during
more normal periods. As this indicates, the *policy* environment plays no small
role in determining the relative balance of influences on exchange rates.

Furthermore, the relative importance of the determinants is apt to depend
upon the analyst's time horizon. Those concerned with predicting and explaining
long-term exchange rate trends may be justified in focusing primarily on monetary forces. But anyone charged with interpreting exchange rates over the short-
and medium-term cannot afford to ignore real interest rates or the real factors
affecting commodity supplies and demands. Because disturbances in credit markets that produce real interest fluctuations are often very short-lived, domestic
interest rates and the value of home currency could well vary together on a daily
or intra-day basis—as market traders frequently assert—while moving in opposite directions over longer periods, as economists have frequently found. These
observations suggest again that practical analyses of exchange rates will generally
need to combine the analytical rigor of the asset approach with a more flexible
and eclectic view of their determinants than has usually been incorporated in
specific models.

From a modeling perspective, this means that testing between alternative simple models becomes less urgent than incorporating the eclectic view of exchange
rate determinants taken by earlier writers within the more rigorous formal
frameworks developed in recent years. For the policymaker, the implication is
that actual exchange rate movements will often not be nearly as easy to interpret
as some of the simpler models might suggest—almost as difficult to 'explain',
perhaps, as the stock market. Even more important, mechanical rules relating
domestic policies to exchange market developments—such as those suggested

by several analysts[45]—pose considerable risks when the factors determining exchange rates are potentially many yet often not observable directly. The reason is that such rules, while designed to be beneficial given a particular type of disturbance to exchange markets, can have harmful consequences under other disturbances.[46]

Theory and experience have both underscored another basic policy lesson, namely that floating rates do not automatically bring greater stability or smoother adjustment to the real sector, nor do they necessarily insulate that sector from changes in policy, anymore than under fixed exchange rates. Indeed, since nominal and real exchange rates have tended to vary closely together under floating, policy actions or other factors that cause instability in exchange markets may well have adverse real consequences. Likewise, floating rates have often been criticized for failing to reduce current account imbalances. But the lesson of the absorption approach—that current account deficits inevitably result when policy or other factors cause domestic spending to exceed production—is no less valid under the current regime than it was during the Bretton Woods era. Floating rates may be said to have allowed greater current account imbalances because of the greater divergences in national economic conditions they can accommodate, but floating rates are hardly the cause of these imbalances.

Theory and experience too have severely tempered hopes that floating rates would allow policymakers much greater autonomy than they enjoyed under fixed exchange rates. If anything, the necessity for stable and credible policies has increased with the adoption of floating, given the critical dependence of market determined exchange rates on expectations about the future course of policy. Indeed, the near crises in the exchange markets in November 1978 and October 1979 demonstrated graphically that uncertainty about government policies can have dramatic effects on real exchange rates, with potentially adverse consequences for the real economy. Thus the notion that domestic policies can be formulated without worrying about any real-sector repercussions of their exchange rate consequence has been shown to be overly optimistic, at best.

Furthermore, the limited degree to which floating exchange rates insulate a nation from the consequences of policies pursued by its neighbors has also become increasingly apparent. European officials have complained that U.S. monetary and fiscal actions disrupt their own economics and limit their policy options. These complaints may be exaggerated, but the experience with the high dollar in recent years has often supported such contentions. This experience has confirmed what several exchange rate models have predicted, namely that even shifts in purely financial policies can, by temporarily changing real exchange rates, distort international trade flows, affect real income abroad, and adversely alter the medium-term unemployment-inflation trade-offs faced by foreign authorities. Policy conflicts, then, may have been diminished by the move to floating exchange rates, but they have not been banished altogether.

Taken as a whole, these observations point to a more basic conclusion that has been emphasized by many observers, as well as throughout this volume: exchange rates, as with financial prices generally, are largely reflections of more fundamental economic forces originating with government policies and the preferences, capabilities, and expectations of the public sector. The exchange rate regime itself does not determine these forces, but it does shape the way in which they affect financial and real sectors. Thus the increased turbulence and uncertainty in financial markets, including the foreign exchanges, in recent years, is most plausibly attributed to variations in economic policies and other fundamental economic conditions, and to their divergence across countries, rather than a product of the floating exchange rate regime itself. That this conclusion is increasingly taken for granted is perhaps the best indicator of the contributions made by the theoretical frameworks we have discussed. Despite their limitations, they have substantially clarified the fundamental forces determining exchange rates and the ways in which they are transmitted to foreign exchange and domestic markets, and in so doing have contributed to a deeper understanding of the floating rate system.

NOTES TO CHAPTER 2

1. Several excellent recent surveys of theoretical and empirical analyses of exchange rates include R. Dornbusch, "Exchange Rate Economics: Where Do We Stand?" *Brookings Papers on Economic Activity*, no. 1 (1980): 143–85; J. A. Frenkel, "Flexible Exchange Rates in the 1970s" Working Paper No. 450, National Bureau of Economic Research, (February 1980): J. F. Helliwell, "Policy Modeling of Foreign Exchange Rates," *Journal of Policy Modeling* 1 (1979): 425–44; M. Mussa, "Empirical Regularities in the Behavior of Exchange Rates and Theories of the Foreign Exchange Market," in K. Brunner and A. Meltzer, eds., *Policies for Employment, Prices and Exchange Rates* (Carnegie–Rochester Conference Series on Public Policy, vol. II, 1979): 9–57; R. G. Murphy and C. Van Dyne, "Asset Market Approaches to Exchange Rate Determination: A Comparative Analysis," *Weltwirtschaftliches Archiv* 116, no. 4 (1980): 627–56.

2. The simplest models in the elasticity approach were strictly of a partial-equilibrium nature, in that the effects of devaluation were calculated using elasticities of export and import demands and supplies only. The validity of such models depended on "ceteris paribus" assumptions about the factors underlying monetary and income variables affecting exchange rates and the balance of payments, as a number of scholars, including Haberler, made clear. For excellent expositions, see G. Haberler, "The Market for Foreign Exchange and the Stability of the Balance of Payments: A Theoretical Analysis," *Kyklos* 3 (1949): 193–218; F. Machlup, "The Theory of Foreign Exchanges," *Economica* 6 (November 1939 and February 1940).

3. See S. S. Alexander, "Effects of a Devaluation on a Trade Balance," *IMF Staff Papers* 2 (April 1952): 263–78.

4. See S. S. Alexander, "The Effects of Devaluation: A Simplified Synthesis of Elasticities and Absorption Approaches," *American Economic Review* 49 (March 1959): 22–42 and F. Machlup, "Relative Prices and Aggregate Spending in the Analysis of Devaluation," *American Economic Review* 45 (June 1955): 255–78.

5. See H. S. Houthakker & S. P. Magee, "Income and Price Elasticities in World Trade," *Review of Economics and Statistics* 51 (May 1969): 111–25; M. Goldstein and M. S. Khan, "The Supply and Demand for Exports: A Simultaneous Approach," *Review of Economics and Statistics* 60 (May 1978): 275–86.

6. An early and important exception may be found in M. Friedman, "The Case for Flexible Exchange Rates," in *Essays in Positive Economics* (Chicago: University of Chicago Press, 1953).

7. See S. C. Tsiang, "The Role of Money in Trade Balance Stability: Synthesis of the Elasticity and Absorption Approaches," *American Economic Review* 51 (December 1961): 912–36 and Harry G. Johnson, "Towards a General Theory of the Balance of Payments," in *International Trade and Economic Growth* (Cambridge, Mass.: Harvard University Press, 1958).

8. See Robert A. Mundell, *International Economics* (New York: Macmillan, 1968) and J. M. Fleming, "Domestic Financial Policies under Fixed and Flexible Exchange Rates," *IMF Staff Papers* 9 (September 1962): 369–79.

9. See J. E. Meade, *The Balance of Payments* (London: Oxford University Press, 1951); Mundell, *International Economics*; and Fleming, "Domestic Financial Policies Under Fixed and Flexible Exchange Rates."

10. See J. R. Artus, "Exchange Rate Stability and Managed Floating: The Experience of the Federal Republic of Germany," *IMF Staff Papers* 23 (July 1976): 312–34 and G. Stevens, et al., "Modeling Bilateral Exchange Rates in a Multi-Country Model," *Proceedings* of the Fourth Pacific Basin Central Bank Econometric Modeling Conference, Tokyo, November 1979.

11. See W. H. Branson and T. D. Willett, "Policy Toward Short-Term Capital Movements: Some Implications of the Portfolio Approach," and N. C. Miller and M.v.N. Whitman, "The Outflow of Short-term Funds from the United States: Adjustment of Stocks and Flows," both in F. Machlup, W. S. Salant, and Lorie Tarshis, eds., *International Mobility and Movement of Capital* (New York: National Bureau of Economics Research, 1972). See also W. H. Branson, *Financial Capital Flows in the U.S. Balance of Payments* (Amsterdam: North–Holland, 1968) and Thomas D. Willett and F. Forte, "Interest Rate Policy and External Balance," *Quarterly Journal of Economics* 82 (May 1969).

12. For early critical reviews of the experience with floating exchange rates, see Charles P. Kindleberger, "Lessons of Floating Exchange Rates," in Karl Brunner and Allan Meltzer, eds., *Institutional Arrangements and the Inflation Problem*, Carnegie–Rochester Conference Series of Public Policy, 3 (1976): 51–77; and Ronald McKinnon, "Floating Foreign Exchange

Rates 1973–1974: The Emperor's New Clothes," pp. 79–114 of the same volume.

13. Among many examples, see James Meade, *The Balance of Payments* (London: Oxford University Press, 1951); Leland Yeager *International Monetary Relations* 2nd ed. (New York: Harper & Row, 1976); and Gottfried Haberler, *The Theory of International Trade* (New York: William Hodge, 1936).

14. For a discussion of factors affecting the risk premium see Clas Wihlborg, "Currency Risks in International Financial Markets" Princeton *Studies in International Finance*, no. 44 (December, 1978); Jeffrey A. Frankel, "The Diversifiability of Exchange Risk" *Journal of International Economics* 10 (May 1979); Michael Dooley and P. Isard, "Capital Controls, Political Risk, and Deviations from Interest Parity," *Journal of Political Economy* 88 (April 1980).

15. P. Isard, "Factors Determining Exchange Rates: The Role of Prices, Interest Rates, the Current Account and Risk," International Finance Discussion Paper no. 171 (Federal Reserve Board of Governors, 1980).

16. This equalization does *not* reflect any arbitrage process. As shown in equation (2.4), the home foreign real interest rate differential equals (assuming a zero risk premium) the expected change in the real exchange rate, which measures the relative price of home goods in terms of foreign goods. Assuming no long-term trend in relative prices, the home and foreign real interest rates must become equal in the long run. More generally, the long-run real interest rate differential will equal the long-run average change or trend in the real exchange rate.

17. See the discussions in Yeager, *International Monetary Relations* and Haberler, *The Theory of International Trade*.

18. See H. G. Johnson, "The Monetary Approach to the Balance of Payments: A Nontechnical Guide," *Journal of International Economics* 7 (August 1977).

19. For an evaluation, see M. Bazderich, "Does a Strong U.S. Economy Mean a Weak Dollar?" *Economic Review* (Federal Reserve Bank of San Francisco, Spring 1979).

20. See the Pigott and Sweeney chapter on "Purchasing Power Parity and Exchange Rate Dynamics" in this volume; and C. Pigott, R. J. Sweeney and T. D. Willett, "Some Aspects of the Behavior and Effects of Floating Exchange Rates," paper presented to the Conference on Monetary Theory and Policy, Konstanz, Germany (June 1975). Another discussion of the relative volatility of real and nominal exchange rates compared to relative national price levels can be found in Michael Mussa, "Empirical Regularities in the Behavior of Exchange Rates and Theories of the Foreign Exchange Market."

21. R. Dornbusch, "Expectations and Exchange Rate Dynamics," *Journal of Political Economy* 84 (December 1976).

22. For a more detailed discussion of the relations among short- and long-term real interest rates and exchange rates, see C. Piggott, "Real and Financial

Influences on the Dollar," *Proceedings of the Fifth Pacific Basin Central Bank Economists' Conference* (Bank of Canada: Vancouver, September 1981). As equation (2.4) indicates, an increase in the real interest rate for any term raises the current real exchange rate above the level expected to prevail at maturity. In effect, the anticipated real depreciation of the home currency, expressed at an annual rate, must offset the annualized real home-foreign interest differential (on a risk-adjusted basis). However, real interest fluctuations normally can be regarded as leaving the *long-run* real exchange rate unaffected. Thus the 'adjustment' to changes in long-term real interest rates is made by the current real exchange rate only, in accordance with (2.4). A one percent rise in the home ten-year real interest rate then requires (given the risk premium) an expected future depreciation of the real exchange rate of one percent annually over a ten-year horizon—which means the current real exchange rate must rise by roughly 10 percent. The impact of increases in shorter term real interest rates on the current real exchange rate is then given by the change in the longer term real interest rate it is associated with. Thus a rise in the one-year real interest rate itself (that is, with no change in real interest rates expected to prevail a year or more from now), translates into a ten basis point increase in the ten-year real interest rate, and hence raises the current real exchange rate by roughly one percent.

Admittedly, the above calculations must be modified if there is imperfect capital mobility, that is, if the risk premium in (2.4) rises with the domestic real interest rate. However, increases in long-term real interest rates will still have greater impacts than equal increases in short-term real rates *unless* the degree of mobility is markedly less for longer term than shorter term maturities.

23. Again, see Pigott, "Real and Financial Influences on the Dollar." Long-term interest rates (nominal and real) are approximate averages of current and expected future short-term rates. Hence the longer a given change in short-term real interest rates is expected to persist, the greater the impact on long-term rates, and hence the greater the effect on exchange rates.

24. See Bruce Brittain, "Tests of Theories of Exchange Rate Determination," *Journal of Finance* 32 (May 1977). On the question of expectations in the context of sticky prices, see Sven W. Arndt, "On Exchange Rate Dynamics," *Zeitschrift für Wirtschafts—und Sozialwissenschaften* 99, no. 1/2 (1979). The predictions of the Dornbusch model for the statistical behavior of exchange rates are discussed in detail in the Pigott–Sweeney chapter in this volume; and also in Michael Mussa, "A Model of Exchange Rate Dynamics," *Journal of Political Economy* 90, no. 1 (February 1982): 74–104.

25. For two excellent empirical studies of real interest rates, see F. Mishkin, "The Real Interest Rate: An Empirical Investigation," *Carnegie–Rochester Conference on Public Policy*, no. 15 (1981) and "The Real Interest Rate: A Multi-Country Empirical Study," NBER Working Paper No. 1047 (December 1982). See also C. Pigott, "Indicators of Long-Term Real Interest

Rates," *Economic Review* (Federal Reserve Bank of San Francisco, Winter 1984).

26. There is, in fact, considerable and increasing evidence that deviations from PPP persist in the long run. See, for example, Pigott and Sweeney, Chapter 4 in this volume, as well as M. B. Darby, "Does Purchasing Power Parity Work?" Proceedings of the *Sixth West Coast Academic/Federal Reserve Economic Research Seminar* (Federal Reserve Bank of San Francisco, Fall 1982); C. Pigott, "The Importance of Real Factors in Determining Exchange Rates," *Economic Review of the Federal Reserve Bank of San Francisco* (Fall 1981); and J. A. Frankel, "Flexible Exchange Rates in the 1970s."

27. These portfolio approaches can be viewed as extensions to open economies of the models developed by Tobin and others. See J. Tobin, "Money and Economic Growth," *Econometrica* 33 (1965) and D. Foley and M. Sidrauski, "Portfolio Choice, Investment and Growth," *American Economic Review* 50 (March 1970). Early contributions to this approach include R. Dornbusch, "A Portfolio Balance Model of the Open Economy" *Journal of Monetary Economics* 1 (1975); W. H. Branson, "Stocks and Flows in International Monetary Analysis," in A. Ando, et al., eds., *International Aspects of Stabilization Policy* (Boston: Federal Reserve Bank of Boston, 1974); and D. Foley and M. Sidrauski, *Monetary and Fiscal Policy in a Growing Economy* (New York: Macmillan, 1971).

28. For tests of whether there is a risk premium in forward exchange rates, see R. Meese and K. Singleton, "Rational Expectations, Risk Premia, and the Market for Spot and Forward Exchange," International Finance Division Discussion Paper, No. 165 (Board of Governors of the Federal Reserve, July 1980); L. P. Hanson and R. J. Hodrick, "Forward Rates as Optimal Predictors of Future Exchange Rates," *Journal of Political Economy* 88 (October 1980); Jeffrey Frankel, "A Test of Perfect Substitutability in the Foreign Exchange Market," *Southern Economic Journal* 48 (1982); and P. Isard, "Factors Determining Exchange Rates." Generally the most direct tests (and probably the most powerful) reject the hypothesis of no risk premium at all (conditional on rational expectations); Frankel fails to reject this hypothesis, but with a more indirect test. However, this finding of itself does not demonstrate that the risk premium is related to the portfolio mix, and indeed Frankel's study suggests it is not. More recent studies examining the impact of sterilized intervention (which, apart from 'announcement' effects, affects exchange rates, if at all, by altering the mix of interest-bearing assets) is very mixed as to its impact. See Maurice Obstfeld, "Exchange Rates, Inflation, and the Sterilization Problem: Germany, 1975–1981," NBER Working Paper No. 963, August 1982; Deborah Danker, Richard Haas, Steven Symansky, and Ralph Tyron, "Small Empirical Models of Exchange Market Intervention: Applications to Canada, Germany, and Japan," (Federal Reserve Board Staff Study, 1983); Bonnie Loopesko, "A Time-Series Study of the Relationship between Exchange Rates, Intervention, and Other Variables, Empirical Evi-

dence from Daily Data" (Federal Reserve Board Staff Study, 1983); and Michael Hutchison, "Intervention, Deficit Finance, and Real Exchange Rates: The Case of Japan," *Economic Review* of the Federal Reserve Bank of San Francisco, Winter 1984. These and related studies generally find that the portfolio mix affects exchange rates for some countries, but not others. However even where there are positive findings, the impact is relatively small and temporary (see Hutchinson). A summary of recent Federal Reserve studies of this issue is given in "Intervention in the Foreign Exchange Markets: A Summary of Ten Staff Studies," *Federal Reserve Bulletin*, November 1983. This concludes that sterilized intervention *can have an effect* on exchange rates—which is not the same as concluding that its magnitude is large or stable enough to be *effective*.

29.   See P. Isard, "Factors Determining Exchange Rates."

30.   See C. Pigott and R. J. Sweeney, Chapter 4 in this volume; M. B. Darby, "Does Purchasing Power . . . ," *op. cit.*; C. Pigott, "Indicators of Long-Term Real Interest Rates"; and J. A. Frankel, "Flexible Exchange Rates in the 1970s."

31.   For attempts to model or account for shifts in long-run real exchange rates, see P. Hooper and J. Morton, "Fluctuations in the Dollar: A Model of Nominal and Real Exchange Date Determination," International Finance Discussion Papers No. 168 (Federal Reserve Board of Governors, October 1980); M. Dooley and P. Isard, "The Portfolio Balance Model of Exchange Rates," Discussion Paper No. 141, International Finance Division, Board of Governors of the Federal Reserve System (May 1979); Isard, "Factors Determining Exchange Rates"; and Stevens, et al., "Modeling Bilateral Exchange Rates in a Multi-Country Model."

32.   See, for example, C. Fred Bergsten, "The U.S.–Japan Economic Conflict," *Foreign Affairs* (Summer 1982); John Williamson, "The Exchange Rate System," *Policy Analyses in International Economics* no. 5 (September 1983).

33.   Bergsten has called for a moratorium on capital outflows from Japan to raise the value of the yen vis-à-vis the dollar. Williamson argues for managed floating exchange rates on similar grounds.

34.   This view is taken, for example, in a recent report to the U.S. government on the "Misalignment of the United States Dollar and the Japanese Yen: The Problem and Its Solution," prepared by Ezra Solomon and David C. Murchison for the Washington law firm of Howrey and Simon. Most of those holding this view do not argue that the current accounts need to be balanced in the long run, but that there is some essentially constant equilibrium surplus or deficit to which (real) exchange rates must ultimately adjust. This is also implicitly the view underlying the Hooper–Morton portfolio balance model of exchange rates referred to earlier.

35.   Both the Livingston survey of short-term inflation expectations and the survey of longer term inflation expectations taken by Robert B. Hoey, Vice President and Chief Economist of Warburg Paribus/A. G. Becker show a decline in the U.S. beginning in 1980. (Some Hoey estimates are listed in Peter Isard, "What's Wrong with Empirical Exchange Rate Mod-

els: Some Critical Issues and New Directions," International Finance Discussion Paper No. 226 (August 1983).

36. Jurg Niehans, *The Appreciation of Sterling: Causes, Effects, Policies*, Center Symposia Series Paper No. CS–11 (Graduate School of Management of the University of Rochester, 1981).

37. See Paul Evans, "Do Large Deficits Produce High Interest Rates," Working Paper, Department of Economics, Stanford University (October 1983), and *The Effect of Deficits on Prices of Financial Assets: Theory and Evidence* (U.S. Department of the Treasury, 1984). However, Michael Hutchison and David Pyle ("The Real Interest/Budget Deficit Link: International Evidence, 1973–1982," processed, 1984), using a cross-country sample, do find evidence that budget deficits raise short-term real interest rates.

38. Typically, the largest deficits for the U.S. have occurred during war periods. It is not entirely surprising that real interest rates were not raised during such periods, since the price controls, material shortages for non-war-related activities, and other special factors could be expedited to discourage investment demand (and stimulate forced saving) to a considerable degree.

39. The view taken here, that increases in real long-term interest rates account for much, if not most, of the dollar's remarkably high real value, is also that taken by the Council of Economic Advisors in the 1984 *Economic Report of the President*, p. 53.

40. Admittedly, the policies producing the deficit may shift supplies and demands for traded (and nontraded) goods in potentially complex ways. However, since these policies are apt to reduce the amount of U.S. goods available to foreigners on world markets, there would seem to some presumption that the U.S. commodity terms of trade, and hence the real value of the dollar, would rise in the long run.

41. Jeffrey Sachs and Charles Wyplosz, "Real Exchange Rate Effects of Fiscal Policy," NBER Working Paper No. 1255 (January 1984) consider the real impacts of fiscal policies in a two country/good world *without* growth. Their approach highlights the critical importance of the tax/expenditure policies underlying a deficit for its real impact as well as the influence of the currency/country risk premium. See also S. Turnovsky, "The Dynamics of Fiscal Policy in an Open Economy," *Journal of International Economics* (1976): 115–42. However, a zero growth context is misleading in some important respects; it means that the budget and current accounts *must* be balanced in the long-run, which is generally not the case in a growth context. This implies, for example, that an initial rise in government expenditure (no change in taxes) leads to a long-run *fall* in expenditure from its base level; the reason is that government interest payments rise from the initial deficits, requiring a fall in expenditure (or rise in taxes) to balance the budget in the long run. Robert Hodrick, "Dynamic Effects of Government Policies in an Open Economy," *Journal of Monetary Economics* 6 (April 1980) considers a growth context, but in a one-good world so that real exchange rate impacts are suppressed.

42. Again, this is *not* an arbitrage proposition. The U.S.–foreign long-term real interest differential effectively measures the extent to which the real value of the dollar is now above the level expected to prevail in the long run. Eventually the real dollar must fall back to its long-run level (essentially by definition), even if this long-run level has changed. As this happens, U.S. and foreign real interest rates must also come back into alignment.

43. The ultimate impact of permanent budget deficits on the real value of the dollar depend mainly upon how the policies underlying those deficits affect the demand relative to supply for U.S. versus foreign goods. (See, for example, Sachs and Wyplosz, "Real Exchange Rate Effects of Fiscal Policy." Given that the U.S. deficit reflects a sharp increase in defense expenditures (as well as a reduction in personal income taxes) it seems reasonable to suppose that the impact, on balance, is to shift world demand (private *and* public) toward U.S. products, making it likely that the real value of the dollar will be permanently raised if the deficits persist indefinitely.

44. See Pigott, "Indicators of Long-Term Real Interest Rates."

45. In particular, that proposed by Ronald McKinnon in "An International Standard for Monetary Stabilization," *Policy Analyses in International Economics* no. 8 (March 1984). McKinnon's proposal is based on his view that currency fluctuations are dominated by shifts in portfolio preferences; see R. McKinnon, "Currency Substitutions and Instability in the World Dollar Standard," *American Economic Review* 72 (June 1982).

46. In particular, under real disturbances to exchange markets, for example, from fiscal policy or from oil price changes. For a critique of McKinnon see C. Radcliffe, A. Warge, and T. D. Willett, "Currency Substitution and Instability in the World Dollar Standard: Further Comments," Working Paper of the Department of Economics, Claremont Graduate School (1983).

3 INTEREST RATE CHANGES, INFLATIONARY EXPECTATIONS AND EXCHANGE RATE OVERSHOOTING
The Dollar-DM Rate

Thomas D. Willett, Waseem Khan and A'ida Der Hovanessian

INTRODUCTION

There has been considerable interest in the relationships among interest rates, exchange rates, and inflationary expectations. Many exchange market analysts focus heavily on the effects of international interest rate differentials in influencing the ups and downs of currencies. Generally such discussions assume that an interest rate increase will cause a currency to appreciate (i.e., its exchange rate to fall), and recent theoretical analysis, due especially to Rudiger Dornbush, has shown that in a Keynesian world such exchange rate fluctuations may be substantially magnified, causing exchange rate changes in the short run to overshoot longer run equilibrium levels substantially.[1] Many commentators have argued that this has been a major explanation of the observed volatility of key exchange rates under floating rates (particularly the $-DM rate), and in an influential paper, Jeffrey Frankel has found empirical support for this view.[2] However such scenarios are directly counter to the implications of the monetary models of exchange rates, which have also received a great deal of popular attention and empirical support. In these models, interest rate increases are mirrored by currency depreciation rather than appreciation.

The original working title of this paper was "Interest Rates, Exchange Rates, and Inflationary Expectations." Willett is the prime author of the text, while Khan and Der Hovanessian are the prime authors of the appendixes. Financial assistance from Texaco and helpful comments from Jeffrey Frankel, Steven Kohlhagen, Richard Sweeney, and Edward Tower are gratefully acknowledged.

49

While both of these approaches have been provided with published empirical support, a number of other studies have failed to find strong simple relationships of either sign between interest rate and exchange rate changes.[3] In this paper we discuss some of the major theoretical issues involved in analyzing the relationships between interest rates and exchange rates and present further empirical evidence that neither the monetarist nor Keynesian's explanation is fully satisfactory.

The reason is not hard to find. Whether an interest rate increase relative to those abroad should be expected to be accompanied by an appreciation or a depreciation of the currency depends crucially on whether the change in the nominal interest rate represents primarily a change in the expected real rate of interest due, for example, to the liquidity effects of a tightening of monetary policy or whether it is primarily the result of a change in inflationary expectations. In the former (Keynesian) case, which is assumed in many market commentaries, we would indeed expect the currency to appreciate, while in the latter case, emphasized in many monetarist models, we would expect higher interest rates to be accompanied by a falling currency.

The empirical evidence suggests that both explanations have been important in explaining short-term interest rate movements in recent years and thus that neither provides a simple dominant explanation of the relationship between interest rates and exchange rates. The monetarists have certainly been correct in that inflationary expectations have often played a major role in determining interest rate changes and that we cannot safely assume that high nominal interest rates mean tight monetary policy; on the other hand, we have also had fluctuations in short-term interest rates that cannot plausibly be explained in terms of changing inflationary expectations. The long duration of periods of negative real short-term interest rates on an ex post basis in many industrial countries during the 1970s is clearly incompatible with the assumptions of reasonable processes of expectations formation and a positive (much less constant) real rate of return on short-term assets such as was prevalent during the 1950s and 1960s.[4]

Attempting to distinguish between the real and inflationary expectations components of nominal interest rate changes is quite important not only for exchange rate forecasting but also for analysis of the empirical importance of various hypotheses about the causes of the high degree of exchange rate volatility that has been experienced during the current period of floating. Even with respect to real interest rate changes, however, there may be considerable variability in the relationships between interest rate and exchange rate changes. In the following section the basic outline of Rudiger Dornbusch's influential analysis of exchange rate overshooting is presented and several complicating factors such as less than infinite capital mobility and the effects of uncertainty are considered. In subsequent sections, the effects of changes in inflationary expectations on interest rate-exchange rate relationships are discussed and the difference is emphasized between changes in the expected trend rate of changes of exchange rates and changes in the base or initial equilibrium exchange rate from which the expected trend originates. Changes in inflationary expectations will only affect the former in a simple quantity theory world, but resulting effects on velocity and uncertainty may have a substantial impact on the latter. Section VI considers the recent effort by Jeffrey Frankel to model the exchange rate effects of both the real and inflationary expectations components of nominal interest rate changes and the need to extend the analysis to take into account the term structure of inflationary expectations is emphasized. Recent analysis of the possibility of much more substantial and prolonged exchange rate overshooting due to differentials in long-term interest rates is discussed in the concluding section. Appendixes A and B extend and critique the Frankel analysis and present new empirical results.

THE EFFECTS OF REAL INTEREST RATE CHANGES

A great deal of attention has been focused on the recent model presented by Rudiger Dornbusch in which the exchange rate responses to unanticipated money supply changes will overshoot the resulting change in the long-run equilibrium rate because of the combination of high international capital mobility and more rapid adjustment in foreign exchange and domestic financial markets than in goods markets. In traditional macroeconometric models, an unanticipated one-shot increase in the money supply will lead to a temporary fall in the real short-term interest rate. However, if capital is perfectly mobile internationally, there can be no difference in interest rates internationally unless they are exactly offset by expected changes in exchange rates. Thus, if interest rates fell at home relative to abroad, the home currency would immediately have to depreciate sufficiently below its long-run equilibrium value so that it would be expected to appreciate back toward this long-run equilibrium value at a rate equal to the interest rate differential. The initial overshooting would be greater the larger was the change in the interest differential and the longer the differential was expected to be maintained.

Estimates of the relationships between changes in interest rate differentials and exchange rate movements have been used to calculate the magnitude of such exchange rate overshooting. However, the accuracy of such estimates of exchange rate overshooting are critically dependent upon the adequacy of the specification of the estimating equations being used. If, in fact, the cause of the interest rate change has not been correctly identified, we would expect econometric estimates to be quite unstable over time periods in which the relative importance of causes of interest rate differentials differed, and we could have little confidence in the results of overshooting estimates of any one particular regression.

Figure 3-1. Relationships among Interest Rates, Exchange Rates, and Money Supply Change.

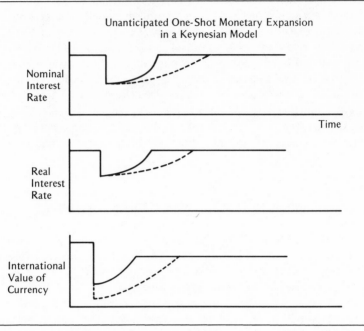

Unanticipated One-Shot Monetary Expansion
in a Keynesian Model

Nominal
Interest
Rate

Time

Real
Interest
Rate

International
Value of
Currency

Note: – – – – indicates slower adjustment speeds.

This will be true even when changes in inflationary expectations play no role in the changes in nominal interest rate differentials. As is illustrated in Figure 3-1 in a Dornbusch-type model, the amount of overshooting in response to a decline in interest rates is a function of how long the resulting interest differential is expected to persist, but the expected duration of the differential (specifically the rate at which the differential is expected to close) may vary considerably depending on the cause of the interest rate change.

Dornbusch's original analysis considers an unanticipated one-shot change in the money supply. In this case, the amount of the initial interest rate decline would be a function of the interest elasticity of the demand for money, and the expected duration of the differential would depend on the speed with which the domestic economy adjusted to work off this unexpected increase in liquidity. These adjustment speeds may differ considerably from one economy to another. In particular, in models that emphasize direct feedback from exchange rate changes to domestic prices (this is not considered in the original Dornbusch paper but is in a later paper by Dornbusch and Krugman)[5] it is often argued that adjustments will take place more rapidly in more open economies. Where adjustment speeds did differ significantly from one economy to another, it could make an important difference in which economy the interest rate change occurred.

Other causes of changes in real interest rates must also be taken into account; the expected duration of changes in interest rates associated with cyclical up-turns and downturns may differ from episode to episode and from those asso-ciated with changes in monetary policy. The story could be repeated with other causes for shifts in the demand for money, some of which might be expected to be quite temporary and others of quite long duration. Indeed, there is certainly the possibility of shifts in real interest rates that are expected to be permanent. In models such as Dornbusch's that assume infinite capital mobility (i.e., perfect asset substitutability), such a permanent change in the expected real rate of interest could not occur, as it would require infinite initial overshooting. Where less than perfectly elastic capital mobility is assumed, it becomes possible for expected rates of return on financial instruments in different countries to differ. Overshooting could still occur, but it would be less than in the case of infinite capital mobility. Other recent models have pointed to the possibility of under-shooting as well.[6]

There appears to be considerable range of opinion today about how high international capital mobility is. Those who have started with null hypotheses of rational expectations and the capital asset pricing models have tended to assume highly integrated financial markets and have tended to take the absence of find-ings of significant risk premiums in forward rates in most studies to date as strong evidence for the perfect substitutability hypothesis. On the other hand, those who have adopted more traditional approaches have tended to view inter-national capital mobility as significant, but considerably less than perfectly elas-tic, and this view is supported by the numerous econometric studies of the inter-est sensitivity of international capital flows that have been carried out in this tradition.[7]

This question of the actual degree of capital mobility facing different coun-tries and the implications for the magnitude of interest rate induced exchange rate overshooting needs a good deal more analysis, as does recognition that the exchange rate path following the initial overshooting is unlikely to remain un-disturbed over the time period of the expected closing of the interest differen-tial. The current interest differential is known with certainty, while there may be considerable variance to expectations of the future price path. With risk aversion this would suggest that the initial overshooting and consequent mean expected rate of appreciation would have to be greater than that indicated in the perfect certainty version of Dornbusch's analysis.[8]

The amount of initial overshooting would presumably be greater, the greater was the amount of uncertainty about future exchange rate shocks and the less the extent to which the exchange rate risk resulting from such shocks could be diversified away at zero or low costs.[9] Under the assumption that the probabil-ity distribution of expected exchange rate paths becomes broader the further the time horizon in question, the longer expected duration of the interest differential would increase the initial overshooting by more than proportionately in relation to the perfect certainty effects.

Thus, consideration of less than infinitely elastic capital mobility and uncertainty about exchange rate disturbances have opposing influences on the expected degree of interest rate-related overshooting. We have little basis at present for judging which of these effects would be the stronger. Given that the interest cum expected appreciation sensitivity of capital flows is likely to vary over different ranges and the amount of exchange rate uncertainty can vary tremendously from one period to another, we should not be surprised to find estimates of exchange rate overshooting coefficients that differ quite a bit from one period to another, as well as from one pair of countries to another.

CHANGES IN INFLATIONARY EXPECTATIONS IN A SIMPLE QUANTITY THEORY WORLD

The likelihood of unstable empirical relationships between interest rate and exchange rate changes is increased still further when one considers that nominal interest rate changes are often the result of changes in inflationary expectations rather than expected real rates of interest. Suppose, for example, that the cause of an interest rate decline is a decline in the expected rates of long-run monetary growth and inflation. Then, in a simple quantity theory world (as is illustrated in Figure 3-2) there would be no immediate impact of the interest rate changes on exchange rates.[10] This change in inflationary expectations would change the expected equilibrium trend of the nominal exchange rate by an amount equal to the change in the expected rate of inflation, but there would be no change in the base—for example, the current equilibrium rate to which this trend is applied.[11] In such a world where this was the only type of disturbance, there would be zero coefficient for the regression of short-run changes in exchange rates on changes in interest rates (assuming no initial trend), but a coefficient of plus one on the regression of the interest differential $(r_h - r_f)$ on the rate of currency appreciation or depreciation (a coefficient of minus one on the rate of exchange rate change (e')).

In a world composed of both types of disturbances, a simple regression of $\Delta(r_h - r_f)$ on Δe would bias downward estimates of the amount of overshooting in response to unanticipated temporary changes in the rate of monetary growth.

It is important to note that the explanations of the dramatic and sizable fall of the dollar during 1977-78 that focused on changes in the inflationary outlook are not consistent with such a simple quantity theory world. It is quite true that this fall of the dollar did coincide with an increase in expectations of U.S. inflation relative to that abroad, but such a shift in expected inflation rate differential could not plausibly have been more than 4 or 5 percent (and was, in

Figure 3-2. Change in the Rate of Monetary Expansion in a Quantity Theory Model.

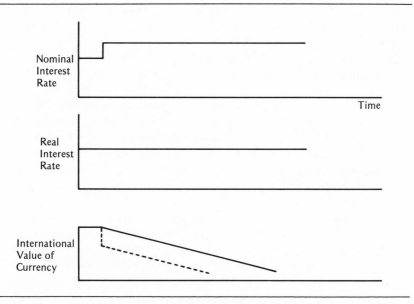

Note: – – – – indicates uncertainty and velocity effects.

fact, probably a good bit less than this). As noted above, in a simple quantity theory world this shift in inflationary expectations would change interest rates and the trend of exchange rates by an equal amount but would have no effects on the current short-run equilibrium exchange rates. While the worsening of inflationary expectations in the United States in 1977–78 undoubtedly played a role in the fall of the dollar over this period, the size of the decline over this period cannot be explained on simple quantity theory grounds.

INFLATIONARY EXPECTATIONS
AND VELOCITY EFFECTS

In more sophisticated models, however, changes in inflationary expectations may have sizable immediate effects on exchange rates. One mechanism noted in the recent exchange rate analysis by Frankel is through the effects of inflation on velocity and the demand for real cash balances where the interest elasticity of the demand for money is non-zero.[12] Expectations of higher rates of inflation increase the expected "tax" on non-interest bearing money balances (and those that bear fixed rates of interest). The resulting incentives to economize on real cash balances results in a one-shot increase in the price level because of the

resulting increase in velocity. Under the ceteris paribus assumption of no permanent real shocks, purchasing power parity will hold in the long run and the
resulting increase in domestic prices because of the one-shot increase in velocity
will lead to a one-shot increase in the domestic price level and a corresponding
change in the level of the equilibrium exchange rate path.

In an efficient foreign exchange market, the exchange rate would change
immediately by the full amount of the one-shot velocity effect plus any overshooting that might occur even though it might take some time for domestic
prices to adjust fully. Thus, just as with the Dornbusch overshooting case of temporary unanticipated monetary expansions, there could be a sizable initial
change in the real exchange rate. Unlike the Dornbusch case, however, there
would be no exchange rate overshooting. The initial deviation from PPP would
be closed entirely through domestic prices rather than exchange rate adjustments (for this discussion I assume no independent feedback from exchange rate
changes to domestic prices).

Jeffrey Frankel in a recent study estimates this one-shot effect of changed
inflationary expectations to be quite large, with a 1 percent change in the U.S.-
German long-run inflation differential leading to a depreciation of the dollar
against the mark of the order of 6 percent. Preliminary work by Hooper and
Morton on an effective exchange rate measure of the dollar finds results of the
same order of magnitude.[13] If these estimates are in the correct ballpark, explanations of the fall of the dollar that place a major emphasis on the worsening of
inflationary expectations in the United States begin to take on a good deal more
plausibility (although there could still be a role for the influences of changed
expectations about equilibrium real exchange rates because of changed expectations about economic growth rates and current account balances).

Estimates of this magnitude seem quite on the high side, however, in terms of
the various estimates of the interest elasticity of the demand for money. Note
also that if the interest elasticities of the demand for money differ significantly
across countries, as appears to be the case, we should look separately at the
expected rate of inflation in each country, rather than just at the expected
differential.[14]

UNCERTAINTY EFFECTS OF HIGHER RATES
OF INFLATION

There is, however, an additional rationale for why a change in the expected rate
of inflation may have a quite large immediate impact on the exchange rate.
There is a growing body of evidence that higher rates of inflation tend to be
more variable and less predictable.[15] As has been emphasized by Richard Sweeney, increased uncertainty about price level developments makes a country a less
attractive place for investment and can lead to a sizable decline in the equilib-

rium foreign exchange value of a country's currency.[16] If the increased uncertainty effects that are likely to accompany higher rates of inflation are taken into account, short-run exchange rate effects of changes in inflationary expectations of the size estimated by Frankel, or even larger, begin to become quite plausible. Initial attempts by Der Hovanessian and Makin to include risk proxies in exchange rate equations have not found strong results, but this seems likely to be due as much or more to the difficulties in empirical estimation of short-run exchange rate models as to the possible relative unimportance of risk considerations in exchange rate determination.[17]

THE DORNBUSCH AND FRANKEL MODELS

While the need to distinguish between the real and inflationary components of interest rate changes has become widely acknowledged, few published studies have attempted to take this distinction directly into account in empirical research. Two of the first of such studies are the recent papers by Dornbusch and Frankel.[18] These studies include both short- and long-term interest differentials in a monetary approach model for the dollar–D-mark exchange rate.

Frankel hypothesizes that changes in the long-run interest rate differential reflect changes in inflationary expectations (he also tries several other proxies), while changes in the short-term interest differential in excess of changes in long-run inflationary expectations reflect changes in real interest rates. In his published estimates he finds empirical support for his hypothesis of a positive coefficient of the long-run interest differential on the exchange rate (i.e., increases in domestic long-term rates are due primarily to changes in inflationary expectations and are associated with currency depreciation). While holding long-run interest differentials constant, he finds a negative coefficient for changes in the short-term interest differential, indicating that these are predominantly changes in real rates so that short-term interest rate increases lead to currency appreciation. Thus, he argues that his theory is a significant improvement over the initial simple monetarist models that assumed that changes in short-term interest rates were positively associated with exchange rate changes and the simple Keynesian–Dornbusch model that abstracted from inflationary expectations. Consistent with his theory, Frankel uses the coefficients on his short-term interest rate differential, holding constant the proxies for long-run inflationary expectations, to derive elements of the magnitude of short-run exchange rate overshooting and the coefficients of the long-run interest differential as a proxy for inflationary expectations to derive estimates of the one-shot effect of changes in the long-run expected inflation rate differential on the level of the exchange rate.

There is a serious question whether we can place much confidence in these estimates, however, because of severe instability of the coefficients. The results reported by Dornbusch using the same type of equation but a somewhat different time period are quite different, with the coefficients on the short-term interest rate differential frequently being positive rather than negative. Further evidence of the instability of coefficient estimates in these types of models resulting both from differences in time periods and econometric techniques is presented in Appendix A. Later work by Frankel himself has also found considerable instability.[19]

THE TERM STRUCTURE OF INFLATION RATE EXPECTATIONS

Another potentially important source of the instability of these types of estimates results from the failure to take into account the fact that there can be quite sizable shifts in the term structures of interest rates and inflationary expectations.[20] In periods of prolonged low inflation we have become accustomed to a term structure with short-term interest rates lying below long-term rates. On the other hand, in the recent periods of very high inflation we have very frequently observed just the reverse, with short-term rates rising far above long-term rates. While the variability in short-term rates has undoubtedly at times reflected sizable shifts in short-term expected real interest rates, it has also often reflected changes in expectations about near-term inflation over, say, the next three months or even a year or two that differ considerably from changes in expectations of the average rate of inflation over the next ten or twenty years. Casual observation suggests that a good bit of the variations in short-term nominal interest rates in recent years has been due to changes in expectations about the cause of inflation over the next few months or years that are associated with much less change about expectations of longer run rates of inflation. Thus, one can have a sizable change in short-term relative to long-term interest rates without there being any change in expected real interest rates.

Even under the assumption that the long-run real rate of interest is constant, one cannot take changes in long-term interest rates as a good indicator of changes in short-run inflationary expectations. We need to also attempt to break down the change in short-term interest differentials into expected real and short-term inflationary expectations components. An initial effort along these lines using several simple proxies for short-run inflationary expectations has been undertaken by Khan. (See Appendix B.) While the empirical results using these proxies have yielded only mixed results, given the large observed shifts in the term structure of interest rates, it would seem that this may reflect more the difficulties of obtaining good estimates of expectations than it does the lack of importance of the term structure of inflationary expectations.

CONCLUDING REMARKS

We have learned quite a bit in recent years about the complexities of the possible relationships between interest rates and exchange rates. Unfortunately as yet, we have been much less successful in identifying stable empirical relationships. We have, however, amassed a good deal of negative knowledge. This at least provides the useful function of warning us to be wary of assuming that particular views of these relationships — such as, that higher interest rates will strengthen the dollar — will almost always hold. In this case, recognition of our ignorance is itself a sign of progress.

At this point a similar conclusion should be drawn about recent assertions that in the 1980s sizable long-term real interest rate differentials have lead to a huge overshooting of the spot rate of the dollar. For example, the 1984 Report of the Council of Economic Advisers reports estimates of real international interest rate differentials for ten-year bonds on the order of 3 percent and suggests that this may have caused an approximately 30 percent overshooting of the real exchange rate of the dollar in order to generate expectations of 3 percent a year depreciation for ten years to offset this interest differential. Such analysis is subject, however, to the same caveats about the conflicting effects of uncertainty and less than infinite capital mobility discussed above in the context of short-term interest differentials. We believe that this should be a priority area for future research.[21]

NOTES TO CHAPTER 3

1. See Rudiger Dornbusch, "Expectations and Exchange Rate Dynamics," *Journal of Political Economy* 84, no. 6 (December 1976): 1161–76.

2. See Jeffrey Frankel, "On the Mark, The Theory of Floating Exchange Rates Based Upon Real Interest Differentials," *American Economic Review* 69, no. 4 (September 1979): 610–22.

3. For survey articles that conclude that there is substantial empirical support for the monetary approach to exchange rates, see John Bilson, "Recent Developments in Monetary Models of Exchange Rate Determination," *IMF Staff Papers* 26, no. 2 (June 1979): 201–23; and Michael Musa, "Empirical Regularities in the Behavior of Exchange Rates," in Karl Brunner and Allan Meltzer, eds., *Policies for Employment, Prices, and Exchange Rates* (Carnegie–Rochester Conference Series on Public Policy, Vol. II), pp. 9–57. For a more recent survey which finds considerably less systematic empirical support for short-run monetary models, see Waseem Khan and Thomas D. Willett, "The Monetary Approach to Exchange Rates," *Kredit und Kapital*, 1984/Heft 2: 199–222. Specifically on the instability of estimates of the relationships between interest rates and exchange rates, see, for example, Ira J. Kaylin, Charles Pigott, Richard J. Sweeney, and

Thomas D. Willett, "Annexes, The Effect of Interest-Rate Changes on Exchange Rates During the Current Float," in Carl H. Stern, et al., eds., *Eurocurrencies and the International Monetary System* (Washington, D.C.: American Enterprise Institute, 1976), pp. 223–34; Bruce Brittain, "Tests of Theories of Exchange Rate Determination," *Journal of Finance* 32 (May 1977): 519–29; and Rudiger Dornbusch, "Monetary Policy Under Exchange Rate Flexibility," in *Managed Exchange Rate Flexibility: The Recent Experience*, Federal Reserve Bank of Boston Conference Series, No. 20, 1978, pp. 90–122.

4.   This point has been emphasized in David Howard, "The Real Rate of Interest in International Financial Markets," International Finance Discussion Papers No. 136 (Federal Reserve Board of Governors, April 1979). A recent study by E. Fama, "Short-Term Interest Rates as Predictors of Inflation," *American Economic Review* 65 (June 1975): 269–82, did purport to find evidence consistent with the hypothesis of rational expectations and a constant real short-term interest rate in the United States, but this study has been subjected to severe criticism. See Charles Nelson and William Schwert, "On Testing the Hypothesis That the Real Rate of Interest is Constant," *American Economic Review* 69 (June 1977): 478–86; John Carlson, "Short-Term Interest Rate as Predictors of Inflation: Comment," *American Economic Review* 67 (June 1977): 469–75; and John Elliot, "Measuring the Expected Real Rate of Interest: An Explanation of Macroeconomic Alternatives," *American Economic Review* 67 (June 1977): 429–44.

5.   See Rudiger Dornbusch and Paul Krugman, "Flexible Exchange Rates in the Short-Run," *Brookings Papers on Economic Activity* 3 (1976): 537–75.

6.   For a demonstration of the effects of less than infinite capital mobility and references to analysis showing the possibility of undershooting, see Jacob Frenkel and Carlos Rodriguez, "Exchange Rate Dynamics and the Overshooting Hypothesis," *IMF Staff Papers* 29, no. 1 (March 1982): 1–30.

7.   See, for example, the analysis and references presented in Victoria Farrell, "Capital Mobility and the Efficacy of Fiscal Policy under Alternative Exchange Rate Systems," in Carl H. Stern, John H. Makin, and Dennis E. Logue, eds., *Eurocurrencies and the International Monetary System* (Washington, D.C.: American Enterprise Institute for Public Policy Research, 1976): 234–42.

8.   On this point, see Susan Schadler, "Sources of Exchange Rate Variability, Theory and Empirical Evidence," *IMF Staff Papers* 24 (July 1977): 253–96; and Ronald McKinnon, "The Exchange Rate and Macroeconomic Policy: Changing Postwar Perceptions," *Journal of Economic Literature* 19 (June 1981): 550–52.

9.   Eaton and Turnovsky have recently presented an alternative analysis in which decreases in risk aversion increase the size of exchange rate movements in response to changes in domestic asset supplies. See Jonathan Eaton and Stephen J. Turnovsky, "Covered Interest Parity, and Exchange Rate Dynamics," *Economic Journal* 93 (September 1983): 555–75. Re-

conciliation of these two apparently conflicting aspects of uncertainty and risk aversion should be an important topic for future research.

10. For simplicity, this analysis assumes that changes in inflationary expectations leave real rates of interest unchanged. It has often been argued that in reality real balance effects and (at least short-run) elasticities of wages with respect to expected inflation of less than one will cause higher expected rates of inflation to lower the real interest rate, while Michael Darby, "The Financial and Tax Effects of Monetary Policy on Interest Rates," *Economic Inquiry* 13, no. 2 (June 1975): 266-76, has pointed out that if after tax real rates of return are to remain constant, nominal rates will have to rise by more than the increase in expected inflation. (He suggests that this tax factor is on the order of 1/3.) For a more recent analysis, that includes the effects of taxes on short-term interest rates, see Maurice Levi and John Makin, "Anticipated Inflation and Interest Rates: Further Interpretation of Findings on the Fisher Equations," *American Economic Review* 68 (December 1979): 801-12. For an application to an open economy, see John Makin, "Anticipated Inflation and Interest Rates in an Open Economy," *Journal of Money, Credit and Banking* 10 (August 1978): 275-89.

11. This point has been emphasized by Peter Isard, "Factors Determining Exchange Rates: The Role of Relative Price Levels, Balances of Payments, Interest Rates and Risk," International Finance Discussion Papers No. 156 (Federal Reserve Board of Governors, April 1980).

12. See Jeffrey Frankel, "On the Mark."

13. See Peter Hooper and John Morton, "Fluctuations in the Dollar: A Model of Nominal and Real Exchange Rate Determination," International Finance Discussion Papers No. 168 (Federal Reserve Board of Governors, October 1980).

14. On this point, see James Rasulo and D. Sykes Wilford, "Estimating Monetary Models of Balance of Payments and Exchange Rates: A Bias," *Southern Economic Journal* 47, no. 1 (July 1980): 136-46.

15. See, for example, Deborah Frohman, Leroy O. Laney, and Thomas D. Willett, "Uncertainty Costs of Inflation," *Voice* of the Federal Reserve Bank of Dallas (July 1981): 1-9, and references cited there.

16. See Richard J. Sweeney, "Risk, Inflation, and Exchange Rates," in the Proceedings of the West Coast Academic/Federal Reserve Economic Research Seminar, Federal Reserve Bank of San Francisco (May 1979), pp. 142-61.

17. See Aida Der Hovanessian, "Risk and the Foreign Exchange Market" (unpublished Ph.D. dissertation, Claremont Graduate School, 1981); John Makin, "Exchange Rate Behavior Under Full Monetary Equilibrium: An Empirical Analysis," National Bureau of Economic Research Working Paper No. 647 (March 1981); and Appendix A.

18. See Rudiger Dornbusch, "Monetary Policy Under Exchange Rate Flexibility," in *Managed Exchange Rate Flexibility: The Recent Experience*, Federal Reserve Bank of Boston Conference Series No. 20 (1978), pp. 90-122; and Jeffrey Frankel, "On The Mark:The Theory of Floating Exchange Rates Based upon Real Interest Differentials."

19. See Jeffrey Frankel, "On the Mark: A Response to Various Comments" (Department of Economics, University of California at Berkeley, April 1981) (Mimeo.); and "On the Mark: Reply," *American Economic Review* 71, no. 3 (December 1081): 1075–82.

20. Recent discussions and analysis which do focus on term structure issues include Joseph Bisignano, "Monetary Policy Regimes and International Term Structures of Interest Rates," Federal Reserve Bank of San Francisco *Economic Review* No. 3 (Fall 1983): 7–26; Peter Isard, "An Accounting Framework and Some Issues for Modelling How Exchange Rates Respond to the News," and comment by Jeffrey Frankel in Jacob Frenkel, ed., *Exchange Rates and International Macroeconomics* (Chicago: University of Chicago Press, 1983): 19–65; Charles Pigott, "Indications of Long-Term Real Interest Rates," Federal Reserve Bank of San Francisco *Economic Review* No. 1 (Winter 1984): 45–63; and Charles A. Wyplosz, "The Exchange and Interest Rate Term Structure under Risk Aversion and Rational Expectations," *Journal of International Economics* 14 (February 1983): 123–39.

21. See also the discussion of this issue in Chapter 18.

APPENDIX 3A
THE FRANKEL MODEL:
CRITIQUE AND FURTHER EVIDENCE

The well known recent empirical study by Jeffrey Frankel examined the behavior of the mark/dollar exchange rate from July 1974 to February 1978.[1] In constructing his empirical model Frankel combined the two well-known variants of the monetary approach—for example, the flexible-price and sticky-price versions—into a single equation and concluded that his model provides sufficient evidence of interest rate induced exchange rate overshooting.

In our recent research on the Frankel model, we found that the model is extremely sensitive to econometric techniques, time periods, and data sources used. Any change in these factors subatantially undercuts Frankel's original conclusions with respect to exchange rate overshooting.[2,3]

More specifically, to correct for first-order serial correlation Frankel employs the Cochrane-Orcutt (CORC) iterative process as is normally done. But as Sargan has demonstrated, this may not be the most efficient method of removing first order serial correlation among the residuals.[4] The CORC iterative process consists essentially of the minimizing of a quadratic function at each step for a certain value of rho, the serial correlation coefficient. The desired value of rho is achieved where the standard error of the regression is a minimum. Since this quadratic function is a bounded decreasing function, the sequence of values of rho necessarily converges to a limit that may be one of the many local minima available. Hence, the desired value of rho may not be achieved, and the estimated coefficients would be inefficient and possibly inconsistent.

To avoid these problems, an alternative method—the Hildreth-Lu (HILU) grid search technique—could be employed. The HILU technique specifies a grid of values for rho whereby an iteration is performed at each value of rho. The final value selected for rho is that where the standard error of the regression is a minimum.

Application of the HILU technique to the Frankel model yielded significantly different results, which, as shown in Table 3A-1 are quite poor as seen in the reduced magnitude and significance of the estimated coefficients. For example, in equation (3) the relative money supply coefficient is insignificantly different than zero and the relative real income variable, though statistically significant, is highly reduced in magnitude and quite different from the income elasticity estimates reported by domestic money demand studies. Furthermore, the insignificance of the interest differential coefficient suggests that there has been no incidence of interest rate induced exchange rate overshooting.

Table 3A-1. The Frankel Sticky-Price Model.

Results of Changes in Econometric Techniques, Sample Period and Data Sources, and the Effect of Risk Variables.

Estimated Techniques	Constant	$\ln(e_{t-1})$	$\ln(m/m^*)$	$\ln(y/y^*)$	$(r-r^*)$	$(\pi-\pi^*)$	$(\sigma-\sigma^*)$	R^2	S.E.	D.W.	RHO
July 1974 to Feb. 1978											
(1) OLS	-3.33* (0.12)		0.87* (0.20)	-0.72* (0.19)	-0.34 (2.04)	27.13* (2.59)		0.79	0.0285	0.95	—
(2) CORC	-3.80* (0.22)		0.37 (0.33)	-0.33 (0.19)	-0.37 (1.01)	7.29 (4.38)		0.90	0.0184	1.38	0.96
(3) HILU	-3.37* (0.20)		0.49 (0.29)	-0.41* (0.17)	-0.45 (0.95)	4.42 (3.95)		0.92	0.0121	1.56	1.05
(4) OLS	0.87* (0.02)		0.028 (0.025)	-0.587* (0.248)	-8.239* (2.840)	20.891* (3.264)		0.55	0.0459	0.61	—
(5) CORC	0.57* (0.16)		0.008 (0.009)	-0.447 (0.227)	-0.316 (1.572)	-7.257 (6.811)		0.87	0.0245	1.88	0.98
(6) HILU	1.067* (0.081)		0.009 (0.009)	-0.522* (0.212)	-0.408 (1.456)	-11.066 (6.187)		0.88	0.0236	2.11	1.05
Jan. 1974 to Dec. 1979											
(7) OLS	-3.62* (0.06)		0.064* (0.026)	0.424 (0.383)	10.150* (2.36)	9.74* (3.75)		0.70	0.0581	0.42	—
(8) CORC	-4.09* (0.11)		0.009 (0.007)	-0.295 (0.160)	0.638 (0.683)	0.372 (3.130)		0.98	0.0203	1.54	0.98
(9) HILU	-11.50 (11.20)		0.019 (0.173)	-0.281 (0.159)	0.629 (0.674)	0.061 (3.121)		0.98	0.0184	1.62	1.00

								$\bar{R}^2$	S.E.	D.W.	RHO
(10) OLS	0.90* (0.03)		0.002 (0.045)	0.490 (0.363)	10.952 (3.027)	9.513* (4.331)		0.63	0.0844	0.31	—
(11) CORC	0.55* (0.14)		0.005 (0.012)	-0.194 (0.240)	1.072 (1.278)	-4.073 (5.665)		0.95	0.0311	2.39	0.98
(12) HILU	0.51* (0.17)		0.004 (0.012)	-0.173 (0.236)	1.172 (1.252)	-2.281 (5.478)		0.95	0.0300	2.10	1.00
(13) HILU	-0.22 (0.21)	0.960* (0.049)	-0.103 (0.088)	-0.074 (0.145)	0.123 (0.308)		-11.038 (7.262)	0.96	0.022	1.94	0.20
(14) HILU	-0.20 (0.22)	0.967* (0.050)	-0.098 (0.091)	-0.073 (0.149)	0.017 (0.283)		-1.431 (2.752)	0.96	0.022	1.94	0.22
(15) HILU	-0.23 (0.23)	0.962* (0.052)	-0.118 (0.096)	-0.084 (0.153)	0.008 (0.267)		0.470 (0.627)	0.97	0.022	1.96	0.28

Notes:

1. Parenthesized figures are standard errors.
2. An asterisk on each variable indicates a foreign country variable. An asterisk on each estimated coefficient indicates statistical significance at the 5 percent level.
3. The dependent variable in all equations is $lne_t = ln\,(DM/\$)$ spot exchange rate.
4. S.E. is the standard error of the regression; D.W. the Durbin–Watson statistic; and RHO the serial correlation coefficient.
5. All equations were estimated with data from the Federal Reserve Bulletin, Economic Report of the President, World Financial Markets of Morgan Guaranty Trust and the Deutsche Bundesbank monthly reports, with the exception of equations (4, 5, 6, 10, 11 and 12) that were estimated with data from the IMF's International Financial Statistics.
6. $(\sigma - \sigma*)$ represents the risk differential. The following proxies for risk were used in equations (13, 14 and 15), respectively: a three-month moving variance of CPI inflation, the lagged three-month moving variance of CPI inflation, and Foster's measure of risk (see Aida Der Hovanessian "Risk in the Foreign Exchange Market").

Note that the higher value of rho obtained by using the HILU technique is accompanied by a lower standard error of the regression and a higher Durbin–Watson statistic when compared to those obtained by employing the CORC method, thus indicating maximum elimination of first-order residual autocorrelation. A value of rho greater than unity implies nonstationarity in the residuals but does not qualitatively affect the above conclusions.

The results of the Frankel model fared even worse when the sample period was extended from January 1974 to December 1979. As shown in Table 3A-1 equations (7, 8, 9) both the magnitude and statistical significance of all estimated coefficients are lower than those reported by Frankel; in particular, the evidence on the interest differential coefficient is very weak and indicates no exchange rate overshooting whatsoever.

In addition, the Frankel model is highly susceptible to changes in data sources. In particular, when data from the IMF's International Financial Statistics tape was employed, the results for both the original and the extended time periods differed significantly from those obtained by using data from the original sources. These results are reproduced in equations (4, 5, 6, 10, 11, 12) in Table 3A-1. Note, for example, that in the equations corrected for serial correlation, the inflation differential coefficients are insignificantly different from zero and carry the incorrect (negative) sign. The interest differential coefficients indicate Keynesian liquidity effects for the July 1974–February 1978 period and inflationary effects for the January 1974–December 1979 period. However, the results remain statistically insignificant in both cases. Evidence on the real income coefficient for both periods is quite similar to that obtained by using data from the original sources. But note that the estimated coefficients are not statistically significant and also are substantially lower than estimates reported in the domestic money demand studies. Estimates on the money supply coefficients that are derived by using the IFS data are substantially lower in magnitude and significance than those derived by employing data from the original sources, particularly in the July 1974–February 1978 sample period. The reader would note once again the advantages of using the HILU technique to correct for serial correlation.

Furthermore, in an attempt to modify the Frankel model, risk variables were introduced into the empirical specification as additional explanatory variables. The results, shown in Table 3A-1, equations (7, 8, 9), suggest two possible effects of the risk factor. One relates to exchange rate appreciation caused by an increase in inflation adjusted real returns. As Makin has lately shown, a rise in inflation volatility causes risk-averse investors to seek a risk premium as compensation for uncertainty in the purchasing power of their financial assets over commodities.[5] The resulting increase in real interest rates attracts foreign capital and causes the exchange rate to appreciate. This argument may find some support in the results of equations (7) and (8). Secondly, as is well known, inflation-augmented risk that tends to lower real returns reduces the relative attractiveness of a country for investment purposes, thereby reducing the demand for its money and hence generating an exchange rate depreciation. The results in equation (9) tend to be supportive of the latter argument.

In summary, we do not find Frankel's conclusion regarding interest rate induced overshooting in the DM/$ exchange rate to hold generally. Further evidence on this issue is provided in Appendix B. Our results also indicate that Frankel's model is highly sensitive to its empirical characteristics, which include data sources, sample periods, and econometric techniques. Any change in these factors yields substantial changes in the depreciation and overshooting aspects of the exchange rate.

NOTES TO APPENDIX 3A

1. Jeffrey Frankel, "On the Mark," *American Economic Review* 69, no. 4 (September 1979): 610–21.

2. For a more detailed discussion of data, sample period, and estimation technique problems in the Frankel model, see Waseem Khan, "Interest Rates and Exchange Rates; Techniques and Methodology: A Critique and Some Evidence," Clarement Working Paper (February 1981), and "The Monetary Approach to Exchange Rates: Theory and Empirical Evidence" (unpublished Ph.D. dissertation, Claremont Graduate School, 1981). Frankel also finds that his model does not hold up well when it is applied to later data. See Frankel, "On the Mark: Reply," *American Economic Review* 71: no. 5 (December 1981): 1075–82. See also Stephen E. Maynes and Joe A. Stone, "On the Mark: Comment," *American Economic Review* 71, no. 5 (December 1981): 1060–67; and Robert A. Driskill and Steven M. Sheffrin, "On the Mark: Comment," *American Economic Review* 71, no. 5 (December 1981): 1068–74.

3. See Aida Der Hovanessian, "Risk in the Foreign Exchange Market" (unpublished Ph.D. dissertation, Claremont Graduate School, 1981).

4. See J. D. Sargan, "Wages and Prices in the United Kingdom: A Study in Econometric Methodology," in P. E. Hart, et al., *Econometric Analysis for National Economic Planning* (London: Butterworth, 1964), pp. 25–63.

5. The inflation-induced increase in real interest rates and the resulting exchange rate appreciation is explained in detail in John H. Makin, "Exchange Rate Behavior Under Full Monetary Equilibrium: An Empirical Analysis," National Bureau of Economic Research Working Paper No. 647 (March 1981).

APPENDIX 3B
INTEREST RATES, INFLATIONARY EXPECTATIONS, AND EXCHANGE RATES

In order to investigate the effects of changes in the real and nominal components of short-term interest rates on changes in the exchange rate, five different proxies for inflationary expectations were constructed. These proxies included the following:

1. Inflationary expectations over the next three months were assumed to equal those experienced over the last three months;
2. The inflationary expectations over the next three months were assumed to equal those experienced over the last three months, *plus* the difference between that and the three month rate preceeding it;
3. Inflationary expectations assumed to prevail over the next three months were derived by using the method specified by Mullineaux;[1]
4. Inflationary expectations assumed to hold over the next three months were derived by using an ARIMA model as specified by Howard;[2]
5. The Livingston[3] six-month and twelve-month-ahead inflation forecasts were used (a) by adjusting following Carlson's[4] method and (b) by taking the average of all survey respondents in each period.

These proxies for inflationary expectations were then used to derive the real components of short-term nominal interest rates, and subsequently both were used in the Frankel model. To increase the generality of the analysis the model was estimated for the DM/$ and the £/$ exchange rates over various periods (see notes to Table 3B-1). These results are reproduced in equations (1) through (8) and (10) through (17) in Table 3B-1.

As is evident, the results are poor. For example, none of the relative money supply coefficients are significantly close to their hypothesized (in the monetary approach) value of unity. The real income coefficients, though they maintain their correct signs (negative according to the monetary approach) are statistically significant only in a handful of cases. But almost all of them are very low in magnitude, significantly lower than the income elasticity estimates reported in the domestic money demand studies.

Evidence on the real interest differential coefficients indicates a mixture of liquidity and inflationary effects where only the latter are statistically significant and that, too, in the £/$ case. The absence of significantly negative real interest differential coefficients indicate no evidence of overshooting for either of the exchange rates. The inflationary expectations proxies, though all maintain their correct (positive) signs, are statistically significant in only half the cases. Since the estimated coefficients are quite low in magnitude (at least compared to what Frankel had reported), we refrain from drawing significant conclusions.

None of the proxies for inflationary expectations employed in the Frankel model yielded results as hypothesized by Frankel.[5] This analysis suggests the lack of a good measure of inflationary expectations. Since the proxies used above are those commonly employed in the domestic inflation predictions literature, our results are indicative of this problem in a more general context.

NOTES TO APPENDIX 3B

1. See Donald Mullineaux, "Inflation Expectations and Money Growth in the United States," *American Economic Review* 70, no. 1 (March 1980): 149–61.

2. A detailed specification of the ARIMA model is given in David Howard, "The Real Rate of Interest on International Financial Markets," International Finance Discussion Paper No. 136 (April 1979).

3. The Livingston six-month and twelve-month-ahead forecast data was graciously provided by David Resler of the Federal Reserve Bank of St. Louis.

4. This method is specified in John Carlson, "A Study of Price Forecasts," *Annals of Economic and Social Measurement* 6 (Winter 1977): 27–56.

5. Jeffrey Frankel, "On the Mark," *American Economic Review* 69, no. 4 (September 1979): 610–21. In a following paper, "On the Mark: A Reply," *American Economic Review* 71: no. 3 (December 1981): 1075–82, Frankel uses a monthly moving average of CPI inflation over the past twelve months to proxy the expected rate of inflation. Although Frankel reports a significant result for this inflationary expectations proxy, our further work using this type of proxy did not find robust results.

Table 3B-1. Proxies for Inflationary Expectations, Real Interest Rates, and the Exchange Rate (*corrected for serial correlation*).

	Constant	$\ln(m/m^*)$	$\ln(y/y^*)$	$(r-r^*)$	$(\pi-\pi^*)$	R^2	D.W.	S.E.	RHO
ln DM/$									
a_1	-4.91* (0.18)	-0.033 (0.172)	-0.272 (0.161)	0.871 (0.710)	1.943 (1.551)	0.98	1.54	0.021	1.00
b_2	-4.85* (0.18)	-0.026 (0.174)	-0.301* (0.150)	0.792 (0.680)	2.123 (1.430)	0.98	1.54	0.021	1.00
c_3	-4.98* (0.20)	-0.030 (0.178)	-0.371 (0.200)	0.980 (0.621)	2.450 (1.401)	0.98	1.60	0.020	1.00
d_4	-3.72* (0.61)	0.590 (0.410)	-0.692* (0.271)	-0.622 (0.420)	1.789* (0.812)	0.91	1.65	0.022	0.95
e_5	-3.45* (0.82)	0.030 (0.540)	-0.223 (0.178)	1.213 (1.001)	4.013* (1.012)	0.85	1.45	0.051	-0.31
f_6	-3.82 (0.73)	0.009 (0.290)	-0.298* (0.132)	1.411 (0.983)	4.230* (0.972)	0.89	1.49	0.047	-0.16
g_7	-3.02* (0.61)	0.051 (0.211)	-0.392* (0.186)	1.351 (1.150)	4.123* (1.311)	0.81	1.21	0.056	-0.16
h_8	-3.13 (0.60)	0.062 (0.216)	-0.387 (0.205)	1.721 (1.311)	4.119* (1.173)	0.83	1.19	0.051	-0.28
i_9	-5.07* (0.18)	0.024 (0.172)	-0.270 (0.160)	0.710 (0.670)	0.261 (0.860)	0.98	1.58	0.081	1.00
ln £/$									
a_{10}	-1.47 (1.95)	0.043 (0.175)	-0.187 (0.131)	2.571* (0.890)	3.541* (1.570)	0.97	1.24	0.021	1.00
b_{11}	-2.19 (2.58)	0.041 (0.176)	-0.201 (0.130)	2.481* (0.880)	2.370* (1.151)	0.97	1.22	0.021	1.00

						S.E.	D.W.	RHO	
c_{12}	-1.72 (1.60)	0.072 (0.136)	-0.201 (0.142)	2.713* (0.810)	3.732* (1.230)	0.98	1.35	0.021	1.00
d_{13}	0.62 (0.42)	0.870 (0.910)	-0.651 (0.680)	0.135 (0.242)	0.771 (1.001)	0.90	1.34	0.022	1.00
e_{14}	-0.75* (0.29)	0.052 (0.220)	-0.450 (0.231)	-0.981 (0.999)	1.820 (1.320)	0.82	1.45	0.065	0.91
f_{15}	-0.83* (0.20)	0.057 (0.131)	-0.430 (0.242)	-0.920 (1.310)	1.320 (1.022)	0.87	1.65	0.061	0.97
g_{16}	-0.85* (0.30)	0.411 (0.523)	-0.398* (0.148)	-0.320 (0.981)	1.977 (1.563)	0.77	1.40	0.073	0.88
h_{17}	-0.87* (0.30)	0.445 (0.511)	-0.372 (0.178)	-0.362 (0.822)	1.451 (0.890)	0.73	1.37	0.065	0.86
i_{18}	-3.16 (4.30)	0.064 (0.174)	-0.161 (0.130)	2.573* (0.871)	2.391* (0.870)	0.97	1.25	0.021	1.00

Notes: Parenthesized figures are standard errors. An asterisk on each variable indicates a foreign country variable; an asterisk on each figure indicates statistical significance at the 5 percent level. All equations are corrected for serial correlation using the Hildreth–Lu grid search technique. RHO is the coefficient of serial correlation; $S.E.$ is the standard error of the regression, and D.W. is the Durbin–Watson statistic. Due to data limitations equations (1, 2, 3, 9, 10, 11, 12 and 18) are estimated over January 1974–December 1979, while equations (4 and 13) are estimated over 1971: I–1977: III, and equations (5, 6, 7, 8, 14, 15, 16 and 17) are estimated over 1972–78. Inflation proxies used are:

a. The previous three-month inflation rate is expected to prevail over the next three months;
b. The previous three-month inflation rate plus the difference between that and the three-month rate preceding it is expected to prevail over the next three months;
c. The inflation rate was calculated by using the technique specified by Mullineaux;
d. The inflation rate was calculated by using an ARIMA model as demonstrated by Howard;
e. The Carlson-adjusted Livingston six-month-ahead inflation forecast;
f. The Carlson-adjusted Livingston twelve-month-ahead inflation forecast;
g. The average of the Livingston six-month-ahead inflation forecast;
h. The average of the Livingston twelve-month-ahead inflation forecast;
i. A three-month moving average of the actual ex post CPI rate of inflation.

Sources: Federal Reserve Bulletin, Economic Report of the President; Deutsche Bundesbank monthly reports and Statistical Supplement; Economic Trends, H.M.S. Central Statistical Office.

4 PURCHASING POWER PARITY AND EXCHANGE RATE DYNAMICS
Some Empirical Results

Charles Pigott and Richard J. Sweeney

I. INTRODUCTION

The relationship between relative national price levels and exchange rates has been extensively investigated since the theory of Purchasing Power Parity (PPP) was first developed. Since then, the theory has waxed and waned in popularity and indeed until recently had come to be widely viewed as, at best, a pedagogical tool. However, the advent of floating exchange rates and the development of the monetary approach to exchange rate determination have revived interest in PPP, both as a theoretical tool for analyzing exchange rate changes and as a practical guide for foreign exchange market intervention.

Broadly stated, PPP implies that relative national price levels and corresponding exchange rates move in offsetting directions. Scholars have distinguished several versions of the theory, depending upon the extent to which offsetting ultimately occurs and the length of time it requires (see Yeager 1976, Frenkel 1978, Balassa 1964, and Officer 1976). The strongest formulation—that exchange rate changes immediately and completely offset changes in relative national price levels—has never been seriously advocated since deviations from PPP are frequently observed.[1] Probably the most widely accepted view is that price and exchange rate changes are eventually, but not immediately, offsetting. Under this hypothesis, exchange rates and relative national price levels adjust with lead/

We thank Thomas D. Willett for many helpful comments and discussions. Some of the work on this project was done while Richard J. Sweeney was visiting at the Institute for International Economic Studies, University of Stockholm. The usual Federal Reserve disclaimer applies in full.

lag relationships, *temporary* deviations from PPP occurring because of capital movements, lagged adjustment of trade flows to changes in relative prices (i.e., "J" curves), "sticky" prices in commodity markets, and, possibly, to slower adjustment of expectations by agents in goods, compared to financial, markets. Weaker formulations of the theory allow systematic and permanent departures from PPP arising from changes in productivity and tastes, shifts in comparative advantage, and variations in tariffs and other trade barriers and in transport costs.[2] Others require only that *average* changes in relative national price levels offset *average* changes in exchange rates.

Which of these versions of PPP is empirically (most) valid is of potentially great importance for policy. It has frequently been proposed that monetary authorities adopt a rule of intervening in the foreign exchange markets whenever observed deviations from PPP exceed a certain amount. (See, for example, OPTICA 1977.) Underlying this suggestion is the presumption that exchange rate changes eventually offset fully all changes in relative national prices, so that deviations from PPP are temporary departures from long-run equilibrium that the market will eventually "correct." Then authorities *may* under such circumstances be able to reduce the variability of the real (or price-adjusted) exchange rate by countering PPP deviations through intervention.[3] The results of empirical studies of PPP using cross-section as well as time-series data have been widely interpreted as supporting this relatively strong version of the theory. (See OPTICA 1977, Brillembourg 1976, Dennis 1976, Kemp 1976, Kern 1976, and King 1977.)

Such an interpretation of the evidence on PPP is unwarranted. More recent studies have discussed the "collapse" of PPP (Frenkel 1981) after the sample period of the earlier studies and have also provided some evidence that deviations from PPP tend to be reversed in the long run (Dornbusch 1978, Frenkel 1978). However, this paper's major point is *not* that PPP collapsed after the earlier sample but that previous techniques were inadequate and biased toward accepting PPP. Thus, we use data from the floating rate period up to the end of 1976. More generally, we argue that the model underlying many empirical studies of the theory fails to distinguish adequately among its alternative versions, leading to tests that are often biased toward acceptance of relatively strong formulations. In many of these studies (and in virtually all those reporting the strongest results in support of PPP), exchange rate changes are regressed on changes in relative national price levels, using a cross-country or pooled cross-country and time-series sample, and where both the slope and intercept are required to be the same for all countries. Section II shows that this model confuses two types of possible relations between relative inflation rates and exchange rate changes: that prevailing across countries between the unconditional mean (or average) of changes in relative price levels and changes in exchange rates; and that between price and exchange rate changes, about their unconditional means, for a *given* country. The results of the regression model have been widely interpreted as supporting the hypothesis that exchange rates offset variations in relative national prices in the long run. In fact, because of the misspecification inherent in the model, the results are equally consistent with the hypothesis that for a given country price and exchange rate changes about their unconditional means are *independent*.

Section III argues that more appropriate tests of PPP support a version in which only the unconditional means of relative national and exchange rate changes are systematically related. This means that a nation with a higher average inflation rate than another can be expected to experience the higher average rate of exchange rate depreciation. It does *not* imply that an above average increase in the price level today will systematically lead to an offsetting depreciation in the current or future exchange rate. This suggests that observed deviations from PPP are permanent in the sense that they cannot be expected to disappear in the long run and thus do not provide a standard for foreign exchange market intervention as proposed by OPTICA. These results prove the contention that the support provided for "strong" PPP by previous regression studies is spurious. However, while we argue that the data support a weaker version of the theory than is often assumed to hold, this does not mean that PPP has no empirical relevance. Indeed, the apparent relation between average relative inflation rates and average exchange rate changes provides strong support for the monetarist proposition that the trend in exchange rates is largely determined by national monetary policies.

II. A COMPARISON OF EMPIRICAL RESULTS

Let $\Delta p_i(t)$ stand for the change in period t in the natural logarithm of the price index of a country i, expressed relative to that of some reference nation, say the United States. Generally, the weights applied to individual goods' prices will differ from one country's index to another.[4] Similarly, let $\Delta \epsilon_i(t)$ be the first difference of the logarithm of the price of base currency in terms of that of country i. Then we can write,

$$\Delta \epsilon_i(t) = a_i + \xi_i(t), \ E[\xi_i(t)] = 0, \ \text{for all} \ i = 1, I \ \text{and} \ t. \qquad (4.1a)$$

$$\Delta p_i(t) = \beta_i + \omega_i(t), \ E[\omega_i(t)] = 0, \ \text{for all} \ i = 1, I \ \text{and} \ t. \qquad (4.1b)$$

In this, β_i is the *unconditional* mean of the change in the log of relative price for country i; over a sufficiently long time, the average value of observed changes in the log of relative price will thus approach β_i. Similarly, α_i is the unconditional mean of the change in the log of the exchange rate. The $\omega_i(t)$ and $\xi_i(t)$, on the other hand, are the stochastic, or nondeterministic, components of relative price and exchange rate changes, respectively. Apart from the restriction that the stochastic terms have stationary distributions with zero unconditional means, they may conform to any bivariate stochastic process (although the arguments below will usually assume they are normal); in particular, they may be serially correlated as well as cross-correlated with one another at any lag.

Hypotheses about PPP can be stated in terms of relations between the $\omega_i(\ )$ and the $\xi_i(\ )$ for a given country and/or in terms of the relation across countries between the α_i and β_i. Under one formulation, which we will refer to as "weak" PPP. the unconditional means vary in proportion as in (without loss of generality),

$$\alpha_i = \beta_i, \text{ all } i = 1, I \tag{4.2}$$

while the $\omega_i(\ )$ and $\xi_i(\ )$ are independent for each i. Thus if *average* changes in the log of relative prices are plotted against the corresponding average change in the exchange rate for a series of countries, the scatter of points will tend to lie along a line whose slope is unity (at least if the average is taken over a sufficiently long time period). However a scatter of actual relative price and exchange rate changes for a *given* country will be roughly circular on average, indicating no relation. Clearly this version is substantially weaker than that generally considered in the recent literature.

On the other hand, a "strong" version of PPP is obtained if in addition to equation (4.2) above, the stochastic terms for each country are deterministically related as

$$\xi_i(t) = A^i(L) \omega_i(t), \ A^i(1) = 1 \tag{4.3}$$

where $A^i(\ )$ is a lag polynomial and $A^i(1)$ refers to the sum of its coefficients.[5] In this case, an innovation in relative prices $(\omega_i(t))$ leads over time to a completely offsetting change in the exchange rate, although variations in exchange rates and relative prices will generally *not* be perfectly correlated at any particular lag. Intermediate, "semi-strong," versions of PPP can be obtained by supposing that the stochastic terms each consist of two components, one pair of which conforms to equation (4.3) while the other pair are independent, or by relaxing the condition that the sum of the coefficients of the lag polynomials, $A^i(\ )$, be unity, or, more generally, from any bivariate Box–Jenkins model of the innovations. Since we are concerned below with testing the alternative of strong PPP against that of weak PPP, we will not pursue the intermediate cases further.

The alternative PPP versions can also be defined in terms of the "real" exchange rate, defined as an index of relative national price levels expressed in a common currency. The logarithm of the real exchange rate for country i, $x_i(t)$, can thus be written as

$$x_i(t) \equiv \epsilon_i(t) - p_i(t) = \sum_{j=-\infty} [\xi_i(j) - \omega_i(j)], \text{ all } i. \tag{4.4}$$

Another way of characterizing strong PPP is to say that the real exchange rate, $x_i(\ )$, is a *stationary* stochastic process—that is, that its unconditional mean does not vary over time. It is easy to see that this is implied by (4.2) and (4.3), because the trend in price and exchange rates then has the same "slope" *and* any innovation in relative prices is eventually fully offset by exchange rate changes. Thus at any time, present deviations from PPP, that is the average of $x_i(\ )$, must be expected to dissipate. Under weak PPP, on the other hand, $x_i(t)$ is nonstationary because a given innovation in relative prices cannot be expected to be offset by exchange rates, however long the horizon. For example, if $\xi_i(\ )$ and $\omega_i(\ )$ are white noises, the real exchange rate does a random walk under weak PPP; $x_i(t)$ varies in a manner analogous to the total excess of heads over tails recorded in a sequence of tosses of a fair coin. Finally, semi-strong PPP implies that some portion of observed deviations from PPP are temporary, while some are permanent.[6]

Generally, strong PPP is likely to characterize actual price and exchange rate relations only when the primary source of variation in each is monetary in origin. This is because money stock changes are essentially neutral in the long run, changing national price levels in proportion while leaving relative prices, and thus the real exchange rate, unchanged. As in Dornbusch's (1976) model of exchange rate dynamics, short-run deviations from PPP may occur when the only disturbances are monetary, but in that case the deviations must disappear in the long run.[7] On the other hand, changes in the *real* supplies and demands for commodities that lead to permanent changes in relative prices will also generally cause permanent departures from PPP. Thus, real shocks tend to reduce the strong correlations between price and exchange rate changes implied by strong PPP. In this sense, the strength of the correlation between relative national price levels and exchange rate changes provides a rough measure of the relative importance of real and monetary shocks.

Finally, the above distinctions among versions of PPP have potentially important implications for policy as well as for the design of empirical tests. Under strong PPP, the "real" exchange rate deviates in a partially predictable manner about its long-run equilibrium; if, as *may* but need not be the case, such deviations are associated with predictable fluctuations in exchange rate changes about their unconditional mean, a basis for profitable stabilizing foreign exchange market intervention may exist. Clearly no such basis exists under weak PPP because all observed $x_i(t)$ then represent expected long-run equilibria.

An Incorrectly Specified Regression Model

Several empirical studies of PPP (OPTICA 1977, King 1976, and Kemp 1977) have used the following regression model:

$$\Delta\epsilon_i(t) = a + b\,\Delta p_i(t) + u_i(t), \ i = 1, I; \ t = 1, T \qquad (4.5)$$

where $u_i(t)$ is a classical (stationary) disturbance with żero mean. In some cases, the sample is a pure cross section $(T = 1)$, where the price and exchange rate changes are *averages* taken over some (often long) period. Notice that the parameters a and b (which are estimated using Ordinary Least Squares, sometimes with a correction for first-order serial correlation of the residuals) are forced to be the same for all countries. This model has provided the greatest apparent support for PPP (under the current float) in the sense that the hypothesis, $a = 0$ and $b = 1$, usually *cannot* be rejected.[8]

Clearly, however, the relation (4.5) cannot be a correct specification under all the versions of PPP discussed above. The equation implies that the expected value of the exchange rate change conditional upon a given change in corresponding relative national prices is the same regardless of the country. But suppose that weak PPP is empirically valid, and (for illustrative purposes) that the price and exchange rate innovations are serially uncorrelated. Then the expectation of $\Delta \epsilon_i(t)$ is α_i, regardless of the change in relative prices ($\beta_i + \omega_i$). Hence relation (4.5) is incorrectly specified under weak PPP, unless the α_i are the same for all nations. Needless to say, this is unlikely to be the case since the unconditional mean of the exchange rate change is largely a function of the *long run* rate of national inflation, and national inflation rates are likely to differ.

The difficulty with (4.5) is that it confuses the two sources of price and exchange rate changes: that across countries in the unconditional means, α_i and β_i; and the within-country deviations of price and exchange rate changes about their unconditional means. Under weak PPP, the statement, "the conditional expected value of the exchange rate change varies proportionally with the corresponding change in relative national prices," is true of the unconditional means but not of the innovations. Intuitively it is clear that the estimate of b obtained from (4.5) will then reflect the relative importance in the sample of the two sources of variation in price and exchange rate changes—and will provide a biased estimate of the true relations among each set. This is most easily seen from Figure 4-1. Each "circular" scatter represents a plot of $\Delta p_i(t)$ against $\Delta \epsilon_i(t)$ for a single country, assuming that weak PPP applies. The points about which the country scatters cluster are estimates of the α_i and thus tend to lie along a 45 degree line. The regression line obtained by estimating (4.5) will tend to be upward sloped if the unconditional means of the exchange rate changes vary across countries. Evidently, the problem can be remedied by allowing each country to have its own intercept, that is by estimating,

$$\Delta \epsilon_i(t) = a_i + b \Delta p_i(t) + u_i(t). \tag{4.5'}$$

This is correctly specified for weak PPP with $b = 0$ and $Ea_i = \alpha_i$.

Figure 4-1 thus suggests that the estimate of b from (4.5) is biased toward unity under weak PPP, and that the bias will be greater the larger the differences among the β_i compared to the variance of the stochastic source of relative price changes, $\omega_i(\ )$. Detailed analysis, available from the authors on request, shows that this is so. This result simply reflects that fact that high inflation countries tend to be those with relatively rapid exchange rate depreciation—that is, it

Figure 4-1. Scatter Diagram of Changes in Prices and Exchange Rates.

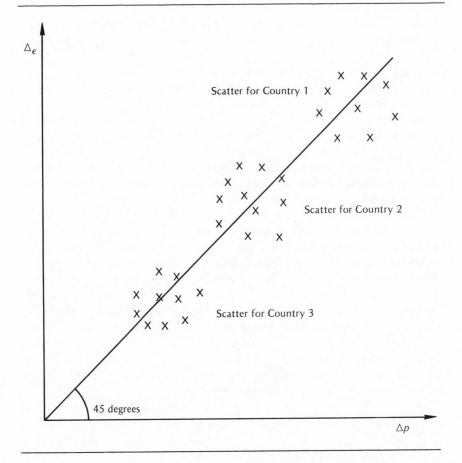

captures the relation between the unconditional means of exchange rate and relative national price level changes. Thus, it is not valid to conclude from such results (as OPTICA 1977 does) that the same relation applies to the within-country variations in prices and exchange rates.

Consider a fixed sample of K observations for each of I countries. Suppose that the sample is subdivided so that there are K/k observations per nation, each of which is the change over (nonoverlapping) intervals of k original periods. A common finding of recent studies of PPP using the model (4.5) is that the estimate of b tends to increase as k increases—that is, as the differencing interval is lengthened. This result is frequently interpreted (King 1977 and Brillembourg 1976) as implying that PPP holds in the long run. However, it will tend to occur under weak PPP—where there is *no* tendency for the real exchange rate to converge to a fixed value in the long run[9] – because the bias in $\hat{b}$ is systematically and positively related to k.

The analysis thus shows that the regression model (4.5) is apt to provide a misleading indication of the extent to which price and exchange rate changes offset one another. Since the estimate of b is likely to be near unity (at least for quarterly or annual changes) whether or not price and exchange rate changes for a given country are related, the model cannot discriminate between weak and strong versions of PPP. Furthermore, the previous arguments are no less valid if the unconditional means, α_i and β_i, are not actually fixed over time but shift at discrete intervals; each sample-period for which these terms are fixed is then analogous to one of the nations and the analysis above goes through as before. Thus, the results derived from (4.5) reported in several recent studies cannot be taken as substantial support for the proposition that a change in relative national prices will eventually be offset by exchange rates.

As indicated earlier, the regression model (4.5') provides a more appropriate test of the relation between price and exchange rate changes for individual countries since it explicitly allows for variations in the unconditional means across countries. Results for this model estimated on a sample of ten industrial countries are reported in the lower half of Table 4-1. In contrast to the results from the incorrectly specified model (upper portion of the table), the hypothesis that $b = 1$ can be rejected in all but one case, and generally the hypothesis that $b = 0$ cannot be rejected.[10] It is interesting to note that Brillembourg (1976) found that the hypothesis that price and exchange rate changes are independent could be rejected for only two of the eleven major industrial countries he examined; his results are particularly significant since his test explicitly allowed for lags between exchange rate and relative price variations.

However, these results cannot be taken as conclusive, particularly as we must still ask why the model (4.5') leads to these estimates of b that are significantly different from zero, and in one case not significantly different from one, when the changes are expressed over fairly long intervals, such as eighteen months.[11] One possibility is that the unconditional means of the price and exchange rate changes in fact have changed over time, so that it is insufficient to allow only one constant for each country in order to remove the bias. Suppose, that is, in Figure 4-1 the different scatters of points represent the relations between price and exchange rate changes for a given country for different periods when (presumably) long-run inflation rates differ. Since (4.5') only allows for one intercept per country, the regression line will again tend to be sloped upward even when price and exchange rate changes in each period are unrelated. We now proceed to examine this possibility further.

Table 4-1. Slope Coefficients for Pooled Cross-Section, Time-Series Regressions of Percentage Rate of Change of Exchange Rates as Functions of Relative Rates of Inflation, March 1973–December 1976.

Difference Interval	*Country Constants Constrained to be Equal*	
	CPI	*WPI*
1 month	0.18989 (0.17711)*	0.08938 (0.0884)
3	0.7377** † (0.28896)	0.56156** (0.14298)
6	1.1658** † (0.37093)	0.43572** (0.17178)
12	1.51905** † (0.3818)	0.6531** † (0.20328)
18	1.2552** † (0.1808)	0.8395** † (0.13442)
	Separate Constants for Each Country	
	CPI	*WPI*
1	−0.06959 (0.19302)	0.00494 (0.0916)
3	0.31094 (0.36362)	0.4459** (0.1602)
6	0.65534 (0.56956)	0.2351 (0.19905)
12	1.5038 (0.83811)	0.40769 (0.28118)
18	0.71265** † (0.2532)	0.3855** (0.17846)

The base country is the United States. The other countries are the rest of the Group of Ten plus Switzerland.

* Standard errors of estimates are in parentheses.
** Significantly different from zero (95 percent).
† *Not* significantly different from unity (95 percent).

Source: International Financial Statistics.

III. SHIFTS IN THE UNCONDITIONAL MEANS OF PRICE AND EXCHANGE RATE CHANGES

The sample period witnessed sharp variations in money growth and inflation for particular countries. Thus, it is not implausible to suspect that the unconditional means of relative national price changes (which are likely to be primarily influenced by average relative money growth rates) and of exchange rate changes have shifted. Here we consider two approaches to the testing of the relation be-

Table 4-2. Estimated Slope Coefficients: March 1973–December 1976.

	Country Constants Constrained to be Equal	
Difference Interval	CPI	WPI
1 month	-0.03095 (0.21291)*	-0.02462 (0.0996)
3	0.45901 (0.35884)	0.4522** (0.16831)
6	0.85335 (0.4637)	0.31421 (0.204689)
12	1.044** † (0.3536)	0.51922** (0.12966)
	Separate Constants for Each Country	
	CPI	WPI
1	-0.2278 (0.23613)	-0.07476 (0.10294)
3	0.13506 (0.44605)	0.38934** (0.18707)
6	0.58417 (1.7178)	0.20159 (0.24544)
12	-0.63454 (0.710451)	0.30344** (0.1357)

* Standard errors of estimates are in parentheses.
** Significantly different from zero (95 percent).
† *Not* significantly different from unity (95 percent).
Source: International Financial Statistics.

tween the stochastic components of price and exchange rate variations, ω_i and ξ_i, in the presence of (possible) shifts in the α_i and β_i. One is based on time-series analysis; two other (related) methods are based on attempts to divide the sample so that the unconditional means are fixed in at least one of resulting subsamples.

With the forty-seven observations of the sample, time-series methods give rather imprecise estimates. Nevertheless, the evidence seems to show that some countries (for example, Switzerland) had stationary processes generating Δp and $\Delta \epsilon$ with their autocorrelation functions (ACFs) showing no significant spikes and their cross-correlation functions (CCFs) showing no lead-lag relationships. Other countries (for example, Italy) showed evidence of nonstationarity in their ACFs and some contemporaneous and lead-lag relationships in their CCFs. When Δp and $\Delta \epsilon$ were differenced, the CCF relationship vanished.

Another approach is to consider only the first thirty-three months of the period of generalized floating that began in March 1973 rather than the first forty-five months as we did above. We do this for two reasons. First, a number of observers believe that the float "settled down" after the first two to two and one half years. Such a qualitative change might well be associated with a shift in the α_i and β_i. Indeed, we find some exchange rates becoming less volatile, and others (for example, the United Kingdom and Italy) more volatile. Secondly, March 1973-December 1975 is the period others (e.g., King 1977) examined.

Table 4-2 shows some interesting changes (lack of data precluded 18 month differencing intervals) as compared with Table 4-1. In every case where a coefficient is significant in Table 4-1, it is *larger* than in Table 4-2. Of course, these estimates are not independent across differencing intervals, and no coefficient differs by two standard errors. Nevertheless, *the results are consistent with the view that changes in the means of the processes generating exchange rate changes and relative inflation rates have contributed to statistical results that have been misleadingly interpreted as showing a relationship between $\Delta\epsilon$ and Δp that is not there.*

A final approach is to try to separate the set of countries into those where the constants have shifted and those where they have not. Recall that the model in equations (4.1a) and (4.1b) implies that the ACFs for both exchange rate changes and relative price changes should be essentially zero *unless* there have been mean shifts, in which case the ACFs should show positive, declining coefficients. Further, as was shown above, such mean shifts will tend to bias upward from zero the slope coefficient in pooled regressions even when separate country constants are included. Hence, we tried to divide the sample of countries into two groups—stationary and nonstationary countries. This division was done by examining ACFs, *before* CCFs were examined. Tables 4-3 and 4-4 show the results.

Table 4-3 shows that, compared to Table 4-1, the number of significant slope coefficients falls noticeably in the single constant case when nonstationary countries are excluded from the sample, which suggests that nonstationarity was present.[12] In the separate constant case, estimated slope coefficients generally fall when going from Table 4-1 to Table 4-3, and the estimated coefficient at eighteen months lag for the CPI becomes statistically insignificant.[13]

In Table 4-4, the results (particularly for CPIs) seem much closer to those of Table 4-1 than do Table 4-3's.[14] We tentatively conclude that nonstationarity plays a significant role in the results we have found.

Table 4-3. Estimated Slope Coefficients: March 1973–December 1976.

Difference Interval	"Stationary" Countries	
	Country Constants Constrained to be Equal	
	CPI	WPI
1 month	0.0051 (0.224)*	-0.229 (0.133)
3	0.536 (0.454)	0.376 (0.280)
6	0.817 (0.579)	0.050 (0.333)
12	1.44** † (0.597)	0.807** † (0.341)
18	1.15** † (0.243)	0.673** (0.131)
	Separate Constants for Each Country	
1	-0.093 (0.232)	-0.259 (0.136)
3	0.287 (0.528)	0.330 (0.302)
6	0.469 (0.782)	-0.066 (0.377)
12	1.35 (1.08)	0.799 (0.472)
18	0.631 (0.376)	0.488** (0.099)

*Standard errors of estimates are in parentheses.
**Significantly different from zero.
† *Not* significantly different from unity.
Source: International Financial Statistics.

Notes to Tables 4-3 and 4-4: From the original Group of Ten countries, the stationary group excludes the United Kingdom, Germany, and Italy for CPI inflation rate experiments. For the WPI inflation rates, the stationary group excludes the United Kingdom, France, Italy, and Japan.

Table 4-4. Estimated Slope Coefficients: March 1973-December 1976.

"Nonstationary" Countries

Country Constants Constrained to be Equal

Difference Interval	CPI	WPI
1 month	0.327 (0.305)*	0.273** (0.116)
3	0.724 (0.419)	0.536** (0.154)
6	1.20** (0.554)	0.444** (0.191)
12	1.40** (0.641)	0.387 (0.297)
Separate Constants for Each Country		
1	-0.026 (0.349)	0.243** (0.120)
3	0.330 (0.530)	0.504** (0.167)
6	0.834 (0.887)	0.377 (0.212)
12	1.68 (1.50)	0.243 (0.380)

*Standard errors of estimates are in parentheses.
**Significantly different from zero.
†*Not* significantly different from unity.
Source: International Financial Statistics.

IV. SUMMARY AND CONCLUSIONS

A number of authors, using cross-section regression, have found a strong, PPP-type relationship between exchange rate changes and changes in relative national price levels. Many of them explicitly conclude that if a single country has, say, a quarter of particularly high inflation relative to abroad, it can then expect to see this sooner or later reflected in a proportionate depreciation of its exchange rate. We show that the regression results are just as consistent with a model in which mean (relative) inflation and depreciation rates are related but deviations around these averages are totally unrelated.

These cross-section regressions have thus been very poor, nondiscriminating tests of the validity of the PPP theory. Further, such regressions have been used by some (see, for example, OPTICA 1977) to argue for exchange market intervention based upon PPP considerations. The statistical results given here raise serious doubts about the accuracy of their view.

Other authors have argued that PPP will hold only with a lag. Thus, in pooled cross-section time-series regressions they predict and observe that the slope coefficient of the regression relating changes in exchange rates to changes in relative prices grows larger and more significant as the interval is changed from month-to-month changes to quarter-to-quarter changes, and so forth. We show that this tendency would be observed even if deviations from means of exchange rate and relative price changes were entirely unrelated, provided the average rates for a country are equal *and* the regression contains only a single constant (as in King 1977 and Brillembourg 1976). When separate constants are used for each country, estimates of the slope coefficient are substantially altered. All fall in algebraic value, and most are no longer significant.

Nevertheless, some slope coefficients remain significant at longer differencing intervals, even with separate country constants. We conjecture that this might well be due to shifts in the mean inflation and depreciation rates for various countries. Time-series analysis yields results consistent with this hypothesis for a number of countries. When the sample of countries is divided between those that, on the basis of cursory time-series analysis, seem to display such shifts and those that do not, cross-section time-series regressions on both subsets produce results that lend some, but by no means conclusive, support to this view.

Theoretical discussions have made many distinctions concerning different meanings of purchasing power parity but seldom the distinctions considered here. Proposals for intervention based on PPP are often predicated on the simple view that changes in relative national price levels lead to changes in exchange rates and that the simple relationship is stable and significant enough to be of practical use. The results reported here suggest that this view is simply not valid and that the evidence used to support it has been badly misinterpreted. Instead, our results support a relatively weak but important version of PPP that implies a positive relationship between average rates of depreciation and of changes in relative national prices, but no relation between price and exchange rate changes about these averages. This latter, "weak," version of PPP accords with neoclassical predictions but provides no basis for intervention based upon PPP considerations to improve exchange market performance.

NOTES TO CHAPTER 4

1.   Except, that is, in the trivial case when the basket of goods used to calculate the national price index consists of traded goods only *and* is identical across countries.

2.   For example, the controversy over possible "productivity biases" in PPP is essentially over whether one country's price index can persistently

change at a rate different from another's when both are expressed in a common currency (see Officer 1976 for a discussion and further references).

3.   Whether they will be able to do so — or more generally whether such a policy would be desirable — will depend upon the mechanism determining price and exchange rate changes and their interactions. Suppose, for example, that domestic goods prices respond slowly and at different speeds to changes in the domestic money stock, while the exchange rate moves immediately to its long-run level. Intervention that pushed the exchange rate back to a level consistent with PPP would push it away from its long-run equilibrium and could conceivably delay adjustment in domestic goods markets (by affecting demand) further. Moreover, to the extent that exchange rates directly affect alternative domestic prices differently, such intervention may push some relative prices back toward their long-run equilibrium while pushing others away. Intervention, that is, is likely to be at best a second-best policy when there are imperfections in goods markets, and it could even reduce welfare compared to a policy of nonintervention.

4.   When this is the case, a change in relative prices must (as a matter of arithmetic) lead to a change in relative national price levels expressed in the same currency — that is, in the real exchange rate. Departures from PPP are thus equivalent to changes in relative prices.

5.   We could also add a *transient* noise of the form $C(L)\,\psi(t)$ where $\psi(t)$ is a white noise and $C(1) = 0$.

6.   We could model this by relaxing the restriction that $A(L) = 1$ and/or by adding uncorrelated errors to equations (4.1a) and (4.1b) while maintaining $A(L) = 1$.

7.   Recall that in Dornbusch's (1976) formulation, a once and for all increase in money causes the exchange rate to overshoot — that is, it leads to a temporary change in the real exchange rate. The real rate then adjusts in a serially correlated fashion back to its original level in the absence of further disturbances.

7.   See Kemp (1977) and OPTICA (1977).

9.   Denoting the n-month difference operator as Δ^n,

$$\Delta^n \epsilon(t) = n\alpha + \sum_{j=1}^{n} \xi(t+1-j)$$

$$\Delta^n p(t) = n\beta + \sum_{j=1}^{n} \omega(t+1-j).$$

If the $\xi(\ )$ and $\omega(\ )$ are independent, so will be the n-period price and exchange rate changes, regardless of the length of the differencing interval.

10.   At the very least, the estimated slope coefficients in the second portion of Table 4–1 drop dramatically and in a way not to be expected if the single-intercept model is the appropriate specification. If this specification is correct, inclusion of separate country intercepts will reduce degrees of

freedom and lessen the efficiency of the parameter estimates, but it will *not* bias downwards the estimates. The standard errors do not increase drastically from the first to the second portion of the table. But if the standard error had not increased, the coefficient for the WPI for the twelve-month lag would have been significantly different from zero *and* from unity; the coefficient for the WPI for the six-month lag would have been insignificantly different from zero and unity, while that for the CPI for a twelve-month lag would have been significantly different from one (but not zero) under the same circumstances. Of course, the coefficient estimates are not independent within, or across, the two portions of the table.

11.   Note, however, that it is only the slope coefficient for the CPI at an eighteen-month lag that remains both significant and not different from unity in Table 4–1. The comparable slope coefficient for the WPI is significantly different from zero *and also* from unity, but it is hard to know what PPP interpretation to give a slope coefficient of 0.3855. A slope coefficient of unity but a low adjusted R^2 would be consistent with PPP considerations and the view that other factors beyond it determine the exchange rate. A zero-slope coefficient is consistent with weak PPP.

12.   Intuitively, in the single-constant case, the b is likely to be higher if the sample includes three scatters as in Figure 4–1 than if shortening the sample eliminates one of the scatters. It is also true that shortening the sample will tend to reduce b more if this eliminates one of the outlying scatters in Figure 4–1.

13.   It remains, however, statistically insignificantly different from unity—the standard error grows by around 50 percent between the two tables and the estimated coefficient falls. See Note 10 for a discussion of the effect on estimates and their standard errors of including separate country constants.

14.   Degrees of freedom limited the maximum differencing interval to only twelve months rather than eighteen months.

BIBLIOGRAPHY

Balassa, B. 1964. "The Purchasing Power Parity Doctrine: A Reappraisal," *Journal of Political Economy* 72 (December): 584–96.

Box, G., and G. Jenkins. 1976. *Time Series Analysis*, 2nd ed. San Francisco: Holden–Day.

Brillembourg, A. 1976. "Purchasing Power Parity—Tests of Causality and Equilibrium," International Monetary Fund. (Mimeo.)

Dennis, G. 1976. "Price and Quantity Adjustments in Exchange Rate Forecasting," *Euromoney* (August): 52–56.

Dornbusch, R. 1976. "Expectations and Exchange Rate Dynamics," *Journal of Political Economy* 84 (December): 1161–76.

Dornbusch, R. 1978. "Monetary Policy Under Exchange-Rate Flexibility," in *Managed Exchange-Rate Flexibility: The Recent Experience*, Conference

Series No. 20, Proceedings, Federal Reserve Bank of Boston (October): 90–122.

Frenkel, Jacob A. 1981. "The Collapse of Purchasing Power Parities During the 1970s," *European Economic Review* 16: 145–65.

Frenkel, J. 1978. "Purchasing Power Parity: Doctrinal Perspective and Evidence from the 1920s," *Journal of International Economics* 8: 169–91.

Kemp, D. 1976. "The U.S. Dollar in International Markets: Mid-1970 to Mid-1976," Federal Reserve Bank of St. Louis *Review* (August): 7–14.

Kern, D. 1976. "Inflation Implications in Foreign Exchange Rate Forecasting," *Euromoney* (April): 62–69.

King, D. 1977. "The Performance of Exchange Rates in the Recent Period of Floating: Exchange Rates and Inflation Rates," *Southern Economic Journal*, pp. 1582–87.

Officer, L. 1976. "The Purchasing-Power-Parity Theory of Exchange Rates: A Review Article," *IMF Staff Papers*, pp. 1–60.

OPTICA Report. 1977. Brussels.

Pigott, C., and R. J. Sweeney. 1978. "Price and Exchange Rate Dynamics," Claremont Men's College. (Mimeo.)

Yeager, L. 1966. *International Monetary Relations: Theory, History, and Policy*, 2nd ed. New York: Harper & Row.

5 TESTING THE EXCHANGE RATE IMPLICATIONS OF TWO POPULAR MONETARY MODELS

Charles Pigott and Richard J. Sweeney

Over the past two decades, the monetary approach to the balance of payments has had a large impact on analysis and interpretation of exchange rate and international financial developments. In the 1970s, this approach was applied extensively to short-run exchange rate analysis, and the analysis of overshooting based on the monetary approach has received a good deal of attention. There have been many attempts at empirical verification of various short- and long-run models based on the approach, using a variety of statistical techniques. During the mid-1970s, regression equations based on various monetary approach models seemed to work well. By the late 1970s, however, many researchers were concluding that monetary approach equations were no longer working.[1]

Section I examines a class of models that can generate the range of results found in the monetary approach literature and focuses on the full and partial price adjustment mechanisms.[2] Section II argues that neither adjustment scheme produces predictions that accord well with the observed auto- and cross-correlation patterns in price, exchange rate, and real interest rate series—both predict more and stronger correlation than is found. The overshooting case in particular is grossly at variance with the data.[3] This section uses data from the early period of the float when monetary approach models enjoyed their greatest empirical success.

The argument is illustrated by Figures 5-1 and 5-2 and Tables 5-1 and 5-2. Figure 5-1 shows the theoretical autocorrelation function for inflation where

San Francisco Federal Reserve Bank and Claremont McKenna College and Claremont Graduate School, respectively. The authors wish to thank Sven W. Arndt, Angelo Mascaro, John Rutledge, and especially Thomas D. Willett.

91

changes in the money supply are generated by a simple process, for both the full and partial price adjustment mechanisms that have been discussed in the literature. Neither looks very much like the sample autocorrelation functions reported in Table 5-1. Similarly, Figure 5-2 shows the theoretical cross-correlation function for inflation leading and lagging changes in exchange rates under the two price adjustment mechanisms. However, estimated cross-correlation functions do not show the predicted patterns, as for example in Table 5-2.

One defense against these charges is the argument that the predictions have been drawn from monetary models that are incompletely specified since they do not explicitly incorporate sources of disturbance other than the money supply. That is, if other disturbances are included, the augmented model *might* generate results more consistent with the data. There are two problems with this defense. First, if such augmented models were consistent with the data, this would mean that these other disturbances swamp money supply shocks, and thus money supply shocks would be of trivial importance relative to other disturbances; this is the opposite of the view generally held by those modeling in this vein. Second, most other forms of disturbances would *not* make the partial price adjustment mechanism yield predictions consistent with the data. For example, permanent *random* money supply shocks set off positively correlated price changes. These could be offset by fiscal changes that were negatively correlated with the initial money supply shocks and were also negatively autocorrelated. The partial adjustment mechanism and overshooting thus seem pretty firmly at variance with the data.

Section III concludes that short-run monetary models of the international economy are inadequate as now formulated. This does not mean that it is appropriate to reject the monetary approach, but rather that reformulation is required to make models more complicated but also more adequate.

I. THE MODEL

Assume the usual two-country world and focus on the home country, which is small relative to the foreign nation in the sense that the latter's prices, interest rates, and income are fixed.[4] Each government issues its own money, held only by its own citizens. Government activity consists of transfers to citizens, entirely financed by money creation. The home country demand for money depends only on current real income, the domestic price of the home good, and the domestic interest rate. The demand for each commodity depends only on their relative prices and the current real income in both countries.[5]

Structural Equations

The demands for money, bonds and the home good have the following forms:

$$m_t - p_t = -\lambda r_t + \bar{y} , \quad \lambda > 0 \tag{5.1}$$

$$r_t = \bar{r}_f + E_t \epsilon_{t+1} - \epsilon_t \tag{5.2}$$

$$y_t^d = -\gamma_1 (P_t - \epsilon_t) + \gamma_0 , \quad \gamma_1 > 0, \tag{5.3}$$

where m_t, p_t, y_t, ϵ_t are, respectively, the natural logarithms of the domestic money stock, the domestic price of the home good, domestic real production (assumed constant), and the price of foreign exchange; $\bar{r}_f$ and r_t refer to the foreign and domestic interest rates while y_t^d refers to the natural logarithm of the demand for domestic commodities. Finally, the variable $E_t \epsilon_{t+1}$ refers to the log of the value of the exchange rate expected at period t to prevail in period $t + 1$.[6]

From equation (5.1) the interest elasticity of the demand for money (taken as positive) is λ and the income elasticity of the demand for real balances is for convenience) unity. Equation (5.2) follows from the bonds being perfect substitutes ex ante: The domestic yield must equal the foreign (payable in foreign currency) plus the expected percentage depreciation of the home currency. In equation (5.3), the log of home aggregate demand depends on the log of the relative price of the two goods expressed in domestic currency, $p_t - \epsilon_t$, where γ_1 is the price elasticity (taken as a positive number) of aggregate demand.

Money Stock Behavior

Suppose the money stock has two components, a transient element, e, which disappears in the next period, and a permanent element, δ_t, plus a trend growth rate u,

$$m_t = m_o + e_t + \sum_{j=1}^{t} (u + \delta_j) ,$$

$$m_t - m_{t-1} = u + \delta_t + (e_t - e_{t-1}) , \tag{5.4}$$

or where e and δ are serially correlated, mutually independent, zero mean random variable.[7]

Output Pricing

All of the models cited above assume asset markets clear at all times, in the sense that r and ϵ adjust instantly to make asset stocks and demands equal. Two price adjustment mechanisms are investigated.

A: "Full" Adjustment: Define the monetary equilibrium price level p_t^*, as that for which $\bar{y} = y_t^d$: from equation (5.3):

$$p_t^* = (\gamma_0/\gamma_1) - (1/\gamma_1)\bar{y} + \epsilon_t. \qquad (5.5)$$

The actual price level p_t is assumed to equal the market clearing level p_t^*. In this sense both commodity and asset markets are assumed to clear instantaneously in such models; this is the crucial property in determining exchange rate dynamics within the models, since, from (5.5), p^* *mimics* ϵ.

B: "Partial" Price Adjustment: Dornbusch (1976) assumes that prices adjust to their perceived long-run equilibrium values in successive increments.[8] In placing his nonstochastic, continuous time model in discrete time terms and making it stochastic, a number of versions of the process could be written (all having very similar implications). The version used here is

$$p_t - E_{t-1}p_t^* = -\beta(E_{t-1}p_t^* - p_{t-1}), \qquad 0 \le \beta \le 1 \qquad (5.6)$$

where $E_{t-1}p_t^*$ is the market clearing value of p_t for t expected at time $t-1$. In other words, producers set a price for period t prior to knowing all the variables that determine demand during that period (in particular, prior to knowing m_t and ϵ_t). If $\beta < 1$, commodities markets can be said to adjust more slowly than asset markets.

Formally, it proves useful to allow for a "mixed" pricing scheme whereby some adjustment of prices to currently realized conditions is allowed. That is, assume p_t is determined as

(a) $p_t^{\sim} - E_{t-1}p_t^* = -(E_{t-1}p_t^* - p_{t-1}), \qquad 0 \le \beta < 1$

(b) $p_t = p_t^{\sim} + (1-\theta)p_t^*, \qquad 0 \le \theta \le 1.$ $\qquad (5.7)$

$\theta = 1$ gives the "partial" adjustment scheme described by equation (5.6); $\theta = 0$ gives the "full" adjustment of commodity prices assumed in most of the papers cited above. The "mixed" process is admittedly somewhat artificial but proves economical in deriving results; only extreme cases will be considered explicitly, however.

Solution of the Model

Assume rational expectations. It can be shown that under these circumstances the endogenous variable p_t, t, r_t are linear functions of the exogenous disturbances determining the money stock.

Here the solutions of the two polar cases will be analyzed.[9]

Case 1: $\theta = \beta = 0$ ("full" adjustment):

(a) $p_t - p_{t-1} = u + \delta_t + (\lambda + 1)^{-1} (e_t - e_{t-1})$

(b) $\epsilon_t - \epsilon_{t-1} = u + \delta_t + (\lambda + 1)^{-1} (e_t - e_{t-1})$

(c) $r_t = \bar{r}^f + u - (\lambda + 1)^{-1} e_t$. \hfill (5.8)

Case 2: $\theta = 1, \quad 1 > \beta > 0$ ("partial" adjustment):

(a) $P_t - P_{t-1} = (\beta/\Delta)(p_{t-1} - p_{t-2}) + a_0(1-\beta)/\Delta \delta_{t-1}$
$$+ (a_0(1-\beta)/\Delta)u ;$$

(b) $\epsilon_t - \epsilon_{t-1} = a_0(m_t - m_{t-1}) + (1 - a_0)(p_t - p_{t-1})$
$$- (a_0/\Delta)(e_t - e_{t-1})$$
$$= a_0(\delta_t + u) + (1 - a_0)(p_t - p_{t-1}) + \frac{1}{\lambda}$$
$$(e_t - e_{t-1}) ;$$

(c) $r_t = \bar{r}^f - (1/\lambda)e_t + (1 - a_0) [(\beta/\Delta)(p_t - p_{t-1})$
$$+ (1/\Delta)a_0(1-\beta)\theta \delta_{t-1}] + \frac{a_0}{\lambda} u ;$$

where

$$a_0 = -1 + (1 - \beta)(\lambda - 1) - [(1-\beta)^2 (\lambda - 1)^2$$
$$+ u/\lambda(1-\beta)]^{\frac{1}{2}} / 2\lambda(1-\beta) - 1 > 0 ;$$

$$\Delta = 1 + (a_0 - 1)[\theta(1-\beta) + (1-\theta)] > 0 . \hfill (5.9)$$

II. COMPARISONS OF THE DATA WITH PREDICTED
AUTO- AND CROSS-CORRELATIONS PATTERNS

The models in Section I predict patterns of serial and cross-correlation expected under both the full and partial price adjustment mechanisms. As seen below, these predicted patterns are grossly at variance with the data.

This section considers the impact of monetary disturbances and exchange rate's overshooting, the (closely related) question of the autocorrelation structure of price and exchange rate changes, the relation between interest rate changes and price and exchange rate variations, and the behavior of the purchasing power parity adjusted exchange rate in the presence of purely money supply disturbances.

Consider the predictions of the two models for the simple money supply assumed above.[10] (Of course, the results vary with the process assumed, but the

Figure 5-1. Examples of Autocorrelation Structures of Inflation Rates.*

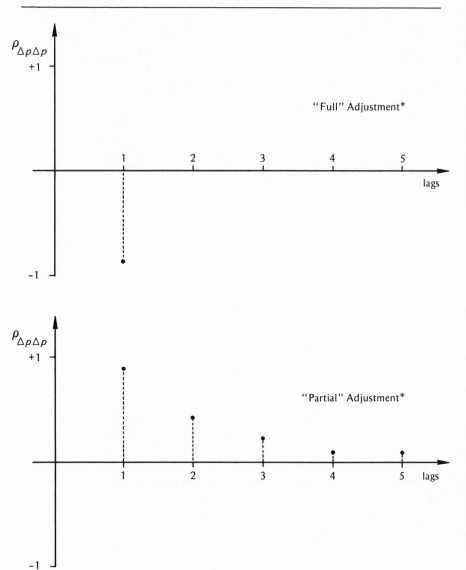

*For the money supply process $\Delta m_t = u + \delta_t + e_t - e_{t-1}$ when δ and e are white noises.

flavor is much as below.) Under both price adjustment schemes, there is strong cross-correlation of charges in prices and exchange rates, as Figure 5-2 illustrates. Both prices and exchange rates will display autocorrelation that is massive and persistent in the partial price adjustment case, as in Figure 5-1. The real exchange rate—the exchange rate adjusted by relative national price levels—is stationary but shows patterns of autocorrelation, as does the real rate of interest. There is a pattern of cross-correlation between changes in interest rates and exchange rates. (The technical details of deriving these results are available on request from the authors.)

These theoretical results derive their importance by their distinct deviations from real world data. The data used are all selected from periods where regression equations based on the monetary approach seemed to work. However, even in this period, the data are at odds with the predicted auto- and cross-correlation patterns. Table 5-1 shows that the inflation rate for the U.S. Consumer Price Index (CPI) over five-year periods is essentially a white noise process. There is not the autocorrelation predicted by the models.[11]

Table 5-2 shows the ACFs for changes in the Swiss-U.S. exchange rate and WPIs. Both are essentially white, though there is an economically meaningless spike at lag 6. Further, the cross-correlation function (CCF) shows no significant relationship (the sign at lag zero is incorrect) compared to the model's predictions. Table 5-3 shows the autocorrelation function (ACF) and partial autocorrelation function (PACF) for the Swiss real exchange rate vis-à-vis the United States, where the nominal exchange rate is adjusted by the relative WPIs of the two countries. The pattern seems consistent with nonstationarity, *not* the stationarity predicted by the models.

Table 5-1. Sample Autocorrelations of the Percentage Rate of Change of the U.S. CPI.

Lag	1953: 2-1958: 1	1958: 2-1963: 1	1963: 2-1968: 1	1966: 6-1971: 5
1	0.19	-0.05	0.19	0.35*
2	0.25	0.02	0.13	0.24
3	0.11	-0.16	-0.01	0.24
4	0.16	-0.05	0.01	0.19
5	0.06	-0.09	0.13	0.26*
6	0.00	0.04	0.18	0.20
7	0.10	-0.02	-0.05	0.13
8	0.18	-0.11	0.07	0.29*
9	0.20	-0.05	0.05	0.24
10	0.18	-0.08	0.06	0.11
11	-0.01	-0.12	0.02	0.09
12	-0.03	0.12	0.12	0.20

Standard error = $1/\sqrt{59}$ = 0.13.
*Significantly different from zero at the 95 percent confidence level.
Source: NBER Data Bank.

Figure 5-2. Examples of Cross-Correlation Structures of Changes in Prices and Exchange Rates.*

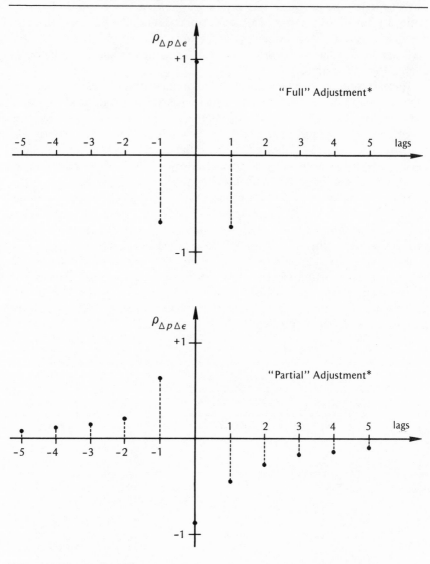

*For the money supply process $\Delta m_t = u + \delta_t + e_t - e_{t-1}$ when δ and e are white noises.

Table 5-2. Switzerland/U.S. (April 1973-February 1977)
Autocorrelation Functions.

Changes in the Swiss Relative to U.S. WPI	Changes in the Swiss/U.S. Exchange Rate
-0.10	0.19
-0.05	0.07
0.09	-0.06
-0.13	-0.24
0.08	-0.07
0.24	-0.38*
-0.23	0.03
0.04	0.05
-0.13	0.03
-0.23	0.14
0.17	-0.13
0.06	-0.08

Cross-Correlation Functions	
Changes in Relative WPIs Lagging Changes in the Exchange Rate	Changes in the Exchange Rate Lagging Changes in Relative WPIs
-0.15	-0.15
0.14	0.12
0.11	0.12
0.04	0.07

Lag	Changes in Relative WPIs Lagging Changes in the Exchange Rate	Changes in the Exchange Rate Lagging Changes in Relative WPIs
4	0.08	-0.06
5	-0.18	0.13
6	0.17	0.08
7	-0.09	0.09
8	-0.17	-0.06
9	0.05	-0.18
10	-0.06	0.01
11	0.03	-0.09
12	-0.18	0.00

$N = 47$.
$2/\sqrt{47} = 0.29$.
*Significantly different from zero at the 95 percent confidence level.

Source: International Financial Statistics.

Table 5-3.   Level of the Real Exchange Rate: Swiss Francs versus U.S. Dollars (*April 1973–February 1977*).

Lag	Autocorrelation	Partial Autocorrelation
1	0.45*	0.45*
2	0.17	−0.05
3	−0.17	−0.29
4	−0.25	−0.08
5	−0.32*	−0.17
6	−0.20	−0.03
7	−0.16	−0.12
8	−0.00	0.01
9	−0.02	−0.13
10	−0.00	−0.10
11	0.05	0.06
12	0.11	0.12

*Standard Error = $1/\sqrt{47}$ = 0.146.

Table 5-4.   First Difference of the Real Exchange Rate: Swiss Francs versus U.S. Dollars (*April 1973–February 1977*).

Lag	Autocorrelation	Partial Autocorrelation
1	0.02	0.02
2	−0.05	−0.05
3	−0.06	−0.06
4	−0.20	−0.20
5	−0.01	−0.01
6	−0.31*	−0.35*
7	−0.02	−0.06
8	0.12	0.03
9	0.04	−0.02
10	0.07	−0.07
11	−0.03	−0.05
12	0.02	−0.07

*Significantly different from zero at the 95 percent confidence level.
Source: International Financial Statistics.

Table 5-3 also shows the ACF and PACF for the first difference of the Swiss-U.S. real exchange rate; the spike at lag 6 has no meaningful economic interpretations: The changes are essentially random and do *not* display the autocorrelation patterns predicted by the models.

Previous work by Kaylin, Pigott, Sweeney, and Willett shows virtually no systematic relationships between interest rates and exchange rates.[12]

The great contrast between the models' predictions and the data is illustrated by Figures 5-1 and 5-2, which show examples of the auto- and cross-correlation patterns (for a particular money supply process—more complex processes tend not to mitigate the model's inadequacies). An acceptable model ought to generate results consistent with these empirical observations. In particular, the notion of exchange rate overshooting is grossly at variance with the data.

Overshooting

Exchange rate overshooting has received considerable attention in recent literature.[13] In a wide variety of theoretical models a monetary disturbance will induce a greater initial exchange rate change than the change in the long-run equilibrium value. Interest in the overshooting question has also been stimulated by the fact that, under the current float, bilateral exchange rates generally have been considerably more variable than stock changes; overshooting has been one reason advanced for the greater variability of exchange rate changes.[14] This issue has important policy implications as well, for if significant overshooting occurs in exchange markets, a case exists in principle for official intervention.[15]

In the present context, overshooting of the exchange rate in response to a permanent change in the money stock occurs under Case 2. In contrast to the full adjustment case, an increase in the money stock must initially be absorbed by a fall in the domestic interest rate, requiring a decline in the exchange rate below its long-run equilibrium value.

Figures 5-1 and 5-2 illustrate the implied price and exchange rate patterns. These results reflect the reaction to a one-shot disturbance analyzed by Dornbusch.[16] *Past* exchange rate changes reflect past changes in the money stock, which lead to price changes in the same direction. However, exchange rate changes subsequent to a disturbance tend to be negatively correlated with prior price changes, because of the "correction" required by the initial overshooting. Given a single money stock increase, and initial depreciation, the exchange rate appreciates (ϵ_t falls) in subsequent periods as prices increase toward their long-run equilibrium. Empirical evidence seems to contradict the implications of this model. First, there simply does not exist the massive serial correlation of inflation rates or changes in exchange rates predicted by this model. Second, nothing is observable resembling the cross-correlation pattern on inflation rates and exchange rates that the model predicts. (The predicted behavior of interest rates and the real exchange rate is discussed below.)

Interest Rates, and Price and Exchange Rate Changes

Equation (5.2) requires equality of the expected yield in home currency of the domestic and foreign assets. This means that a fall in domestic rates must be associated with a subsequent appreciation of home currency, since r_f is constant. This relation must hold regardless of the behavior of domestic prices.[17] The results in Table 5-4 contradict this prediction.

The partial adjustment case implies a distinctive behavior of interest rates, particularly the term structure. For example, a random permanent increase in m_t leads to a fall in the current short-term interest rate relative to all expected future short-term rates: Er_{t+i} Er_{t+i+1}, and Er_{t+i} approaches the foreign rate (plus the expected long term rate of inflation) as i becomes large but is below it for all finite i. In contrast, under full price adjustment, the short-term interest rate is expected to equal its long-run equilibrium value once money stock changes equal their unconditional expected value, u. Moreover, under the partial adjustment case, nominal interest rates tend to be below their long-run values, while price changes are above their long-run mean.

Behavior of the Purchasing Power Parity Adjusted Exchange Rate

Note that the log of the purchasing-power-parity adjusted exchange rate $P_t - \epsilon_t - \bar{p}_f$ is assumed fixed, is a *stationary* stochastic process, so long as the disturbances are in the money supply. While the proposition is obvious enough, since the long-run relative prices are unaffected by money stock changes, it is not trivial as p_t and ϵ_t are *not* individually stationary.[18]

The stationarity of $p_t - \epsilon_t - \bar{p}_f$ may be taken as one stochastic formulation of purchasing-power-parity theory. The alleged tendency for purchasing power parity to hold in the long run refers here to the fact that the limit:

$$\text{Lim } E_t \left(p_{t+i} - \epsilon_{t+i} - \bar{p}_f \right) = \gamma_0 / \gamma_1 - \bar{y}/\gamma_1 - \bar{p}_f$$

where the left-hand expression refers to the conditional expected value of the price adjusted exchange rate at $t + i$, given information available at t. The above would hold regardless of the price formation mechanism (provided it were stable) and regardless of the process determining money stock changes. However, as Table 5-3 illustrates, actual measured price-adjusted exchange rates do *not* appear to have been stationary under the current float.

The differences in the behavior of the price-adjusted exchange rate under the two price adjustment mechanisms parallel those of interest rates. In particular, under Case 1, the price-adjusted exchange rate is at its long-run equilibrium value in every period. Under the partial adjustment mechanism, an innovation in the money stock leads to a gradual adjustment of the price-adjusted exchange rate back to equilibrium. In particular, a permanent money stock increase shifts the real exchange rate against the home country—that, indeed, is the mechanism by which prices are induced to adjust to their new equilibrium—and they adjust gradually back to their original value in subsequent periods.

Suppose that nonmonetary shocks make the real exchange rate nonstationary. After differencing to make the real exchange rate stationary, money supply disturbances would leave no cyclical patterns in the full adjustment case but distinct patterns in the partial adjustment case. Thus, the results in Table 5-2 seem at first glance consistent with the full adjustment mechanism but distinctly inconsistent with the partial adjustment mechanism. It is possible to argue that the cyclical behavior set off by the partial mechanism is just offset by negatively (but highly) correlated nonmonetary disturbances; but there is not an a priori reason to assume this is so and it is a conjecture for which no empirical support has been offered.

III. CONCLUSIONS

Our focus has been on the implications of alternative commodity price formation processes for price and exchange rate dynamics, and how well these models' predictions conform to the data. A very simple model was used, but, nonetheless, the results provide useful insights into the short-run behavior of exchange rates implied by a number of recent papers. Explicit consideration of the stochastic structure of the models generated important implications that were compared with the data.

Under partial price adjustment in goods markets, both price and exchange rate changes, as well as interest rates, display an autoregressive structure, even if money stock changes are of the simplest (white noise) form. This property is imparted by the internal dynamics of the partial adjustment mechanism; it implies that the autocorrelations of price changes (or interest rates or exchange rate changes) will be non-zero at any lag. Since this property is an intrinsic element of the model, it must hold under any (additive) disturbances.[19] In particular, exchange rate variability may exceed that of money stock changes simply because there are real disturbances to equilibrium. We have noted that purchasing power parity adjusted exchange rates appear not to have been stationary under the current float, which suggests the presence of such disturbances.

The framework examined here could be extended in a number of ways. In particular, income dynamics could be studied by adding a labor market and examining the implications of alternative wage formation mechanisms. Moreover, relaxation of the assumption that market participants possess complete information about the current values of the endogenous and exogenous variables, as well as of all structural parameters, could prove interesting.

NOTES TO CHAPTER 5

1. For documentation of the failure of estimated short-run monetary approach models, see Waseem Khan and Thomas D. Willett, "The Monetary Approach to Exchange Rates: A Review of Recent Empirical Studies," *Kredit und Kapital* 17 (January 1984): 199–22.

2. These models include Robert J. Barro, "A Stochastic Equilibrium Model of an Open Economy Under Flexible Exchange Rates," *Quarterly Journal of Economics* 92 (February 1978): 149–64; John F. O. Bilson, "The Monetary Approach to the Exchange Rate: Some Empirical Evidence," *IMF Staff Papers* 25 (March 1978): 47–75; Guillermo A. Calvo and Carlos A. Rodriquez, "A Model of Exchange Rate Determination with Currency Substitutes and Rational Expectations," *Journal of Political Economy* 85 (June 1977): 617–25; Rudiger Dornbusch, "Expectations and Rational Exchange Rates," *Journal of Political Economy* 84 (December 1976): 1161–76; Pentti J. K. Kouri, "The Exchange Rate and the Balance of Payments in the Short Run and in the Long Run," *Scandinavian Journal of Economics* 78, no. 2 (1976): 280–304; and Michael Mussa, "The Exchange Rate, the Balance of Payments and Monetary and Fiscal Policy Under a Regime of Controlled Floating," *Scandinavian Journal of Economics* 78: no. 2 (1976): 229–48. These focus almost entirely upon short-run behavior–investment and growth are not considered explicitly. However, they are all intellectual descendants of the portfolio balance, open economy models developed by Duncan I. Foley and Miguel Sidrauski, *Monetary and Fiscal Policy in a Growing Economy* (New York: McMillan, 1971), especially chapter 16, and Rudiger Dornbusch, "A Portfolio Balance Model of the Open Economy," *Journal of Monetary Economics* 1 (January 1975): 3–20.

3. Rudiger Dornbusch, "Expectations and Rational Exchange Rates." There are, of course other versions of overshooting; see Richard Levich, "Overshooting in the Foreign Exchange Market" Group of Thirty Occasional Paper No. 4. (New York University, August 1979).

   The approach of this paper is not the only way of testing for overshooting; see Robert Driskill, "Exchange Rate Dynamics: An Empirical Investigation," *Journal of Political Economy* 89 (April 1981): 357–71; Bruce Brittain, "Tests of Theories of Exchange Rate Determination," *Journal of Finance* 32 (May 1977): 519–29; and Michael Keran and Stephen Zeldes, "Effects of Monetary Disturbances on Exchange Rates, Inflation, and Interest Rates," *Economic Review* of the Federal Reserve Bank of San Francisco (Spring 1980): 7–29.

4. John F. O. Bilson, "The Monetary Approach to Exchange Rates," discusses a two-country world explicitly, but the interactions of the models are quite simple and do not lead to substantially different outcomes from those developed here. Proceedings of the Fall 1978 Academic Conference, Federal Reserve Bank of San Francisco (1979), pp. 142–61, and Richard J. Sweeney, "Risk, Exchange Rates, and Capital Formation" (Claremont, 1979) (Mimeo.), consider a two-country model with markets for goods, bonds, and money in each country and in the latter shows some of the differences between the closed- and open-economy cases.

5. These assumptions, widely adopted in the literature, make analysis manageable, but it is important to recall what is thereby omitted. In particular, the demands for money and commodities are assumed to depend on current and not expected future prices. This assumption is quite restrictive

for the sort of analysis pursued here, where prices will vary in a complex manner over many periods, because intertemporal substitutions of consumption and money holding induced by such price variations are, in effect, excluded. Some indications of the complexity of intertemporal consumption-investment decisions are produced by papers by William A. Brock, "A Simple Perfect Foresight Monetary Model" *Journal of Monetary Economics* 1 (April 1975): 133–50, whose discussions are by far the most lucid of the ones we have examined. Richard J. Sweeney, "Risk, Inflation and Exchange Rates," and "Risk, Exchange Rates and Capital Formation," modifies the following model by considering a two-country world in which the expected real rate of interest in each country influences aggregate demand in that country and both expected real rates of interest (adjusted for risk) influence the demands for home and foreign country bonds.

6. γ_0 includes the foreign price, taken as given, and also the influences of domestic and foreign production, both of which are assumed fixed. γ_0 is assumed to have a random term in mimeo, Appendix B, available on request from the authors, at The Claremont Center for Economic Policy Studies, The Claremont Graduate School, Claremont, Calif. 91711.

7. Appendix A to this paper included in the Working Paper version investigates more elaborate forms of money stock behavior. The present assumptions suffice to reveal key differences in the two pricing cases discussed below. More elaborate money stock supply functions are revealing but do not crucially alter results regarding the auto- and cross-correlation patterns the models imply for observable endogenous variables. Appendix A is available from The Claremont Working Papers. See Note 6.

8. Rudiger Dornbusch, "Expectations and Rational Exchange Rates."

9. These are found, with the derivations, in the mimeo Appendix A, available at the address in Note 6.

10. Appendix A considers some more complex money stock processes; Appendix B discusses the effects of real shocks that alter the long-run equilibrium price-adjusted exchange rate. Both appendixes are available upon request from the authors, at the address in Note 6.

11. A more detailed discussion of the evidence and its implications is in Richard J. Sweeney, "On the Efficiency of Goods Markets" (U.S. Treasury Department) (Mimeo.) and "Efficient Information Processing in Output Markets: Tests and Implications," *Economic Inquiry* XVI (July 1978): 313–31. In particular, the period as a whole as well as the first and last subperiods show signs of nonstationarity.

12. Ira J. Kaylin, Charles Pigott, Richard J. Sweeney, and Thomas D. Willett, "The Effects of Interest Rate Changes on Exchange Rates During the Current Float," in Carl H. Stern, Dennis Logue, and John Makin, eds., *Eurocurrencies and the International Monetary System* (Washington: American Enterprise Institute, 1976): 223–34.

13. Marina v. N. Whitman, "The Locomotive Approach to Sustaining World Recovery: Has It Run Out of Steam?" in William Fellner, ed., *Contemporary Economic Problems: 1978* (Washington: American Enterprise Insti-

tute, 1978), pp. 245–83, and Rudiger Dornbusch, "Expectations and Rational Exchange Rates."

14. See, again, Rudiger Dornbusch, "Expectations and Rational Exchange Rates." There is, of course, no necessary connection between the variability of the two changes unless money stock changes are the only disturbances. The mimeo Appendix B introduces real, permanent disturbances to aggregate demand, and in this case the variance of exchange rate changes can easily exceed that of money stock changes even in the absence of overshooting.

15. Such intervention could be successful in reducing exchange rate variability, and while the authorities would not make money in the Dornbusch type of overshooting, neither would they lose money.

16. Rudiger Dornbusch, "Expectations and Rational Exchange Rates."

17. It is useful in this regard to distinguish between alternative money stock processes and alternative price formation mechanisms. Even where price adjustment is full, a rise in the domestic money stock may be associated with a rise or a fall in the exchange rate, depending upon the stochastic structure of money stock variations.

    For example, under Case 1, a permanent change in the money stock (δ) leaves interest rates unaffected, because prices adjust fully within the period and no further changes in the money stock are expected. A positive transient money stock change (which we might regard as a disturbance perfectly negatively correlated with a disturbance next period) induces a decline in the interest rate. If, on the other hand, successive money stock changes are highly positively correlated, a rise in the domestic money stock could lead (initially) to a *rise* in the domestic interest rate.

18 A case where the real exchange rate is not stationary is discussed in the mimeo Appendix B, available upon request from the authors at the address in Note 6.

19. Or at least for "almost all" disturbance structure in probability sense.

6 STABILIZING OR DESTABILIZING SPECULATION? EVIDENCE FROM THE FOREIGN EXCHANGE MARKETS

Richard J. Sweeney

I. INTRODUCTION

Many economists view a high degree of variability in price as per se undesirable. Intuitively, objections to exchange rates changing in response to temporary, short-run, self-reversing changes in demand and supply are well taken. Such an increase in demand, for example, will drive up the exchange rate (if only normal, nonspeculative supply is forthcoming), only to find the exchange rate later falling as demand returns to its previous level. These transitory price movements give misleading signals to resource allocation.[1]

But such price movements also offer profit opportunities to speculators. When demand rises, presumably some speculators will sell their currency holdings when the rate has risen a little in the expectation of rebuying when the rate falls back to its old level. In the limit, such activity would reduce transitory price changes to a level consistent with storage, transactions, and interest costs, *if* the temporary nature of the shocks is recognized. There is reason to doubt government interveners would be any better than private market participants at distinguishing between transitory and permanent shocks.

Efficient speculation will not only tend to offset price reactions to short-run, self-reversing changes but will help cause rapid adjustment to permanent changes to the extent speculators correctly interpret the shocks. If demand rises permanently, the long-run equilibrium rate also rises. A speculator will profit if he buys at the current rate, before it moves to the new long-run value. Floods of such purchases will drive the rate quickly to its new equilibrium value. Again, government should be no better than the private market at foreseeing such

107

changes and correctly distinguishing them from short-run shocks, unless they are due to government actions being kept secret from the public. Thus, speculation should much reduce cycles in exchange rates that are due to short-run, self-reversing shifts while causing the market quickly to reflect all long-run changes.

In Section II, the above arguments are developed in more detail and rigor. Section III examines some practical problems in testing for efficiency. Section IV discusses the results of efficiency tests on daily exchange rate data. Serial correlation tests give statistical evidence of some degree of inefficiency but may not be evidence of economic inefficiency. Filter rule tests give substantial evidence of inefficiency and show how it may be exploited through buy-and-sell rules. Section V offers a brief summary and some conclusions.

II. IMPLICATIONS OF EFFICIENT INFORMATION PROCESSING

Figure 6-1 pictures the demand and supply curves for some hypothetical good. It need not be foreign exchange, since the argument is perfectly general. The deterministic equilibrium price is $\bar{P}_0$. Introduce a stochastic element into the system by adding a random term, u_t, to the demand curve, $q_t^d = D(P_t)$, where q^d is the quantity demanded. The system is then the demand curve

$$q_t^d = D(P_t) + u_t \ , \tag{6.1}$$

and the supply curve

$$q_t^s = S(P_t) \ . \tag{6.2}$$

Suppose that $q_t^d = q_t^s$—that is, the market clears in every instant, t. If both (6.1) and (6.2) are linearized, price may be written as

$$P_t = \bar{P}_0 + cu_t \ , \tag{6.3}$$

where the equilibrium value of P is $\bar{P}_0$, in the absence of any error term. The cyclical variations in P_t will depend on the patterns in u_t.

To investigate such patterns, assume that u_t is a classical, serially uncorrelated error term with a zero mean. If the current realization u_t is negative, demand is lower than normal—say, the demand curve falls to D_1 and P to P_1. In the next period, price will depend on u_{t+1}, but the best guess is that u_{t+1} will equal zero and the price will be $\bar{P}_0$. Anyone buying now and selling next period has the mathematical expectation of making a per-unit gross profit of $\bar{P}_0 - P_1$.[2] Of course, transaction, interest, and storage costs must be netted from any such profit, and the interest rate must be appropriately adjusted for risk. But ignoring these for the moment, it is clear that the speculators will tend to buy the good when price falls below $\bar{P}_0$, and this buying will keep price from falling as far as

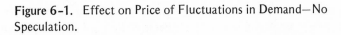

Figure 6-1. Effect on Price of Fluctuations in Demand—No
Speculation.

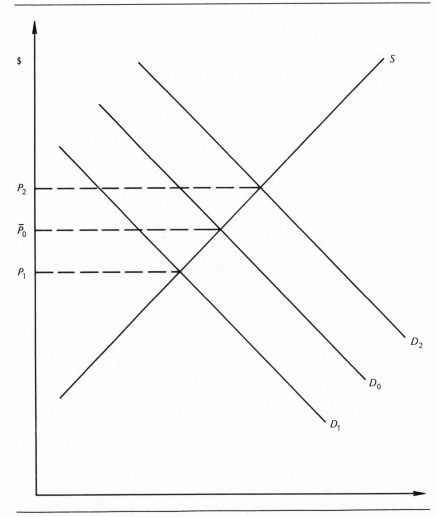

otherwise. Of course, when u_t is positive, giving say D_2 and P_2, speculators will sell off their accumulated inventories and this will tend to limit the price rise. In the limit, with no risk aversion and zero transaction, storage, and interest costs, speculators will hold price exactly at $\bar{P}_0$.[3] For if it ever falls, speculators will try to buy unlimited quantities, to sell whenever price rises above $\bar{P}_0$.

More elaborate patterns in the error terms are possible. In particular, there may be serial correlation. Suppose that a negative u_t is very likely to be followed by a positive u_{t+1} of approximately equal absolute value. Then, in the absence of speculation, price will tend to cycle between P_1 and P_2, setting up substantial profit opportunities and creating incentives for speculators to stabilize such cycles.

The one type of error term *not* stabilized is permanent shocks to the system or changes in expectations of future developments, e_t, which are expected to shift the demand curve permanently. In this case, suppose demand is written as

$$q_t^d = D(P_t) + u_t + \sum_{j=0}^{t} e_j ,$$

depending on both transitory shocks (u) and permanent shocks (e). If the market clears in each period (and the demand and supply curves have been linearized), the price is

$$P_t = \bar{P}_0 + c_1 u_t + c_2 \sum_{j=0}^{t} e_j . \tag{6.4}$$

$\bar{P}_0$ is the equilibrium price (in the absence of shocks) in the initial period ($t = 0$), and $c_2 \sum_{j=0}^{t} e_j$ represents how this "normal" price has evolved over time. Thus, the long-run equilibrium price at time t is

$$\bar{P}_0 + c_2 \sum^{t} e . \tag{6.5}$$

Now, presumably speculators will try to smooth out the u_t as before. The e_t are permanent changes, however, so that attempts to offset them would lose money for speculators. If the demand curve, net of any u_t, shifts permanently to D_2 in Figure 6-1, attempts to hold P at $\bar{P}_0$ would lose money and would be frustrated by other speculators who would buy large quantities in the expectation that price will, in the end, rise to P_2. Indeed, the only way systematically to make money on such shocks is to recognize them as soon as possible and buy before P rises. This sort of speculation ensures that price tends very quickly to reflect permanent, long-run changes.

It may be very difficult to sort out temporary, self-reversing from permanent shifts. However, the market cannot make *consistent* mistakes, for such consistency would itself set up discernible cycles in the rate that would then be stabilized out at a profit.

Permanent changes need not, of course, be independent of each other. For example, suppose that a positive e_t is often followed by an e_{t+1} of approximately the same size. Efficient speculators should come to recognize this dependence and, when observing e_t, should raise P_t to incorporate not only e_t but also the best guess (based on e_t) of how e_{t+1} will affect price. To the extent speculation is efficient, then, only the completely random unforecastable component of e_{t+1} will affect P_{t+1}. Thus, in such a case it does no harm to assume the e_t are simply uncorrelated since any discernible correlation is stabilized out.[4]

When all the influences of the u_t have been smoothed out, price may be written as

$$P_t = \bar{P}_0 + c_2 \sum_{j=0}^{t} e_j \; . \tag{6.6}$$

Taking first differences, and assuming without loss of generality that $c_2 = 1$,

$$\Delta P_t \equiv P_t - P_{t-1} = e_t \; . \tag{6.7}$$

For purposes of testing for efficiency, it is important to recognize that the e_t are serially uncorrelated. While the e_t and their degree of serial correlation are unobservable, the ΔP_t *are* observable. The properties of ΔP_t can then be used to infer the properties of e_t, in particular to see if a random process is generating ΔP_t. Series whose changes are serially correlated are often said to "do a random walk" or the changes are said to be generated by a random walk process.[5]

The U.S. stock markets have been extensively tested, and by and large stock prices have been found to do a random walk. The typical test involves calculating the linear correlation coefficients for ΔP_{t+1} and ΔP_t, ΔP_{t+2} and ΔP_t, and so forth, for a fairly large number of lags. While the observed ΔP are not perfectly random, the patterns are small and not economically exploitable once transactions, interest, and storage costs are taken into account.[6]

While the U.S. stock markets have been judged quite efficient in light of correlation tests, it is important to note that a number of difficulties can arise in some markets that have not arisen, as practical matters, in testing stock markets.

Bounds on Size of Cycles

Begin by taking account of the transaction, interest and storage costs of speculation, which have been ignored so far. Suppose that demand rises during the course of the month from D_1 to D_2 and falls back to D_1 the next month, in a steady cyclical fashion. If there are no transactions or storage costs, profit-motivated, efficient speculation will tend to ensure that the percentage appreciation in price, $(P_2 - P_1)/P_1$ must be smaller than the interest rate for borrowing money for one month. For example, if the yearly call money rate is 6 percent, the appreciation from trough to peak must not exceed (approximately) 0.5 percent per month or it would be profitable to speculate. Indeed, the day-to-day rise would not be able to exceed 1/356th of 6 percent without drawing in speculators. That is, even in an efficient market, there may very well be cycles once interest costs are allowed. Transaction and storage costs merely reinforce this possibility and can be analyzed in the same fashion. This means, then, that prices in an efficient market need not do a random walk in the strict statistical sense.

This qualification may have great relevance for testing for efficiency in the market for fresh strawberries but little relevance for testing for efficiency in some other markets. Suppose the change in price at time t is composed of a deterministic component, b_t, and a stochastic component, e_t, where e_t is serially uncorrelated with itself and independent of all b_t. Then,

$$\Delta P_t = b_t + e_t \ ,$$

the variance of P_t is

$$\sigma^2_{\Delta P_t} = \sigma^2_{b_t} + \sigma^2_e \ ,$$

the covariance between ΔP_t and ΔP_{t+j} is

$$\sigma_{\Delta P_t \Delta P_{t+j}} = b_t \cdot b_{t+j} \ ,$$

and the correlation coefficient at lag j is

$$r_j = \left(b_t \cdot b_{t+j}\right)/\left(\sigma^2_{b_t} + \sigma^2_e\right) \ .$$

Suppose that we are dealing with daily data and a cycle that reverses itself daily. Then b_{t+j} is equal to $-b_t$ for all odd j and $+b_t$ for all even j. Thus, for say $j = 1$,

$$r_1 = \frac{-b^2}{b^2 + \sigma^2_e} \ .$$

If there is no stochastic element, $r_1 = -1$. But in exchange markets, σ^2_e is likely to be very large relative to b^2 and hence r_1 will almost exactly equal zero.

For example, if the interest rate is 6 percent, then at most $b = 6/365$ and

$$r = \frac{\dfrac{-(6)}{(365)^2}}{\dfrac{(6)^2}{(365)^2} + \sigma^2_e} = \frac{-36}{36 + (365)^2 \, \sigma^2_e} \ .$$

Now, if the variance of the stochastic term is one-half of 1 percent—which is not entirely unusual for exchange markets—then $\sigma^2_e = 0.5$ and $(365)^2 \sigma^2_e = 66,612$, and r in absolute value is less than 0.001.

This discussion has so far neglected the foreign country's interest rate and the implications of the possible assumption that the expected rate of change in the exchange rate equals the exchange rate. However, Sweeney (1984a) shows that virtually all the variance of exchange rate changes is due to the error term rather than changes in the interest rate differential. In other words, it still makes sense to test for whether exchange rate changes are essentially random.

Positive Drift in Price

The mean of e_t need not be zero and may be positive. Introduction of an interest rate allows rationalization of this fact. With zero interest costs, the fact that

next period's price is expected to be greater than today's would cause speculators to bid up the price today. In fact, with a zero interest rate and positive
means, the price will shoot off to infinity. However, with a 6 percent risk-
adjusted interest rate, the e_t can have a mean such that price tends to increase by
(no more than) 0.5 percent per month.

Generalized price inflation is the most pervasive reason for a positive mean in
the rate of increase of a particular good's price.[7] In succeeding periods, the
demand and supply intersection shifts upward by proportionate amounts approximately equal to the overall inflation rate. An increase in the inflation rate
from 4 percent to 5 percent will cause the interest rate to rise say from 6 percent
to about 7 percent.

Risk-Adjusted Interest Rates

What interest rate is it appropriate to use in making speculative decisions to buy
and sell? One of the most popular models in modern finance theory—the capital
asset pricing model (CAPM)—implies that the appropriate rate is the rate on a
risk-free asset, *adjusted* for the risk of holding the speculative good in a balanced
portfolio—in fact, in a market portfolio, where all assets are held in their proportions to the total market. The risk factor depends on the covariance of the
rate of return on this good with the market's return, and on the variance of the
market's rate of return. Unless the covariance term is zero or negative, the appropriate rate will be larger than the risk-free rate but likely still small enough so
that random walk tests are appropriate, especially in financial markets where
transactions and storage costs are low and random components are large.

Filter Rule versus Serial Correlation Tests

Correlation tests look for *linear* relationships. It has been recognized, though,
that there might be correlations of a nonlinear variety. Such correlations would
show that speculators are not doing a very sophisticated job. In fact, just this
sort of nonlinear correlation lies behind many "chartist" notions of the stock
market, where rather particular nonlinear patterns are judged to imply profit
opportunities. There is an infinite number of possible nonlinear patterns, so it
is conceptually impossible to refute the hypothesis that some patterns exist—
there's neither world enough nor time. However, certain simple buy-and-sell
rules have been examined. There are often of the form, "If P rises by X percent
above its past low value, buy; sell when P falls Y percent below its past high
value." The X and Y percent figures are designed to filter out price rises and falls
that are insignificant, and hence the rules are often called filter rules. By and
large, such filter rules have failed to detect any inefficiencies in U.S. stock markets, *after* account was taken of transaction costs, and the like.

It is important to note, however, that the profits made from such buy-and-sell rules must always be compared to the profits from simply buying into the market and holding on—that is, the buy-and-hold strategy. One way to look at this is that chartists think they can "beat the market" so their profits have to be compared with what the market would yield. Another view notes that people holding stocks expect a positive return, either in the form of dividends or in the form of price appreciation (or a combination). Hence, rules that sometimes get one into the market can be expected to make some profits as opposed to holding cash. But can they make more than simply staying in the market? That is the real test.

Filter rules are often useful when it is suspected that the distribution of e is subject to change in variance or indeed does not have a finite variance. In such a case, the standard statistical tests, based on the assumption of a given normal distribution (which thus has a finite variance), will too often incorrectly reject the null hypothesis of no serial correlation. If filter rules on the same data do not make abnormal profits, this may indicate such problems with the serial correlation tests. For example, Logue, Sweeney, and Willett find significant serial correlation in the Canadian/U.S. forward market that, however, filter rules could not exploit.[8]

Filter rules offer a means of trying to detect non-linear dependencies. For example, when Logue and Sweeney examined the French franc/U.S. dollar spot market, these serial correlation tests found no relationship; however, a substantial number of these filter rules beat an "up" market.[9]

As they have been used in the literature, filter rules are not a statistical test with confidence bounds, and so forth. Rather, they are an indicator that must be used with sophistication and discretion. As noted, one serious failure is to neglect comparison with buy-and-hold profits. In an up market, profits from filter rules are to be expected (anything that gets you into an up market should tend to make you profits), but not as much as with buy-and-hold; in an up market, you are better off to stay in the market rather than go in and out. In a "down" market, getting out of the market periodically is better than staying in, so filter rules should be expected to beat buy-and-hold even in an efficient market. In a market with a zero mean for the process generating ΔP_t, we expect any rule to make zero abnormal profits over a long enough time period, and an average of several rules to make zero abnormal profits as well.

Even efficient markets can go through down periods, where filter rules beat buy-and-hold. Thus, for down periods filter rules can be misleading. It is important to note that when filter rules make profits by chance in one period, they should still have no forecasting value about which rules (if any) will make profits next period. Hence, splitting the sample is often a useful check.

Many of the problems in using filter rules are avoided by using the statistical filter rule test developed in Sweeney.[10] The test uses the statistic X, based on the mean rate of return to buy-and-hold versus the mean rate of return to the filter rule. The expected value of X is zero, and in large samples X is normally distributed if random disturbances to the exchange rate have finite variance.[11]

III. EMPIRICAL RESULTS

Many of the empirical results in the literature are based on data from the first two or three years of the generalized managed float that began in March 1973. Many researchers detected disturbing signs of inefficiency, using both serial correlation and filter rule tests. Some argued that the results justified rejection of efficiency—for example, Dooley and Shafer.[12] Others argued that more evidence was needed, especially since one might expect the system to take some time to settle down after the change in exchange rate regimes. Some, but by no means all, of the controversies from these earlier years can be resolved by examining later evidence.

To start, consider the first 692 business days of the float from 1 April 1973, as discussed in Logue, Sweeney, and Willett.[13] They find more autocorrelation than would be expected in most of the exchange rates they examined for the U.S. dollar versus the currencies of Germany, France, Italy, Japan, United Kingdom, Switzerland, and the Netherlands. However, they note that significant spikes often occur at peculiar lags (for example, at a lag of 6 days or nine days), that the spikes that are significant vary with changes in the subsample used, and that the variance of the process generating exchange rate changes alters substantially over subperiods (sometimes by a factor of two or three). They conclude that for many of the currencies, it is not clear that there are any exploitable patterns in the data.

When they examine filter rule results, they find that substantial profits could often have been made. They note, however, that rules that are profitable in one period are often not profitable subsequently. Further, for many countries much of the profit is concentrated in the first one-third of their sample. They argue that the markets may have taken perhaps a year to adapt to the new exchange rate regime and thus at first showed signs of inefficiency, but later did not.

The data used for the current study were obtained from the Board of Governors of the Federal Reserve System. In general, for each currency there are 1830 business days since 1 April 1973, thus carrying the analysis into 1980. The data were cleaned to take account of missing observations and obviously incorrect entries and were checked to some extent with alternative sources.

Serial Correlation Tests

Table 6-1 gives some serial correlation results for the 1830 observations broken into periods of one-third each. For each country, Table 6-1 reports the lag at

Table 6-1.   Autocorrelation Results.*

	First 610 Observations	Second 610 Observations	Third 610 Observations
Belgian Franc	2, 4, 7, 8, 9, 12	1, 4, 5, 8, 10, 12	2, 5, 6, 10
Canadian Dollar	1, 5, 11	1, 7	1, 3, 5, 11
Deutsche Mark	2, 8, 11	1, 4, 8	4, 6, 10
French Franc	2, 10, 11	2, 10, 11	10
Italian Lira	2, 4, 10	1, 3, 4, 6, 7, 8	2, 3, 10, 11
Japanese Yen	10, 12	4, 7, 12	1, 9, 10, 12
Swiss Franc	2, 6, 7	4, 8, 9, 11	X
Swedish Krone	2, 4, 8, 10	X	X
Spanish Peseta	X	X	1, 10, 11, 12
U.K. Pound Sterling	1, 5	4, 5, 9	1, 9

*The row for each currency contains the lags at which spikes are either significant at the 95 percent confidence level, or "suspicious" by being (approximately) 1½ standard errors or more from zero.

X = No suspicious or significant spikes at any lags.

Source: Data from Board of Governors of The Federal Reserve System.

which "suspiciously" large autocorrelation coefficients occur, coefficients that are significant at the 95 percent confidence level or are at least one-and-a-half standard errors from zero.

Often the suspicious spikes appear not to be very stable over time—for example, with the DM. Some of the spikes occur at lags that are hard to interpret—for example, lag 10 for the French franc. (A two-week cycle is implausible; in addition, these are trading days, so ten-day periodicity would be disturbed by holidays.) In general, it seems (to me) that plausible speculative strategies should be based on spikes at the first two or three lags—for example, if there is a positive significant spike at lag 1, buying the currency after an appreciation. On the other hand, the Canadian dollar shows a positive, significant spike at lag 1 in every period. This suggests that one could have successfully bet that changes in the Canadian rate would tend to be followed the next day by further changes in the same direction. (The coefficient was generally small, even if quite significant; thus any forecast about tomorrow's change, based on today's change, could easily be swamped by tomorrow's error, and transactions costs would be incurred.) The Canadian government's strategy of leaning against the wind seems a plausible reason both for the existence of the pattern and for its persistence in a world of private speculators.

Overall, then, the serial correlation tests suggest at least a few instances of inefficiency but in many instances give quite ambiguous results. These conclusions based on 1830 daily observations seem little different from those of Logue, Sweeney, and Willett, who used 691 observations.

Filter Rule Tests

While the filter rule results are subject to debate, they seem to offer substantial evidence of inefficiency. These tests use the X statistic, which is based on daily rates of return to buy-and-hold (R_{BH}) versus daily rates of return to filter strategies (R_F). This test is described in two papers by Sweeney.[14]

Table 6-2 shows that a substantial fraction of rules produced significant X values. For example, the buy-and-sell filter of one-half of 1 percent for the Belgium franc gave an $X = 0.035$, which is highly significant relative to the 95 percent confidence bounds (0.010, 0.060). Out of the seventy cases given by the ten rules and seven countries, twenty-three cases are significant.[15] Of course, these X statistics should be adjusted for transactions costs before concluding that excess profits can be made. As discussed by Sweeney,[16] transactions costs in foreign exchange markets are small enough for large customers, and filters larger than one-half of 1 percent trigger few enough transactions, that transactions costs will alter the results only for the smallest filters.

A major question is whether knowledge of these results would have helped obtain profits after the first 610 trading days. Table 6-3 shows that many rules gave significant X values in the next 1220 trading days. There are sixteen significant cases of the seventy total, somewhat smaller than in the first 610 days.

Table 6-4 sheds light on how helpful the results in Table 6-2 are in exploiting the profit potential revealed in Table 6-3. First, nine rules significant in the first period are also significant in the second. However, fifteen rules were significant in the first period but not in the second, while there were eleven rules significant in the second period but not the first. Two further counts may be more revealing. The row $\Sigma \neq /N$ shows the second period's average values for rules that were significant in the first period. In other words, suppose the first period's significant rules were used in the second period. For every country, $\Sigma \neq /N$ is positive. Further, for the average X in the second period, $\Sigma / 7$, for eight of the countries, $\Sigma \neq /N > \Sigma / 7$.

As a second experiment, for each country pick the three best rules in Table 6-3, based on X values, and use these in the second period. The resulting average X values for the second period are shown in the row for $\Sigma / 3$. For every country, $\Sigma / 3$ is positive, and $\Sigma / 3 > \Sigma / 7$ for every country but Japan. The weight of the evidence seems (to me) to indicate substantial inefficiency in most if not all exchange markets considered.

IV. SUMMARY AND CONCLUSIONS

This paper began with a simple, intuitive introduction to the notion of intertemporal efficiency of prices (Section I) and to popular tests of inefficiency

Table 6-2. Filter Rule Results: First 610 Observations.

	0.5 Percent	1 Percent	2 Percent	3 Percent	4 Percent	5 Percent	10 Percent
Belgian Franc	0.035* (0.010) (0.060)	0.029 (0.004) (0.054)	0.024 (-0.001) (0.049)	0.028 (0.003) (0.053)	0.026* (0.001) (0.051)	0.033 (-0.008) (0.057)	0.007 (-0.012) (0.027)
Canadian Dollar	0.004 (-0.001) (0.010)	0.005 (-0.001) (0.010)	0.006* (0.001) (0.011)	0.004 (-0.001) (0.010)	0.003 (-0.001) (0.008)	0.002 (-0.002) (0.006)	0 (0) (0)
Deutsche Mark	0.019 (-0.009) (0.047)	0.026 (-0.002) (0.055)	0.035* (0.007) (0.063)	0.018 (-0.010) (0.046)	0.043* (0.015) (0.071)	0.031* (0.003) (0.059)	-0.006 (-0.032) (0.020)
French Franc	0.027* (0.001) (0.053)	0.034* (0.008) (0.061)	0.031* (0.005) (0.057)	0.027* (0.002) (0.052)	0.036* (0.013) (0.060)	0.041* (0.017) (0.065)	0.018 (-0.005) (0.041)
Italian Lira	0.028* (0.010) (0.045)	0.020* (0.006) (0.038)	0.016 (-0.001) (0.033)	0.016 (-0.001) (0.033)	0.008 (-0.007) (0.026)	-0.005 (-0.022) (0.013)	-0.005 (-0.021) (0.011)
Japanese Yen	0.005 (-0.011) (0.021)	0.007 (-0.010) (0.024)	0.017* (0.001) (0.034)	0.008 (-0.010) (0.025)	0 (-0.017) (0.018)	-0.002 (-0.019) (0.015)	-0.015 (-0.025) (-0.005)
Swiss Franc	0.034 (-0.008) (0.056)	0.026* (0.004) (0.068)	0.023 (-0.009) (0.055)	0.030 (-0.002) (0.062)	0.027 (-0.005) (0.059)	0.026 (-0.006) (0.058)	0.013 (-0.015) (0.041)
Swedish Krone	0.013 (-0.011) (0.037)	0.030* (0.006) (0.054)	0.016 (-0.008) (0.041)	0.021 (-0.004) (0.045)	0.035* (0.010) (0.059)	0.025* (0.001) (0.069)	0.003 (-0.015) (0.021)
Spanish Peseta	-0.002 (-0.013) (0.009)	-0.007 (-0.018) (0.004)	0.002 (-0.007) (0.012)	0 (-0.009) (0.008)	-0.005 (-0.014) (0.004)	0 (-0.003) (0.003)	0 (0) (0)
U.K. Pound Sterling	0.009 (-0.007) (0.024)	0.015 (-0.001) (0.030)	0.024* (0.008) (0.039)	0.017* (0.002) (0.033)	0.010 (-0.006) (0.025)	0.004 (-0.012) (0.020)	-0.006 (-0.018) (0.007)

*Significant at the 95 percent confidence level.

Source: Data from Board of Governors of The Federal Reserve System.

Table 6-3. Filter Rule Results: Last 1220 Observations.

	0.5 Percent	1 Percent	2 Percent	3 Percent	4 Percent	5 Percent	10 Percent
Belgian Franc	0.009 (-0.005) (0.022)	0.017* (0.003) (0.031)	0.010 (-0.004) (0.024)	0.006 (-0.008) (0.019)	-0.001 (-0.013) (0.011)	-0.001 (-0.008) (0.011)	-0.008 (-0.018) (0.004)
Canadian Dollar	0.012* (-0.005) (0.018)	0.012* (0.005) (0.019)	0.004 (-0.003) (0.011)	0 (-0.006) (0.007)	-0.003 (-0.010) (0.003)	0.004 (-0.002) (0.011)	0 (-0.006) (0.007)
Deutsche Mark	0.008 (-0.006) (0.022)	0.014* (0) (0.028)	0.008 (-0.006) (0.022)	0 (-0.014) (0.014)	-0.001 (-0.011) (0.010)	-0.002 (-0.011) (0.007)	-0.007 (-0.018) (0.004)
French Franc	0.013 (-0.001) (0.026)	0.014* (0.001) (0.028)	0.006 (-0.008) (0.019)	0.005 (-0.008) (0.019)	0.005 (-0.008) (0.018)	-0.005 (-0.018) (0.009)	-0.016* (-0.029) (-0.003)
Italian Lira	0.022* (0.008) (0.036)	0.015* (0.001) (0.029)	0.000 (-0.014) (0.014)	0.003 (-0.011) (0.017)	0.005 (-0.009) (0.018)	-0.004 (-0.018) (0.009)	0 (-0.009) (0.009)
Japanese Yen	0.020* (0.004) (0.030)	0.027 (0.010) (0.043)	0.010 (-0.005) (0.036)	0.010 (-0.005) (0.026)	0.009 (-0.005) (0.023)	0.018* (0.006) (0.031)	0.022* (0.007) (0.037)
Swiss Franc	0.015 (-0.005) (0.036)	0.023* (0.004) (0.043)	0.012 (-0.008) (0.031)	0.019 (-0.001) (0.039)	0.015 (-0.006) (0.035)	-0.002 (-0.021) (0.017)	-0.002 (-0.020) (0.015)
Swedish Krone	0.009 (-0.004) (0.022)	0.015* (0.002) (0.028)	0.009 (-0.004) (0.022)	0.003 (-0.008) (0.015)	0.009 (-0.002) (0.020)	0.002 (-0.010) (0.015)	-0.014* (-0.026) (-0.003)
Spanish Peseta (last 1218 obs.)	0.018 (-0.002) (0.037)	0.019* (0) (0.038)	0.023* (0.004) (0.043)	0.015 (-0.004) (0.034)	0.011 (-0.009) (0.030)	0.006 (-0.014) (0.026)	0.002 (-0.017) (0.022)
U.K. Pound Sterling	0.019* (0.005) (0.033)	0.026* (0.012) (0.040)	0.015* (0) (0.020)	0.024* (0.006) (0.034)	0.018* (0.005) (0.032)	0.007 (-0.006) (0.020)	0.007 (-0.006) (0.020)

*Significant at the 95 percent confidence level.

Source: Data from Board of Governors of The Federal Reserve System.

Table 6-4. Values of X: Final 1220 Observations.

		Belg.	Can.	DM	FR.	IT.	Jap.
0.5%		0.009$^{\neq}$	0.021*	0.008	0.013$^{\neq}$	0.022$^{\neq}$	0.020*
1%		0.017$^{\neq*}$	0.012*	0.014*	0.014$^{\neq*}$	0.015$^{\neq}$	0.027*
2%		0.010	0.004$^{\neq}$	0.008$^{\neq}$	0.006$^{\neq}$	0	0.010$^{\neq}$
3%		0.006$^{\neq}$	0	0	0.005$^{\neq}$	0.005	0.009
4%		-0.001$^{\neq}$	-0.003	-0.001$^{\neq}$	0.005$^{\neq}$	0.005	0.009
5%		0.001	0.004	-0.002$^{\neq}$	-0.005	-0.004	0.018*
10%		-0.007	0	0.007	-0.016	0	0.022*
	7	0.035	0.029	0.020	0.022	0.041	0.116
	$\Sigma/7$	0.005	0.004	0.003	0.003	0.006	0.017
	$\Sigma = /N$	0.008	0.004	0.002	0.006	0.019	0.010
	$\Sigma^3/3$	0.011	0.007	0.008	0.010	0.010	0.016

		SW FR	SW K	SP P	UK		
0.5%		0.015	0.009	0.018	0.019*		
1%		0.023$^{\neq*}$	0.015$^{\neq*}$	0.019*	0.026*		
2%		0.012	0.009	0.023*	0.015$^{\neq*}$		
3%		0.019	0.003	0.015	0.020$^{\neq*}$		
4%		0.015	0.009$^{\neq}$	0.011	0.018$^{\neq*}$		
5%		-0.002	0.002$^{\neq}$	0.006	0.007		
10%		-0.002	-0.014	0.002	0.007		
	7	0.080	0.033	0.086	0.112		
	$\Sigma/7$	0.011	0.005	0.012	0.016		
	$\Sigma = /N$	0.023	0.009	0.000	0.018		
	$\Sigma^3/3$	0.017	0.009	0.019	0.020		

*Rules that for this country generated values of X significant at the 95 percent confidence level in the last 1220 observations (twenty did so).

$^{\neq}$Rules that for this country generated values of X significant at the 95 percent confidence level in the first 610 observations (twenty-four did so).

$\Sigma/3$: Take the three rules with the highest Xs in Table 6-2. Use these rules for the period of Table 6-3. $\Sigma/3$ is the average X value that results in this latter period.

Source: Data from Board of Governors of The Federal Reserve System.

based on serial correlation and filter rules (Section II). Section III discusses serial correlation and filter rule tests on 1830 daily observations on ten exchange rates versus the U.S. dollar on trading days since 1 April 1973 (generalized managed floating began in March 1973). For a number of countries, serial correlation tests indicate patterns that might be used to generate speculative profits and hence are indicative of inefficiency. However, the tests were judged mostly inconclusive, on grounds of either instability of the process or implausibility of the patterns of serial correlation.

Filter rule tests for this period find significant profits in both the first 610 and remaining 1220 days. The profitable rules in the first period seem to have some predictive power for the second period. The evidence is substantial but not perhaps overwhelming to all observers.

These profits may simply be due to inefficiency in the exchange markets due to the behavior of private participants—that is, there may be insufficient stabilizing speculation. However, an argument can be made that the existence of such profits is due to the substantial intervention that governments have pursued in exchange markets. Of course, it is obvious that government intervention can create profitable patterns for speculators to exploit only if there is insufficient stabilizing speculation to offset such intervention. There is evidence that government intervention has been fairly substantial, with central banks tending to "lean against the wind."[17] Do governments or private speculators have a better notion on average about where rates will eventually settle? Some authors argue that governments tend to make losses on their intervention, thus indicating their actions are destabilizing and offer potential profits from counteracting speculation.[18] However, whether government intervention is destabilizing is a complicated issue where definitive results are not yet available.[19] Hence, the filter profits found above may be due to destabilizing private speculation or to speculation that works in a stabilizing direction but is insufficient in magnitude.

NOTES TO CHAPTER 6

1. R. M. Goodwin, "Stabilizing the Exchange Rate," *Review of Economics and Statistics* (February 1964): 160–62. This is not to say that transitory price changes, in response to problems that will be transitory, are inoptimal but rather that the current effect of disturbances on price should be conditional economically on future prices, which can often be conveniently summarized with the long-run equilibrium price level.

2. The analysis here is similar to that in John Muth, "Rational Expectations and the Theory of Price Movements," *Econometrica* (July 1961): 315–35.

3. This neglects the problem that in some instances speculators' stocks may not be large enough to keep $P = \bar{P}_0$ in the face of a positive transitory increase in demand; a rise in price in this case reflects scarcity rather than inefficiency.

4. Suppose that in the absence of knowledge of this period's e_t, the best guess about next period's shock is that it will be zero, or $Ee_{t+1} = 0$; however, suppose that this best guess contingent on knowledge of e_t is $a_1 e_t$, or $E(e_{t+1}|e_t) = a_1 e_t$, and similarly for the next n periods. Then, the best guess about P_{t+n} is that it will equal

$$P_{t-1} + e_t + \sum_{j=1}^{n} a_j e_t \ .$$

In the absence of transactions, storage, and interest costs, P_t will jump to $P_{t-1} + (1 + a_j) e_t$ (n may become infinite but assume $\Sigma a_j < \infty$ to keep the process from being explosive). Of course, positive values of such costs will keep adjustments from being instantaneous. The point is, however, that such costs imply bounds on maximum observable deviations from complete and instantaneous adjustment as the text below argues.

5. If e_t has a non-zero mean a, the process is random walk "with drift" to extent a per period. Empirically, the first differences of the logarithms of price are usually examined. The only change in the above argument is to assume quantities demanded and supplied depend linearly on the log, not the level, of price.

6. A classic survey is Eugene F. Fama, "Efficient Capital Markets: A Review of Theory and Empirical Works," *Journal of Finance* (May 1970): 383–417.

7. *If* the good is reproducible. With nonreproducible resources such as petroleum, the resource is depleted and price rises over time at a rate dependent on the market rate of interest. See Robert Solow, "The Economics of Resources" *American Economic Review* (May 1974): 1–14. Of course, it is well known that in a world of stable prices, firms can allow stockholders to take their return in the form of dividends, with the expected change in stock prices equal to zero. Alternatively, they could provide lower dividends and allow the gains in the form of stock price appreciation; see Merton Miller, "Debt and Taxes," *Journal of Finance* (May 1977): 261–75.

8. Dennis E. Logue, Richard James Sweeney, and Thomas D. Willett, "Aspects of Efficiency in the Canadian/U.S. Foreign Exchange Market," in Arthur B. Laffer and Ernest Tanner, eds., *Studies in U.S. Canadian Economic Relations* (North American Economic Studies Association, forthcoming). See Dennis E. Logue, Richard James Sweeney, and Thomas D. Willett, "The Speculative Behavior of Foreign Exchange Rates During the Current Float." *Journal of Business Research* 6, no. 2 (1978): 159–74 for an evaluation of whether reliable excess profits could be made by filter rules in the early years of the float. See also Bradford Cornell and J. Kimball Dietrich, "The Efficiency of the Market for Foreign Exchange Under Floating Exchange Rates." *Review of Economics and Statistics* LX, no. 1 (February 1978): 111–20. Further, staff members of the Board of Governors of the Federal Reserve System, the Federal Reserve Banks, and the U.S. Department of the Treasury have carried out a number of related studies. These are referred to and discussed in "Intervention in Foreign Exchange Markets: A Summary of Ten Staff Studies," *Federal Reserve Bulletin* (November 1983): 830–36.

9. Dennis E. Logue and Richard James Sweeney, "'White Noise' in Imperfect Markets; The Case of the French Franc/U.S. Dollar Exchange Rate," *Journal of Finance* (June 1977): 761–68.

10. Richard J. Sweeney, "A Statistical Filter Rule Test, With an Application to the Dollar–DM Exchange Rate," Claremont Working Papers, The Claremont Center for Economic Policy Studies, Claremont Graduate School, Claremont, CA, 1981.

11. See Richard J. Sweeney, "A Statistical Filter Rule Test, With an Application to the Dollar-DM Exchange Rate." If the random component of exchange rate changes has an infinite variance, usual statistical criteria do not apply, as with testing the significance of serial correlation coefficients.

12. See Michael P. Dooley and Jeffrey Shafer, "Analysis of Short-Run Exchange Rate Behavior, March 1973 to September 1975," International Finance Discussion Paper No. 76 (Federal Reserve Board, 1976).

13. See Dennis Logue, Richard J. Sweeney, and Thomas D. Willett, "The Speculative Behavior of Exchange Rates."

14. Richard J. Sweeney, "Beating the Foreign Exchange Market," (1984a) and "Some New Filter Rule Tests: Methodology and Results," (1984b). (Unpublished manuscripts.)

15. For any one currency, these cases are not statistically independent and hence no overall test is possible.

16. Sweeney, "Beating the Foreign Exchange Market."

17. For a survey of a variety of evidence, see Hans Genberg, "Effects of Central Bank Intervention in the Foreign Exchange Market," *International Monetary Fund Staff Papers* (September 1981): 451–76. See William Branson, "A Model of Exchange Determination with Policy Reaction: Evidence From Monthly Data." National Bureau of Economic Research Working Papers No. 1135 (June 1983); and Rudiger Dornbush, "Exchange Rate Economics: Where Do We Stand?" *Brookings Papers on Economic Activity*, Vol. 1 (1980): 143–206.

18. See Dean Taylor, "Official Intervention in the Foreign Exchange Market or, Bet Against the Central Bank," *Journal of Political Economy* 90, no. 2 (April 1982): 356–68.

19. See "Intervention in Foreign Exchange Markets: A Summary of Ten Staff Studies," *Federal Reserve Bulletin* (November 1983): 830–36; and also Victor Argy, "Exchange-Rate Management and Practice," *Princeton Studies in International Finance* 50 (1982).

EFFECTS ON INTERNATIONAL TRADE

7 FLEXIBLE EXCHANGE RATES AND INTERNATIONAL TRADE
An Overview

Sven W. Arndt, Marie Thursby,
and Thomas D. Willett

There has been a long history of analysis and debate about the effects of pegged versus flexible exchange rates on international trade and investment. At the time of the creation of the Bretton Woods system at the end of World War II, the majority view among academic economists and the business and official communities involved with international financial issues was that floating rates would be severely harmful to the operation of international trade. This view, based heavily on the experiences of the interwar period, had a major influence on the design of the Bretton Woods system.[1] Flexible rates were widely seen as being inherently unstable and severely damaging to international trade both through the direct adverse effects of exchange rate volatility and through the indirect effects of such volatility on the stimulation of trade barriers.

In the postwar period this view was severely challenged, however, by economists such as Milton Friedman and Gottfried Haberler. It was shown that most of the earlier analysis was based on the (often implicit) assumption that exchange rate movements were caused predominantly by destabilizing speculation and hence reflected disequilibrium conditions. If instead exchange rate movements under flexible rates predominantly reflect changing equilibrium rates in response to changes in an unstable underlying economic environment, then the analysis becomes quite different. It was also pointed out that it was not appropriate to assume that pegged rates were always set at equilibrium levels. Where this was not the case, as became more and more common as the postwar period progressed, strong pressures developed to restrict international trade and payments.

Conceptually at least, private speculation and official intervention (public speculation) could be stabilizing or destabilizing under either pegged or flexible

127

rates. Thus as a first approximation, the question of the comparative effects of pegged versus flexible exchange rates or other exchange rate regimes on international trade and investment comes down to the question of how closely exchange rates under each system approximate equilibrium rates. This major point is formalized in Chapter 8, and provides a major connection between the analysis of the causes of exchange rate movements in Part I and the effects of exchange rate movements in this part. The less are the changes in underlying economic conditions and the less sticky are pegged exchange rates, the more effective this system will be. The more stabilizing is private speculation, the better will flexible rates work.

Until very recently, the main thrust of postwar analysis has been to weaken the initial presumption that pegged rates will have a favorable net effect on resource allocation. Indeed there was some tendency to create a counter-presumption that flexible exchange rates would be more conducive to efficient international trade and investment. This new presumption has itself become increasingly challenged in recent years, however. While it has been frequently argued that the initial depreciation of the dollar that accompanied the initiation of generalized floating made a major contribution to the increasing support of flexible rates by American business, and helped to dampen domestic protectionist pressures, the strength of the dollar in the 1980s has frequently been cited as a major cause of resource misallocation and protectionist pressure.[2]

If the strength of the dollar were due primarily to destabilizing speculation, then the validity of such arguments would be straightforward (although there would of course remain questions about the quantitative magnitudes of these effects). The paper by Feigenbaum and Willett in this part suggests that while there is undoubtedly some basis to the arguments that trade deficits and high values of the dollar contribute to domestic protectionist pressures, the quantitative strength of these effects may be relatively weak compared with those of domestic macroeconomic fluctuations and industry specific considerations. While the operation of the exchange rate regime can certainly influence protectionist pressures, these pressures come predominantly from domestic causes which are independent of the exchange rate regime.

There is perhaps greater scope for differential effects of alternative exchange rate regimes on the efficiency of resource allocation, but the issues here become quite complicated to the extent that exchange rate movements are not due to speculative inefficiencies. As is discussed in Chapters 1 and 2, the normative analysis of a strong dollar due to large budget deficits is a complicated issue necessitating at a minimum a distinction between the best and second-best analysis. Thus while we might agree that a lower budget deficit and lower dollar would be preferred on grounds of allocative efficiency, in the absence of budget deficit restrictions a strong dollar may be efficient, at least from a U.S. perspective. Likewise, while the development of greater stability in underlying economic conditions throughout the world is clearly to be desired and would undoubtedly reduce the volatility of exchange rates, in the absence of the re-establishment of such underlying stability, considerable flexibility of exchange rates is probably a practical necessity. While it is possible that changes in the exchange rate regime can themselves produce changes in the stability of under-lying economic conditions, little factual evidence has been offered to support arguments that the reimposition of pegged rates would by itself foster substan-tially more stable underlying conditions.[3]

Despite the frequency of charges that the adoption of flexible exchange rates has been quite harmful to international trade and investment, there has been little systematic documentation of substantial negative effects. The research presented and surveyed in the following papers generally has failed to find evidence of the sizeable negative effects frequently predicted by critics of float-ing rates, despite the considerable amount of exchange rate volatility that we have experienced.

One major reason for these findings may be that, as many floating rates advo-cates have pointed out, the use of forward markets can substantially reduce the adverse effects of short-term exchange rate volatility. There are costs to obtain-ing forward cover, however, and the nature and magnitude of these costs has been the subject of considerable analysis and debate. To market participants the cost of cover often means the difference between current spot and forward rates, even though the net cost is zero.[4] This is so because, with trade flowing both ways, a dollar-franc rate that is at a premium (positive cost of cover) for trade flowing in one direction will be at a discount (negative cost of cover) for trans-actions moving in the opposite direction. Similarly, when the foreign-exchange market marries a forward sale of dollars for pounds by a British exporter con-cerned about his profits that are expressed in pounds to a purchase of dollars for pounds from the U.S. exporter to Britain who worries about the dollar value of his receipts, exchange risk has been eliminated. Risk premia may develop because holding demands in each direction do not exactly balance, but this does not represent a net cost of forward transactions.

Economists considering the costs of cover have tended to focus on the trans-actions costs of forward transactions (the difference between buying and selling rates). These rose substantially with the initiation of floating, but then subsided. Such transactions costs are more the result of general economic turbulence than a matter of the exchange rate regime. Moreover, even at their height such costs represent a mere fraction of 1 percent for wholesale trade among the major industrial nations.[5]

Another important case in which the use of the forward market may entail an economic cost is when the eventual spot rate falls systematically above or below the current forward rate for that period. Such a bias in the predictions of the forward rate reduces its informational content and implies that the presence of systematic profits or losses affects the choice between covering and speculat-ing. In Chapter 11 Peter Sharp notes that in the presence of risk aversion a forward rate bias is not necessarily inconsistent with market efficiency, although the calculation of "efficient bias" is highly sensitive to model specification.

Empirical estimation of forward rate bias is in itself no simple task. While some evidence of forward rate bias has been found, it is also apparent that forward rates explain only small proportions of subsequent spot rate movements, suggesting that most of the short-run movements in exchange rates have been due to unanticipated developments. While this raises serious questions about the predictive ability of forward rates, risk averse transactors concerned about the effects of short-term variations in exchange rates will continue to find forward contracts a valuable and relatively low-cost method of reducing exchange risk.

Forward markets are not, however, the only means of reducing or eliminating exchange risk. The traditional view that international activities were inherently riskier than domestic activities has been shown to be seriously flawed. It failed to take into account the potential benefits of diversification and to recognize that the real value of one's nominal contracts and assets and liabilities may be significantly influenced by international as well as domestic prices. One of the major insights of modern financial analysis is the need to look at the risks of individual investments or other activities, not in isolation, but in relation to the firm's or individual's total set of investments or activities. The literature on this approach is discussed in Chapter 11. As that analysis illustrates, we are still very far from having developed unambiguous procedures for calculating optimal patterns of diversification, but we do have a good basis for developing reasonable strategies which made major improvements over traditional analysis and these are being increasingly adopted by market participants.[6]

One of the implications of modern financial analysis is that it will not always be a wise strategy for firms to attempt to cover or hedge all of their international transactions, even if the firm is quite risk adverse. Furthermore, hedging or covering will often be more convenient or cheaper through the spot market (international lending or borrowing) than the forward market. Thus the finding that many international transactions are not covered in the forward market is not a necessary indication that firms are either risk neutral or that they are suffering from poor financial practices (although particular examples of each of these explanations can of course be found).

By the same token, however, forward markets do not exist for all currencies even for short-term contracts and even for the major currencies where contracts that do cover trade commitments for up to a year in the future are widely available, it is typically difficult or impossible to obtain cover for long term investments. The availability of low cost cover against exchange rate fluctuations over the short term does little to reduce the risk involved in the decision of whether or not to expand your production capacity to increase export sales over the next ten years. Recent models that have shown exchange risk to be fully diversifiable, and hence irrelevant to efficient decision making, are based on assumptions which abstract from considerations important to many aspects of international business.

Thus the question of the effects of alternative exchange rate regimes on the efficiency of international resource allocation remains an important one, even though the weight of most of the recent research presented and surveyed in the following papers serves primarily to make one cautious of accepting either of the commonly expressed polar views that pegged rates are clearly good for international trade and flexible rates harmful, or the reverse that flexible rates are clearly preferable on efficiency grounds. It is easy to construct hypothetical scenarios contrasting a well functioning pegged rate system with a poorly functioning flexible rate one or vice versa under which the conclusion to be drawn seems obvious. However, comparing actual experiences with each while trying to distinguish between the effects of underlying economic developments and the differences in exchange rate regimes per se is a quite different matter.

As previously discussed, disequilibrium exchange rates and pressures for protectionism can be generated under any type of exchange rate regime. While recent experience clearly shows that the adoption of flexible exchange rates need not stimulate the breakdown in international cooperation and massive increases in protectionism that many critics feared, neither have exchange rate changes closely followed differences in national inflation rates in the short run so as to keep real exchange rate changes relatively small as many floating rate advocates had expected. As was discussed in Part I, one of the major features of recent exchange rate analysis has been the development of a better understanding of the important role which financial market conditions play in exchange rate determination. Even where speculation is efficient, financial market developments can cause substantial changes in short-term equilibrium exchange rates which in turn can have important effects on the real sectors of the economy.

Analysis of the effects of changes in real exchange rates on resource allocation can be quite complicated. Three different major types of private costs should be distinguished. The first are static efficiency costs incurred when transactions take place at disequilibrium exchange rates. Such costs are measured along standard demand and supply curves and may be found under pegged exchange rates when the balance of payments is in disequilibrium and under floating rates when destabilizing speculation is present.[7] There is no systematic evidence suggesting that one type is more likely to generate this kind of cost than another. Views on this will be heavily dependent on the judgments reached about the relative importance of the causes of exchange rate volatility discussed in Part I. The greater the role played by destabilizing or insufficiently stabilizing speculation, the less well would flexible rates score on this criteria.

The second are the effects on the volume of trade brought about by exchange rate uncertainty. Uncertainty generally reduces economic activity, shifting demand and supply curves inward and reducing their elasticities.[8] This outcome, however, holds for uncertainty in general, including uncertainty due to the underlying economic environment. Thus, to conclude that floating rates harm international trade on this score, it is necessary to show that a regime of floating generates inherently more uncertainty. The proposition that exchange rate uncertainty reduces the volume of trade is examined in Chapter 10, which surveys the recent studies on this subject and presents new results. The bulk of the evidence examined suggests that there have not been large negative uncertainty effects on aggregate international trade under floating rates but some evidence of uncertainty effects on patterns of bilateral trade has been found. The general failure to find large negative effects may be due in part to the substantial increases in the uncertainties facing domestic economic activities in most countries over this period, which has limited the degree to which international trade and investment has become especially risky.[9]

The third type of costs are associated with resource shifts, which may be especially troublesome when temporary exchange rate changes are perceived by resource owners as permanent and when reallocation is governed by wage/price rigidities and sector specificities and factor immobilities. With respect to temporary exchange rate movements, critics have asserted that they generate uneconomic wrenchings of resources back and forth among the sectors affected and that this constitutes a major failing of floating rates. Once again, however, little systematic evidence in support of this contention has been presented.[10] In Chapter 9 Willett and Flacco discuss reasons why fluctuations in exchange rates are likely to produce only limited short-term resource reallocation effects when exchange rate movements are quite volatile. They also consider a number of externality arguments concerning possible reasons why the social costs of exchange rate fluctuations may exceed the private costs.

While short-term fluctuations in exchange rates appear to have produced less damage than many expected, medium-term swings in exchange rates do seem likely to have more substantial effects. In the case of the dollar, the low real value in the late 1970s and high value in the early 1980s can be "blamed" to a much greater degree on U.S. economic policies than on destabilizing speculation and hence the associated resource allocation costs should not be ascribed primarily to floating rates per se. Nor have these effects been nearly as large as implied by popular charges that the recent strong dollar and associated trade deficits are deindustrializing America.[11] But these costs may still be substantial.

In a world of high factor mobility and wage and price flexibility this would not be the case. However, short-term, wage/price rigidities, immobilities and other distortions may have serious consequences for the speed and efficiency of resource reallocation in response to a permanent change in the real exchange rate, regardless of whether that change occurs under a pegged or floating nominal exchange rate. A real appreciation lowers the home currency price of traded goods relative to nontraded goods. If nominal wages in the traded goods sector decline in proportion to the fall in product prices, the product wage in this sector will remain unaltered and hence employment will remain unchanged. Any tendency for money wages in that sector to be sticky, however, raises product wages relative to productivity and generates unemployment in the traded goods sector. If economy-wide employment levels are to be preserved, labor must be mobile intersectorally and nominal wages must fall in the nontraded goods sector in order to absorb workers released in the traded goods sector. If the other factors of production are sector-specific and immobile in the short run, the outcome involving factor returns and factor allocations in the two sectors will differ in the short run from the long-run result.[12]

In our judgment such rigidities are sufficiently important for the U.S. economy in the short- and medium-terms so that they should be of concern to U.S. policymakers. While the recent strength of the dollar has been a source of considerable benefit in reducing U.S. inflation (see Part III), it has also imposed resource allocation costs. The lesson that we would draw from this conclusion is not that we need much heavier official intervention to manage the foreign exchange value of the dollar, but rather that the likely consequences on the exchange rate and resource allocation in export and import competing industries need to be considered in the formulation of U.S. macroeconomic policies.

NOTES TO CHAPTER 7

1. For discussion and references to the historical development of analysis of the effects of pegged versus flexible exchange rates on international trade see Flacco et al. (1984), and Willett (1977: 38–40).
2. For recent discussions of the interrelationships between exchange rates and trade policy and references to earlier literature see Bergsten and Williamson (1984), Flacco et al. (1984), Krugman (1982), and Richardson (1982) and (1984).
3. This is a subject, however, that we believe deserves more careful study.
4. See, for example, Machlup (1970) and Sohmen (1969).
5. See, for example, Frenkel and Levich (1977), McCormick (1979) and the survey by Kohlhagen (1984).
6. For recent discussion of business reactions to floating rates and developments in the management of exchange risk, see Dreyer, Haberler, and Willett (1978, part III), and Lessard (1979).
7. See, for example, Hause (1966) and Johnson (1966) and the recent generalization by Feldman and Tower (1984). Trade at such disequilibrium rates is often called false trading. See, for example, McKinnon (1979).
8. For discussions and references of the theoretical literature on the effects of uncertainty on international trade, see Farrell, et al., (1983), Pomery (1979), and Chapter 10 in this volume.
9. On the negative effects of domestic inflation uncertainty on employment and production see Frohman, Laney, and Willett (1981) and the references cited there.
10. Indeed, the main paper published in the last several years on this subject, Thursby (1981), found that resource reallocation costs hadn't risen with the shift from pegged to flexible rates. See also, however, the results of the

recent study on "Exchange Rate Volatility and World Trade," IMF (1984), that was published after this volume was completed.

11. For a useful critical examination of the evidence on this issue, see Lawrence (1983).

12. For further analysis on these points see Arndt (1983) and (1984).

REFERENCES

Arndt, Sven W. 1984. "Comment on Flacco, Laney, Thursby, and Willett: Exchange Rates and Trade Policy," *Contemporary Policy Issues* 4 (January): 19-22.

Arndt, Sven W. 1983. "Allocation and Adjustment in an Economy with Imperfections," in E. Wille, ed., *Beitrage zur Gesamtwirtschaftlichen Allokation.* New York: Verlag Peter Lang, pp. 185-203.

Bergsten, C. Fred, and John Williamson. 1983. "Exchange Rates and Trade Policy," in William R. Cline, ed., *Trade Policy in the 1980s*. Cambridge, Mass.: M.I.T. Press for the Institute for International Economics, pp. 99-120.

Dreyer, Jacob S., Gottfried Haberler, and Thomas D. Willett. 1978. *Exchange Rate Flexibility.* Washington, D.C.: American Enterprise Institute for Public Policy Research.

Farrell, Victoria S., Dean A. DeRosa, and T. Ashby McCown. 1983. "Effects of Exchange Rate Variability on International Trade and Other Economic Variables: A Review of the Literature," Board of Governors of the Federal Reserve System, *Staff Studies* 130 (December).

Feldman, David H., and Edward Tower. 1984. "The Welfare Economics of an Unstable Real Exchange Rate," Duke University. (Unpublished manuscript.)

Flacco, Paul R., Leroy O. Laney, Marie C. Thursby, and Thomas D. Willett. 1984. "Exchange Rates and Trade Policy," *Contemporary Policy Issues* 4 (January): 6-18.

Frenkel, Jacob A., and Richard H. Levich. 1977. "Transaction Costs and Interest Arbitrage: Tranquil Versus Turbulent Periods," *Journal of Political Economy* 85, no. 6 (December): 1209-226.

Frohman, Deborah A., Leroy O. Laney, and Thomas D. Willett. 1981. "Uncertainty Costs of High Inflation," *Voice* of the Federal Reserve Bank of Dallas (July): 1-9.

Hause, J.C. 1966. "The Welfare Cost of Disequilibrium Exchanges Rates," *Journal of Political Economy* 74, no. 4 (August): 15-26.

International Monetary Fund. 1984. "Exchange Rate Volatility and World Trade: A Study by the Research Department of the I.M.F., "Occasional Papers of the I.M.F. (July).

Johnson, Harry G. 1966. "The Welfare Costs of Exchange-Rate Stabilization," *Journal of Political Economy* 74, no. 5 (October): 512-18.

Kohlhagen, Steven W. 1984. "The Behavior of Transaction Costs and the Accuracy of Forward Rate Forecasts During the Current Float." *Claremont Working Papers*, Claremont Center for Economic Policy Studies.

Krugman, Paul. 1982. "The Macroeconomics of Protection with a Floating Exchange Rate," in Karl Brunner and Allan H. Meltzer, eds., *Monetary Regimes and Protectionism*. Carnegie–Rochester Conference Series on Public Policy, Vol. 16 (Spring): 141–81.

Lawrence, Robert Z. 1983. "Is Trade Deindustrializing America? A Medium-Term Perspective," *Brookings Papers on Economic Activity*, Vol. 1, pp. 129–61. Comment and Discussion, 162–71.

Lessard, Donald R., ed. 1979. *International Financial Management*. Boston: Warren, Gorham, and Lamont.

McCormick, Frank. 1979. "Covered Interest Arbitrage: Unexploited Profits? Comment," *Journal of Political Economy* 87, no. 2 (April): 411–17.

McKinnon, Ronald I. 1979. *Money in International Exchange: The Convertible Currency System*. New York: Oxford University Press.

Machlup, Fritz. 1970. "The Forward-Exchange Market: Misunderstandings Between Practitioners and Economists," in George N. Halm, ed., *Approaches Toward Greater Flexibility of Exchange Rates*. Princeton, N.J.: Princeton University Press.

Pomery, John. 1979. "Uncertainty in International Trade," in Rudiger Dornbusch and Jacob Frenkel, eds., *International Economic Policy*. Baltimore, MD: Johns Hopkins University Press.

Richardson, J. David. 1984. "The New Nexus among Trade, Industrial, and Exchange-Rate Policies," and "Comments," in Tamir Agmon, et al., eds., *The Future of the International Monetary System*. Lexington, Mass.: Lexington Books.

Richardson, J. David. 1982. "Four Observations on Modern International Commercial Policy under Floating Exchange Rates," in Karl Brunner and Allan H. Meltzer, eds., *Monetary Regimes and Protectionism*. Carnegie–Rochester Conference Series on Public Policy, Vol. 16 (Spring): 187–220.

Sohmen, Egon. 1969. *Flexible Exchange Rates*, revised edition. Chicago: University of Chicago Press.

Thursby, Marie. 1981. "The Resource Reallocation Costs of Fixed and Flexible Exchange Rates: A Multicountry Extension," *Journal of International Economics* 11, no. 4 (November): 487–93.

Willett, Thomas D. 1977. *Floating Exchange Rates and International Monetary Reform*. Washington, D.C.: American Enterprise Institute for Public Policy Research.

8 ON THE COSTS OF DISEQUILIBRIUM UNDER PEGGED AND FLEXIBLE EXCHANGE RATES

Charles Pigott, Richard J. Sweeney, and Thomas D. Willett

INTRODUCTION

Recent developments in economic analysis have suggested that with well functioning markets, international capital mobility, and stabilizing speculation the most important determinants of macroeconomic stability and the efficiency of resources allocation in open economies will be macroeconomic policies and the patterns analysis of economic disturbances, with the choice of exchange rate regime having much more limited, and in some cases no, effects.[1] This suggests that in comparing alternative exchange rate systems, it is important to examine the implications of various imperfections in their operations as well as under ideal conditions.

In the following section we present an illustration framework comparing the costs of disequilibrium exchange rates under the assumption that each suffers from the major deficiency alleged by its critics, that the adjustable peg is managed in a sticky fashion that adjusts too slowly to changing economic conditions, and that floating exchange rates are characterized by excessive short-run variability due to an absence of rational, efficient, stabilizing speculation. To keep the analysis manageable we assume that the only source of change in equilibrium exchange rates is different rates of inflation between the countries in question. Holding the frequency of parity adjustments constant under the adjustable peg, the comparative costs of flexible rates decline as the difference in inflation rates increases and as the variance of the stochastic terms reflecting destabilizing speculation declines. Likewise, the relative performance of the adjustable peg improves with increases in the frequency of adjustment. In this model, as the time periods for official adjustment and as the excessive variance due to destabilizing speculation go to zero, the performance of the adjustable peg and freely floating rates becomes identical with both tracking a moving equilibrium caused by different trend rates of inflation.

Of course, the assumption of no changes in equilibrium real exchange rates is quite unrealistic. In the concluding section we discuss some implications of dropping this assumption and suggest directions for research that would take changes in equilibrium real exchange rates into account.[2]

A SIMPLE MODEL

This section makes a formal comparison of the costs of excessive variability of exchange rates under the two regions of floating versus adjustable pegged exchange rates. Floating rates are taken as being costly due to poorly behaved speculation that keeps the nominal exchange rate, e_t, away from its equilibrium value for more or less extended time periods. Pegged rates are taken as costly in not allowing the exchange rate to adjust in response to differential inflation rates. To fix ideas suppose the real exchange rate at $t = 0$ — the exchange rate adjusted for relative national price levels — is in long-run equilibrium. Further, suppose the equilibrium real exchange rate is constant over time. The natural logs of the home and foreign country price levels and the exchange rate are p, p' and e (expressed as unity of foreign currency per domestic unit), respectively, so the log of the real exchange rate at time t is $p_t - p_t' - e_t$, and the deviation of this rate from its equilibrium value is then

$$(p_t - p_t' - e_t) - (p_0 - p_0' - e_0) \ . \tag{8.1}$$

Under pegged rates, $e_0 = e_t$ as long as the pegged rate has not been adjusted. The per period rate of change in the (log of the) relative national price levels is $\Delta(p - p')$, which is the difference of the inflation rates in the two countries, and is taken as a constant u under both fixed and floating rates. Thus,

$$(p_t - p_t') = (p_0 - p_0') + \sum_{j=1}^{t} u = (p_0 - p_0') + tu \ , \tag{8.2}$$

and under pegged rates, the deviation of the real exchange rate from its equilibrium value is wholly *deterministic* and is

$$(p_t - p_t' - e_t) - (p_0 - p_0' - e_0) = (p_0 - p_0' - e_0 + tu) - (p_0 - p_0' - e_0)$$
$$= tu \ . \tag{8.3}$$

Under flexible rates, the trend change in e just offsets the trend change u in relative national price levels. However, e_t is also subject to *stochastic* disturbances, z_t. Thus,

$$e_t = e_0 + \sum_{j=1}^{t} u + z_t = e_0 + tu + z_t \ .$$ (8.4)

The deviation of the real exchange rate from its equilibrium level under flexible rates is then found by substituting (8.2) and (8.4) into (8.1),

$$(p_t - p_t' - e_t) - (p_0 - p_0' - e_0) = tu - tu - z_t = -z_t \ .$$ (8.5)

Thus, under floating rates it is only the uncertain disturbance, z_t, that keeps the real exchange rate from its equilibrum level. Under fixed rates, there is a predictable but growing wedge equal to $t \cdot u$ between the actual and equilibrium real exchange rate, where this divergence is due to continuing differences in inflation rates (u).

To illustrate the elements involved in choosing between flexible and pegged exchange rates in these circumstances, suppose that in any given period the loss to society is proportional to the *squared* deviation of the actual real exchange rate from its equilibrium for that period.[3] Then for any given time t, the loss ($L(t)$) under fixed rates is proportional to

$$L(t) = [(p_t - p_t' - e_t) - (p_0 - p_0' - e_0)]^2 = (tu)^2$$

(where period 0 is that at which the rate was first fixed); the loss under floating rates, $L^*(t)$ is

$$L^*(t) = (z_t)^2 \ .$$

In comparing the two regimes, we thus compare the anticipated *cumulative* loss incurred over a given interval.

Now suppose z_t is stationary in the sense that its unconditional mean is constant over time and its variance is finite. (Heuristically, this means that z_t does not grow explosively as time passes.) For any t (as viewed from $t = 0$), the expected loss, $E[L^*(t)]$ is simply the variance of z_t, which, since z_t is stationary, is *bounded* for all t. In contrast, the expected loss at t under fixed rates, $E[L(t)] = t^2 u^2$, grows without bound as time progresses. Thus, for sufficiently large t, the pre-period loss under floating will always be less than that incurred under a pegged rate system. It follows that for a sufficiently long interval, the expected cumulative loss under floating will always be less than that under the alternative – and, in this sense, floating will be the better system.

To illustrate, consider three possible specifications of the process followed by z_t, all of which are linear functions of a serially uncorrelated (random) disturbance, a_t. In the first case, $z_t = a_t$ is a random but transitory shock to the real exchange rate. The expected loss in each period is thus the same or $E[L^*(t)] = \sigma_a^2$, the variance of a_t. In the second case,

$$z_t = bz_{t-1} + a_t = b^0 a_t + ba_{t-1} + b^2 a_{t-2} + \ldots, |b| < 1 \qquad (8.8)$$

so the process is a geometrically declining moving average on the random disturbances, a. Viewed at time 0, the expected loss at t is simply

$$E[L^*(t)] = \sum_{j=0}^{t} b^{2j} \sigma_a^2 = \frac{1 - b^{2(t+1)}}{1 - b^2} .$$

Note that in both cases the expected per-period loss is uniformly bounded for all t, as asserted above.

Finally, that floating can dominate fixed rates even if z_t is *not* stationary can be seen from the following illustration. Suppose changes in z_t are random, so $z_t - z_{t-1} = a_t$. Then $z_t = a_0 + a_1 + \ldots a_t$ and

$$E[L^*(t)] = t\sigma_a^2 .$$

Since this grows more slowly than the fixed rate loss, $t^2 u^2$, plainly for sufficiently large t, $E[L^*(t)] < E[L(t)]$ as in the case where z_t is stationary.

These three cases are summarized in Table 8-1. The general case for stationary z_t is depicted in Figure 8-1. The locus, EL, gives the expected loss at t under a fixed rate regime (where exchange rates are initially set at their equilibrium at $t = 0$); the locus EL^* gives the corresponding loss under floating. Furthermore, the cumulative loss up through t can be approximated by the area under the respective curves.

Now from the above arguments we know that the loss under floating rates grows more slowly than that under the pegged rate system. Hence there must be

Table 8-1. Comparative Pre-Period Losses from Fixed and Floating Rates.

| | Cases: | | |
	I	*II*	*III*
Expected loss at t as viewed at u:			
Pegged Rate*	$t^2 u^2$	$t^2 u^2$	$t^2 u^2$
Floating	σ_a^2	$\dfrac{1 - b^{2(t+1)}}{1 - b^2} \sigma_a^2$	$t\sigma_a^2$

*With rates initially set at $t = 0$.
Source: Author's calculations.

Figure 8-1. Costs Under Alternative Exchange Rate Regimes.

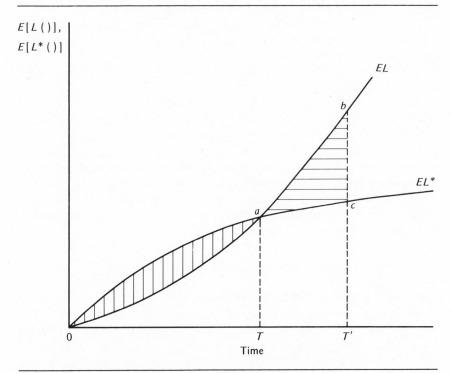

a time, T, as shown in Figure 8-1, after which $E[L^*(t)] < E[L(t)]$. T is interpreted as follows. From the point of view of $t = 0$, the best guess is that the marginal costs of the distortions imposed by the pegged exchange rate and differential inflation rates will be less than the costs of the likely disturbances due to destabilizing speculation in every period $t < T$. Thus, ex ante we can expect growing pressure beyond T to move to floating exchange rates or to change the pegged rate, if these are the only two policy choices possible. This time T is larger the greater is the variance or the disturbance, σ_a^2, the longer this disturbance persists (the more serially correlated are the z_t), and the smaller the drift away from equilibrium under fixed rates, u.

If the pegged rate is adjusted at T, the pegged rate system is superior to floating, with this advantage measured ex ante by the area below the EL^* and above the EL curves in Figure 8-1. Clearly, however, there is some $T' > T$ such that if the pegged rate is on average adjusted at T', the two exchange rate systems are equally costly in expected value terms. (The area below EL and above EL^* from T to T' exactly offsets the area from $t = 0$ to T; indeed, it is this condition from which T' is found.) Thus, under a wide range of assumptions about how severe and prolonged is destabilizing speculation, floating rates will be preferable to pegged rates *if* these are not adjusted for long enough intervals.

As the model stands, optimum policy is neither floating, permanently fixed rates, nor an adjustable peg but is rather a gliding parity where the change in parity every period is $\Delta e = -u$. This gives $\Delta(p - p' - e) = 0$ for all t, and since the equilibrium real rate was assumed to be $(p_0 - p_0' - e_0)$, the system is kept always at equilibrium.

The government whose rate is attacked may not have sufficient reserves to offset the pressures generated by the speculative flows that caused the z_t under floating; the other government may not be willing to supply its currency in such large quantities as to hold the rate. Further, the above analysis is biased in favor of the gliding parity by making optimum policy straightforward and easily knowable; in every period, the differential inflation rate u is known and optimum policy is to set $\Delta e = -u$. In other words, just as the private market is allowed scope for mistakes through the z_t, in realistic comparisons, governments must also be allowed scope for error.

CONCLUDING REMARKS

For analytic simplicity, the analysis presented, while useful we hope for helping to clarify several important issues in the traditional debate over the effects of pegged versus flexible exchange rates on resource allocation, has been loaded against the efficiency of both pegged and flexible exchange rates. With no real disturbances and a constant inflation rate differential, the optimum exchange rate regime on resource allocation grounds would be a PPP-based crawling peg. Official management to keep nominal exchange rates close to this equilibrium would not be difficult to implement. On the other hand, it is difficult to believe that under such stable underlying conditions there would be any serious deficiencies in private speculation such that official intervention would be needed to establish equilibrium exchange rates.

In reality, of course, the underlying factors determining inflation rates are far from predictable, and there have been (and are likely to continue to be) frequent changes in equilibrium real exchange rates, sometimes of considerable magnitude.[4] Consequently, observed real exchange rate variations will generally reflect a combination of shifts in long-run equilibria, short-run adjustments of the real rate when nominal exchange rates anticipate future inflation, transient fluctuations in real interest rates, or "irrational" or inefficient speculation.

None of these sources of real exchange rate changes is directly observable. Each, though, is likely to imply a different optimal course for exchange rate policy; for example, it is doubtful that official intervention would be justified in any but (possibly) the last case, unless there are important externalities or market failures calling for intervention as a second-best solution. However, as the analytics of such cases have not been satisfactorily worked out, this is not likely to provide a practical basis for intervention in the foreseeable future.[5] Thus, at present, the safest criteria for evaluating the microefficiency implications of alternative exchange rate policies is to compare the degree to which they allow market rates to track their underlying equilibria — where due allowance is made for the practical difficulties of making such comparisons.

Phrased this way, the major question becomes to what extent under different exchange rate regimes are officials or private speculators better able to identify and move nominal exchange rates toward levels in harmony with ongoing changes in equilibrium real exchange rates, and what are the relative costs of the mistakes that will inevitably be made under any strategy? There has been a good deal of analysis of the effects of different types of disturbances (around equilibrium trends) on the stability of economic activity under pegged versus flexible exchange rates.[6] Straightforward extensions can be used to investigate the effects on microeconomic resource allocation as well,[7] but such models assume usually that disturbances are random shocks around trend. Under such circumstances, in the presence of efficient price speculation there would in general be no major difference between fixed and flexible exchange rates.[8]

Given the mixed evidence on the behavior of private speculation, at present we cannot safely rely exclusively on the results from analysis, that makes any one particular set of assumptions about the efficiency or inefficiency of speculative behavior to derive conclusions about the comparative effects of alternative exchange rate regimes. What is required is a more comprehensive analysis of the effects of various transitory and permanent disturbances under different types of assumptions about the behavior of private speculation and official exchange rate policies and also about domestic policy reaction functions. This will be an enormous task that lies well beyond the scope of this study. We suspect that, as in the cases of the effects of alternative exchange rate regimes on inflation and the stabilization of aggregate economic activity, the number of possible, plausible scenarios is so great that it will prove virtually impossible to merge a sufficiently comprehensive analytical framework with empirical observation to draw strong general conclusions, at least anytime in the near future. In the process of such searches, however, we have gained and should continue to gain many important insights that improve the quality of our analysis of contemporary problems, even if we cannot consider them definitive.

NOTES TO CHAPTER 8

1. See Edward Tower and Thomas D. Willett, *The Theory of Optimum Currency Areas and Exchange-Rate Flexibility*, Special Papers in International Economics, No. 11, May 1976 (Princeton: Princeton University Press); and Walter Enders and Harvey Lapan, "Stability, Random Disturbance, and the Exchange Rate Regime," *Southern Economic Journal* (July 1979): 49–70.

2. Charles Pigott and Richard Sweeney, "Purchasing Power Parity and Exchange Rate Dynamics: Some Empirical Evidence," in this volume show that the real exchange rate does seem to be subject to permanent changes, and in fact it can be reasonably approximated as a random walk. See also Michael Darby, "Does Purchasing Power Parity Work?" in the Proceedings of the Fall 1981 Academic Conference, Federal Reserve Bank of San Francisco. Such behavior will arise from permanent disturbances to the goods sector from shifts in tastes or in technical progress.

3. This assumption of a quadratic loss function, while quite common in the literature on the theory of economic policy, is admittedly somewhat arbitrary. As was discussed in Chapter 7, there are a number of different types of costs caused by disequilibrium exchange rates and exchange rate variability, and their quantitative magnitudes may vary considerably from industry to industry. Derivation of a precise aggregate loss function is well beyond the state of current analysis, but given our present state of knowledge, our assumption of a quadratic loss function does not seem unreasonable. This should obviously be an important area for further research, however.

4. See Michael Darby, "Does Purchasing Power Parity Work?"; and Charles Pigott, "The Influence of Real Factors on Exchange Rate," *Economic Review* of the Federal Reserve Bank of San Francisco (Fall 1981).

5. See the section on externality arguments for official intervention in Thomas D. Willett, "Alternative Approach to International Surveillance of Exchange-Rate Policies," *Managed Exchange-Rate Flexibility* (Boston: Federal Reserve Bank of Boston, 1978).

6. For discussion and references, see Richard J. Sweeney, "Automatic Stabilization from Exchange Rate Regimes," Chapter 15 in this volume.

7. See, for example, the excellent papers by Walter Enders and Harvey Lapan, "Stability, Random Disturbance and the Exchange Rate Regime"; and "The Exchange Rate, Resource Allocation, and Uncertainty," *Southern Economic Journal* (April 1981): 924–40.

8. Again, see Edward Tower and Thomas D. Willett, "The Theory of Optimum Currency Areas"; and Walter Enders and Harvey Lapan, "Stability, Random Disturbance and the Exchange Regime."

9 THE REALLOCATION EFFECTS OF EXCHANGE RATE FLUCTUATIONS UNDER UNCERTAINTY WITH EFFICIENT SPECULATION

Thomas D. Willett and Paul R. Flacco

INTRODUCTION

Traditionally one of the most influential arguments against floating exchange rates has been the concern that exchange rate volatility would impose substantial resource reallocation costs on domestic economies. As exchange rates went up and down resources would be wrenched back and forth from one industry to another, generating high frictional unemployment and other costs of shifting resources. In fact, however, while unemployment has tended to be high during the current system of widespread managed floating and exchange rates have often tended to be quite volatile, it does not appear that large rapid shifts in resource allocation accompanying short-term exchange rate fluctuations have been a major cause of unemployment and other resource adjustment costs. At least amid the many criticisms of our experience with floating that have been raised, few have focused on this problem, and no published study of which we are aware has attempted to show that this has been a serious problem.[1]

A commonly offered explanation for the lack of short-run resource allocation responsiveness to even sizable exchange rate movements is that firms distinguish between what are expected to be permanent and what are only temporary movements in the exchange rate, with little adjustment being made to the latter.[2] While such behavior is seemingly quite plausible, it is to a large degree inconsistent with the existence of an efficient foreign exchange market. With sufficient stabilizing private speculation, exchange rate fluctuations will generally not reflect temporary developments; otherwise, profit opportunities would exist from buying temporarily undervalued currencies and selling temporarily overvalued currencies. Thus, in efficient markets, expected changes in exchange rates would be limited primarily to trends.

There are several necessary caveats to this proposition involving the possibilities of efficient risk premiums and stock-flow interactions, but probably the most important type of commonly discussed exception is the possibility of exchange rate overshooting that mirrors temporary changes in international interest rate differentials.[3] In such analysis, the expected spot exchange rate change offsets the interest differential, leaving no scope for excess speculative cum arbitrage profits. In this case, the whole structure of forward rates does not overshoot, however, so that trade based on medium-term forward rates would be unlikely to be affected substantially, and the empirical studies in Part I raised substantial doubts about the quantitative importance of such possible efficient market overshooting.

While the empirical evidence available to date is far from definitive, it suggests that most of the observed volatility of exchange rates among the major industrial countries has been unanticipated and cannot be accounted for either by destabilizing or insufficiently stabilizing private speculation or by interest rate induced exchange rate overshooting (see the papers in Part I of this volume). This suggests that while individual business firms may view particular short-term exchange rate movements as temporary, it is unlikely to have been typically true of the market as a whole. Thus, we need to look elsewhere for a full explanation of why there does not appear to have been a great deal of short-run volatility in resource allocation in response to fluctuations in exchange rates.

We believe that this can largely be explained by taking into account the degree of uncertainty about future prices cum exchange rate changes and the costs of short-run adjustments. Thus, even assuming that the current price is always approximately equal to the mean expected future price, where there are costs of adjustment that are an increasing function of the speed of adjustment — that is, adjustment costs are convex — responses to shifts in price incentives will be dampened.[4] Furthermore, where there are significant irreversible aspects to changing employment levels or the capital stock, adjustments to changing conditions are likely to be further dampened when uncertainty is present.[5]

This point will be discussed in the following section. In the final section we go on to discuss some of the important aspects of the social efficiency of the reallocation responses to exchange rate fluctuations. Combined with the role which the availability of forward cover can play in reducing exchange risk, we believe that the analysis in this chapter does help to explain why short-term exchange rate volatility does not appear to have imposed as heavy reallocation costs as many had feared. Probably more serious problems come from large exchange rate movements which are maintained for lengthy periods of time such as the weak dollar of the last several years of the 1970s followed by the strong dollar of the early 1980s. These may induce much more substantial reallocation costs which should be the subject of future research.

THE DAMPENING EFFECTS OF UNCERTAINTY
AND IRREVERSIBILITIES ON THE REALLOCATION
EFFECTS OF EXCHANGE RATE FLUCTUATIONS IN
EFFICIENT MARKETS

Even ignoring risk aversion, profit maximizing firms would have a status quo "bias" against changing levels of input use where fixed cost commitments are involved if there is the possibility of reversals in the change in price incentives. In an efficient speculative market, after the change in current price,[6] the probability of a reversal in price and of a further change in the same direction normally will be approximately equal.[7] The greater the probability of a reversal, the greater is the incentive to avoid taking on increased fixed cost investments. Likewise, given the probability of a reversal of the price change, the greater are the fixed costs involved in least cost variation in output levels, the smaller will be the likely initial output responses to changes in price incentives.[8]

Note that important fixities are not limited to variations in capital where resale is costly. Skilled labor also has important elements of quasi-fixity.[9] Given significant hiring and training costs, firms often have strong incentives to carry workers during periods of low demand as long as there is a reasonable prospect of the fall in demand being reversed. Likewise, when workers are let go, severance pay may be involved. Such costs of hiring and firing mean that as long as it is not known with certainty that the changed market conditions are permanent, changes in labor use in response to changing market conditions will be dampened. The higher the fixed costs involved, the less will be the variation in labor utilization for a given pattern of fluctuations in demand and the greater is the portion of this change that will take the form of variation in the hours worked per person, rather than variations in the numbers of workers employed by a particular firm.[10] Both of these factors will reduce the amount of transitional unemployment resulting from fluctuations in demand resulting from exchange rate variations.

This treatment gives an alternative meaning to statements that resource reallocation will be more sluggish in response to temporary rather than permanent changes.[11] With efficient speculation, we can reinterpret temporary as meaning that considerable uncertainty surrounds the expected future price path. In the face of irreversibilities in adjustment costs, the higher the level of uncertainty, the less should be the initial output and employment responses to changes in demand.

This dampening of initial responses will be even greater when it is believed that, by waiting, better estimates of future developments can be made. Often large rapid exchange rates movements are the results of unsettling developments that are initially accompanied by considerable uncertainty about what the exact long-run price and exchange rate effects will be. Decisionmakers may often feel that as time passes they will gain a better idea of the future pattern of exchange rates. Thus, by delaying resource adjustments that have irreversibility and fore-going the implied expected profits, decisionmakers are investing in an expected acquisition of information. This effect would be stronger, the larger the magnitudes of the irreversibilities and the greater the expected narrowing of the probability distribution of expected future exchange rates.

We would also expect that, over time, firms would adjust to a more uncertain environment by changing the production process so that the input mix would use more variable relative to fixed factors if this were technically feasible. If the firm could choose between a plant size and production process with lower minimum average cost and less elastic marginal cost versus one with a higher minimum average cost but more elastic marginal cost, then the greater the expected fluctuation in demand, the more likely the firm would be to construct the latter plant. In turn, this mix would increase the short-run responsiveness of resource allocation to exchange rate fluctuations. Thus, we would expect that if the level of uncertainty associated with (but not necessarily caused by) the widespread adoption of flexible exchange rates remains high, the short-run responsiveness of exports and imports to exchange rate fluctuations would probably increase over time as input mix adjustments were made. The amount of resource reallocation per unit of exchange rate change would still remain less than if the degree of expected exchange rate variability were reduced, however.

EFFICIENCY ASPECTS OF RESOURCE REALLOCATION RESPONSES TO EXCHANGE RATE FLUCTUATIONS

These propositions about the effects of uncertainty and the extent of exchange rate fluctuations in dampening the responsiveness of resource reallocation should hold even if the causes of fluctuations are at times due to erratic destabilizing speculation, rather than just to efficient speculative responses to disturbances in underlying conditions. The economic welfare-effects of these two cases of course differ greatly. Where the cause of exchange rate fluctuations is destabilizing speculation, the resulting reallocation costs imposed on the economy are a dead-weight loss that must be added to the static disequilibrium costs of incorrect price signals.

On the other hand, where speculation is efficient, economic decisionmakers have a correct perception of the underlying probability distribution, and private and social costs are equal, profit maximizing firms will adjust to changing exchange rates in a socially efficient manner.[12] We believe that some of the early predictions that flexible rates would lead to a great deal of resource reallocation and frictional unemployment may have stemmed from implicit assumptions that firms would respond to exchange rate changes under flexible rates as they did under pegged rates—that is, they assumed that the changes would be "permanent" for several years (there would be a narrow distribution of expected future rates) and would not modify their responses in an environment in which the behavior of future exchange rate changes was a good deal more uncertain.

Indeed, if market participants did systematically underestimate the likelihood of future changes, flexible rates would lead to "excessive" resource reallocation costs. At present, however, we know of no objective way to ascertain the "true" degree of dispersion of probabilities of exchange rate changes in any particular episode for use as a benchmark, nor do we see particularly strong reasons to believe that the market would be likely to err systematically in either over- or underestimating the relevant probability distribution functions. Thus, while we find such possibilities to be an interesting issue that may merit future attention, we do not see any basis at present for believing that flexible rates will cause serious inefficiencies on this score. We certainly have not seen the huge short-term wrenching of resources back and forth that would evidence strong myopia on the part of the economic system in adjusting to uncertainty about future exchange rate changes.

A second source of potential microeconomic inefficiency as a result of efficient exchange rate fluctuations results from possible divergencies between private and social costs. Where employment and resource allocation decisions are made by firms that do not bear the full marginal costs of their decisions, exchange rate fluctuations may create incentives for greater or less than optimal short-run resource responsiveness.[13] For example, where there is short-run wage inflexibility, the marginal cost curve facing the firm may be a good deal more elastic than the social cost curve for the economy as a whole. In such circumstances, exchange rate fluctuations in response to changing expectations about medium-term equilibrium conditions would cause greater transitional unemployment than would be socially optimal.

As the recent literature on labor contracting and firm pricing emphasizes, however, short-run wage and price rigidity often results from longer term contracting considerations that serve in part as risk-sharing arrangements.[14] The welfare economics of such implicit and explicit contracting is an exciting but complicated area from which we are not prepared to draw strong conclusions at present. We would note, however, that implicit or explicit understandings are likely to have an important influence on firm behavior in a manner that reduces the extent to which the short-run cost of adjustment is placed exclusively on labor. In long-run equilibrium, the greater the fluctuations in wages and employment, the higher will be the supply prices of risk-averse workers to that firm. When such longer run consequences are taken into account, the short-run marginal cost of the firm becomes less elastic, reducing short-run responses to changing prices.

On the other hand, a perhaps quantitatively more significant factor is the extent to which unemployment insurance shifts the costs of layoffs to the taxpayer from firms and workers alike. As a consequence the private marginal cost curve facing the firm at below average output may be much more elastic than the social cost curve, leading to excessive short-run adjustments in response to changing exchange rates.[15] This can present a potential second-best case for limiting exchange rate fluctuations to less than would occur in an efficient foreign exchange market or, in Richard Cooper's words, "to create the possibility that the welfare maximizing rate will fluctuate less than the efficient market rate."[16]

We would caution, however, against jumping quickly to policy recommendations for systematic official interventions in the foreign exchange market to lean against the wind on these grounds. Changes in real exchange rates are only one source of shifts in demand for firms. Even if official intervention could be effective in systematically limiting the range of short-run fluctuations in exchange rates, this could still leave a major domestic problem of excessive temporary unemployment from fluctuations in domestic conditions, and it is not at all clear at present whether the benefit cost ratio of such an intervention strategy would be greater than one. This analysis does further highlight, however, the need for far greater policy attention to the structural and government policy factors that contribute to substantial divergencies in private and social costs of resource adjustments and temporary unemployment.

NOTES TO CHAPTER 9

1. To date empirical studies on the effects of floating rates on resource allocation have focused primarily on the level of international trade. For an interesting study of reallocation effects during the earlier Canadian experiment with floating, see Marie Thursby, "The Resource Reallocation Cost of Fixed and Flexible Exchange Rates," *Journal of International Economics* (February 1980): 79-90, and for a generalization to the recent floating experience see Marie Thursby, "The Resource Allocation Costs of Fixed and Flexible Exchange Rates: A Multicountry Extension," *Journal of International Economics* (November 1981): 487-93.

    These studies do not find estimates of reallocation costs to have been significantly higher under flexible rates.

2. See, for example, Jürg Niehans, "Some Doubts About the Efficiency of Monetary Policy Under Flexible Exchange Rates," *Journal of International Economics* (August 1975): 275-87.

3. See Rudiger Dornbusch, "Exchange-Rate Expectations and Monetary Policy," *Journal of Political Economy* (August 1976): 1161-76.

4. See Stephen J. Nickell, *The Investment Decisions of Firms* (Cambridge: Cambridge University Press, 1978), pp. 25-49, for a discussion of the sluggish investment response of the firm when adjustment costs are present.

5. Irreversibility is used here not in the strict sense that a decision cannot literally be undone, but rather in the more general sense that it cannot be

reversed without incurring significant additional costs. For models of the firm's investment decision under uncertainty in a dynamic context where there is a single stable distribution of future price, and when adjustment costs and irreversibility are present, see Richard Hartman, "The Effect of Price and Cost Uncertainty on Investment," *Journal of Economic Theory* 5 (October 1972): 258–66; "Adjustment Costs, Price and Wage Uncertainty and Investment," *Review of Economic Studies* 40 (April, 1973): 259–68; Stephen J. Nickell, "Uncertainty and Lags in the Investment Decisions of Firms," *Review of Economic Studies* 44 (June 1977): 249–63; and *The Investment Decision of Firms.*

For general surveys and references to the literature on the effects of uncertainty on resource allocation, see John Hey, *Uncertainty in Microeconomics* (New York: New York University Press, 1979), and specifically in an international context, see John Pomery, "Uncertainty in International Trade," in Rudiger Dornbusch and Jacob Frenkell, eds., *International Economic Policy* (Baltimore: Johns Hopkins University Press, 1979), pp. 112–157; and Victoria S. Farrell with Dean A. DeRosa and T. Ashby McCown, *Effects of Exchange Rate Variability on International Trade and Other Economic Variables: A Review of the Literature* (Washington, D.C.: Board of Governors of the Federal Reserve System, Staff Studies, No. 130, December 1983). See also the interesting recent analysis in Leonard Cheng, "Ex Ante Plant Design, Portfolio Theory, and Uncertainty Terms of Trade," *Journal of International Economics* (February 1980): 25–52.

6. For some decisions the relevant prices will be forward rather than spot prices.

7. Technically, the expected value of possible additional price changes remains zero, as was the expectation of the original price change with efficient speculation. Note that this need not necessarily mean that the distribution of price is symmetrical.

8. These points and the propositions put forward later in this paper seem intuitively obvious and are generally consistent with the existing results in the literature. It would be useful to have a more formal analysis of these issues, however; for example, looking at the effects of risk aversion and different types of adjustment costs.

9. The classic article is Walter Oi, "Labor as a Quasi-Fixed Factor," *Journal of Political Economy* (December 1962): 538–55.

10. See, for example, Stephen J. Nickell, "Unemployment and the Structure of Labor Costs," in Karl Brunner and Allan Meltzer, eds., *Policies for Employment, Prices, and Exchange Rates* (Carnegie–Rochester Conference Series No. 11, 1979), pp. 187–222, for the result that fixed costs in the decision to hire labor (in the form of institutionally imposed firing costs) reduces overall employment fluctuations and increased fluctuations in hours worked.

11. It is, of course, likely that adjustments from inventories will be greater when price changes are expected to be reversed soon, and this may also occur to some extent with the utilization of variable factors of production; but there are adjustments that tend not to carry substantial reallocation

costs. Such more rapid responsiveness of sales to temporary fluctuations in price would not be expected to be a major cause of frictional unemployment, however.

12.   See, for example, Michael Mussa, "Dynamic Adjustment in the Heckscher-Ohlen–Samuelson Model," *Journal of Political Economy* 86, no. 5 (October 1978): 775–91.

13.   For earlier discussions on this point see Richard N. Cooper, "I.M.F. Surveillance Over Exchange Rates," in Robert Mundell and Jacques Pollak, eds., *The New International Monetary System* (New York: Columbia University Press, 1977), pp. 69–83; and Thomas D. Willett, "Alternative Approaches to International Surveillance of Exchange-Rate Policies," in *Managed Exchange Rate Flexibility* (Boston: Federal Reserve Bank of Boston, 1978), 148–72.

14.   For a recent contribution and references to the rapidly growing literature on this subject, see Robert Hall and D.M. Lillien, "Efficient Wage Bargains Under Uncertain Supply and Demand," *American Economic Review* 69 (December 1979): 868–79.

15.   On the effects of unemployment insurance on the amount of unemployment, see, for example, Martin Feldstein, "The Effect of Unemployment Insurance on Temporary Layoff Unemployment," *American Economic Review* (December 1978): 834–46; and "The Private and Social Costs of Unemployment," *American Economic Review* (May 1978): 155–58. For a provocative analysis concluding that a public subsidy to unemployment insurance promotes labor mobility, see H.M. Polemauchakis and B. Weiss, "Fixed Wages, Layoffs, Unemployment Compensation, and Welfare," *American Economic Review* (December 1978): 909–17.

16.   Richard N. Cooper, "I.M.F. Surveillance," p. 72.

10 THE UNCERTAINTY EFFECTS OF FLOATING EXCHANGE RATES
Empirical Evidence on International Trade Flows

Marie C. Thursby and Jerry G. Thursby

There have been wide swings in opinions on uncertainty effects of flexible exchange rates since the pre-Bretton Woods era,[1] and to some extent it is lack of empirical evidence that has fostered the development of these diverse opinions. Prior to the early seventies the only evidence was the type presented in Leland Yeager's extensive survey on exchange risk as an obstacle to trade flows.[2] He presents data on trade volume, trade volume relative to GNP, and growth in trade for several European economies for 1919–31 and for Thailand, Peru, Canada, and the world for 1928–63. As Yeager himself remarks, the crudeness of these data limits the interpretation of evidence no matter what correlation one finds between the indexes and periods of flexible rates. Nonetheless, he finds neither strong evidence that floating rates decreased or enhanced world trade.

The introduction of floating rates in the early seventies provided both the impetus and data for new studies. This chapter presents a survey of these and additional empirical results. Since the behavior of transactions costs and efficiency of exchange markets has been discussed elsewhere in this volume, we shall limit our attention to studies of the uncertainty effects of floating rates on trade flows. We survey only empirical studies, referring the reader to Farrell, et al., for a survey of the theoretical literature.[3] Both the evidence from other studies and our results are mixed. These generally support the view that whatever the net effects of the change in exchange rate regimes may have been, these have not yet proven to be as large as had been suggested by many of the participants in the debate about fixed versus flexible exchange rates. While, in general, studies of world trade do not show significant uncertainty effects on aggregate trade, there is limited evidence that exchange rate volatility affects the pattern of that trade.

153

RECENT EMPIRICAL STUDIES

Two types of issues have been addressed by looking at trade flows. One is whether short-run resource reallocation costs of flexible rates exceed those of fixed rates. This is the issue, of whether destabilizing speculation or cyclical changes in equilibrium rates will induce firms to reallocate resources unnecessarily (or temporarily). The second, and related, issue is whether the level of trade will be lower under flexible (than fixed) rates because of uncertainty about the future value of the exchange rate.

In the case of temporary reallocation effects, Thursby's results for a sample of twenty countries suggest that even during periods of substantial exchange rate flexibility unnecessary reallocation effects are not a significant disadvantage of flexible rates.[4,5] These studies compare a proxy measure of reallocation costs under exchange rates for 1972–79 with a simulated fixed exchange rate. It is shown that under fairly simple assumptions, the reallocation effects of export related disturbances are directly related to changes in exports, so that the study compares quarterly fluctuations in the quantity of exports under flexible rates with those under a system that differs only in the flexibility of the rate. Of the twenty countries studied, only for two (Italy and Ireland) are export fluctuations significantly different under the two systems; and for those two, the flexible rate induced less fluctuation.

To examine whether export fluctuations did not differ in general because firms adjusted slowly to profit changes or because signals for reallocation were no different with the fixed and flexible rate, these studies also examined the mean difference in fluctuation in the value of exports under the two systems. On the assumption that exporters use only domestic inputs, fluctuation in export profits differs under the two systems only if export value fluctuation is significantly different. Export value fluctuation was significantly different only for Italy, Ireland, Japan, and the United Kingdom. Results for Japan and the United Kingdom suggest that the flexible rate signaled less reallocation but that slow adjustment could have prevented export quantity data from showing any difference in output fluctuation. Since the sample of countries varies by degree of industrialization and openness, it is interesting that in no case does the flexible rate appear to have caused significantly larger reallocation effects than would a fixed rate during the same period.

These results are consistent with results of regression analyses of the effect of exchange risk on aggregate trade flows. Table 10-1 summarizes the format and results of eight recent studies of the relation between trade flows and various proxy measures of exchange risk. In the studies by Clark and Haulk, Makin, Kenen, and Akhtar and Hilton, aggregate imports or exports are regressed on a proxy measure of exchange risk.[6] Of these, only Akhtar and Hilton find a significant effect of exchange risk on exports and imports. Their results may be due to their later sample or their specification.

On the other hand, each of the three studies of bilateral trade flows finds limited evidence that exchange risk affects trade flows.[7] Hooper and Kohlhagen estimated reduced form price and quantity equations for sixteen bilateral trade flows. As noted in column 4 of Table 10-1, their exchange risk proxy is significantly related to the volume of trade only for the case of United States-United Kingdom trade. They do, however, find a significant relation between exchange risk and prices in the majority of their cases. Cushman modifies Kohlhagen and Hooper's equations by replacing nominal measures of costs and exchange rates with real variables. He estimates these equations for the same data set to find that in a large number of cases real exchange risk affects the volume of U.S. and German bilateral trade flows. For a few of the cases he finds a significant relation between real exchange risk and prices.

Finally, the last two studies surveyed report a significant relation between their trade flow variable and exchange risk proxy. Abrams estimates a variant of the gravity equation for bilateral trade and finds that two measures of flexibility in the previous year's exchange rate are related to flows.[8] One measure reflects changes in trend in the exchange rate and the second measures variability of the rate around trend. When each is entered independently they are significant, but when both are included in the same equation they are insignificant; so he is unable to distinguish between the two types of fluctuations in importance. In addition, Abrams used his regression results to compare the level of trade during the period to trade in the case where rates were as stable as they were in a pre-float period. As stable rates for comparison he used the 1970 and 1971 rates. If rates during 1974-76 had been as stable in 1970, he estimates that as much as 19 percent more trade would have occurred. But using the 1971 rate as a comparison, he estimates that 1 percent less trade would have taken place.

The Coes study of Brazil is the only one of those surveyed that presents results disaggregated by industry.[9] The combined implication of the studies surveyed is that the only significant trade effects of exchange rate fluctuation are on the pattern of trade flows rather than the level of world trade.

REAL AND NOMINAL EXCHANGE
RATE FLEXIBILITY

For a sample of twenty countries for 1973-77 we have conducted several tests to augment these results.[10] The major reason for doing this is that greater nominal exchange rate variability need not increase exchange risk appropriately measured.[11] Nonetheless, of the studies we survey in Table 10-1, only Kenen, Cushman, and Coes employ measures of real exchange rate variability.[12] Neither

Table 10-1. Empirical Studies of the Trade Effects of Exchange Risk.

Study	Dependent Variables	Exchange Risk Proxy*	Significance	Data	Time	Countries
Clark & Haulk	Aggregate real imports and exports	Standard deviations of forward exchange rate over previous four quarters	No	Quarterly	1952–62	Canada
Makin	Aggregate real imports	Standard deviation of spot (forward) exchange rate	No	Quarterly	1960–73	U.S., Germany, Japan, Canada
Kenen	Growth aggregate real exports and fixed capital formation	Mean and standard deviation of absolute monthly percentage change in nominal and real spot exchange rates	No	Annual Cross Section	1974–76	33 countries
Akhtar & Hilton	Aggregate export and import volume and prices	Standard deviation of effective nominal exchange rate	Yes for German export and import volume and U.S. export volume	Quarterly	1974–81	U.S., Germany
Hooper & Kohlhagen	Bilateral export volume and prices	Average absolute differences between the previous forward and current spot rate	Price effect significant in a majority of cases; volume effect significant only for US–UK flow	Quarterly	1965–75	U.S., Germany, Japan, U.K., France
Abrams	Bilateral export volume	Variance of previous year's spot exchange rate; variance of monthly changes in previous year's exchange rate	Yes when only one proxy is entered	Annual (pooled cross section time series)	1973–76	19 developed countries

Cushman	Bilateral export volume and prices	Standard deviation of current relative to previous real rate	Volume effects significant for seven cases; price effects significant in a few cases	Quarterly	1965–77	Same as Hooper & Kohlhagen
Coes	Exports/Production disaggregated by industry	Integral difference in cumulative distribution of monthly real exchange rate and "certain" exchange rate	Yes for all but two cases	Annual	1957–74	Brazil

* Unless specified all exchange rates are in nominal terms.

Sources: Clark and Havlk (1982); Makin (1976); Kenen (1980); Akhtar and Hilton (1984); Hooper and Kohlhagen (1978); Abrams (1980b); Cushman (1983); and Coes (1981).

Table 10-2. Percentage Change in Exports/GNP (1973-77).

Country	Value	Country	Value
Austria	1.958	Norway	0.502
Belgium	0.566	Portugal	1.971
Denmark	1.641	South Africa	1.511
Finland	0.436	Spain	1.993
France	1.301	Sweden	-1.998
Germany	-1.842	Switzerland	0.295
Greece	-2.001	Turkey	1.876
Italy	2.000	United Kingdom	-1.999
Japan	-0.638	United States	-0.008
Netherlands	1.677	Canada	1.289

Source: Data are annual, taken from OECD, *Main Economic Indicators and Statistics of Foreign Trade.*

Kenan nor Coes examine bilateral trade flows, and Cushman examines only U.S. and German trade, so that it would be useful to examine the relation between real exchange rate variation and bilateral trade for a larger sample of countries. Our results are consistent with the majority of earlier studies since we find that while aggregate world trade has not suffered under the recent float, for some countries we find a significant relation between bilateral trade flows and an exchange risk proxy.

As a crude measure of trade effects, we calculated the growth of export quantity relative to GNP for each country during the sample period. As shown in Table 10-2, the ratio of exports to GNP increases for all but six of the twenty countries. This result is consistent with Yeager's results for earlier periods and with Blackhurst and Tumlir's calculation of exports relative to production during the period 1955-79.[13]

In order to examine the relation between exchange rate changes and trade flows, we calculated the same measures used by Kenen.[14] First we calculated the trade weighted algebraic mean of the percentage change in bilateral exchange rates,

$$MN = S_{ij} MN_{ij}$$

where S_{ij} is the share of the value of i's exports to j in i's total exports, and MN_{ij} is the mean percentage change in the nominal rate (N_{ij}) of exchange between currencies i and j. MC and MW are the trade weighted algebraic means of percentage changes in real rates, where C_{ij} (W_{ij}) is the nominal rate multiplied by the CPI (WPI) in country j relative to the CPI (WPI) in country i. Second, we calculated the trade weighted mean of the absolute values of percentage changes in each series, denoted by AN, AC, and AW. While these are measures of exchange rate variability, they reflect trend in the exchange rate series; so as a measure of variability around trend, both Kenen and we calculated the trade weighted standard deviation of percentage changes in each series, which we denote as SN, SC, and SW.

Table 10-3 presents these measures using monthly data for 1973-77. The results are consistent with Kenen's for the earlier time period since only in the case of the trade weighted algebraic mean are the measures for real rates lower in magnitude than the nominal measures. Even in that case, MC and SW are lower in magnitude for less than half of the countries.

For the cross country data, we regressed each of these variability measures against the growth in exports relative to GNP during the period. For none of the variability measures was the relation significant, so that our results are consistent with Clark and Haulk, Makin, and Kenen's findings of no significant relation between aggregate trade and exchange rate variability for 1974-76.

We tested the relation between bilateral trade flows and exchange rate variation by pooling cross-section and yearly time series data for 1973-77. We estimated regressions of the following form:

$$X_{ij} = \alpha_1 + \alpha_2 ADG_{ij} + \alpha_3 V_{ij} + \alpha_4 ME_{ij}$$

where X_{ij} is the value of exports for i to j in constant 1975 dollars,

$ADG_{ij} = | GNP_i - GNP_j |$,

V_{ij} = variability measure for rate of exchange between currencies i and j, and

ME_{ij} = mean percentage change in the exchange rate.

Trade and GNP data are yearly, and exchange rate data are monthly, so that V_{ij} and ME_{ij} refer to monthly changes within the year.

According to the Linder hypothesis, countries with similar levels of income tend to trade with each other;[15] hence, we would expect $\alpha_1 > 0$ and $\alpha_2 < 0$. If bilateral trade flows are not affected by exchange rate uncertainty, $\alpha_3 = 0$. On the other hand, either $\alpha_3 \gtrless 0$ are consistent with significant uncertainty effects on the bilateral flows since X_{ij} is measured in value terms.[16] If exchange risk lowers the level of trade $\alpha_3 < 0$, but if exporters increase prices in response to increased risk $\alpha_3 > 0$. ME_{ij} is included as a general measure of trend in an exchange rate series. We expect $\alpha_4 < 0$ since a revaluation is expected to reduce the dollar value of exports, ceteris paribus.

Our results, in general, support the Linder hypothesis, but since our interest is primarily in the effect of exchange rate variability, we report only the estimates α_3 and α_4. Table 10-4 presents these estimates (expressed in elasticity form) for three measures of V_{ij} for each of the three exchange rate series (N_{ij}, C_{ij}, W_{ij}). As before MN_{ij}, MC_{ij}, MW_{ij} refer to mean percentage changes in the nominal rate of exchange between i and j and the mean percentage change in the real rates based on the CPI and WPI, respectively. A, S, and R refer to the three variability measures where, as before, A refers to the absolute percentage change in the series and S is the standard deviation of the percentage change. R was cal-

Table 10-3. Real and Nominal Exchange Rate Variability.

	MN	SN	AN	MC	SC	AC	MW	SW	AW
Austria	-0.007	0.066	0.037	0.002	0.132	0.058	0.003	0.132	0.062
Belgium	-0.004	0.026	0.019	-0.007	0.042	0.025	-0.003	0.071	0.042
Canada	0.001	0.011	0.008	0.002	0.044	0.020	-0.000	0.086	0.045
Denmark	-0.004	0.028	0.020	-0.015	0.043	0.031	-0.014	0.082	0.048
Finland	-0.002	0.059	0.026	-0.006	0.081	0.036	-0.006	0.088	0.039
France	-0.002	0.029	0.021	-0.008	0.038	0.027	-0.006	0.055	0.033
Germany	-0.008	0.040	0.023	0.002	0.079	0.032	0.001	0.110	0.038
Greece	0.001	0.029	0.013	-0.003	0.073	0.032	-0.002	0.079	0.034
Italy	0.009	0.032	0.023	0.001	0.049	0.030	-0.002	0.080	0.037
Japan	-0.004	0.026	0.014	-0.008	0.041	0.022	-0.005	0.064	0.034
Netherlands	-0.004	0.026	0.019	-0.003	0.065	0.036	-0.002	0.068	0.036
Norway	-0.004	0.027	0.019	-0.008	0.045	0.027	-0.007	0.073	0.041
Portugal	0.004	0.033	0.020	-0.004	0.052	0.033	-0.003	0.063	0.033
South Africa	0.008	0.076	0.020	-0.028	0.220	0.045	-0.026	0.224	0.050
Spain	0.002	0.017	0.008	-0.002	0.030	0.016	-0.000	0.040	0.023
Sweden	-0.002	0.031	0.020	-0.012	0.178	0.060	-0.014	0.055	0.036
Switzerland	-0.009	0.030	0.023	-0.008	0.057	0.034	-0.007	0.177	0.066
Turkey	0.004	0.026	0.015	-0.005	0.053	0.028	-0.002	0.077	0.034
United Kingdom	0.006	0.026	0.018	0.023	0.040	0.031	0.023	0.066	0.040
United States	0.001	0.022	0.014	0.001	0.053	0.026	-0.001	0.088	0.047

culated as an alternative measure of variability around trend since the mean may not remove all trend. To form R we regressed the percentage change in the rate against a quadratic function of time and calculated the standard deviation of the residuals of the regression (R).

As can be seen from the even numbered columns, the coefficient of the general trend measure (M) is significant in few cases (roughly a quarter) no matter which exchange rate series is used.[17] Results for V_{ij} vary by measure and exchange rate series. For most cases $\alpha_3 < 0$, but as shown in columns (13), (15), and (16) the coefficient of V_{ij} where the real rate is based on the WPI is rarely significant. For both the nominal rate and the CPI based real rate series, $\alpha_3 < 0$ and is significant for a substantial number of cases. If the absolute mean is used as a measure of V_{ij}, α_3 is significant in fourteen of the twenty countries for both N_{ij} and C_{ij}. For the two measures of variation around trend, the coefficient associated with the elasticity is significant in roughly half of the cases. Finally, when the standard deviation of the quadratic regression residuals is used as the measure of variability, the least number of α_3 estimates is significant.[18]

In summary, our results for aggregate trade flows are consistent with previous studies that fail to show a significant reduction in the rate of growth of trade as a result of exchange rate variability. On the other hand, our bilateral trade results provide support for the hypothesis that exchange rate variability affects the pattern of trade. As noted earlier this result is consistent with previous studies of bilateral flows, with the primary differences being that we employ measures of both real and nominal exchange rate variation, as well as additional measures of variability.

Table 10-4. Bilateral Trade Regression Results.

Country	(1) AN_{ij}	(2) MN_{ij}	(3) SN_{ij}	(4) MN_{ij}	(5) RN_{ij}	(6) MN_{ij}	(7) AC_{ij}	(8) MC_{ij}	(9) SC_{ij}
Austria	-1.130*	-0.063	-0.554*	-0.107	-0.753*	-0.106	-1.339*	-0.017	-0.933*
Belgium	-1.950*	0.203	-0.596	0.117	-0.691	0.134	-2.062*	0.139	-0.764
Canada	-4.029*	0.165	-2.277*	0.070	-2.175*	0.068	-3.982*	0.038	-3.225*
Denmark	-1.653*	0.005	-1.067	0.040	-0.909	0.034	-2.514*	0.126*	-1.297
Finland	-3.111*	0.103*	-1.423*	0.046	-1.505*	0.039	-3.237*	0.039	-2.598*
France	-0.356	-0.008	0.001	0.001	-0.006	0.001	-0.614*	-0.012	-0.042
Germany	-0.658	0.115	-0.172	0.075	-0.197	0.079	-0.677*	0.254*	-0.170
Greece	-1.039*	0.011	-0.270	0.029	-0.313	0.031	-0.741	0.211	-0.216
Italy	-1.138*	-0.088*	-0.576*	-0.073*	-0.584*	-0.072*	-0.083	0.046	0.341
Japan	-6.911*	1.439*	-4.533*	1.179*	-3.920*	0.865*	-5.196*	0.284	-4.874*
Netherlands	-3.238*	-0.115	-0.991	-0.149	-0.985	-0.151	-4.719*	-0.014	-2.792*
Norway	-3.302*	-0.038	-1.642*	0.022	-1.506*	0.014	-1.709*	-0.014*	-2.247*
Portugal	-1.150*	0.294	-0.215	0.142	-0.231	0.142	-1.546*	0.175	-0.518
South Africa	-0.552	-0.071*	-0.168	-0.067*	-0.176	-0.067*	-0.496	-0.127	-0.173
Spain	-0.960*	0.168	-0.642*	0.196*	-0.639*	+0.197*	-1.450*	0.036	-0.757*
Sweden	-0.513	0.302*	0.037	0.283*	-0.042	0.283*	-0.772	0.097	-0.276
Switzerland	-6.396*	1.647*	-2.389*	0.595	-2.578*	0.624*	-3.484*	0.808*	-2.574*
Turkey	-0.909	0.291*	-0.153	0.222	-0.205	0.223*	-0.517	-0.054	-0.146
United Kingdom	-0.298	0.193*	-0.080	-0.193*	0.088	-0.193*	0.710	0.089	0.790*
United States	-0.465	+0.001	-0.823*	-0.001	-0.790*	-0.001	-1.748*	-0.026	-1.317*

Table 10-4. continued

Country	(10) MC_{ij}	(11) RC_{ij}	(12) MC_{ij}	(13) AW_{ij}	(14) MW_{ij}	(15) SW_{ij}	(16) MW_{ij}	(17) RW_{ij}	(18) MW_{ij}
Austria	-0.037	-0.666*	-0.033	-0.341*	-0.161*	-0.212*	-0.144*	-0.192*	-0.146*
Belgium	0.172	-0.683	0.175	-0.664	-0.279	-0.389	-0.256	-0.375	-0.258
Canada	-0.043	-3.240*	-0.065	-0.413	0.194	-0.245	0.186	-0.225	0.184
Denmark	0.150*	-1.218	0.154*	0.015	0.097	0.038	0.106	0.034	0.105
Finland	0.022	-2.437*	0.021	-0.352*	0.128	-0.180	0.110	-0.169	0.109
France	0.011	-0.025	0.012	-0.140	0.002	-0.075	0.004	-0.074	0.004
Germany	0.243*	-0.158	0.244*	0.275*	0.429*	0.201*	0.430*	0.194*	0.431*
Greece	0.232	-0.190	0.234	-0.056	0.084	-0.001	0.098	0.004	0.101
Italy	0.049	0.385	0.048	0.150	-0.007	0.145	0.008	0.145	0.012
Japan	0.318	-4.929*	0.458	-0.329	-0.430	-0.150	-0.400	-0.139	-0.397
Netherlands	0.029	-2.679*	0.049	-0.066	-0.082	-0.004	-0.055	-0.0004	-0.053
Norway	-0.015*	-2.572*	-0.015*	0.291	0.118*	0.213	0.120*	0.212	0.121*
Portugal	0.068	-0.494	0.070	-0.366	0.013*	-0.182	0.009	-0.177	0.009
South Africa	-0.150	-0.164	-0.150	-0.047	-0.068	-0.022	-0.071	-0.012	-0.073
Spain	0.060	-0.706*	0.057	-0.210	0.142*	-0.126	0.135*	-0.103	0.129*
Sweden	0.082	-0.172	0.077	-0.135	0.148	-0.093	0.149	-0.085	0.147
Switzerland	0.674*	-2.358*	0.685*	-0.519	0.332	-0.417	0.303	-0.412	0.303
Turkey	-0.059	-0.171	-0.064	-0.206	-0.294	-0.111	-0.292	-0.109	-0.294
United Kingdom	0.032	0.773*	0.016	-1.941*	0.560*	-1.082*	0.343*	-1.005*	0.331*
United States	-0.053	-1.043*	-0.051	-0.116	-0.005	-0.086	-0.005	-0.077	-0.005

*Indicates that the coefficient associated with the elasticity is significant at the 5 percent level.

NOTES TO CHAPTER 10

1. See Flacco, Laney, Thursby, and Willett (1984) for a discussion of the evolution of opinions.
2. Yeager (1976).
3. See Farrell, De Rosa, and McCown (1983). See also IMF (1984), which was published too late to be included in our survey, but which offers analysis broadly similar to that presented here.
4. Thursby, Marie, "The Resource Reallocation Costs of Fixed and Flexible Exchange Rates," *Journal of International Economics* (February 1980): 79–90; and "The Resource Reallocation Costs of Fixed and Flexible Exchange Rates: A Multicountry Extension," *Journal of International Economics* (1981).
5. The countries studied are Austria, Belgium, Canada, Denmark, France, Germany, Italy, Japan, Netherlands, Norway, Sweden, Switzerland, United Kingdom, United States, Brazil, Finland, Greece, Ireland, Spain, and Turkey.
6. Clark and Haulk (1972); Makin (1976); Kenen (1980); and Akhtar and Hilton (1984).
7. Cushman (1983); Hooper and Kohlhagen (1978); and Abrams (1980b).
8. R. Abrams, "Actual and Potential International Trade Flows." (See Table 10–1 for complete reference).
9. D. V. Coes, "The Crawling Peg and Exchange Rate Uncertainty."
10. Data are for Austria, Belgium, Canada, Denmark, Finland, France, Germany, Greece, Italy, Japan, Netherlands, Norway, Portugal, South Africa, Spain, Sweden, Switzerland, Turkey, United Kingdom, and the United States.
11. This result would be consistent with those of Thursby, "The Reallocation Costs," 1980 and 1981.
12. P. Kenen, "Exchange Rate Variability"; and D. Coes, "The Crawling Peg and Exchange Rate Uncertainty."
13. Richard Blackhurst and Jan Tumlir, *Trade Relations Under Flexible Exchange Rates* (Geneva: GATT, September 1980).
14. P. Kenen, "Exchange Rate Variability," p. 5.
15. This hypothesis focuses on demand as a determinant of trade flow and concludes that potential trade between two countries is a positive function of the similarities in their demand. Since income is a major determinant of demand, it is inferred that potential trade between two countries is a negative function of differences in their levels of GNP.
16. Data sufficient to calculate bilateral quantity indexes are not available.
17. Note that when $\alpha_4 < 0$ the elasticity may be positive or negative.
18. It should be noted that when the trend measure is omitted from the regressions the results for the variability measures are qualitatively the same.

BIBLIOGRAPHY

Abrams, R. 1980a. "International Trade Flows Under Flexible Exchange Rates." Federal Reserve Bank of Kansas City, *Economic Review* 65 (March): 3-10.

Abrams, R. 1980b. "Actual and Potential International Trade Flows with Flexible Exchange Rates." Federal Reserve Bank of Kansas City, (January). (Unpublished.)

Akhtar, M. A., and R. Spence Hilton. 1984. "Effects of Exchange Rate Uncertainty on German and U.S. Trade," Federal Reserve Bank of New York, *Quarterly Review* (Spring): 7-16.

Blackhurst, R., and J. Tumlir. 1980. "Trade Relations Under Flexible Exchange Rates," GATT Studies in International Trade 8. Geneva: General Agreement on Tariffs and Trade.

Clark, Peter B., and Charles J. Haulk. 1972. "Flexible Exchange Rates and the Level of Trade: A Preliminary Analysis of the Canadian Experience." Federal Reserve Board. (Unpublished.)

Coes, Donald V. 1981. "The Crawling Peg and Exchange Rate Uncertainty," presented at ANPEC/Ford Foundation Conference on Crawling Pegs, Rio de Janeiro, October 1979, in John Williamson, ed., *Exchange Rate Rules*. London: Macmillan Press.

Cushman, David. 1983. "The Effects of Real Exchange Rate Risk on International Trade." *Journal of International Economics* (August): 45-63.

Flacco, Peter, Leroy Laney, Marie Thursby, and Thomas Willett. 1984. "Exchange Rates and Trade Policy." *Contemporary Policy Issues* (January): 6-18.

Hooper, Peter, and Steven W. Kohlhagen. 1978. "The Effect of Exchange Rate Uncertainty on the Prices and Volume of International Trade." *Journal of International Economics* 8 (November): 483-511.

Kenen, Peter B. 1980. "Exchange Rate Variability." Princeton University. (Unpublished.)

Makin, John H. 1976. "The Impact of Exchange Rate Variability Upon Trade Flows in Four Industrial Countries." *Eurocurrencies and the International Monetary System*. Washington, D.C.: American Enterprise Institute.

Thursby, Marie. 1980. "The Resource Reallocation Costs of Fixed and Flexible Exchange Rates." *Journal of International Economics* (February): 79-90.

_____. 1981. "The Resource Reallocation Costs of Fixed and Flexible Exchange Rates: A Multicountry Extension." *Journal of International Economics* (1981): 487-93.

Yeager, Leland. 1976. *International Monetary Relations: Theory, History, and Policy*. New York: Harper and Row, 1976, Chapter 12.

11 DETERMINANTS OF FORWARD EXCHANGE RISK PREMIA IN EFFICIENT MARKETS

Peter A. Sharp

The large fluctuations in exchange rates during the recent period have produced considerable intervention in exchange markets by monetary officials as well as considerable discussion about the effectiveness of intervention, in particular sterilized intervention.[1] The concerns in this debate have included the issues of imperfect substitutability of international assets, the relevance of portfolio balance methods of exchange rates, the diversifiability of exchange risk, and the efficiency of foreign exchange markets. These concerns have motivated considerable research interest in the forward exchange market and the issue of forward risk premia. The presence of forward risk premia would support the imperfect substitutability of assets denominated in different currencies and would bolster the case for such intervention. This paper examines models of forward exchange risk premia based on international capital asset pricing models for the determinants of those risk premia. It argues that the emphasis on the role of outside nominal assets is secondary to the role of outside real assets, and that recent empirical evidence supporting the existence of forward rate bias should not be interpreted as evidence of risk premia.

The International Capital Asset Pricing Models yield equilibrium relationships for forward exchange risk premia, by extending models of domestic financial market equilibrium under uncertainty to a multicurrency and multinational world. The most widely used models to study the effects of uncertainty in general equilibrium are the Sharpe–Linter–Mossin capital asset pricing model and

I would like to express my appreciation to Thomas D. Willett and Richard J. Sweeney for their helpful comments on earlier drafts of this paper.

167

the Arrow–Debreu state preference model.[2] The capital asset pricing model assumes investors optimize their portfolio holdings of risky assets according to the Markowitz mean-variance criterion. The model is subject to extensive criticism on both theoretical and empirical grounds.[3]

In one extension of the model, Merton examines capital markets in an intertemporal framework using continuous time.[4] Merton's work forms the basis of the pioneering models by Solnik and by Kouri of international capital markets. Using a continuous time model, both Solnik and Kouri assume preferences and investment opportunities to be independent over time, so that their results are consistent with a static model but allow the linearization of returns. Grauer, Litzenberger, and Steehle (GLS) employ the elegant Arrow–Debreu state preference model to derive nonlinear asset pricing relationships. The work of Solnik, Kouri, and GLS forms the basis of the finance theory approach to questions in international financial markets.[5]

All these works obtain expressions for equilibrium forward risk premia relationships. A critical distinction occurs between the work by Solnik and the works by Kouri and GLS. Solnik's model depicts a market without inflation (or at most certain inflation) but with uncertain future exchange rates. Exchange rates fluctuate in real terms. Kouri and GLS model a world in which there is uncertain inflation, but exchange rate changes are tied to price level changes— that is, purchasing power parity strictly holds. In their models uncertainty arising from real exchange rates is absent. Since the two approaches investigate distinct sources of uncertainty, the equilibrium relationships are different.

Solnik finds that equilibrium forward risk premia vary with measures of aggregate world risk aversion and the variance and covariance of exchange rates weighted by the value of net indebtedness (or net external investment) among residents of the various countries. The risk premia are directly related to the value of the cumulative current account deficit.

Kouri and GLS find forward risk premia related to measures of aggregate world risk aversion, and the covariance of exchange rates (restricted though to nominal fluctuations) with real returns on aggregate world assets. In their models, net indebtedness among countries is unrelated to forward risk premia, except to the extent that the distribution of wealth affects aggregate world risk aversion. This implies that a country's cumulative current account deficit (or surplus) does not affect the rate of return it must pay (receive) to finance that deficit (or surplus).

The different results occur because of the different sources of uncertainty. In Solnik's model, future real exchange rates are uncertain. Foreign bonds are risky. Domestic bonds are risk free. In order for a cumulative net debt between countries to be financed in the private bond market, either domestic residents issue liabilities in the foreign currency or foreign residents hold bonds denominated in the domestic currency. In order for domestic residents to issue unhedged liabilities in a foreign currency willingly, they must expect to pay a lower real return to compensate for the risk of an unexpected appreciation of the foreign currency. In order for investors in the foreign country to hold domestic country bonds willingly, they must expect to receive a higher rate of return. In either case, or any combination of the two methods of financing, a risk differential between the two currencies would exist.

In contrast, when there is no real exchange rate uncertainty, domestic and foreign bonds yield returns that are uncertain because of changes in inflation rates only. In this case, although domestic and foreign bonds are imperfect substitutes, their risk does not depend upon the residency of the investor.[6] Domestic borrowers would agree with foreign lenders on which currency or combination of currencies would minimize their risk for a given expected return. More formally, under real exchange rate uncertainty, the set of portfolios that are efficient, that maximizes return for a given level of risk, vary according to the residence of the investor. In the absence of real exchange rate uncertainty, the set of efficient portfolios does not vary with the residence of the investor, and asset preferences depend on attitudes toward risk but not on country of residence.

Equilibrium models studying inflation rate uncertainties, but ignoring real exchange rate uncertainty, are the more abundant of the two approaches. Frankel, using a model in which strict purchasing power parity prevails, argues that no forward risk premium exists if two conditions are met: exchange rates are independent of returns on real capital, and no outside nominal assets exist. Outside nominal assets are government debt that is not discounted by the public's perception of future taxes required to repay the debt and the portion of money stock that is outside.[7] Indeed, if returns are independent of exchange rates and no outside nominal assets exist, the covariance of exchange rates with returns on world wealth is zero. This condition, however, is sufficient for zero-risk premia only if real exchange rates are constant, or if there is no foreign indebtedness.

Fama and Farber, emphasizing the special role that purchasing power parity plays in restricting such analysis to inflation uncertainty, find a forward premium that results from differential purchasing power risks across currencies.[8] Their study explicitly assumes that money and one-period bonds have identical risk characteristics. They demonstrate that if at least part of the money stock is outside money, an equilibrium risk premium can exist because nominal bonds can be used to hedge the purchasing power of the risk associated with holding transactions balances. This link between money and bonds implies that the forward exchange rate depends on the differential risks contained in their respective currencies, even if all nominal bonds are inside assets.

Kouri extends the analysis of international financial markets under inflation uncertainty to the case in which lenders and savers have different endowments and varying degrees of uncertainty about future real income. He concludes that risk premia are related to the net supplies of outside assets and covariance between real incomes and prices. He finds that nominal asset demands, not price levels, should be stabilized to reduce uncertainty.[9] Stapleton and Subrahmanyam examine the effects of monetary policy in a pure quantity theory of money world in which velocity is constant. The equilibrium forward risk premium results from inflation uncertainty, money supply uncertainty, or both.[10] Dornbusch develops a rational expectations macroeconomic model in which a forward risk premium equilibrium condition is a key equation in the model. He concludes that the importance of such portfolio considerations in interest rate determination and monetary policy depends critically on the specification of the demand for money.[11]

Financial market models under real exchange rate uncertainty are more limited. Kouri and de Macedo consider both inflation uncertainty and real exchange rate uncertainty in a model in which the menu of assets is restricted to one-period nominal bonds.[12] They find that, in the absence of a forward risk premia, all portfolios have the same real return, so that all investors would select portfolios that minimize the variance of real return. Under real exchange rate uncertainty and no inflation in any country, all investors minimize risk by choosing portfolios totally dominated by their domestic currency asset. With no real exchange rate variability but with inflation that is deterministic, all investors choose the same portfolio, regardless of their own country. In general, investors have no preference for their own currency's bonds.

Kouri and de Macedo estimate hypothetical portfolios of five currencies for investors who calculate real returns using the wholesale price indices of their respective countries. The minimum variance portfolio for residents of Germany, the United States, and the United Kingdom consists primarily of domestic currency nominal assets, thus closely approximating Solnik's model in which investors find portfolios of home country bonds to be the least risky. However, residents of Japan and France hold substantial portions of foreign assets. If the value of the supplies of assets do not match the minimum variance portfolio demands, a forward premium must exist in equilibrium. The difference between the actual supplies and the demands of the minimum variance portfolio is termed the speculative portfolio. In his paper, Dornbusch also briefly considers this case.[13] Stulz reports on a model in which both real exchange rate uncertainty and internal price level uncertainty are considered in a continuous time model.[14]

A simple expositional model of the equilibrium forward risk premium in a two-country format is as follows:

$$\rho = \phi \left[\text{cov}(x, R) + \text{cov}(x, \chi) \frac{E}{W} \right] \quad [15]$$

(11.1)

where:

ρ = forward risk premium on the foreign currency;

ϕ = measure of aggregate world risk aversion;

x = rate of appreciation of the foreign currency;

χ = real rate of appreciation of the foreign currency;

R = rate of return on total world assets of both countries, excluding gains and losses from exchange rate fluctuations;

E = net indebtedness by residents of the foreign country to residents of the domestic country;

W = total value of world wealth.

Under purchasing power parity, $\mathrm{cov}(x, \chi) = 0$, so that the model becomes the model developed by Kouri;[16] that is

$$\rho = \phi\left[\mathrm{cov}(x, R)\right] . \tag{11.2}$$

When changes in exchange rates are independent of returns on world assets, the first covariance term is zero. If there is no inflation, then the $\mathrm{cov}(x, \chi) = \mathrm{var}(x)$. The model becomes a two-country version of the expression derived by Solnik;[17] that is,

$$\rho = \phi\left[\mathrm{var}(x)\,\frac{E}{W}\right] . \tag{11.3}$$

EXCHANGE RATE UNCERTAINTY

Expression (11.2) and the first covariance term in (11.1) have an intuitive interpretation. When, for example, the $\mathrm{cov}(x, R)$ is negative, it means that the foreign currency F appreciates in bad times, (i.e., R declines), and depreciates in good times, (i.e., R increases). Thus, an investor can reduce his overall risk by investing in assets in currency F. Bonds and other assets in currency F represent hedges. Hence, such assets would yield lower returns in efficient markets. If, for example, investors perceive the British pound to be relatively protected against an oil embargo and thus to be a hedging vehicle for returns on other assets, the expected returns on pounds sterling would be lower than returns on assets in other countries. Although the covariance term is written without a time subscript, it could fluctuate over time. If neither currency is a hedging vehicle, this first term is zero.

The second covariance term of (11.1) states that the forward risk premium varies directly with the net indebtedness (net external investment) between residents of the foreign country and residents of the domestic country. If residents of the foreign country, for example, are indebted to residents of the domestic country, either domestic residents must hold currency F assets or foreign residents must hold liabilities in currency D, the domestic currency. Since currency F assets are the riskier of the two for domestic residents, expected yields on these assets must be higher in order for them to hold such assets. Likewise, currency D liabilities are riskier to foreign residents than currency F liabilities. Thus, foreign residents would demand a lower rate to incur them, and so foreign assets must yield a higher rate of return.

In the absence of an exogeneous supply of outside forward cover, the foreign exchange risk cannot be diversified away. Domestic residents would want to cover their holdings of foreign assets by selling currency F forward for currency D. Foreign residents holding currency D *liabilities* would also cover by selling currency F forward for currency D. That is, even in the absence of outside nominal assets, net indebtedness in the presence of real exchange rate uncertainty creates risk that is nondiversifiable. Although exchange rate fluctuations imply risk for both domestic and foreign residents, they cannot eliminate these risks simply by making forward contracts with each other if there is a net debt that must be financed. Both creditors as well as debtors would want to hedge their risk by entering forward contracts the same way.[18]

The empirical magnitude of this effect, however, is another matter. Net investment positions that are observed represent very small portions of total world wealth. Ibbotson and Siegel made rough estimates of this aggregate market value of world investable wealth. Their estimates are probably conservative, excluding non–U.S. real estate and personal holding such as automobiles, although including all government debt as wealth. Their estimates for 1975 and 1980 were $5.3 trillion and $11.5 trillion, respectively, while, for example, estimates of the net investment position of the United States in 1975 and 1980 were 93.6 billion and 122.7 billion, respectively. The magnitude of $\frac{E}{W}$, therefore, is small and the magnitude of changes in $\frac{E}{W}$ will typically be smaller still.[19]

INFLATION RATE UNCERTAINTY

A special case occurs when purchasing power parity strictly holds, so that exchange rate changes reflect changes in the internal purchasing power of each currency. Such a result arises when there are no barriers to trade and all individuals consume identical consumption bundles. Real exchange rates do not change. The one-period equilibrium forward risk premium relationship becomes the expression (11.2).

Conspicuously absent in (11.2) is the term that depends upon the net indebtedness of residents of the foreign country to residents of the domestic country. This occurs because, although assets are imperfect substitutes, residents of each country have no particular preference for assets denominated in their own currency. This is, the set of efficient portfolios that investors face are identical regardless of the country in which they are residents. Net indebtedness between residents of each country cannot affect the forward risk premium except through changes in aggregate world risk aversion, ϕ, which depends on the distribution of world wealth.

The forward risk premium, under purchasing power parity, is zero if the covariance of the exchange rate and return on total world wealth is zero. To the extent that changes in the supplies of nominal outside assets affect changes in the covariance of real world wealth with the exchange rate, these changes may affect the forward risk premium. Under purchasing power parity the rate of appreciation of the exchange rate is equal, in continuous time, and to a close approximation in discrete time, to the differences in inflation rates:

$$x = \P_d - \P_f \tag{11.4}$$

where: $\P_d$ = domestic inflation

$\P_f$ = foreign inflation.

Then, since cov $(\P_d - \P_f, R)$ = cov $(\P_d, R)$ - cov $(\P_f, R)$, the purchasing power parity forward rate of equation (11.2) may be expressed as:

$$\rho = \phi \left[\text{cov}(\P_d, R) - \text{cov}(\P_f, R) \right] . \tag{11.5}$$

This form, equivalent to (11.2) under purchasing power parity, shows the forward risk premium to be the result of different degrees of inflation risk in the underlying currencies.

EFFECTS OF CHANGES IN NOMINAL OUTSIDE ASSETS

The role of outside assets in the determination of the forward risk premium has been emphasized by Frankel.[20] The role of outside assets, nominal as well as real, in the determination of the forward risk premia is seen by writing the rate of return on world wealth, R, explicitly as a weighted average of the sum of returns on each of the components of total world wealth.

$$R = r_d \frac{B_d}{W} + r_f \frac{XB_f}{W} + k_d \frac{K_d}{W} + k_f \frac{XK_f}{W} \tag{11.6}$$

where: $W = B_d + XB_f + K_d + XK_f$

r_d, r_f are real returns on nominal domestic and foreign bonds;

k_d, k_f are real returns on domestic and foreign capital;

B_d, XB_f are the value of domestic and foreign bonds, nominal outside assets; and

K_d, XK_f are the value of domestic and foreign capital, real outside assets.

Substituting R into cov (x, R) of expression (11.2) yields:

$$\rho = \phi \left[\text{cov}\,(x, r_d)\,\frac{B_d}{W} + \text{cov}\,(x, r_f)\,\frac{XB_f}{W} + \text{cov}\,(x, k_d)\,\frac{K_d}{W} \right.$$
$$\left. + \text{cov}\,(x, k_f)\,\frac{XK_f}{W} \right] \,. \tag{11.7}$$

Expression (11.7) clearly shows the role of outside assets. In particular, if one assumes that returns on domestic and foreign capital are uncorrelated with changes in the exchange rate, the last two terms are zero. Then the forward risk premium varies only with the first two terms, and changes in nominal outside assets acquire substantial importance. Their salient role, however, appears only because the impact of net indebtedness and the impact of real assets were both assumed away.

Expressions (11.2) and (11.7) could also represent a forward risk premium in a nonpurchasing power parity world in which $\frac{E}{W}$ is zero. If inflation rate uncertainty is also assumed zero, only the supplies of real assets and the covariance of exchange rates with returns on real assets would affect the forward premium. Changes in the relative supplies of outside nominal assets would have no effect since the covariances of exchange rates with returns on nominal assets would be zero. If inflation rate uncertainty were positive but much smaller than uncertainty about returns on real assets, changes in the relative supplies of nominal outside assets through sterilized intervention would have an imperceptible impact on the forward risk premium. In effect, it would require the shifts in relative asset supplies to be large enough to alter the covariance of exchange rates with returns on total world wealth.

DIVERSIFIABILITY OF EXCHANGE RISK

Some perspective on the arguments for the diversifiability of exchange risk is gained from examining (11.1). If exchange risk is diversifiable, there would be no forward premium because there can be no systematic risk. Systematic risk arises from two sources. First, there is the relationship between exchange rate changes, x, and returns on total world assets—that is, cov (x, R). Secondly, there is real exchange rate uncertainty, cov (x, χ), and net foreign indebtedness, E. Exchange risk is diversifiable only if these terms are zero—that is, if

$$\rho = \phi \left[\text{cov}\,(x, R) + \text{cov}\,(X, \chi)\,E/W \right] = 0 \,.$$

Kouri and Frankel have argued that exchange risk may be diversifiable.[21] Their argument depends on a particular set of conditions that make these terms zero. That is, if

(1) there is no real exchange rate uncertainty;
(2) returns on capital are uncorrelated with exchange rate changes; and
(3) there are no nominal outside assets.

These conditions are sufficient to imply that the forward risk premium is zero, since (1) implies that cov $(x, X) = 0$, and condition (2) and (3) imply that cov $(x, R) = 0$.

These, however, are not the only conditions implying the diversifiability of exchange risk. Sufficient conditions are also:

(1) there is no inflation rate uncertainty;
(2) returns on capital are uncorrelated with exchange rate changes; and
(3) the ratio of net indebtedness between countries to total world wealth $\left(\frac{E}{W}\right)$ is zero.

Both arguments for the diversifiability of exchange risk depend on making the empirically incorrect assumption of the exchange rate being uncorrelated with returns on total assets.[22] The effect of these assumptions is to make exposed assets behave like zero-beta assets.[23]

EMPIRICAL EVIDENCE

Testing for the existence of forward rate bias is extensive. Kohlhagen and Levich provide surveys of early studies that generally conclude the forward premium to be an unbiased, but generally poor, predictor of the subsequent change in the spot rate.[24] More recent studies seriously challenge this view of an unbiased forward rate. Meese and Singleton reject the hypothesis of a nonvarying ex ante risk premium, lending support to the view of a time-varying forward risk premium.[25] Hansen and Hodrick, using overlapping data, find evidence that forward rate forecasts could be improved by using lagged ex post differences between the forward rate and the subsequent future spot rate for some currencies during the recent floating period. They further find evidence during the period of the 1920's in the pound/mark and pound/franc exchange rates of a mean bias.[26] Bilson finds forward premia to be significantly negatively related to subsequent rates of depreciation.[27] Robicheck and Eaker find significant covariance between exchange rate changes and returns on a world market portfolio, proxied by returns on the S &P 500.[28] Geweke and Feige, and Hakkio also, find the forward rate to be a biased estimate for the future spot rate during the recent period.[29] Cumby and Obstfeld reject the hypothesis that return differentials between similar assets in different currencies reflect only expected changes in the exchange rate.[30]

Relatively few studies, however, attempt to estimate the effect of the various determinants on the forward premium. Difficulties in measuring national wealth, outside bonds, real capital, net foreign indebtedness, as well as ex ante expected returns limit empirical implementations. Roll and Solnik present evidence in support of the hypothesis that real exchange risk is a factor in explaining the forward risk premia.[31] They use Solnik's model and estimate returns based on 1971–75 data for eight countries. Because data limitations prevent their using net indebtedness measures to weight their exchange risk measures, they report results using an equally weighted average and find a positive measure for most currencies using each of the seven currencies as a base. As noted in discussing this paper, the appropriate weights would be very small fractions and of different signs. Given the problems involved, the authors are justifiably skeptical that the results represent tests of the hypothesis.

Dooley and Isard test for the existence of forward risk premia.[32] Starting with a two-country portfolio balance model, in which wealth is held as outside money and outside bonds, they solve the model for the forward risk premium. They estimate the forward risk premium of the dollar/mark using estimates of German, U.S., and the rest of the world levels of wealth and German supplies of money. Their estimated risk premiums explain only a small proportion of the actual change in the ex post change in the spot rate with respect to the forward rate. Dooley and Isard conclude that in the portfolio balance model, or at least their representation of it, expected exchange rate changes can play only a small part of observed exchange rate changes.

Frankel reports running many regressions of the ex post risk premia of the dollar/mark exchange rate on various measures of money, bonds, and income in each country. He is unable to reject the null hypothesis of no risk premia.[33]

While evidence of forward exchange rate bias mounts, there exists little evidence that such bias is related to a risk premium. Indeed, the bias measured by Hanson and Hodrick would imply that assets dominated in pounds would have been riskier than assets dominated in marks during the 1920s if the bias represented a risk premium. Bilson indicates that the mean return would have been too large to be explained by the risk premium hypothesis and hence doubts the speculative efficiency of the foreign exchange market.[34] Sharp finds that the covariances of exchange rates with returns on world assets, while significant, to be unrelated to forward bias in a manner suggested by the theory.[35] While measurement problems make inferences from the data hazardous, there does not appear any firm basis on which to link observed bias with risk premia. The signs and magnitude of forward bias suggest some other explanations, such as market segmentation, inelastic speculative demand, or other market imperfections may be more relevant than explanation based on risk premia.

CONCLUSIONS

International capital asset pricing theories explicitly model the effects of uncertainty of exchange rates, returns on nominal assets, and returns on real assets on international interest differentials. Such theories seem to support the imperfect substitutability of domestic and foreign bonds and, hence, the possible effectiveness of foreign exchange intervention in which the relative supplies of those national bonds are changed while the national money supplies are left unchanged. While the theories do confirm the effect of such changes on expected return differentials, or on foreign exchange rate risk premia, the effects of such intervention should be imperceptible in a world in which the magnitude of inflation uncertainty is small relative to the magnitude of the uncertainty about returns on real assets and in which outside nominal assets represent a small fraction of total world wealth. In a world in which exchange rates vary in real terms and real assets are the major component of wealth, foreign exchange risk premia would be primarily determined by systematic variation of exchange rates with returns on real assets. A secondary effect would be proportional to the magnitude of the external debt as a percentage of world wealth. While these asset pricing models may not portray actual international asset pricing behavior, they do not give much support to the effectiveness of sterilized intervention.

NOTES TO CHAPTER 11

1. For recent surveys, see Dale Henderson and Stephanie Sampson, "Intervention in Foreign Exchange Markets: A Summary of Ten Staff Studies," *Federal Reserve Bulletin* (November 1983): 830–36; Ralph W. Tyron, "Small Empirical Models of Exchange Market Intervention: A Review of Current Literature," Staff Study 134, Board of Governors Federal Reserve System (September 1983); Robert Solomen, "Official Intervention in Foreign Exchange Markets: A Survey," *Brookings Discussion Papers in International Finance* 1 (June 1983).

2. Harry M. Markowitz, "Portfolio Selection," *Journal of Finance* (March 1952): 77–91; William F. Sharpe, "Capital Asset Prices: A Theory of Market Equilibrium Under Conditions of Risk," *Journal of Finance* (September 1964): 425–42; John Linter, "The Valuation of Risk Assets and the Selection of Risky Investments in Stock Portfolios and Capital Budgets," *Review of Economics and Statistics* (February 1965): 13–37; Jan Mossin, "Equilibrium in a Capital Asset Market," *Econometrica* (October 1966): 768–83; Kenneth S. Arrow, "The Role of Securities in the Optimal Allocation of Risk Bearing," in *Essays in the Theory of Risk Bearing* (Chicago, Illinois: Markham Press, 1971), ch. 4; and Gerald Debreu, *Theory of Value* (New York: John Wiley and Sons, 1959).

3. The capital asset pricing model is subject to all the criticism of using mean and variance as objects of choice in a utility function. This has been defended as a useful approximation. See Hain Levy and Harry M. Markowitz, "Approximating Expected Utility by a Function of Mean and Variance," *American Economic Review* (June 1981): 308–17, and references cited therein. For recent criticism in the empirical implementation, see Richard Roll, "A Critique of the Asset Pricing Theory's Tests," *Journal of Finan-*

cial Economics (March 1977): 129–76; Pao L. Cheng and Robert Grauer, "An Alternative Test of The Capital Asset Pricing Model," *American Economic Review* (September 1980): 660–71; Stuart M. Turnbull and Ralph A. Winter, "An Alternative Test of the Capital Asset Pricing Model: Comment," *American Economic Review* (December 1982): 1194–95; Richard J. Sweeney, "An Alternative Test of the Capital Asset Pricing Model: Comment," *American Economic Review* (December 1982): 1196–1200; and Pao L. Cheng and Robert L. Grauer, "An Alternative Test of the Capital Asset Pricing Model: Reply," *American Economic Review* (December 1982): 1201–1207.

4. Robert C. Merton, "Optimum Consumption and Portfolio Rules in Continuous-Time Model," *Journal of Economic Theory* (December 1971): 373–413; and "An Intertemporal Capital Asset Pricing Model, *Econometrica* (September 1973): 867–87.

5. Bruno H. Solnik, *European Capital Markets* (Lexington, Massachusetts: Lexington Books, 1973), or "An Equilibrium Model of the International Capital Market," *Journal of Economic Theory* (August 1974): 500–24; Frederick L. A. Grauer, Robert H. Litzenberger, and Richard H. Steehle, "Sharing Rules and Equilibrium in an International Capital Market Under Uncertainty," *Journal of Financial Economics* (June 1976): 233–356; and Pentti Kouri, "International Investment and Interest Rate Linkages Under Flexible Exchange Rates," in Robert Z. Aliber, ed., *The Political Economy of Monetary Reform* (Montclair, New Jersey: Allanheld, Osman and Co., 1977).

6. Economic residency refers to the basket of goods investors use to measure their real returns from an asset. This basket of goods reflects consumption preferences among tradable goods as well as the geographic availability of nontradable goods. Since the latter contribute a large share to an investor's consumption bundle, economic residency is a relevant distinction. Economic residency does not depend upon a monetary unit in which an investor calculates his nominal returns, only on the commodity bundle in which he calculates real returns. In a purchasing power parity model, economic residency ceases to be a distinction between investors. In this sense, a purchasing power parity model is a multicurrency domestic model.

7. Jeffrey Frankel, "The Diversifiability of Exchange Risk," *Journal of International Economics* (August 1979): 379–93. The extent to which government debt remains undiscounted by the general public is the subject of continuing theoretical and empirical controversy. For recent contributions and references to this debate, see Roger C. Kormedi, "Government Debt, Government Spending, and Private Sector Behavior," *American Economic Review* (December 1983): 994–1010; and Charles I. Plosser, "Government Financing and Asset Returns, *Journal of Monetary Economics* (May 1982): 325–52.

8. Eugene Fama and Andre Farber, "Money, Bonds, and Foreign Exchange," *American Economic Review* (September 1979): 639–49.

9. Pentti J. K. Kouri, "The Effect of Risk on Interest Rates: A Synthesis of the Macroeconomic and Financial Views," NBER Working Paper No. 643 (March 1981).

10. Richard C. Stapleton and Marti G. Subrahmanyam, "Uncertain Inflation, Exchange Rates, and Bond Yields," Salomon Brothers Center for the Study of Financial Institutions, New York, April 1980.

11. Rudiger Dornbusch, "Exchange Risk and the Macroeconomics of Exchange Rate Determination," in Robert Hawkins, Richard Levich, and Wihlborg, ed., *The Internationalization of Financial Markets and National Economic Policy* (Greenwich, Conn.: JAI Press, 1982).

12. Pentti J. K. Kouri and Jorge Brage de Macedo, "Exchange Rates and the International Adjustment Process," *Brookings Papers on Economic Activity* 1 (1978), pp. 111–50.

13. Rudiger Dornbusch, "Exchange Risk and Macroeconomics."

14. Rene Stulz, "The Forward Exchange Rate and Macroeconomics" (Rochester, New York: University of Rochester, 1980).

15. For a deviation of this formula in an N country world as well as a two-country world, see Peter A. Sharp, "Forward Exchange Risk Premia in Efficient Markets," Claremont Graduate School, 1984.

16. This form closely corresponds to the expression derived in Pentti Kouri, "International Investment and Interest Rate Linkages," p. 85.

17. See Bruno H. Solnik, "An Equilibrium Model": 517.

18. See Jeffrey Frankel, "Diversifiability of Exchange Risk," for an argument that such risks are offsetting. This argument is supported by a model in which exchange rates do not fluctuate in real terms.

19. See Roger G. Ibbotson and Laurence B. Siegel, "The World Market Wealth Portfolio," *Journal of Portfolio Management* (Winter 1983): 5–17, for annual estimates of world wealth broken into asset class from 1960 through 1970. Figures for the international investment position of the United States were obtained from *Survey of Current Business*, August 1975 and August 1981 issues.

20. Jeffrey Frankel, "Diversifiability of Exchange Risk."

21. Pentti Kouri, "International Investment and Interest Rate Linkages Under Flexible Exchange Rates": 84–85; and Jeffrey Frankel, "The Diversifiability of Exchange Risk."

22. The portfolio balance model, which has been used to examine the relationship between intervention and exchange rates, generally omits real assets by assuming wealth to consist solely of money and government bonds. Privately issued bonds and stocks are excluded on the grounds that these private securities will net out when all such claims are aggregated, even though the real assets on which these privately issued bonds are based are excluded from wealth. Omitting real assets from these models greatly exaggerates the impact that changes in the supplies of nominal assets may have on relative interest rates or risk premia. Whether domestically issued government debt is an outside asset or whether it is an imperfect or perfect substitute with debt issued by a foreign government may be essentially irrelevant if claims on capital are close substitutes with foreign debt. Papers that find a lack of an empirical relationship between changes in outside nominal assets and forward risk premia are discussed below.

23. Beta is the covariance of an asset's returns with the returns on the true market portfolio, divided by the variance of returns on the market port-

folio. A zero-beta asset is therefore an asset whose returns are uncorrelated with returns on the true market portfolio. See Fischer Black, "Capital Market Equilibrium with Restricted Borrowing," *Journal of Business* (July 1972): 444–55.

24. Steven Kohlhagen, *The Behavior of Foreign Exchange Markets*; and Richard Levich, "On the Efficiency of Markets in Forward Exchange."

25. Richard A. Meese and Kenneth Singleton, "Rational Expectations, Risk Premia, and the Market for Spot and Forward Exchange," Federal Reserve Board of Governors, 1980).

26. Peter Lars Hansen and Robert J. Hodrick, "Forward Exchange Rates as Optimal Predictors of Future Spot Rates: An Econometric Analysis," *Journal of Political Economy* (October 1980): 829–53. See also, Lars Peter Hansen and Robert J. Hodrick, "Risk Averse Speculation in the Forward Foreign Exchange Market: An Econometric Analysis of Linear Models," in Jacob A. Frenkel, ed., *Exchange Rates and International Macroeconomics* (Chicago: University of Chicago Press, 1983).

27. John F. O. Bilson, "The Speculative Efficiency Hypothesis," *Journal of Business* (July 1981): 435–51.

28. Alexander A. Robichek and Mark R. Eaker, "Foreign Exchange Hedging and the Capital Asset Pricing Model," *Journal of Finance* 33 (June 1978): 1011–18.

29. John F. Geweke and Edgar Fiege, "Some Joint Tests of the Efficiency of Markets for Forward Exchange," *Review of Economics and Statistics* (August 1979): 334–41.

30. Robert F. Cumby and Maurice Obstfeld, "A Note on Exchange-Rate Expectations and Nominal Interest Differentials: A Test of the Fisher Hypothesis," *Journal of Finance* (June 1981): 697–703.

31. Richard Roll and Bruno Solnik, "A Pure Foreign Exchange Asset Pricing Model," *Journal of International Economics* (May 1977): 161–80.

32. Michael P. Dooley and Peter Isard, "The Portfolio Balance Model of Exchange Rates."

33. Jeffrey A. Frankel, "Tests of Rational Expectations in the Forward Exchange Market," *Southern Economic Journal* (April 1980): 1083–1101.

34. John F. O. Bilson, "The Speculative Efficiency Hypothesis.

35. Peter A. Sharp, "Forward Exchange Risk Premia in Efficient Markets."

12 DOMESTIC VERSUS INTERNATIONAL INFLUENCES ON PROTECTIONIST PRESSURES IN THE UNITED STATES

Susan Feigenbaum and Thomas D. Willett

There has been considerable interest in the influence of fluctuations in the domestic economy and developments in the international sector on protectionist pressures. Most observers of trade policy developments would agree that the likelihood of an industry seeking and securing protectionist policy support increases when the industry is in economic distress, particularly when it appears that this distress is not primarily of the industry's own making. Thus, while the traditional public choice view that protectionist policies result from the greatest political effectiveness of small well-organized (industry) groups than that of large unorganized groups (consumer-voters) gives important insight into the policy process, the political system does provide some checks on protectionist attempts, frequently requiring a broad measure of general sympathy for an industry's plight before protectionist policies will be implemented by the government.[1]

Economic hardships thus increase both the demand for protection by particular groups and the likelihood that such efforts will be successful. The early 1980s in the United States provides a clear example of this. The combination of a severe domestic recession and a strong dollar and huge trade and current account deficits was accompanied by a substantial increase in protectionist pressures.

There has been considerable disagreement among informed observers, however, about the relative influence on protectionist pressures of the state of the domestic economy versus direct international factors such as the strength of the dollar and state of the trade balance.[2] This debate is particularly relevant for predicting the course of protectionism in the face of domestic economic recov-

181

ery combined with widespread expectations of a continued strong dollar and weak trade balance.

What does historical experience tell us about the relative importance of these factors when their influences conflict? This question is difficult to answer because we have no good general measure of the overall degree of protectionist pressures or policy actions. And, of course, the historical record will often be a less secure guide to the future of political actions taken by a small and changing group of relevant actors than to the average market reactions of large numbers of economic actors. Despite these important caveats, however, we believe that systematic historical analysis can shed important light on the issue. In this study we make a preliminary effort in this direction by following the suggestion of Takacs (1981) to use the number of escape clause cases brought before the International Trade Commission as one important indicator of protectionist pressures. We should stress that such analysis clearly needs to be extended in future research to attempt to take into account broader measures of protectionist pressures that may be developed.[3]

Earlier work by Takacs (1981) and us (Feigenbaum, Ortiz, and Willett 1984) showed that in simple regressions of domestic unemployment, capacity utilization, import penetration (the ratio of imports to GNP), and the trade balance on the cases brought before the ITC, all of these variables were statistically significant. However, when the effects of the changes in trade legislation in 1962 and 1974 are taken into account through the use of dummy variables, the significance of the international variables tended to disappear.

In this study, we extend our previous work to focus on the post-1962 period and include three measures of the real exchange rate (using, respectively, wholesale prices, export unit values, and value added deflators) as well as import penetration and the trade and current account deficits. The results are reported in Table 12-1. We find that over the period investigated (1963-81), while they generally have the expected sign, none of these international variables yields a consistently significant degree of explanation. On the other hand the state of the domestic economy is significant in almost all of the equations.

While we report here only the results for our capacity utilization measure, our previous study found that using the unemployment rate instead gives roughly similar results. We also ran lagged values of the independent variables and did not find them to offer significant explanatory power. This is particularly interesting in light of the argument by Bergsten and Williamson (1983) that the strength of the dollar is an important leading indicator of protectionist pressures.[4]

We should note also that the dummy for the 1974 trade act is consistently significant, and, as would be expected from its loosening of the criteria for receiving escape clause protection, it has a positive sign. While not statistically significant, we find all but one of the signs on the inflation variable to be negative, suggesting that increasing concern about inflation may offer a mild counter to protectionist pressures.

As indicated above, cases brought to the ITC are only one of the major channels of protectionist pressure. Thus, while it would be premature to conclude that exchange rates and the trade balance have no impact on protectionist pressures in the United States, our analysis does offer some support to those who have argued that the state of the domestic economy is of greater importance.

NOTES TO CHAPTER 12

1. On the public choice approach to explaining trade policy see, for example, Amacher, Tollison and Willett (1978); Baldwin (1982); Frey (1984); and Olson (1982) and the references cited in these works. For discussions of recent developments in U.S. trade policies, see Cline (1983) and Destler (1980), and for theoretical discussions and empirical evidence on how macroeconomic conditions are likely to influence regulatory policies in general, see Peltzman (1976) and Amacher, et al. (forthcoming). For particular emphasis on the role of public opinion, which generally reflects considerable support for protectionist policies when they are seen as measures to save American jobs, see Amacher, Tollison, and Willett (1978) and McElrath (1984).
2. See, for example, the conflicting views expressed in Bergsten, et al. (1982).
3. This would seem to be particularly important as the general qualitative evaluations recently offered by Bergsten and Williamson (1983) differ substantially from the results of our quantitative study reported below.
4. The full set of results is available from the authors upon request. Write in care of The Claremont Center for Economic Policy Studies, Department of Economics, Claremont Graduate School, Claremont, CA 91711.

Table 12-1. Determinants of Protectionist Pressures.

Constant	Real Exchange Rate (Wholesale Prices)	Real GNP	Capacity Utilization Rate – Manufacturing	Trade Balance	Import Penetration – Imports/GNP	Balance of Goods and Services	Consumer Price Index	1974 Trade Act Dummy	Adjusted R^2	Durbin-Watson Statistic
20.048** (2.195)	-0.149 (-1.760)								0.104	2.055
47.548 (1.608)	-0.032 (-0.205)	0.002 (0.252)	-51.012* (-2.874)						0.362	2.170
61.761 (1.785)	-0.051 (-0.321)	-0.005 (-0.435)	-56.523* (-2.948)	-0.094 (-0.817)					0.348	2.314
57.365 (1.777)	-0.107 (-0.589)	0.011 (0.804)	-56.061* (-2.949)		-106.090 (-0.809)				0.347	1.958
66.908 (1.928)	-0.091 (-0.559)	-0.002 (-0.259)	-59.714* (-3.061)			-0.126 (-1.056)			0.367	2.390
56.022 (1.971)	-0.086 (-0.590)	0.009 (1.050)	-59.113* (-3.383)				-0.661 (-1.666)		0.430	2.361
60.714 (1.814)	-0.088 (-0.571)	0.006 (0.422)	-60.600* (-3.229)	-0.035 (-0.293)			-0.616 (-1.403)		0.390	2.387
55.748 (1.779)	-0.083 (-0.468)	0.009 (0.646)	-59.010* (-3.179)		3.894 (0.026)		-0.668 (-1.372)		0.386	2.370
60.666 (1.760)	-0.097 (-0.601)	0.007 (0.611)	-60.767* (-3.168)			-0.036 (-0.259)	-0.594 (-1.226)		0.389	2.383
32.286 (1.243)	0.041 (0.306)	-0.006 (-0.783)	-34.184** (-2.066)					6.300* (2.553)	0.534	2.509
32.231 (0.976)	0.041 (0.287)	-0.006 (-0.556)	-34.157 (-1.754)	0.0003 (0.0029)				6.303* (2.278)	0.498	2.509

48.752 (1.977)	-0.096 (-0.698)	0.011 (1.055)	-40.442* (-2.666)		-218.610** (-2.080)			7.853* (3.356)	0.623	2.783
50.996 (1.701)	-0.017 (-0.120)	-0.009 (-1.225)	-42.686* (-2.402)			-0.121 (-1.199)		6.242 (2.569)	0.548	2.769
33.818 (1.044)	0.004 (0.026)	0.003 (0.244)	-39.230** (-2.009)	0.039 (0.355)			-0.489 (-1.239)	5.787** (2.109)	0.518	2.767
48.704 (1.897)	-0.098 (-0.676)	0.011 (1.015)	-40.013* (-2.406)		-226.850 (-1.528)		0.039 (0.082)	7.982* (2.752)	0.592	2.776
49.197 (1.599)	-0.026 (-0.178)	-0.005 (-0.393)	-44.645* (-2.427)			-0.076 (-0.618)	-0.299 (-0.668)	5.718** (2.195)	0.528	2.781
32.754* (2.335)			-36.191* (-2.202)					3.582* (2.379)	0.536	2.467

(Table 12-1. continued overleaf)

Table 12-1. continued

Constant	Real Exchange Rate (Export Unit Values)	Real GNP	Capacity Utilization Rate – Manufacturing	Trade Balance	Import Penetration – Imports/GNP	Balance of Goods and Services	Consumer Price Index	1974 Trade Act Dummy	Adjusted R^2	Durbin–Watson Statistic
-4.992 (-0.326)	0.087 (0.581)								-0.038	1.612
34.326 (1.554)	0.069 (0.588)	0.004 (0.925)	-49.943* (-2.825)						0.375	2.079
45.365 (1.666)	0.058 (0.486)	-0.002 (-0.216)	-54.960* (-2.850)	-0.082 (-0.716)					0.354	2.222
35.454 (1.551)	0.051 (0.406)	0.009 (0.661)	-52.763* (-2.728)		-50.949 (-0.426)				0.339	1.984
41.461 (1.894)	0.012 (0.087)	0.011 (1.731)	-58.421* (-3.236)				-0.600 (-1.442)		0.417	2.335
43.325 (1.760)	0.058 (0.486)	0.002 (0.555)	-56.954* (-2.904)			-0.097 (-0.859)			0.364	2.252
45.010 (1.680)	0.010 (0.085)	0.009 (0.743)	-59.679* (-3.082)	-0.030 (-0.249)			-0.559 (-1.214)		0.375	2.360
41.464 (1.832)	0.017 (0.134)	0.008 (0.584)	-57.233* (-3.001)		41.046 (0.306)		-0.677 (-1.359)		0.377	2.434
42.389 (1.733)	0.012 (0.094)	0.011 (1.228)	-58.999* (-3.015)			-0.014 (-0.102)	-0.570 (-1.094)		0.373	2.340
30.328 (1.608)	0.070 (0.708)	-0.007 (-1.331)	-33.279** (-2.033)					6.152* (2.588)	0.547	2.381
29.987 (1.223)	0.071 (0.679)	-0.007 (-0.889)	-33.081 (-1.726)	0.002 (0.022)				6.171* (2.353)	0.512	2.381

33.203 (1.888)	0.010 (0.101)	0.011 (0.973)	-38.617* (-2.494)		-179.97 (-1.800)			7.859* (3.272)	0.610	2.665
40.514 (1.974)	0.058 (0.586)	-0.009 (-1.617)	-40.881* (-2.351)			-0.110 (-1.177)		6.303* (2.684)	0.559	2.653
30.560 (1.256)	0.031 (0.288)	0.002 (0.210)	-38.117 (-1.953)	0.040 (0.362)			-0.454 (-1.116)	5.830* (2.229)	0.521	2.700
33.072 (1.749)	0.010 (0.100)	0.011 (0.933)	-38.451* (-2.235)		-182.500 (-1.316)		0.013 (0.028)	7.902 (2.676)	0.577	2.659
40.305 (1.905)	0.039 (0.361)	-0.004 (-0.431)	-42.685* (-2.332)			-0.076 (-0.635)	-0.231 (-0.488)	5.921* (2.329)	0.532	2.702
32.754* (2.335)			-36.191* (-2.202)					3.582* (2.379)	0.536	2.467

(Table 12-1. continued overleaf)

Table 12-1. continued

Constant	Real Exchange Rate (Value-Added Deflator)	Real GNP	Capacity Utilization Rate—Manufacturing	Trade Balance	Import Penetration—Imports/GNP	Balance of Goods and Services	Consumer Price Index	1974 Trade Act Dummy	Adjusted R^2	Durbin-Watson Statistic
10.723 (1.983)**	-0.060 (-1.280)								0.034	2.080
40.446 (2.192)	0.016 (0.317)	0.004 (0.876)	-52.010* (-2.899)						0.365	2.121
51.152** (2.181)	0.014 (0.259)	-0.002 (-0.175)	-56.978* (-2.945)	-0.086 (-0.757)					0.346	2.269
40.869** (2.157)	0.004 (0.075)	0.011 (0.772)	-54.449* (-2.860)		-62.559 (-0.500)				0.332	2.018
49.844* (2.309)	0.005 (0.098)	0.002 (0.440)	-58.444* (-2.984)			-0.100 (-0.859)			0.354	2.322
43.373* (2.440)	-0.005 (-0.095)	0.012 (1.740)	-58.608* (-3.308)				-0.623 (-1.531)		0.417	2.374
46.829** (2.020)	-0.004 (-0.083)	0.009 (0.750)	-59.865* (-3.143)	-0.029 (-0.245)			-0.582 (-1.283)		0.375	2.395
43.433* (2.361)	0.001 (0.002)	0.008 (0.628)	-57.837* (-3.118)		38.109 (0.272)		-0.690 (-1.412)		0.376	2.453
44.564** (2.052)	-0.006 (-0.103)	0.011 (1.231)	-59.220* (-3.068)			-0.014 (-0.104)	-0.595 (-1.195)		0.373	2.384
34.430* (2.189)	0.032 (0.729)	-0.006 (-1.043)	-35.644** (-2.182)					6.375* (2.660)	0.548	2.425
34.179 (1.595)	0.032 (0.699)	-0.006 (-0.706)	-35.491 (-1.875)	0.002 (0.018)				6.392* (2.409)	0.513	2.425

34.239* (2.341)	0.001 (0.021)	0.011 (1.021)	-38.881* (-2.542)		-182.200 (-1.788)			7.889* (3.310)	0.609	2.690
44.354* (2.459)	0.020 (0.455)	-0.008 (-1.352)	-42.317* (-2.444)			-0.106 (-1.099)		6.437 (2.705)	0.555	2.693
31.990 (1.501)	0.017 (0.556)	0.003 (0.267)	-39.195** (-2.060)	0.039 (0.365)			-0.451 (-1.125)	5.955** (2.243)	0.523	2.706
34.200* (2.201)	0.001 (0.016)	0.011 (0.973)	-38.812* (-2.304)		-183.97 (-1.294)		0.005 (0.012)	7.909* (2.678)	0.577	2.688
42.440* (2.255)	0.015 (0.809)	-0.003 (-0.332)	-43.834* (-2.439)			-0.068 (-0.570)	-0.261 (-0.574)	5.968* (2.316)	0.530	2.927
32.754* (2.335)			-36.191* (-2.202)					3.582* (2.379)	0.536	2.467

t-statistics in parentheses.
  *Significant at 1 percent level.
 **Significant at 5 percent level.

REFERENCES

Amacher, Ryan C., et al. Forthcoming. "The Behavior of Regulatory Activity over the Business Cycle," *Economic Inquiry*.

Amacher, Ryan C., Robert Tollison, and Thomas D. Willett. 1978. "The Divergence Between Theory and Practice," in Walter Adams, et al., eds., *Tariffs, Quotas, and Trade*. San Francisco: Institute for Contemporary Studies.

Baldwin, Robert. 1982. "The Political Economy of Protectionism," in Jagdish N. Bhagwati, ed., *Import Competition and Response*. Chicago: University of Chicago Press.

Bergesten, C. Fred, et al. 1982. *From Rambouillet to Versailles: A Symposium*. Princeton, N.J.: Princeton Essays in International Finance, No. 149 (December).

Bergsten, C. Fred, and John Williamson. 1983. "Exchange Rates and Trade Policy," in William R. Cline, ed., *Trade Policy Issues in the 1980s*. Cambridge, Mass.: M.I.T. Press for the Institute for International Economics.

Cline, William R., ed. 1983. *Trade Policy in the 1980s*. Cambridge, Mass.: M.I.T. Press for the Institute for International Economics.

Destler, I.M. 1980. *Making Foreign Economic Policy*. Washington, D.C.: The Brookings Institution.

Feigenbaum, Susan, Henry Ortiz, and Thomas D. Willett. 1984. "Protectionist Pressures and Aggregate Economic Conditions." *Claremont Working Papers*, The Claremont Center for Economic Policy Studies. Forthcoming in *Economic Inquiry*.

Feigenbaum, Susan, and Thomas D. Willett. 1984. "Political Parties, Economic Conditions, and Protectionist Policies: Evidence from the U.S. International Trade Commission." *Claremont Working Papers*, The Claremont Center for Economic Policy Studies.

Frey, Bruno S. 1984. "The Public Choice View of International Political Economy," *Industrial Organization* 38, no. 1 (Winter): 199–223.

McElrath, Erin. 1984. "American Voter Perspectives on Trade Protectionism: A Public Choice Approach," *Claremont Journal of Public Affairs* 11 (Summer): 50–62.

Olson, Mancur. 1982. *The Rise and Decline of Nations*. New Haven, Conn.: Yale University Press.

Peltzman, Sam. 1976. "Toward a More General Theory of Regulation," *Journal of Law and Economics* 19, no. 2 (August): 211–40.

Takacs, Wendy E. 1981. "Pressures for Protectionism: An Empirical Analysis," *Economic Inquiry* 19, no. 4 (October): 687–93.

▌▌▌ INTERNATIONAL EFFECTS ON THE U.S. ECONOMY

13 INTERNATIONAL ASPECTS OF MACROECONOMIC POLICY
An Overview

Thomas D. Willett and Marc Bremer

Over the past decade interest in the influence of international developments on the U.S. economy has increased tremendously. In this respect, the United States has become much more like the smaller countries of the world who have long focused on the importance of international economic developments on their domestic economic well-being.[1] And, just as in other countries, there has been a strong tendency for commentators both to exaggerate the quantitative influence of international interdependence and to emphasize its negative rather than positive aspects.

Thus, for example, with the strong dollar of the early 1980s, popular discussion in the United States tended to focus on the contribution made by the U.S. trade deficit to the depth of the U.S. recession, while discussion in Europe focused on the short-run domestic inflationary pressures stimulated by the corresponding weakness of the European currencies.[2] Although not ignored by economists, the counterpart effects of the strong dollar in reducing the rate of U.S. inflation and the weak European currencies in stimulating trade and employment in the short-run have received much less public attention.

In Chapter 14, Radcliffe, Warga, and Willett show that the international sector has had a nontrivial impact on the U.S. economy through a number of channels but that these efforts have been far from dominant in explaining U.S. economic development on average. Furthermore, even if we limit our analysis to output and employment effects, the easily acquired public impression of the international sector as a typically destabilizing element for the U.S. economy does not hold up. Table 13-1 compares the real and nominal changes in U.S. net exports (as a percent of GNP) with changes in GNP for the United States

193

over the years 1950 to 1982. There is virtually no difference between the actual annual standard deviations of U.S. GNP growth and those that would have occurred if there had been no fluctuations in net exports. The actual standard deviations were 3.40 and 2.81 percent for nominal and real GNP growth, respectively, while the hypothetical standard deviations with no changes in net exports were 3.34 and 2.81 percent, respectively (mean growth rates were 7.8 and 3.4 percent). This suggests that fluctuations in net exports had a stabilizing influence on GNP roughly as often as not.[3]

In fact, calculations summarized in Table 13-2 of the relationships between changes in net exports and estimates of output gaps (deviations from full employ-

Table 13-1. Real and Nominal Changes in U.S. Net Exports and GNP.

	Ratio of the Change in Nominal Net Exports to Nominal GNP	Ratio of the Change in Real Net Exports to Real GNP	Percentage Change in Nominal GNP	Percentage Change in Real GNP
1950	−1.50087	−0.897532	10.9175	8.65501
1951	0.665054	0.724888	15.4625	8.33957
1952	−0.344828	−0.366178	5.19952	3.69347
1953	−0.517994	−0.497114	5.40230	3.79494
1954	0.327154	0.340854	0.00000	−1.20269
1955	0.125000	0.060836	9.05126	6.71969
1956	0.545411	0.416915	5.42500	2.14448
1957	0.450450	0.248611	5.28812	1.81656
1958	−0.889482	−0.910560	1.28379	−0.42409
1959	−0.389424	−0.401829	8.49455	5.99207
1960	0.809477	0.678242	3.81226	2.14771
1961	0.209684	0.105736	3.57354	2.63157
1962	−0.0353982	−0.124953	7.70111	5.77584
1963	0.201106	0.228228	5.61062	4.02349
1964	0.392034	0.387951	6.87112	5.27328
1965	−0.188106	−0.290541	8.37384	6.03605
1966	−0.304233	−0.365556	9.39083	5.97224
1967	−0.0250125	−0.108760	5.76719	2.70106
1968	−0.228990	−0.330782	9.22962	4.61736
1969	−0.0105933	−0.0919456	8.08335	2.78802
1970	0.251838	0.276345	5.15890	−0.183891
1971	−0.241277	−0.204918	8.55243	3.38983
1972	−0.286702	−0.0758917	10.0501	5.65752
1973	1.01779	1.17994	11.8475	5.76777
1974	−0.0557802	0.986921	8.12726	−0.637806
1975	0.864963	0.357259	8.01841	−1.17950
1976	−0.756694	−0.523802	10.8959	5.40760
1977	−0.927905	−0.248230	11.6589	5.50763
1978	0.134017	0.139024	12.8030	5.03030
1979	0.591447	0.892254	11.7335	2.83609
1980	0.455737	0.909091	8.90479	−0.365014
1981	0.0306362	−0.572341	11.5681	1.94030
1982	−0.313982	−0.792952	4.07802	−1.80354

Source: Export and GNP series in The Economic Report of the President 1983.

ment) show the international trade sector to have contributed mildly to the stability of U.S. output more often than not. (Since analysts differ considerably on the importance they ascribe to levels versus changes in output gaps for macroeconomic analysis, we have presented calculations giving the relationships for both levels and changes.) In each combination of calculations, the number of years of stabilizing international influence was either substantially greater or approximately equal to the number of years of destabilizing influence. In no combination of the calculations did the number of destabilizing years substantially exceed stabilizing ones.

These results should not be surprising to those familiar with the economic literature on stabilization policy in open economies.[4] Using simple Keynesian models the early contributions to this literature showed that in the absence of

Table 13-2. Annual Relationships between Levels and Changes in Net Exports and Output Gaps the United States, 1950-82.

Nominal

	G > 0	G < 0			G > 0	G < 0
NE > 0	16	15		Ch: NE > 0	9	7
NE < 0	2	0		Ch: NE < 0	9	8

Stabilizing Years: 16   Stabilizing Years: 17
Destabilizing Years: 17   Destabilizing Years: 16

	Ch: G > 0	Ch: G < 0			Ch: G > 0	Ch: G < 0
NE > 0	17	14		Ch: NE > 0	10	6
NE < 0	0	2		Ch: NE > 0	7	10

Stabilizing Years: 19   Stabilizing Years: 20
Destabilizing Years: 14   Destabilizing Years: 13

Real

	G > 0	G < 0			G > 0	G < 0
NE > 0	18	15		Ch: NE > 0	9	7
NE < 0	0	0		Ch: NE < 0	9	8

Stabilizing Years: 18   Stabilizing Years: 17
Destabilizing Years: 15   Destabilizing Years: 16

	Ch: G > 0	Ch: G < 0			Ch: G > 0	Ch: G < 0
NE > 0	17	16		Ch: NE > 0	10	6
NE < 0	0	0		Ch: NE > 0	7	10

Stabilizing Years: 17   Stabilizing Years: 20
Destabilizing Years: 16   Destabilizing Years: 13

Note: Where Ch: is 'the change in'; NE is net exports and G is the gap between actual and full employment Gross National Product.

This table should be interpreted as follows: Ideally, one would like the stimulus of net exports to counteract the gap between full employment GNP and actual GNP. Therefore if the gap were positive (Full employment GNP – Actual GNP > 0) it would be stabilizing to have net exports be positive. If the gap were negative reflecting overemployment it would be stabilizing to have net exports be negative.

Source: Export and GNP Series in The Economic Report of the President 1983.

international capital mobility, the international sector would have a stabilizing influence on domestic output under fixed rates in the face of domestic disturbances, and a destabilizing influence with foreign disturbances. With flexible exchange rates, the international transmission of disturbances would be eliminated (except for wealth effects related to terms of trade changes) and economies would operate as if they were closed. In other words, economic disturbances would be spread out internationally under fixed rates and bottled up under flexible rates.

When international capital mobility was taken into account, flexible exchange rates could no longer almost completely insulate economies from macroeconomic disturbances abroad, and the differences between the stabilizing properties of fixed versus flexible exchange rates were generally reduced.[5] Indeed, under conditions of very high capital mobility, it would be possible for a domestic boom to be accompanied by exchange rate appreciation rather than depreciation, with the associated increase in the trade deficit generating greater spreading out effects under flexible than fixed rates. As is shown in Appendix B, during the current float, for the industrial countries domestic booms have been associated with currency appreciation roughly as often as with depreciation. Thus, the switch from pegged to flexible exchange rates has probably not had a major impact on the transmission and automatic stabilization effects of the international sector from the perspective of simple Keynesian analysis.

Even before the outpouring of Chicago school-type monetary models of the balance of payments and exchange rate, considerable analysis of the importance of monetary aspects of open-economy macroeconomics had been undertaken. The type of analysis summarized above assumes that fluctuations in aggregate demand (IS curve shifts) were the dominant type of disturbance. Monetary disturbances may be of considerable importance, however, as may the differences in the effects of monetary and fiscal policy under pegged and flexible exchange rates under different degrees of international capital mobility. In a standard Keynesian IS-LM framework, high international capital mobility will reduce the domestic effects of a given change in monetary policy under fixed exchange rates and increase it under flexible exchange rates.[6]

Analysis of the effects on fiscal policy are somewhat more complicated. Under pegged rates, active fiscal deficits will attract capital from abroad, reducing the degree of domestic crowding out and hence increasing the effects of fiscal policy on aggregate demand. Under flexible exchange rates, expansionary fiscal policy may be associated with either exchange rate appreciation or depreciation, depending upon whether the capital flows attracted are greater or less than the worsening of the trade deficit stimulated by domestic expansion. Appreciation would increase the trade deficit, reducing the stimulative effects of the fiscal expansion as compared with fixed rates. With depreciation the strength of fiscal policy would be increased compared with a fixed rate system because of the stimulus to net exports. In both cases, however, the trade balance leakages would reduce the fiscal multiplier as compared with a closed economy (or flexible rates with no capital mobility).

While this simple IS–LM framework suffers from a number of major difficulties, particularly with respect to stock-flow interactions and the role of expectations, it does point to a number of considerations that have empirical importance for the short-run.[7] Recent experience is consistent with the predictions of such analysis that the Reaganomics combination of tight monetary and easy fiscal policy (the cut in government spending more than offset by the tax cuts) has led to a much larger appreciation than would have occurred from the reverse combination of easy monetary and tight fiscal policy. This in turn increased both the depth of the recession and the speed of disinflation.

As is shown in the paper by Pigott, Rutledge, and Willet, the cause of exchange rate changes can have a substantial influence on the effects of such changes. Since this has not been systematically taken into account in past studies, we cannot have great confidence in past efforts to offer precise estimates of the inflationary effects of changes in the dollar. The analysis does suggest, however, that changes in real exchange rates can have significant effects on the price level even for an economy as large as the United States. In his paper, McClure shows that even using conservative estimates of the strength of the impact effects of exchange rate prices on U.S. prices, the substantial appreciation of the dollar may fully explain the speed with which inflation fell. This rapid fall in inflation has probably contributed importantly to the political feasibility of continuing disinflationary policies rather than reversing course in midstream as would be predicted by simple theories of the political business cycle and the behavior of President Nixon. Thus, while floating exchange rates are generally treated as a major cause of inflation in popular discussion, it may be that they have greatly increased the likelihood of bringing inflation under control in the United States. In our judgment, this is an essential prerequisite for restoring global macroeconomic stability. If this does turn out to be the case, the additional difficulties that the magnitude of the appreciation of the dollar has caused for other countries may well turn out to have been worthwhile even from their perspective. However, as is discussed in Chapter 18, a strong case can be made for reducing the U.S. budget deficits and in consequence lowering the external value of the dollar.

Recent developments in the rational expectations literature have been important contributions to our understanding of the limitations of the effects of systematic macroeconomic stabilization policies. While this new classical "policy ineffectiveness" literature has been developed primarily in a domestic context, under the assumptions of these types of models exchange rate behavior, official intervention in the exchange market and international coordination questions would also cease to be relevant policy issues. Official intervention would be unnecessary because of the efficiency of the foreign exchange market and would be ineffective even if attempted because, under the assumption of perfect asset substitutability, such official transactions would stimulate offsetting private capital movements. Furthermore, there would be no case for policy coordination because flexible exchange rates would provide perfect insulation from systematic policy actions. Only unanticipated developments would have short-term real effects that might be transmitted internationally.[8]

The evidence is rather strong, however, that due to short-run wage and price stickiness and other considerations, monetary and fiscal policy changes do have policy-relevant real effects that give importance to many aspects of traditional IS–LM type analysis, at least in the short run. While it is easy for such models to give an exaggerated idea of the ability of governments to fine-tune international policy coordination, their limitations do not rob them entirely of their short-run significance.

Within this context, one of the most important developments has been the increased integration of domestic and international monetary analysis. There is a strong analytic similarity between the domestic literature on the conditions favoring interest rate versus money supply targets and the international literature focusing on the desirability of fixed or flexible exchange rates (i.e., exchange rate or international reserve targets).[9] It has now become understood by economists that in open economies these two sets of questions cannot be safely separated and one must look at the properties of combinations of interest rate, money supply, and exchange rate strategies. Looking at these interrelationships is necessary for determining optimal discretionary policy responses.

The subsequent paper by Richard Sweeney makes an important contribution to this type of literature by showing that classifying disturbances as monetary or real is not sufficient to analyze countries' exchange rate interests, even when macroeconomic objectives are limited only to output stabilization. By using a two-country model with careful attention paid to the role of international capital mobility and sterilization (money supply) policies, Sweeney shows that the desirable policy responses to an increase in the demand for one country's goods depend crucially on whether the counterpart to this increase is a drop in the demand for bonds in the home country or for goods or bonds in the foreign country. Depending upon this pattern, both countries could prefer pegged exchange rates, or both could prefer flexible or one fixed and one flexible.

While Sweeney's model should be extended to take into account price level effects and the role of expectations, such extensions would be unlikely to undercut the important implications that his model has for current international policy debates. Discussion of international policy coordination issues has frequently taken the minimization of nominal or real exchange rate fluctuations as the policy objective and analyzed economic circumstances in terms of a division of countries into the categories of weak and strong. For example, such views have been important in both the vicious circle debates about the alleged destabilizing effects of flexible exchange rates, and the locomotive theory proposals for coordinated economic expansion during the Carter administration.

From the standpoint of modern economic analysis as illustrated in Sweeney's paper, such a policy objective is dangerously oversimplified.

A constant exchange rate is not necessarily a desirable objective for national policy or for international policy coordination, and short-run similarities and differences in preferences toward exchange rate policy may not correspond closely to classifications of countries as weak or strong. What is needed is analysis of desirable combinations of monetary, fiscal, and exchange rate policies in light of the pattern of major disturbances. Unfortunately, however, real-world policy discussions are seldom approached in this manner. A high proportion of international monetary policy issues are based on highly oversimplified or extreme views of how the world operates.

The global monetarist school and officials in many countries adopt the assumption that the world economy is so highly integrated that there is little or no effective scope for independent national macroeconomic policies. While this has long been recognized to be true for very small open economies, an influential group of economists led in the United States by Arthur Laffer, Robert Mundell, and Ronald McKinnon argue that the large industrial countries like Germany and even the United States are now small open economies in the analytical sense.[10] This school usually recommends a system of fixed exchange rates with monetary policy being directed toward the achievement of this objective.

A second more traditional monetarist group sees more scope for independent national policies but argues that discretionary policies are unlikely to work well.[11] This school thus advocates domestic monetary rules combined with flexible exchange rates. Because of the assumption of efficiency in the private foreign exchange market, sterilized official intervention in the foreign exchange market is deemed to be undesirable and would not be very effective even if attempted. Under this view the scope for international policy coordination is limited to agreement on monetary targets.

At the other extreme are the views popular in many official circles that the private foreign exchange markets do not work well, that economic interdependence is quite high, and that internationally coordinated intervention and macroeconomic policies are urgently needed. Unfortunately, however, as discussed above the policy analysis eminating from those holding such views is frequently dangerously oversimplified. The empirical evidence presented in the papers in this section shows convincingly, we believe, that international interdependences are important, even for the United States, but that the strength of such interdependences is commonly exaggerated.

Combined with the empirical studies of exchange rate determinants in Part I, these studies suggest the need for careful consideration of international influences on national economies. As the simulations presented by DeRosa and Smeal in Appendix A illustrate, the strength of Keynesian income linkages among countries is often not trivial, but the amount of interdependence varies tremendously between different pairs of countries. American macroeconomic developments are tremendously important for Canada and Mexico but a good deal less important for European countries than is frequently assumed. Likewise, international developments can have a substantial influence on the U.S. economy. They are not so dominant, however, that they undermine the ability of the United States to follow independent national macroeconomic policies. Nor are sizable real disturbances so rare that a constant nominal or real exchange rate can be safely taken as an automatic guide for U.S. policies.

The monetarist and efficient market critiques of the scope for desirable discretionary monetary, fiscal, and intervention policies are useful in highlighting the substantial limits on what such policies can realistically hope to achieve. The work presented and summarized in this volume strongly suggests that the scope for such discretionary policy considerations is not zero, however. The strongest versions of the rational expectations models do not appear to hold empirically in the short-run, and at times the nature of the predominant economic disturbances and alternative proposed policy strategies are sufficiently clear for the types of economic analysis presented in the papers by Sweeney to be a useful aid in framing policy discussions.

Unfortunately, such technical and real-world policy analysis is still all too seldom brought together. There continue to be tremendous gains to be made in increasing the technical sophistication of real-world policy discussions and the real-world relevance of technical analysis. Our analysis has showed that there is considerable reason to be skeptical of most of the popular simple presentations for international monetary policy. We can be much less confident in concluding at present what optimal practical policy strategies should be. There is still considerable scope for reasonable people to differ in such judgments.

NOTES TO CHAPTER 13

1. See, for example, McKinnon (1981).
2. See, for example, the discussion and references in Flacco et al. (1984).
3. The hypothetical standard deviations used here were calculated from the growth rate of the transformed GNP series:

$$GNP = gnp + CH: NE$$

where CH: NE is the change in net exports.

Use of alternative time periods and types of measures may yield different calculations of net destabilizing influence. The major point is that fluctuations in net exports have not had a terribly strong tendency to either stabilize systematically or destabilize aggregate demand.
4. For discussion and references to this literature, see Chapter 15.
5. See Tower and Willett (1976).
6. The original contributions in this area were by Marcus Fleming and Robert Mundell, and the basics of their analysis are now presented in the interna-

tional chapters of most leading macroeconomics texts. For further discussion and references, see Chapter 2.

7. For recent analysis that considers stock flows, see Branson and Buiter (1983).

8. On these questions, see the discussion and references in Willett (1984).

9. See, for example, Poole (1970).

10. For recent discussions and references to the global monetarist literature, see Whitman (1975), and Willett (1980) and (1983).

11. See, for example, Sachverstandigenrat zur Begutachtung der Gesamtwirtschaftlichen Entwicklung (1977) and Giersch (1977).

REFERENCES

Branson, William H., and Willem H. Buiter. 1983. "Monetary and Fiscal Policy with Flexible Exchange Rates," in Jagdeep S. Bhandari and Bluford M. Putman, eds., *Economic Interdependence and Flexible Exchange Rates*. Cambridge, Mass.: MIT Press.

Flacco, Paul R., Leroy O. Laney, Marie C. Thursby, and Thomas D. Willett. 1984. "Exchange Rates and Trade Policy," *Contemporary Policy Issues* (January): 6–18.

Giersch, Herbert. 1977. "IMF Surveillance Over Exchange Rates," in Robert A. Mundell and Jacques J. Polack, eds., *The International Monetary System*. Columbia University Press, New York.

McKinnon, Ronald. 1981. "The Exchange Rate and Macroeconomic Policy: Changing Postwar Perceptions," *Journal of Economic Literature* (June): 531–57.

Poole, William. 1970. "Optimal Choice of Monetary Policy Instruments in a Simple Stochastic Macro Model," *Quarterly Journal of Economics* 84, no. 2, pp. 197–216.

Sachverstandigenrat zur Begutachtung der Gesamtwirtschaftlichen Entwicklung, (Counsel of Economic Experts). 1977. Jahresgutachten 1976/77, Stuttgart, Mainz.

Tower, Edward and Thomas D. Willett. 1976. "The Theory of Optimum Currency Areas and Exchange Rate Flexibility," *Princeton Special Papers in International Economics* No. 11. Princeton, N.J.: Princeton University Press (May).

Whitman, Marina. 1975. "Global Monetarism and the Monetary Approach to the Balance of Payments," *Brookings Papers on Economic Activity*, No. 3, pp. 491–536.

Willett, Thomas D. 1980. *International Liquidity Issues*. Washington, D.C.: American Enterprise Institute.

Willett, Thomas D. 1984. "Macroeconomic Policy Coordination Issues Under Flexible Exchange Rates," *ORDO*.

Willett, Thomas D. 1983. "U.S. Monetary Policy and World Liquidity," *American Economic Review* (May): 43–47.

APPENDIX 13A
THE INTERNATIONAL TRANSMISSION
OF ECONOMIC ACTIVITY

Dean A. DeRosa and Gary Smeal

This appendix presents calculations of the magnitude of the international transmission of fluctuations in levels of real economic activity among the major industrial countries from a simulation model developed by the authors for the Office of International Monetary Research at the U.S. Treasury. The calculations assume unchanged real exchange rates. A tendency for a country's currency to depreciate during a cyclical upturn would diminish the extent to which the boom was transmitted abroad while an appreciation would increase the amount of transmission.

The crucial parameters in the model are countries' marginal propensities to import and their autonomous expenditure multipliers.[1] In order to bound the likely magnitudes of transmission effects calculations are made using both high and low values of the parameter estimates from various empirical studies. The high set of import elasticity estimates are based on regressions run by the authors for each. These are likely to be biased upwards because of the neglect of supply conditions.[2] These give income elasticities in the range of 1.5 to 2.0. For the low calculations values of 1.0 are assumed.

We also specify two sets of values for the autonomous expenditure multipliers of the industrial countries in the model. The first set consists of short-run (one-year) autonomous expenditure multiplier values associated with increased fiscal expenditures in each of the national models comprising the LINK model, while the second set consists of medium-term (three-year) autonomous expenditures multiplier values, also derived from the LINK model.[3] The LINK multiplier values range from a low of 0.79 for Canada and Austria to a high of 2.58 for the United States, with most values falling between one and two. Generally, as might be expected, values for the medium-term multipliers are greater than those for the short-run multipliers of each country.

We consider the short- and medium-term effects of added expansion of one percentage point by each of the fourteen industrial countries identified separately in our model. Our simulation results are presented in Tables 13A–1 and 13A–2. They were obtained by assuming the one and three year LINK multiplier values in combination with the two alternative sets of income elasticities of import demand.

Tables 13A–1 and 13A–2 present our calculations of the incremental changes in the growth rate of GDP for the major industrial countries included by an increase in the growth rate of each country by 1 percent. The effects induced by each self-expanding country are determined by reading down the appropriate column. Thus, for example, the first columns in Tables 13A-1 and 13A-2 indicate the short- and medium-term effects of unilateral expansion by the United States on economic growth abroad while the first row shows the effects of foreign expansion on the United States.

The simulation results in Table 13A-1, which assume the set of "high" import elasticities, indicate that for most industrial countries one percentage point added expansion leads to increased economic growth in other industrial countries by less than 0.1 percentage points, even after three years. The United States and Germany, however, appear to stand apart from other countries, including Japan, in their ability to stimulate foreign economic growth.

Even in the first year these two countries generally increase growth in other industrial countries by more than 0.1 percentage points. The United States, of course, appears to exercise the greatest influence on Canada, due to the strong economic bonds between these two countries. American stimulus to other countries is generally less than 0.2 percentage points in the first year and not more than 0.25 percentage points after three years.

By contrast, German stimulus to the major European countries is appreciably greater than that afforded by U.S. expansion. Germany appears to exercise the greatest influence on economic activity in Belgium and in the Netherlands; in the first year induced growth is nearly 0.6 percentage points in both countries, while after three years it remains at about 0.5 percentage points. For the other major European countries, German stimulus is often greater than 0.2 percentage points in the first year and more than 0.25 percentage points after three years. Finally, German stimulus to the economies of the United States, Canada, and Japan is very weak, much like the stimulus generally afforded by smaller industrial countries.

Belgium and the Netherlands appear to be very sensitive to added growth by one another and to added growth by other major European countries besides Germany, particularly France. Extreme sensitivity of Belgium and the Netherlands results from the relative openness of these countries. More generally, where the transmission of economic activity between industrial countries appears to be greater than average, underlying bilateral trade flows account for a large share of the recipient country's gross domestic product.

Assuming the alternative set of "low," or unit import elasticities does little to alter the general profile of the simulation results; however, it does significantly reduce the magnitude of the simulated effects. The United States and Germany continue to exercise the greatest influence on other countries, on average. Moreover, Germany again appears to be most important for simulating growth in all European countries and the United States for stimulating growth in Canada, Japan, and the United Kingdom. The influence of the two countries is much smaller, however. With unit income elasticities assumed, added U.S. growth

Table 13A-1. Effects on Multilateral Growth of One Percentage Point Added Economic Expansion in Fourteen Industrial Countries, Assuming "High" Income Elasticities.

(Change of Real GDP in Percentage Points)

| Country | Year | Self-Expanding Country | | | | |
		U.S.	*Canada*	*Japan*	*Austria*	*Belgium*
United States	1	1.00	0.04	0.03	0.00	0.01
	3	1.00	0.09	0.07	0.01	0.03
Canada	1	0.04	1.00	0.04	0.01	0.02
	3	0.28	1.00	0.04	0.01	0.02
Japan	1	0.14	0.01	1.00	0.01	0.01
	3	0.18	0.03	1.00	0.01	0.02
Austria	1	0.09	0.01	0.02	1.00	0.03
	3	0.24	0.04	0.07	1.00	0.09
Belgium	1	0.25	0.03	0.06	0.05	1.00
	3	0.22	0.04	0.06	0.04	1.00
Denmark	1	0.15	0.02	0.04	0.02	0.05
	3	0.19	0.03	0.05	0.03	0.06
France	1	0.11	0.01	0.03	0.02	0.07
	3	0.12	0.02	0.04	0.02	0.08
Germany	1	0.12	0.01	0.03	0.04	0.07
	3	0.15	0.03	0.04	0.05	0.09
Italy	1	0.15	0.02	0.03	0.03	0.06
	3	0.23	0.04	0.06	0.05	0.10
Netherlands	1	0.22	0.03	0.06	0.05	0.21
	3	0.20	0.04	0.00	0.04	0.19
Norway	1	0.19	0.03	0.04	0.02	0.06
	3	0.23	0.04	0.06	0.03	0.08
Sweden	1	0.13	0.02	0.03	0.02	0.05
	3	0.15	0.03	0.04	0.03	0.06
Switzerland	1	0.19	0.02	0.06	0.06	0.06
	3	0.23	0.04	0.08	0.07	0.08
United Kingdom	1	0.21	0.03	0.05	0.02	0.07
	3	0.26	0.05	0.08	0.03	0.10

Note: Results from simulations of the model of world trade and economic activity described in the text, assuming one- and three-year LINK model multiplier values and the set of estimated income elasticities of demand for imports.

increases growth in other industrial countries usually by less than 0.1 percentage point over both short- and medium-term horizons. Even for Canada, U.S. expansion is seen to induce added growth of not more than 0.2 percentage points after one year and not more than 0.15 percentage points after three years.

It is difficult to place confidence bounds on our simulation results given the reduced-form nature of our model and our eclectic approach to choosing param-

Table 13A-1. continued

(Change of Real GDP in Percentage Points) Self-Expanding Country								
Denmark	France	Germany	Italy	Neth.	Norway	Sweden	Switz.	U.K.
0.00	0.02	0.04	0.02	0.02	0.00	0.01	0.01	0.02
0.01	0.05	0.09	0.04	0.05	0.01	0.02	0.02	0.06
0.00	0.03	0.05	0.03	0.02	0.01	0.01	0.01	0.04
0.01	0.03	0.05	0.02	0.02	0.01	0.01	0.01	0.04
0.01	0.03	0.05	0.02	0.02	0.01	0.01	0.01	0.03
0.01	0.05	0.07	0.03	0.03	0.01	0.02	0.01	0.05
0.02	0.07	0.19	0.08	0.04	0.02	0.03	0.05	0.07
0.05	0.20	0.47	0.20	0.12	0.04	0.09	0.12	0.18
0.04	0.43	0.57	0.18	0.28	0.04	0.07	0.07	0.21
0.04	0.35	0.45	0.15	0.24	0.03	0.06	0.07	0.17
1.00	0.10	0.20	0.08	0.06	0.06	0.12	0.03	0.18
1.00	0.13	0.24	0.09	0.08	0.07	0.13	0.04	0.20
0.01	1.00	0.18	0.09	0.06	0.01	0.02	0.04	0.08
0.02	1.00	0.19	0.10	0.07	0.02	0.03	0.04	0.09
0.02	0.13	1.00	0.03	0.08	0.02	0.03	0.04	0.08
0.03	0.17	1.00	0.10	0.11	0.02	0.05	0.06	0.10
0.02	0.17	0.23	1.00	0.07	0.01	0.03	0.05	0.09
0.03	0.25	0.34	1.00	0.11	0.02	0.05	0.07	0.14
0.04	0.29	0.57	0.16	1.00	0.04	0.07	0.06	0.21
0.04	0.26	0.47	0.14	1.00	0.04	0.06	0.06	0.18
0.07	0.12	0.22	0.07	0.08	1.00	0.13	0.04	0.31
0.08	0.15	0.26	0.10	0.11	1.00	0.15	0.05	0.35
0.06	0.10	0.17	0.06	0.06	0.07	1.00	0.03	0.13
0.06	0.12	0.18	0.07	0.07	0.07	1.00	0.04	0.14
0.02	0.15	0.24	0.11	0.07	0.02	0.04	1.00	0.11
0.03	0.19	0.29	0.14	0.09	0.03	0.06	1.00	0.14
0.03	0.13	0.18	0.08	0.08	0.03	0.05	0.05	1.00
0.04	0.17	0.23	0.10	0.11	0.03	0.07	0.08	1.00

eter values. A comparison is possible, however, between the pattern of inter-dependence among industrial countries found by simulating our model and patterns found by simulating other world models.

Deardorff and Stern, and Fair provide useful summaries of patterns of interdependence revealed by simulations of primarily three different world modeling efforts: DESMOS, METEOR, and LINK.[4,5] While these three modeling efforts all basically link the foreign sectors of macroeconometric models for several industrial countries, they differ importantly in their central theoretical develop-

Table 13A-2. Effects on Multilateral Growth of One Percentage Point Added Economic Expansion in Fourteen Industrial Countries, Assuming "Low" Income Elasticities.

(Change of Real GDP in Percentage Points)

| | | Self-Expanding Country | | | | |
Country	Year	U.S.	Canada	Japan	Austria	Belgium
United States	1	1.00	0.02	0.02	0.00	0.01
	3	1.00	0.06	0.04	0.00	0.01
Canada	1	0.20	1.00	0.03	0.00	0.01
	3	0.14	1.00	0.02	0.00	0.01
Japan	1	0.07	0.01	1.00	0.00	0.01
	3	0.08	0.01	1.00	0.00	0.01
Austria	1	0.03	0.00	0.01	1.00	0.01
	3	0.07	0.01	0.03	1.00	0.03
Belgium	1	0.07	0.01	0.03	0.01	1.00
	3	0.06	0.01	0.02	0.01	1.00
Denmark	1	0.05	0.01	0.02	0.01	0.02
	3	0.06	0.01	0.02	0.01	0.02
France	1	0.04	0.01	0.01	0.01	0.03
	3	0.04	0.01	0.02	0.01	0.03
Germany	1	0.04	0.01	0.01	0.02	0.03
	3	0.05	0.01	0.02	0.02	0.04
Italy	1	0.05	0.01	0.02	0.01	0.02
	3	0.08	0.01	0.03	0.02	0.03
Netherlands	1	0.06	0.01	0.02	0.01	0.10
	3	0.06	0.01	0.02	0.01	0.09
Norway	1	0.06	0.01	0.02	0.01	0.02
	3	0.07	0.02	0.03	0.01	0.02
Sweden	1	0.04	0.01	0.02	0.01	0.02
	3	0.05	0.01	0.02	0.01	0.02
Switzerland	1	0.07	0.01	0.03	0.03	0.02
	3	0.08	0.01	0.04	0.03	0.03
United Kingdom	1	0.08	0.02	0.03	0.01	0.03
	3	0.10	0.02	0.04	0.01	0.04

Note: Results from simulations of the model of world trade and economic activity described in the text, assuming one- and three-year LINK model multiplier values and unit income elasticities of demand for imports.

ment and country coverage. National models in the DESMOS and METEOR systems are estimated on the basis of a common theoretical framework, whereas those in the LINK model are strictly the product of different national model builders working independently of one another. Both the LINK and METEOR models include all world trading countries and regions; the coverage of the

Table 13A-2. continued

(Change of Real GDP in Percentage Points)
Self-Expanding Country

Denmark	France	Germany	Italy	Neth.	Norway	Sweden	Switz.	U.K.
0.00	0.01	0.01	0.01	0.01	0.00	0.00	0.00	0.01
0.00	0.02	0.03	0.01	0.02	0.00	0.01	0.01	0.02
0.00	0.01	0.02	0.01	0.01	0.00	0.00	0.00	0.02
0.00	0.01	0.01	0.01	0.01	0.00	0.00	0.00	0.02
0.00	0.01	0.02	0.01	0.01	0.00	0.00	0.00	0.01
0.00	0.01	0.02	0.01	0.01	0.00	0.01	0.00	0.02
0.01	0.02	0.08	0.03	0.01	0.01	0.01	0.02	0.03
0.02	0.06	0.20	0.08	0.04	0.02	0.03	0.05	0.07
0.02	0.19	0.23	0.06	0.13	0.01	0.02	0.02	0.00
0.01	0.15	0.18	0.05	0.11	0.01	0.02	0.02	0.06
1.00	0.03	0.08	0.03	0.02	0.03	0.06	0.01	0.08
1.00	0.04	0.09	0.03	0.03	0.04	0.06	0.01	0.09
0.00	1.00	0.07	0.04	0.02	0.01	0.01	0.01	0.03
0.01	1.00	0.07	0.04	0.02	0.01	0.01	0.01	0.03
0.01	0.05	1.00	0.03	0.03	0.01	0.01	0.02	0.03
0.01	0.07	1.00	0.04	0.04	0.01	0.02	0.02	0.04
0.01	0.08	0.10	1.00	0.03	0.01	0.01	0.02	0.04
0.01	0.11	0.14	1.00	0.04	0.01	0.02	0.03	0.05
0.02	0.11	0.25	0.05	1.00	0.02	0.02	0.02	0.08
0.02	0.09	0.21	0.05	1.00	0.02	0.02	0.02	0.07
0.04	0.04	0.08	0.02	0.03	1.00	0.06	0.01	0.16
0.04	0.04	0.09	0.03	0.04	1.00	0.07	0.01	0.18
0.04	0.04	0.06	0.02	0.02	0.04	1.00	0.01	0.06
0.04	0.04	0.06	0.02	0.03	0.04	1.00	0.01	0.06
0.01	0.06	0.10	0.04	0.02	0.01	0.02	1.00	0.05
0.01	0.07	0.11	0.05	0.03	0.01	0.02	1.00	0.05
0.01	0.05	0.06	0.03	0.03	0.01	0.02	0.02	1.00
0.02	0.06	0.08	0.03	0.04	0.02	0.03	0.02	1.00

DESMOS model, however, is limited to the European Economic Community countries.

To the evidence compiled by Deardorff and Stern and Fair we should also add consideration of results presented recently by Samuelson from a fourth modeling effort, the OECD INTERLINK model.[6] The OECD world model, like the simple transmission model we introduce in this paper, is essentially a simulation model that draws upon existing empirical evidence on the relationships among economic variables in different countries, and combines this information in the form of dynamic multiplier equations in analyzing the international effects of fiscal policy actions originating in the OECD countries.

Comparison of the patterns of interdependence from the four models and the results from our simulation model reveals some interesting relationships. The DESMOS and LINK results are quite similar to ours when we assume the low, unit income elasticities. Only in the case of German expansion do the results from the three models appear to diverge substantially. On the other hand, the INTERLINK model presents results more in line with the version of our simulation model when the high, estimated import elasticity values are assumed. The METEOR model results generally fall in between.[7]

NOTES TO APPENDIX 13A

1. A full description of the model is available from the authors.
2. In an empirical investigation of this problem for the case of U.S. imports, Peter Hooper finds income elasticity estimates fall from about 2.0 to as low as 1.3 when he introduces a variable for foreign output capacity in his regression equation for quarterly U.S. imports over the period 1957–77. See, Peter Hooper, "The Stability of Income and Price Elasticities in U.S. Trade, 1957–77," International Finance Discussion Paper No. 119 (U.S. Federal Reserve Board, July 1978). Our income elasticity estimates for annual imports of goods and services over the period 1960–73 are the United States 1.99, Canada 1.44, Japan 1.29, Austria 1.87, Belgium 1.75, Denmark 1.54, France 1.75, Germany 1.88, Italy 1.96, the Netherlands 1.83, Norway 1.51, Sweden 1.78, Switzerland 1.97, and the United Kingdom 1.77.
3. The LINK model expenditure multiplier values are set forth in Bert G. Hickman, "International Transmission of Economic Fluctuations and Inflation," in Albert Ando, Richard Herring and Richard Marston, eds., International Aspects of Stabilization Policies (proceedings of a conference sponsored by the Federal Reserve Bank of Boston, June 1974), pp. 201–31; and Bert G. Hickman and Stefan Schleicher, "The Interdependence of National Economies and the Synchronization of Economic Fluctuation: Evidence from the Project LINK," Weltwirtschaftliches Archiv (Band 114, Heft 4, 1978), pp. 643–707.
4. Alan V. Deardorff and Robert M. Stern, "International Economic Interdependence: Evidence and Econometric Models," Discussion Paper No. 71 (Research Seminar in International Economics, University of Michigan, January 1977); and Alan V. Deardorff and Robert M. Stern, "What Have We Learned from Linked International Econometric Models? A Comparison of Fiscal Policy Simulations," Banca Nazionale del Lavoro Quarterly Review (December 1979): 415–32.
5. Ray C. Fair, "On Modeling Economic Linkages Among Countries," in Rudiger Dornbusch and Jacob A. Frenkel, eds., International Economic Pol-

icy: Theory and Evidence (Baltimore: Johns Hopkins University Press, 1979), pp. 209–38. Another important recent effort to include the effects of induced exchange rate changes is the U.S. Federal Reserve Board's multi-country model described in Richard Berner, Peter Clark, Howard Howe, Sung Kwack, and Guy Stevens, "Modeling the International Influences on the U.S. Economy: A Multi-Country Approach," International Finance Discussion Papers No. 93 (U.S. Federal Reserve Board, Washington, D.C., November 1976); Richard Berner, et al., "Multi-Country Model of the International Influences on the U.S. Economy: Preliminary Results," International Finance Discussion Papers No. 115 (U.S. Federal Reserve Board, Washington, D.C., December 1977); and Guy Stevens et al., *The U.S. Economy in an Interdependent World: A Multicountry Model* (Washington, D.C.: Board of Governors of the Federal Reserve System, 1984).

6. Lee Samuelson, "The OECD International Linkage Model," OECD Occasional Studies, (Paris: Organization for Economic Cooperation and Development, 1979).

7. Several factors may contribute to these disparate results. The first is that import elasticity estimates in the OECD and our own model are much larger on average than in other models. A second possibility concerns the treatment of traded services in the various models. In particular, whereas in the OECD and our model consistency of total world imports and exports of services in enforced, it is unclear in the LINK and DESMOS models whether some downward bias of transmission is not possible because the models fail to simulate consistency of world trade in services as well as goods. Finally, it is possible that the LINK and DESMOS models assume much smaller propensities by developing countries to absorb imports than the other two models, thereby indirectly producing weaker transmission effects between the major industrial countries.

APPENDIX 13B
THE CYCLICAL BEHAVIOR
OF EXCHANGE RATES
Joachim Harnack

This appendix considers how real exchange rates have moved over the business cycle for the major industrial countries. An exchange rate increase (currency depreciation) would tend to diminish the transmission effects of a domestic boom compared with the constant real exchange rate assumption adopted in the DeRosa-Smeal simulations reported in Appendix A. Currency appreciation would increase these transmission effects. Table 13B-1 uses the direction of change in the growth rate of GNP relative to those abroad as the indicator of fluctuations in economic activity, while Table 13B-2 uses changes in output gaps. All calculations are for the years 1973 through 1978. In each case bilateral exchange rates are calculated against the country's most important trading part-

Table 13B-1. Relation Between Changes in Real Exchange Rates and Changes in GNP Growth[1] (*Annual Data*).

	Midyear Changes				*Year-end Changes*			
	Bilateral		*Multilateral*		*Bilateral*		*Multilateral*	
	−	+	−	+	−	+	−	+
Canada	2	4*	2	4*	3	3	3	3
Japan	1	5*	3	3	3	3	3	3
Austria	3	3	4*	2	3	3	3	3
Belgium	2	4*	2	4*	2	4*	1	5*
Switzerland	4*	2	5*	1	3	3	2	4*
France	3	3	3	3	3	3	2	4*
Germany	2	4*	2	4*	2	4*	2	4*
Italy	4*	2	4*	2	2	4*	4*	2
Netherlands	3	3	1	5*	1	5*	1	5*
Norway	3	3	2	4*	1	5*	2	4*
Sweden	2	4*	3	3	0	6*	1	5*
United Kingdom	3	3	2	4*	4*	2	3	3
United States	−	−	1	5*	−	−	3	3
Totals:								
Including U.S.	−	−	34	44*	−	−	30	48*
Excluding U.S.	32	40*	33	39*	27	45*	27	45*

1. The exchange rate is defined in terms of domestic currency units per foreign currency units or its equivalent in index form.

*Indicates the majority of observations are in this category.

ner while multilateral rates are based on the International Monetary Fund's effective exchange rate calculations.

Positive signs indicate that increases in economic activity are associated with exchange rate decreases (appreciation), thus increasing transmission. In Table 13B-1, we find that in approximately 60 percent of the cases, real exchange rates moved so as to increase rather than decrease the international transmission of domestic economic fluctuation through the Keynesian trade balance mechanism. Table 13B-2 shows that using output gaps instead, these results are reversed. Combined, these results show that there has not been a strong systematic tendency for exchange rates to either appreciate or depreciate with domestic booms. Further research using regression analysis and also considering quarterly relationships yields a similar conclusion.[1]

Table 13B-3 looks specially at the relationships between fiscal stimulus and exchange rate movements. Again we do not find a strong tendency for currencies to depreciate as would be expected in the low capital mobility nor to appreciate as would be the case with very high capital mobility. This suggests that there has been little change in the average strength of the Keynesian transmission effects due to the change in exchange rate regime. Effects are likely to be more variable, however, suggesting that the difficulties of fine-tuning internationally coordinated macroeconomic policies has increased.

Table 13B-2. Relation Between Changes in Real Exchange Rates and Changes in Output Gap[1] (*Annual Data*).

	Midyear Changes				*Year-end Changes*			
	Bilateral		*Multilateral*		*Bilateral*		*Multilateral*	
	+	−	+	−	+	−	+	−
Canada	2	4*	1	5*	2	4*	1	5*
Japan	3	3	4*	2	3	3	4*	2
Austria	4*	2	4*	2	3	3	4*	2
Belgium	4*	2	3	3	5*	1	3	3
Switzerland	5*	1	4*	2	5*	1	6*	0
France	4*	2	3	3	5*	1	3	3
Germany	5*	1	4*	2	4*	2	5*	1
Italy	1	5*	2	4*	2	4*	1	5*
Netherlands	4*	2	3	3	4*	2	4*	2
Norway	3	3	3	3	3	3	2	4*
Sweden	1	5*	3	3	2	4*	3	3
United Kingdom	3	3	2	4*	4*	2	2	4*
United States	−	−	1	5*	−	−	3	3
Totals:								
Including U.S.	−	−	37	41*	−	−	41*	37
Excluding U.S.	39*	33	36	36	42*	30	38*	34

1. The exchange rate is defined in terms of domestic currency units per foreign currency units or the equivalent in index form.
*Indicates the majority of observations are in this category.

Table 13B-3. Relation Between Changes in Effective Real Exchange Rates and Changes in the Impact of the Fiscal Balance[1] (*Annual Data*).

	Real +	Real -
Canada	4*	2
Japan	2	4*
Belgium	3	3
France	1	5*
Germany	4*	2
Italy	3	3
Netherlands	2	4*
Sweden	3	3
United Kingdom	6*	0
United States	2	4*

1. The exchange rate is defined in terms of domestic currency units per foreign currency units or its equivalent in index form. The impact of the fiscal balance is defined as the difference between the cyclically neutral balance and the actual balance, expressed in percent of GNP, as presented in the *IMF Annual Report*, 1980.

*The majority of observations are in this category.

NOTE TO APPENDIX 13B

1. See Joachim Harnack, "The Floating Experience: Exchange Rate Determination and Real Effects" (Ph.D. dissertation, Claremont Graduate School, 1982).

14 INTERNATIONAL INFLUENCES ON U.S. NATIONAL INCOME
Currency Substitution, Exchange Rate Changes, and Commodity Shocks

Christopher Radcliffe, Arthur D. Warga, and Thomas D. Willett

INTRODUCTION

Two of the more important developments in economics over the past decade were the increased recognition of the importance of international influences on the U.S. economy and the development of substantial instabilities in the estimated demand for money functions in the United States. In two recent important contributions Bruce Brittain (1981) and Ronald McKinnon (1982) have suggested that these two elements may be intimately connected. International currency substitution could perhaps help explain the unanticipated fluctuations in velocity that have substantially increased the difficulties of U.S. monetary management over the past decade.

In his influential article, McKinnon even argued that international currency substitution had become so high that the world money supply was a better guide to U.S. price and income developments than was the U.S. money supply. While the strong form of this claim did not hold up to systematic econometric testing, such further work does support the view that international developments do have an important influence on U.S. monetary conditions.[1]

American payments imbalances are automatically sterilized so that such developments do not tend to influence the U.S. money supply. However, exchange rate expectations and international capital flows can have direct and indirect effects on the demand for money. International switching of narrowly defined noninterest-bearing U.S. monetary assets appears to be quite small relative to U.S. aggregates so that direct currency substitution is probably not an important problem for U.S. monetary management.[2] (This is not necessarily the case for a number of other countries such as Germany, Mexico, and Switzerland.[3]) Likely to be more important is what McKinnon has termed indirect currency substitution. International financial flows can influence interest rates and hence the quantity of money demanded, even if there is little direct substitution among narrowly defined national monetary aggregates.[4]

In an important reformulation of his initial analysis, McKinnon argued that under flexible exchange rates, exchange rate changes would be a better indicator of international currency substitution to or from the dollar than foreign money supply developments. McKinnon and Tan (1984) present econometric estimates for the floating rate period which suggest that a 10 percent fall in the dollar with a year lag will stimulate aggregate spending in the United States by 2.5 percentage points. They interpret these results as evidence in support of the importance of international currency substitution.

These results are also consistent with other channels of international influence, however. Traditional international economic analysis emphasizes the effects that exogenous exchange rate changes can have on prices (see the accompanying paper by Pigott, Rutledge, and Willett) and on output via effects on the trade balance and domestic spending through the foreign trade multiplier.[5] As is argued in the accompanying paper by McClure, the focus by McKinnon and Tan on the "Reagan appreciation" of the dollar in 1981–82 leading to the rapid deflation in the United States in 1982–83 is quite consistent with standard analysis of the effects of tight monetary and easy fiscal policy under flexible exchange rates with high international capital mobility.

Furthermore, the two episodes that they single out for discussion of the inflationary effects of currency substitution against the dollar, "the sharp depreciation of the dollar in 1971–73 . . . followed by unusually high inflation in 1973–74," and "the 'Blumenthal' devaluation of the dollar in 1977–78 followed by inflation in 1979–80," are also commonly explained in terms of the major food and oil price increases of these periods (see, for example, Blinder 1982).[6]

We hope that the current emphasis on currency substitution and effects of exchange rate changes will help to correct past tendencies to exclude such considerations from the analysis of the apparent instability in the demand for money and short-run inflationary developments in the U.S. economy.[7] Analysis of international influences should not focus on currency substitution alone, however. As is indicated by the further empirical results presented below, McKinnon and Tan's statistical findings of very strong effects of currency substitution as proxied by exchange rate changes are subject to qualification when alternative specifications are tried. Not only are the results highly sensitive to the U.S. money supply measures used (as McKinnon and Tan note), but food and energy prices give roughly similar results to exchange rate changes, and changing a year or two in the sample period can substantially affect the quantitative estimates, occasionally even causing sign reversals. Exchange rate changes retain their significance in enough equations for us to be convinced that they are an important consideration, but considerably more research will be required before we have a good idea of the relative quantitative importance of the various main channels of international influence.

EMPIRICAL RESULTS

In studying the international influences on the U.S. economy it is important to investigate the possible explanatory power of alternative hypothesis and the robustness of the estimates with respect to alternative plausible specifications and time periods. Consequently, we have run a number of alternative equations including food and energy prices as explanatory variables. Furthermore, because there has been substantial official intervention in the foreign exchange market during the current float, we felt that it was a more appropriate test of McKinnon's full analysis to include both exchange rate changes and the aggregate of foreign money supplies to capture the full effects of exchange market pressures whether officials decided to take them on the rate or on reserves.[8,9] As McKinnon and Tan note, there is a tremendous difference in the results from their initial money supply series and the second series that they use. To emphasize the effects of other factors such as food and energy prices, time period, and the like, we have only used the same two money supply series as McKinnon and Tan. We wish to emphasize, however, that this far from exhausts the major relevant possibilities. There has been substantial controversy among domestic monetary analysts about the best monetary indicators, including not just issues of interest rates versus aggregates, and broad versus narrow aggregates, but also averaged versus unaveraged data and adjustments to the main measures to attempt to take into account such innovations as NOW accounts.[10] During 1980 and 1981, a period in which McKinnon and Tan's two series differ substantially, there was substantial disagreement about the extent of monetary tightening and, indeed, whether monetary conditions were even being tightened at all. While M2 was growing at a rate above its target, the array of M1 figures (M1A and M1B, with and without shift adjustments), gave off a wide range of signals. Thus, we believe that a substantially more detailed analysis of the various monetary indicators is needed before we can begin to have confidence in our estimates of the importance of international currency substitution.

The first equations presented in Table 14-1 replicate the results of McKinnon and Tan in examining the joint impact of M1FED and the dollar exchange rates on GNP for the U.S. (each independent variable is lagged twice). The explanatory power of alternate specifications is then explored with the addition of variables to capture the impact of the food and energy shocks of the 1970s.[11]

Table 14-1. Effects of the Money Supply and Other Variables on Nominal GNP in the United States, 1972-82, Using Federal Reserve M1 Data.

Equation	C	M1FED	M1FED (-1)	Row	Row (-1)	Exch.
(1)	8.54 (2.59)*	1.61 (3.48)* [0.83]	-1.37 (-2.89)* [-0.69]			
(2)	13.0 (5.74)*	1.34 (4.13)* [0.69]	-1.80 (-5.67)* [-0.91]			0.050 (0.860) [0.14]
(3)	9.44 (4.03)*	2.00 (5.13)* [1.03]	-2.38 (-5.86)* [-1.20]			
(4)	10.50 (3.72)*	1.53 (3.81)* [0.79]	-1.79 (-4.29)* [-0.90]			
(5)	12.73 (6.0)*	1.59 (4.45)* [0.82]	-2.33 (-6.89)* [-1.17]			0.107 (1.94) [0.31]
(6)	12.83 (4.78)	1.36 (3.53) [0.70]	-1.85 (-5.01) [-0.93]			0.044 (0.671) [0.13]
(7)	10.50 (4.47)	1.82 (4.70) [0.94]	-2.31 (-5.90) [-1.16]			
(8)	8.85 (1.91)	1.59 (2.71) [0.82]	-1.39 (-2.37) [-0.70]	-0.034 (-0.172) [-0.05]	0.030 (0.166) [0.05]	
(9)	14.5 (4.9)*	1.38 (4.52)* [0.71]	-1.84 (-6.13)* [-0.93]	0.055 (0.509) [0.08]	-0.185 (-1.69) [0.03]	0.005 (0.065) [0.01]
(10)	10.02 (2.98)*	1.99 (4.17) [1.03]	-2.43 (-4.75)* [-1.22]	-0.054 (-0.412) [-0.08]	0.029 (0.237) [0.05]	
(11)	8.95 (2.04)	1.59 (3.53) [0.82]	-1.76 (3.82)* [-0.89]	0.155 (0.899) [0.23]	-0.089 (-0.55) [-0.14]	
(12)	13.12 (3.77)**	1.41 (3.19)** [0.73]	-2.17 (-5.03)* [-1.09]	0.120 (1.12) [0.18]	0.095 (-0.68) [0.15]	0.132 (1.37) [0.38]
(13)	21.70 (10.42)*	1.00 (7.36)* [0.52]	-1.76 (17.6)* [-0.89]	-0.076 (-1.34) [-0.11]	-0.404 (-6.87)* [-0.66]	-0.084 (-2.56) [-0.24]
(14)	12.16 (2.63)	1.87 (3.62)** [0.97]	-2.39 (-4.18)** [-1.20]	-0.034 (-0.174) [-0.05]	-0.076 (-0.51) [-0.12]	

t-statistics in parentheses; beta coefficients in brackets.
*Significant at 5 percent level; **Significant at 10 percent level.

Table 14-1. continued

Exch. (-1)	Food	Food (-1)	Energy	Energy (-1)	$\bar{R}^2$	SER.
					0.55	1.70
-0.265 (-3.96)* [-0.66]					0.84	1.00
	0.127 (1.55) [0.27]	0.273 (3.09)* [0.57]			0.82	1.07
			0.126 (2.73)* [0.51]	-0.018 (-0.378) [-0.07]	0.73	1.31
-0.194 (-2.58)** [-0.48]	0.169 (2.24)** [0.36]	0.104 (1.11) [-0.22]			0.91	0.76
-0.210 (-0.204) [-0.52]			0.049 (0.902) [0.20]	-0.014 (-0.342) [-0.06]	0.80	1.12
	0.086 (1.04) [0.18]	0.230 (2.19)** [0.48]	0.058 (1.27) [0.24]	-0.037 (-0.970) [-0.15]	0.84	1.02
					0.40	1.95
-0.298 (-4.43)* [-0.74]					0.86	0.94
	0.125 (1.25) [0.27]	0.277 (2.59)** [0.58]			0.74	1.28
			0.150 (2.63)** [0.61]	-0.013 (-0.197) [-0.05]	0.67	1.45
-0.276 (-2.40) [-0.69]	0.177 (1.77) [0.38]	0.020 (0.145) [0.04]			0.89	0.82
-0.327 (-9.65)* [-0.81]			-0.002 (-0.11) [-0.01]	-0.109 (5.29)* [-0.43]	0.99	0.30
	0.101 (0.894) [0.22]	0.251 (1.51) [0.53]	0.052 (0.649) [0.21]	-0.065 (-0.911) [-0.26]	0.72	1.33

Table 14-2. Effects of the Money Supply and Other Variables on Nominal GNP in the United States, 1972-82, Using IMF M1 Data.

Equation	C	M1IMF	M1IMF (-1)	Row	Row (-1)	Exch.
(1)	3.50 (1.25)	0.310 (0.825) [0.233]	0.718 (1.89) [0.905]			
(2)	3.60 (0.814)	0.594 (1.06) [0.446]	0.390 (0.697) [0.492]			0.060 (0.363) [0.173]
(3)	2.93 (0.624)	0.332 (0.574) [0.249]	0.798 (1.20) [1.006]			
(4)	4.91 (1.14)	0.215 (0.417) [0.161]	0.642 (1.26) [0.809]			
(5)	7.56 (0.808)	0.403 (0.368) [0.303]	0.153 (0.154) [0.193]			0.066 (0.215) [0.190]
(6)	4.35 (0.706)	0.557 (0.732) [0.418]	0.448 (0.664) [0.565]			0.089 (0.423) [0.256]
(7)	4.70 (0.682)	0.157 (0.205) [0.118]	0.831 (0.964) [1.047]			
(8)	1.36 (0.375)	0.0097 (0.192) [0.073]	1.05 (2.04) [1.323]	0.294 (1.06) [0.429]	-0.147 (-0.602) [-0.239]	
(9)	-2.24 (-0.255)	0.533 (0.800) [0.400]	1.03 (1.14) [1.298]	0.434 (1.08) [0.633]	-0.213 (-0.728) [-0.346]	0.194 (0.776) [0.558]
(10)	0.299 (0.054)	-0.243 (-0.274) [-0.182]	1.60 (1.61) [2.017]	0.428 (1.13) [0.624]	-0.154 (-0.545) [-0.250]	
(11)	2.86 (0.450)	0.092 (0.151) [0.069]	0.944 (1.50) [1.190]	0.314 (0.909) [0.458]	-0.234 (-0.726) [-0.380]	
(12)	8.79 (0.507)	0.235 (0.197) [0.176]	0.525 (0.355) [0.662]	0.337 (0.671) [0.492]	-0.398 (-0.944) [-0.647]	0.064 (0.151) [0.184]
(13)	49.00 (0.74)	1.42 (0.976) [1.066]	-1.90 (-0.489) [-2.395]	-1.30 (-0.573) [-1.896]	-1.23 (-0.916) [1.998]	-0.700 (-0.571) [-2.014]
(14)	1.94 (0.339)	-1.76 (-1.51) [-0.132]	2.25 (2.40) [2.836]	1.20 (2.07) [1.750]	-0.264 (-0.943) [-4.289]**	

t-statistics in parentheses; beta coefficients in brackets.
*Significant at 5 percent level; **Significant at 10 percent level.

Table 14-2. continued

Exch. (-1)	Food	Food (-1)	Energy	Energy (-1)	$\bar{R}^2$, (R^2)	SER.
					0.285 (0.43)	2.14
-0.183 (-1.03) [-0.457]					0.191 (0.51)	2.27
	-0.040 (-0.179) [-0.086]	0.031 (0.164) [0.065]			0.055 (0.43)	2.41
			0.023 (0.254) [0.093]	-0.047 (-0.516) [-0.187]	0.092 (0.46)	2.41
-0.297 (-1.02) [-0.737]	0.015 (0.039) [0.032]	-0.178 (-0.620) [-0.373]			0 (0.56)	2.65
-0.250 (-0.881) [-0.621]			-0.055 (-0.411) [0.223]	-0.018 (-0.165) [0.072]	0 (0.55)	2.70
	-0.083 (-0.300) [-0.177]	0.032 (0.103) [0.067]	0.019 (0.128) [0.077]	-0.059 (-0.50) [0.234]	0 (0.47)	2.90
					0.20 (0.52)	2.26
-0.219 (-1.09) [-0.544]					0.146 (0.67)	2.34
	-0.194 (-0.697) [-0.415]	-0.004 (-0.203) [-0.008]			0 (0.57)	2.60
			0.053 (0.519) [0.215]	-0.056 (0.122) [0.222]	0 (0.57)	2.60
-0.446 (-1.16) [-1.107]	-0.062 (-0.151) [-0.133]	-0.302 (-0.826) [-0.633]			0 (0.75)	2.85
-0.944 (-0.961) [-2.343]			-0.356 (-0.746) [-1.442]	-0.341 (-0.779) [-1.355]	0 (0.74)	2.88
-0.552 (-1.75) [-1.180]		-0.564 (-1.43) [-1.182]	0.343 (1.73) [1.390]	0.016 (0.130) [0.064]	0.198 (0.84)	2.26

Table 14-3. Effects of the Money Supply and Other Variables on Nominal GNP in the United States, 1972-82, Using IMF M2 Data.

Equation	C	M2IMF	M2IMF (-1)	Row	Row (-1)	Exch.
(1)	7.42 (1.96)	-0.149 (-0.468) [-0.155]	0.395 (1.34) [0.445]			
(2)	5.22 (1.36)	0.095 (0.302) [0.099]	0.356 (1.24) [0.401]			-0.045 (-0.362) [-0.129]
(3)	-6.55 (-0.610)	0.488 (0.887) [0.507]	0.676 (1.31) [0.762]			
(4)	0.593 (0.085)	0.146 (0.410) [0.157]	0.582 (1.39) [0.656]			
(5)	10.8 (0.495)	0.039 (0.045) [0.011]	0.054 (0.066) [0.061]			-0.016 (-0.070) [-0.046]
(6)	2.46 (0.304)	0.162 (0.409) [0.168]	0.460 (0.947) [0.518]			-0.057 (-0.373) [-0.164]
(7)	-0.74 (-0.574)	0.515 (0.857) [0.535]	0.728 (1.09) [0.820]			
(8)	6.79 (1.52)	-0.174 (-0.456) [-0.181]	0.318 (0.844) [0.358]	0.065 (0.222) [0.095]	0.086 (0.318) [0.140]	
(9)	6.29 (1.45)	0.255 (0.705) [0.265]	0.555 (1.72) [0.625]	0.034 (0.129) [0.050]	-0.453 (-0.139) [-0.736]	-0.162 (-0.892) [-0.466]
(10)	-10.6 (-0.703)	0.725 (0.872) [0.754]	0.884 (1.20) [0.996]	-0.017 (-0.058) [-0.025]	-0.170 (-0.490) [-0.276]	
(11)	-7.05 (-0.744)	0.108 (0.282) [0.112]	0.920 (1.86) [1.036]	0.442 (1.32) [0.645]	-0.213 (-0.708) [-0.346]	
(12)	18.90 (0.709)	-0.077 (-0.075) [-0.080]	-0.027 (-0.024) [-0.030]	0.200 (0.419) [0.292]	-0.459 (-1.05) [-0.756]	-0.086 (-0.233) [-0.247]
(13)	46.07 (3.33)	1.33 (3.78) [1.383]	-0.696 (-1.51) [-0.784]	-1.19 (-2.72) [-1.736]	-1.61 (-4.33) [-2.615]	-0.757 (-3.65) [-2.178]
(14)	-13.4 (-0.837)	0.915 (0.711) [0.951]	1.02 (1.24) [1.149]	0.170 (0.293) [0.248]	-0.438 (-0.868) [-0.712]	

t-statistics in parentheses; beta coefficients in brackets.
*Significant at 5 percent level; **Significant at 10 percent level.

Table 14–3. continued

Exch. (-1)	Food	Food (-1)	Energy	Energy (-1)	$\bar{R}^2$, (R^2)	SER.
					0 (0.18)	2.55
-0.218 (-1.47) [-0.541]					0.17 (0.50)	2.30
	0.296 (1.21) [0.633]	0.279 (0.940) [0.584]			0 (0.40)	2.52
			0.163 (1.62) [0.660]	-0.01 (-0.081) [-0.040]	0.10 (0.44)	2.44
-0.318 (-1.01) [-0.789]	-0.013 (-0.026) [-0.028]	-0.234 (-0.395) [-0.490]			0 (0.53)	2.75
-0.133 (-0.557) [-0.330]			0.082 (0.521) [0.332]	0.003 (0.029) [0.102]	0 (0.54)	2.53
	0.207 (0.739) [0.443]	0.186 (0.554) [0.390]	0.124 (1.02) [0.502]	-0.004 (-0.034) [-0.016]	0 (0.53)	2.75
					0 (0.215)	2.89
-0.327 (-0.189) [-0.812]					0.164 (0.666)	2.30
	0.407 (1.11) [0.870]	0.371 (0.933) [0.777]			0.41 (0.44)	3.00
			0.270 (2.04) [1.094]	0.064 (0.439) [0.254]	0 (0.62)	2.50
-0.554 (-1.18) [-1.375]	-0.130 (-0.225) [-0.278]	-0.462 (-0.558) [-0.968]			0 (0.71)	3.00
-0.679 (-3.92) [-1.685]			-0.293 (-1.97) [-2.451]	-0.605 (-3.39) [-0.012]	0.799 (0.950)	1.13
	0.360 (0.649) [0.770]	0.291 (0.572) [0.610]	0.196 (0.980) [0.794]	-0.061 (-0.234) [-0.242]	0 (0.689)	3.15

The various regressions show that while the coefficients of the exchange rate variables generally continue to be consistent with the arguments of McKinnon and Tan, there is also evidence for alternative explanations of money demand instability and short-run inflationary developments in the U.S. economy. A high degree of multicollinearity among the explanatory variables makes comparison of these results imprecise, but it would be difficult to argue that any single variable is dominant. When taken singly with M1FED (and its lag) each variable or its lag improves significantly the original specification with M1FED terms only (eqs. 1 through 4), as indicated by a consistent improvement in $\bar{R}^2$ and the standard error of the regression (SER). When the additional variables are estimated in pairs (e.g., both exchange rate and food terms, concurrent and lagged), these results are in general preserved (eqs. 5 through 7). The addition of the food price terms to the exchange rate equation provides a marked improvement in $\bar{R}^2$ and SER, though the t-statistic significance is reduced due to multicollinearity. The exchange rate/energy price equation shows a slight deterioration from the exchange rate equation alone. The food/energy equation is superior to its single-variable counterparts (eqs. 3 and 4) in terms of $\bar{R}^2$ and SER, but again, with the attendant multicollinearity problems. Beta coefficients for the estimated parameters of equations 1 through 7 are also presented to measure the relative contribution of each variable in explaining the variance of GNP.[12] The message that emerges from this table is clear: There are multiple explanations for instability in the relationship between money and GNP in the 1970s, and no single explanation is dominant.

The second half of Table 14-1 (eqs. 8 through 14) repeats the previous specifications but with the addition of the variable ROW (both concurrent and lagged). ROW is the weighted average of domestic money growth rates for nine leading industrial countries, excluding the United States, with the weights corresponding to GNP in 1970. Except for equations 9 and 13, the addition of ROW variables lowers $\bar{R}^2$ and raises SER. Equation 13 is the best fit in terms of these measures, which includes the significant coefficient on lagged energy prices. Equation 9, the exchange rate equation, exhibits an improved fit over its counterpart, equation 2, but an F-test for the coefficients on ROW and ROW (-1) fails at the 5 percent level of significance.

The estimation procedures of Table 14-1 were repeated with alternative measures of money taken from the *International Financial Statistics Yearbook, 1982*. These include M1 (line 34) and M2 ("Quasi-Money," line 35). The results are presented in Tables 14-2 and 14-3, respectively. Both sets of equations yield results structurally similar to Table 14-1 but with consistently poorer fit. However, the summation of the coefficients on the money supply terms generally yields a value between 0.5 and 1.5, suggesting an overall positive effect of monetary expansion on GNP. As noted earlier in this section, this is not the case for McKinnon and Tan's results using M1FED, or in our Table 14-1.

CONCLUDING REMARKS

In summary, we find both that international developments are important for the U.S. economy, but they do not operate through a single simple channel. Further investigation of this subject is likely to require the development of structural models explicitly designed to highlight the major possible interactions between domestic and international influences on the U.S. economy and the impact of U.S. developments on the rest of the world.

A final word concerns policy implications. McKinnon interprets his results as further evidence in support of his view that the United States should place the primary focus of monetary policy on stabilizing exchange rates. We agree that exchange rate behavior can often give useful signals for those concerned with implementing monetary policy. But exchange rate movements are often caused by factors other than excessive ease or tightness of monetary policy, shifts in the demand for money, and destabilizing speculation. Both real factors and foreign monetary developments can also at times be quite important. We do not believe that the available evidence supports the view that a weakening dollar always means that U.S. monetary policy should be tightened and that a strengthening dollar means that monetary policy should be eased. Nor do we yet have a clear single indicator of whether monetary policy is easy or tight.

NOTES TO CHAPTER 14

1. The original McKinnon hypothesis appeared in McKinnon (1982). Our first test of the strong form of the McKinnon hypothesis appears in Radcliffe, Warga and Willett (1984). See also, Goldstein and Haynes (1984) and McKinnon and Tan (1984); summarized in McKinnon et al. (1984) and McKinnon (1984).
2. The relatively small effects of currency substitution on U.S. monetary conditions are demonstrated in Laney, Radcliffe, and Willett (1984). See also Willett (1983).
3. See, for example, Vaubel (1982); Laney (1981); Ortiz (1983); and Melvin (forthcoming). For a recent discussion of the current state of the literature on currency substitution and extensive references, see Willett et al. (1984).
4. This channel of monetary interdependence even under flexible exchange rates had been recognized well before the development of the recent literature on currency substitution. See, for example, the discussion and references in Tower and Willett (1976). A more recent investigation which also shows minimal indirect effects of the international economy on U.S. monetary conditions appears in Darby (1981).
5. The lag pattern found is consistent with initial J-curve effects which keeps major stimulative effects from occurring until the second year. As has been

emphasized by Pigott, Rutledge, and Willett in this volume, in general the actual effects of exchange rate exchanges will not be independent of their causes. This consideration may point us toward the development of more detailed hypotheses that would allow us to discriminate empirically between these alternative explanations.

6. Furthermore, changes in energy and food prices and exchange rates may have nontrivial influences on each other although it is fairly clear that exchange rate changes were not the dominant explanation of short-run developments in U.S. food and energy prices over this period.

7. For examples of important analyses that have overlooked such considerations, see Blinder (1982) and Goldfeld (1976).

8. McKinnon and Tan focus currently on unanticipated changes in exchange rates as possible indicators of currency substitution. As a rough proxy they use the actual changes in nominal exchange rates. Conceptually, we believe that better simple proxies would be the forecast error of the forward rate or changes in the real exchange rate. Empirically, the choice of these proxies may not make a great deal of difference as in the short-run all three have been highly correlated for the United States during the current float, and in some studies the spot rate has given as good or better forecasts as the forward rate. See, for example, Sweeney (1982) and Willett (1982) and studies referenced there. Of more likely empirical importance, one should attempt in future research to estimate the portion of exchange market pressures not due to other factors. While this will inevitably be imprecise, we believe that future efforts along this line would be worthwhile for further research.

9. We would not expect currency switching to have as much effect on foreign money supplies as does McKinnon, because our own work and reading of other studies suggests that there is substantial short-run sterilization by the major industrial countries. See, for example, Willett (1980), Laney and Willett (1982) and the other studies referenced there.

10. On these general issues, see, for example, Cagan and Dewald (1982) and references cited there. For discussions of the difficulties of redefining the U.S. monetary aggregates because of financial innovations over the last several years, see the concluding policy discussions section in Federal Reserve Bank of San Francisco (1982) and Hetzel (1983).

11. The series on GNP, M1FED and exchange rates are taken from McKinnon and Tan (1984) Table 1. December-to-December percentage changes in food and energy price indices are from the *Economic Report of the President* (1983), p. 225. Year-to-year annual averages for these series were also tested with only marginally lower performance.

12. Beta = $CS(X)/S(\text{GNP})$

where:

C = coefficient on the independent variable X;

$S(X)$ = the standard deviation of X;

$S(\text{GNP})$ = the standard deviation of GNP.

BIBLIOGRAPHY

Blinder, Alan S. 1982. "The Anatomy of Double Digit Inflation in the 1970s: NBER Project Report," in Robert E. Hall, ed., *Inflation: Causes and Effects*. Chicago: University of Chicago Press.

Cagan, Phillip, and William G. Dewald, eds. 1982. "Current Issues in the Conduct of U.S. Monetary Policy," special supplement to the *Journal of Money, Credit and Banking* 14, no. 4, part 2, (November).

Darby, Michael R. 1981. "The International Economy as a Source of and Restraint on U.S. Inflation," in *Inflation: Causes, Consequences, and Control*, edited by William A. Gale. Cambridge, Mass.: Oelgeschlager, Gunn and Hain.

Brittain, B. 1981. "International Currency Substitution and the Apparent Instability of Velocity in Some European Economies and in the United States," *Journal of Money, Credit and Banking* 13, no. 2 (May): 135–55.

Federal Reserve Bank of San Francisco. 1982. *Proceedings of Fifth West Coast Academic/Federal Reserve Economic Research Seminar*. San Francisco: Federal Reserve Bank of San Francisco (November).

Frankel, Jacob A. 1983. "Monetary Policy: Domestic Targets and International Constraints," *American Economic Review: Papers and Proceedings* 73, no. 2 (May): 48–52.

Goldfeld, S. M. 1976. "The Case of the Missing Money," *Brookings Papers on Economic Activity* vol. 3: 683–730.

Goldstein, Henry N. and Stephen E. Haynes. 1984. "A Critical Appraisal of McKinnon's World Money Supply Hypothesis," *American Economic Review* 74 (March): 217–24.

Hetzel, Robert L. 1983. "The Relationship Between Money and Expenditure in 1982," Federal Reserve Bank of Richmond *Economic Review* 69 (May/June): 11–19.

Laney, Leroy O. 1981. "Currency Substitution: The Mexican Case," Federal Reserve Bank of Dallas *Voice* (January): 1–10.

Laney, Leroy O., Chris D. Radcliffe and Thomas D. Willett. 1984. "Currency Substitution: Comment," *Southern Economic Journal* 50 (April): 1196–1200.

Laney, Leroy O., and Thomas D. Willett. 1982. "The International Liquidity Explosion and Global Monetary Expansion: 1970–1972," *Journal of International Money and Finance* (August): 141–42.

McKinnon, Ronald I. 1984. *An International Standard for Monetary Stabilization*. Washington, D.C.: Institute for International Economics.

McKinnon, Ronald I. 1982. "Currency Substitution and Instability in the World Dollar Standard," *American Economic Review* 72 (June): 320–33.

McKinnon, Ronald I., and Kong-Yam Tan. 1984. "The Dollar Exchange Rate as a Monetary Indicator: Reply to Radcliffe, Warga, and Willett," *Claremont Working Papers*, Claremont, Calif.: Claremont Center for Economic Policy Studies.

McKinnon, Ronald I., Christopher Radcliffe, Kong-Yam Tan, Arthur Warga, and Thomas D. Willett. 1984. "International Influences on the U.S. Economy: Summary of an Exchange," *American Economic Review* 74 (December).

McClure, J. Harold, Jr. 1984. "Dollar Appreciation and the Reagan Disinflation," Chapter 17 in this volume.

Melvin, Michael. "Currency Substitution and Western European Monetary Unification," *Economica*. (Forthcoming.)

Ortiz, Guillermo. 1983. "Currency Substitution in Mexico: The Dollarization Problem," *Journal of Money, Credit, and Banking* 15 (May): 174–85.

Pigott, Charles, John Rutledge, and Thomas D. Willett. 1984. "Estimating the Inflationary Effects of Exchange Rate Changes," Chapter 16 in this volume.

Radcliffe, Christopher, Arthur D. Warga and Thomas D. Willett. 1984. "Currency Substitution and Instability in the World Dollar Standard: Comment," *American Economic Review* 74 (December).

Sweeney, Richard J. 1982. "Intervention Strategy: Implications of Purchasing Power Parity and Tests of Spot Exchange Market Efficiency," in *The International Monetary System: A Time of Turbulence*, edited by Jacob S. Dreyer, Gottfried Haberler, and Thomas D. Willett. Washington, D.C.: American Enterprise Institute for Public Policy Research.

Tower, Edward and Thomas D. Willett. 1976. *The Theory of Optimum Currency Areas and Exchange-Rate Flexibility*. Princeton, N.J.: Princeton Special Papers in International Economics.

Vaubel, Roland. 1982. "West Germany's and Switzerland's Experiences with Exchange Rate Flexibility," in *The International Monetary System: A Time of Turbulence*, edited by Jacob S. Dreyer, Gottfried Haberler, and Thomas D. Willett. Washington, D.C.: American Enterprise Institute for Public Policy Research.

Willett, Thomas D. 1983. "U.S. Monetary Policy and World Liquidity," *American Economic Review* 73 (May): 43–47.

Willett, Thomas D. 1980. *International Liquidity Issues*. Washington, D.C.: American Enterprise Institute for Public Policy Research.

Willett, Thomas D. and John Mullen. 1982. "The Effects of Alternative International Monetary Systems on Inflationary Biases and Macroeconomic Discipline," *Political Economy of International and Domestic Monetary Relations*, edited by Raymond Lombra and Willard Witte. Ames, Iowa: Iowa State University Press.

Willett, Thomas D., Michael Bordo, Ehsan Choudhri, Douglas Joines, Leroy O. Laney, J. Harold McClure, Michael Melvin, Charles Pigott, and Anna J. Schwartz. 1984. "Currency Substitution and Monetary Interdependence: Recent Research and Policy Implications," *Claremont Working Papers*. Claremont, Calif.: Claremont Center for Economic Policy Studies, Claremont Graduate School. *Contemporary Policy Issues* (Forthcoming).

Willett, Thomas D. 1982. "The Causes and Effects of Exchange Rate Volatility," in *The International Monetary System: A Time of Turbulence*, edited by Jacob S. Dreyer, Gottfried Haberler, and Thomas D. Willett. Washington, D.C.: American Enterprise Institute for Public Policy Research.

15 AUTOMATIC STABILIZATION FROM EXCHANGE RATE REGIMES
A General Equilibrium Approach

Richard J. Sweeney

I: INTRODUCTION

A well-known argument for fixed as opposed to flexible exchange rates turns on the alleged automatic stabilization features of the two systems.[1] It is argued that a nation's internal shocks tend to be dissipated under fixed rates through spilling over into foreign countries, but such shocks would have greater domestic repercussions under flexible rates through being "bottled up." With external shocks, the country is more protected with flexible rates, but the Law of Large Numbers is appealed to in order to argue that *net* external shocks should be of smaller importance for the average country than its internal disturbances. By this argument, each individual country tends to have incentive to adopt fixed rates, and by and large a worldwide system of fixed rates is optimal for all or at least preferable for the majority of countries.

One part of the literature on optimal currency areas is more specific in defining the "shocks" of the above argument. In fact, these are shifts in the export demand function facing a country (external shocks) and autonomous shifts in home consumption demand or government spending (internal shocks). In both cases, only IS curve shifts are considered.[2] Further, the analysis proceeds under the small-country assumption that induced repercussions on foreign countries are negligible or, alternatively, that foreign governments stabilize perfectly.[3] In this literature, it can be shown that shifts in the export demand function are completely neutralized with flexible rates, under the assumptions that the home

The author thanks Sven Arndt, Jacob Dreyer, Angelo Mascaro, John Mullen, Charles Pigott, Edward Tower, and Thomas D. Willett for helpful comments and criticisms.

interest rate is held constant, there are no capital flows (or capital flows are income- and interest-insensitive), and the savings rate is unaffected by exchange rate variations. Briefly, in the absence of capital flows, the increase in export demand induces an exchange rate appreciation until the value of imports again equals exports, to keep balance of payments equilibrium. Because the savings rate does not depend on the exchange rate, the fall in home consumption equals the increase in imports, so the changes in exports and consumption balance to leave home income unchanged.

On the other hand, an autonomous increase in home consumption demand leads, under fixed rates, to an increase in income due to multiplier effects. However, the increase in income drives up home import demand, and under flexible exchange rates, this causes a depreciation in the exchange rate to restrain imports and increase exports. The depreciation-increased exports further stimulate income beyond what it would be under fixed rates. Thus, the argument that a country has better automatic stabilization under fixed rates with internal disturbances, and under flexible rates with external disturbances, is vindicated in this particular simple case.

There has been some work on monetary and capital account shocks in this single country, no-foreign-repercussions model. Modigliani and Askari consider IS curve shifts caused by domestic disturbances (such as changes in the investment or consumption function) and show the preferred exchange rate regime depends on the degree of capital mobility.[4] With *perfectly mobile capital*, taken to mean the domestic interest rate must equal the given foreign rate, fixed rates fully transmit IS shocks: when, say, the IS curve falls, the given interest rate and the new IS curve determine income, and (at least partially unsterilized) reserve flows shift the LM curve through this income-interest point. Floating rates would vary to move the IS curve back to run through the intersection of the given interest rate and the LM curve, and income would then not fluctuate at all. With *immobile capital*, floating rates will depreciate to eliminate balance of trade deficits caused by any IS-induced income expansion and the depreciation-induced export expansion will increase income variations as compared with fixed rates and sterilization.

It remains to consider in a general equilibrium multicountry framework the combined implications of IS, LM, and capital account shocks under a range of assumptions regarding capital mobility and sterilization policy. Recent work has, in fact, indicated the importance of analyzing how different patterns of shocks can influence the desirability of fixed versus flexible exchange rates in the short run. While much of this literature looks at the effects of alternative regimes on the stability of output under the assumption of fixed output prices, this type of framework also is being used now to examine inflation issues as in some of the later generations of vicious circle papers.[5]

The main analytical contributions of the present paper are due to its emphasis on the need to specify more carefully the counterparts of shocks in two-country models, and from its analysis of cases where there are conflicts or agreements among countries on having fixed or flexible exchange rates. For example, there are quite different results from an increase in demand for country A's output, depending on whether the counterpart to this shift is a drop in demand for bonds in A, drop in demand for bonds in country B, or a drop in demand for goods produced in B.

Perhaps the most startling and important conclusion is this: If the typical autonomous shock to aggregate demand in one country is accompanied (through Walras's Law) principally by accommodating shocks in bond markets, then if one country tends to prefer fixed rates for their role in automatic stabilization the other will tend to prefer flexible rates. Thus, in this case, adoption of one particular exchange rate regime among the two considered cannot be based on mutual self-interest but must come about by means of compromises in which automatic stabilization is but one consideration. Further, the sort of shock just described is one where autonomous shocks to aggregate demand are essentially uncorrelated across countries, but if the shocks have positive correlation, the same results hold. However, if the aggregate demand shocks are generally negatively related, as when an autonomous increase in one country's import demand is accompanied by a financing, autonomous decrease in its consumption demand, then *flexible* rates are preferred by both to fixed rates.

Section II shows that in general the exchange rate regime that is better on automatic stabilization grounds for one country is worse for the other in a two-country world, *unless* autonomous aggregate demand shocks are negatively correlated in the two countries. Further, the destabilizing effects of aggregate demand shocks, and preferred exchange rate regimes, depend crucially on the way in which aggregate demand variations are financed by changes in asset demands: an increase in home country aggregate demand with capital immobility will be aggravated by flexible rates if financed by a decrease in demand for *home* bonds but will be mitigated if financed by a decrease in *foreign* bond demand. When capital mobility and sterilization policy are introduced, it can be shown that conflict over choice of regime is essentially the same in the presence of mobile capital. The extent of sterilization is shown to be an important variable in stabilization policy, with the optimum degree of sterilization depending crucially on the pattern of shocks in the world economy. Section III offers a brief summary with conclusions.

II: A GENERAL EQUILIBRIUM MODEL

This section develops a general equilibrium, two-country model to deal with the problems raised above. The model incorporates usual assumptions in the literature, so the contrasting results derived here are clearly dependent on the generalizations of previous work. In particular, exchange rate changes are assumed not to affect either country's saving propensity or demand for money, and prices are constant in the short run considered.[6]

The Model

Consider a system of two countries, with two produced goods, two money supplies, and two bonds, under freely floating rates[7]:

$$P_1 Y_1^d \left(Y_1, Y_2, i_1, E \right) - P_1 Y_1 = ExDY1 = 0 \ . \tag{15.1}$$

$$P_2 Y_2^d \left(Y_1, Y_2, i_2, E \right) - P_2 Y_2 = ExDY2 = 0 \ . \tag{15.2}$$

$$m_1 \left(Y_1, i_1 \right) - M_1 = ExDM1 = 0 \ . \tag{15.3}$$

$$m_2 \left(Y_2, i_2 \right) - M_2 = ExDM2 = 0 \ . \tag{15.4}$$

$$\frac{1}{i_1} B_1^d \left(Y_1, Y_2, i_1, i_2 \right) - \frac{1}{i_1} B_1 = ExDB1 = 0 \ . \tag{15.5}$$

$$\frac{1}{i_2} B_1^d \left(Y_1, Y_2, i_1, i_2 \right) - \frac{1}{i_2} B_2 = ExDB2 = 0 \tag{15.6}$$

where Y_1^d is real aggregate demand for output in country 1, Y_1 is actual output in 1, P_1 is the (constant) price level in 1, i_1 is the yield on perpetuities in 1, E is the price of one unit of country 1's currency in terms of 2's currency (so an increase in E is an appreciation for 1, a depreciation for 2), $ExDY1$ is the value of the excess demand for country 1's output, m_1 is the demand for 1's currency, and $ExDM1$ is the excess demand for 1's currency, B_1^d is the demand for 1's bonds, and $ExDB1$ is the value of the excess demand, and 2's relations are defined similarly.

Since the law of excess demands gives

$$ExDY1 + ExDY2 + ExDM1 + ExDM2 + ExDB1 + ExDB2 = 0 \ , \tag{15.7}$$

the system (15.1) through (15.6) presents five independent equations in the five variables Y_1, Y_2, i_1, i_2, E.

Alternatively, under a fixed rate system, governments react to reserve flows by supplying quantities of their bonds and monies to make the actual exchange rate equal to the equilibrium value. One way to model the process is to suppose that in the absence of reserve inflows (ΔR) to 1, its stocks of money and bonds are $\bar{M}_1$ and $\bar{B}_1$, and with reserve flows are $\bar{M}_1 + \alpha \Delta R$ and $\bar{B}_1 + \frac{1}{i_1}(1 - \alpha) \Delta R$, where $\alpha = 0$ means complete sterilization, $0 < \alpha < 1$ means partial sterilization, and $\alpha = 1$ means completely unsterilized flows. Money and bond stocks in 2 are $\bar{M}_2 - \alpha' \Delta R$ and $\bar{B}_2 - \frac{1}{i_2} (1 - \alpha') \Delta R$ for reserve *inflows* to 1 are exactly equal to *out*flows from 2. Suitably modified versions of equations (15.1) through (15.6) thus yield five independent relations in Y_1, Y_2, i_1, i_2, and ΔR.

The Graphical Framework.

Analysis can most usefully proceed graphically.[8] In Figure 15-1, the curve $Y_1 Y_1$ shows combinations of Y_1 and Y_2 that cause equations (15.1) and (15.3) to be satisfied simultaneously for given values of E and ΔR. [In Figure 15-2, a given value of ΔR fixes the LM curve, and increases in Y_2 cause rightward shifts in the IS curve for a given E, since increases in Y_2 generate increased exports for 1, and the result is the $Y_1 Y_1$ curve of Figure 15-1.] $Y_2 Y_2$ is generated similarly from equations (15.2) and (15,4). $Y_1 Y_1$ is steeper than $Y_2 Y_2$ under very usual assumptions, so that an increase in say consumer demand in 1 that allows a larger Y_1 for any given Y_2, shifts the $Y_1 Y_1'$ curve to $Y_1 Y_1''$ and tends initially to be expansionary for both countries. However, the system does not yet take account of equation (15.5) [or (15.6) for, from equation (15.7), only one or the other must be considered].

To do so, consider the $B^d B_1^s$ curve in Figure 15-2, which shows the locus of points where equation (15.5) is satisfied for given values of B_1, Y_2, and i_2. Now suppose Y_2 increases, and this causes i_2 to rise along 2's LM curve, given by equation (15.4). The simultaneous rise in Y_2 and i_2 can have a number of effects on $B^d B_1^s$. At one extreme, if B_1^d is very insensitive to both Y_2 and i_2, as when there is not much financial integration, $B^d B_1^s$ shifts not at all; the appropriate curve in Figure 15-1, showing where equations (15.3) and (15.5) are satisfied, is the vertical BB_1.[9] Alternatively, if B_1^d is very sensitive to i_2, the increase in i_2 calls forth an upward shift in $B^d B_1^s$ (i_1 would have to rise at the initial Y_1 to keep $B_1^d = B_1^s$ at a higher i_2), and the new $B^d B_1^s$ - LM intersection requires a higher level of Y_1 and i_1. The BB_1 relationship would then have a positive slope. In the same way, the BB_2 curve is derived.

Minimal Financial Integration, Complete Sterilization

The simplest case to consider involves very little financial integration, so that income or interest rate variations in one nation have no influence on the other nation's bond excess demand. This gives the vertical BB_1 and horizontal BB_2 curves (Figure 15-1). Only three of the four relations— $Y_1 Y_1$, $Y_2 Y_2$, BB_1, and BB_2 —need be considered, for from equation (15.7) only three are independent; however, it is convenient to use all four in establishing results. Let all reserve flows be completely sterilized (incomplete sterilization is discussed below). Suppose that Y_1' and Y_2' are full employment, optimum income values, and thus any deviations are viewed as undesirable.

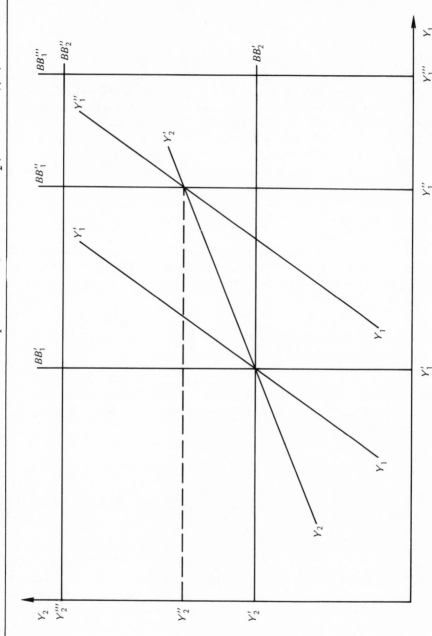

Figure 15-1.   No Capital Flows. An Increase in Y_1^d Financed by a Decrease in B_2^d, Alternatively, by a Decrease in B_1^d.

Figure 15-2. IS–LM Analysis for a Single Country.

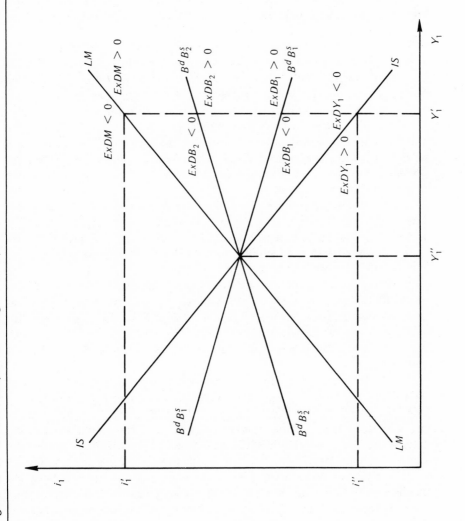

Consider an autonomous increase in 2's demand for 1's exports. From equation (15.7), this increased demand must be financed by some decreased demand; suppose to begin that the demand for 2's bonds falls. The $Y_1 Y_1'$ curve shifts to $Y_1 Y_1''$ and BB_2' shifts up to BB_2'' in Figure 15-1, since with a decreased demand for bonds at Y_2', Y_2 would have to rise to make demand again equal supply. Equilibrium requires the tripartite intersection of the $Y_1 Y_1$, $Y_2 Y_2$, and BB_1 curves, with variations in either E or ΔR serving to shift the curves to such an intersection.

(1) In the fixed rate case, supposing there is complete sterilization, reserve inflows to 1 do not change M_1 and hence do not shift its LM curve, so $Y_1 Y_1$ is unchanged; but such inflows do cause B_1 to rise so that a higher Y_1 would be necessary to equate demand and supply, and thus BB_1' shifts to the right due to reserve inflows. An appropriate quantity of inflows shifts the BB_1' curve to BB_1''. (Note that the reserve outflows from 2 shift the BB_2 curve down, so it must be true that the shift to BB_2'' puts this curve *above* the $Y_1 Y_1'' - Y_2 Y_2'$ intersection.) *In this case, then, reserve flows simply adjust bond supplies to ratify the equilibrium at Y_1'' and Y_2'', as determined by the aggregate demand forces embodied in the $Y_1 Y_1''$ and $Y_2 Y_2'$ curves.*

(2) In the floating rate case, there are no reserve flows, so the BB_1' and BB_2'' curves do not shift. E must vary to run $Y_1 Y_1$ and $Y_2 Y_2$ through the $BB_1' - BB_2''$ intersection. The initial aggregate demand expansion tends to cause Y_1 to rise to Y_1'', but bond market disequilibrium due to such output expansion tends to restrain the expansion. Indeed, in this limiting case of no capital flows, the expansion in 1 is completely offset by an appreciation that returns Y_1 to Y_1' but causes an expansion of 2. As Section I argued, an increase in export demand under flexible rates and no capital mobility has no effect on home income (in this case, where the demand for home bonds does not shift); however, the home appreciation (foreign depreciation) acts to increase foreign aggregate demand and income.

Notice that the expansion in 2 is greater than under fixed rates (Y_2''' versus Y_2''). Thus, 1 prefers floating rates in this case, but 2 prefers fixed to floating rates. But it must not be thought that this conflict in views results only from the particular case chosen. Rather, it is very general and inherent in the way floating rates work. The equilibrium determined by the $Y_1 Y_1'' - Y_2 Y_2'$ intersection (the fixed rate equilibrium) is modified under floating by variations in E (due to bond market disequilibrium), and the change in E causes expansion in the depreciating country and contraction in the appreciating nation. In the depreciating country, the expansionary fluctuation in output is further aggravated, while it is mitigated in the appreciating nation.

The Importance of How Aggregate Demand
Shifts Are Financed

It is worthwhile to examine a variant of the above example. Suppose the export demand increase in 1 is financed by a decrease in foreign holding of 1's bonds. Then the BB_1 curve shifts to the right to BB_1'' in Figure 15-1, and as can be seen 1 suffers a greater increase in Y_1 under flexible than fixed rates (Y_1'' versus Y_1''), and 2 suffers a greater increase under fixed than floating rates. Thus, *the regime a particular country prefers is quite sensitive to the nature of the shock it faces, but the conflict between nations over which regime to adopt persists.*

Note that in a nation's appraisal of regimes it is not enough to specify the shock—its financing must also be specified. In the two examples, the aggregate demand shock was identical, but the difference in financing exactly reversed each nation's preferred regime. As is clear from equation (15.7) every shock must be accompanied by another, accommodating shock.

When Aggregate Demand Shifts Are
Negatively Correlated

However, if the autonomous shock in one country's aggregate demand is essentially *negatively* correlated with an (accommodating) shock in the other's aggregate demand, both countries find it in their interest to adopt a regime of *flexible rates.* To understand this, recall why flexible rates were *not* preferred by both in the preceding example. The autonomous shock to aggregate demand led to too-great aggregate demand and output in both countries, and the induced change in the exchange rate under a flexible rate regime mitigated the rise in one country only at the expense of strengthening the increase in the other. In the new case of simultaneous but negatively correlated autonomous demanded shocks, suppose the increase in, say, 1's aggregate demand is exactly financed by an autonomous decrease in 2's (whether because 2 suddenly wants to import more and consume less home product, in exactly equal amounts, or 1 wants to consume more of its home output by importing just that amount less from 2). Then, under fixed rates with complete sterilization, $Y_1 Y_1$ shifts to the right and $Y_2 Y_2$ shifts down, with the net outcome being an *increase* in Y_1 and *decrease* in Y_2, as in Figure 15-3. Here, an appreciation for 1 tends to mitigate the rise in its aggregate demand while in 2 the fall in demand is cushioned. In fact, if the BB_1 and BB_2 curves do not shift initially, as assumed in this example, the change in the rate under a flexible regime simply returns the system to its previous equilibrium at $Y_1' - Y_2'$. Note that this result requires only that the $BB_1 - BB_2$ intersection not shift initially: the curves need not have the vertical and horizontal slopes pictures for the results to be valid. If shifts in the BB curves are minor relative to

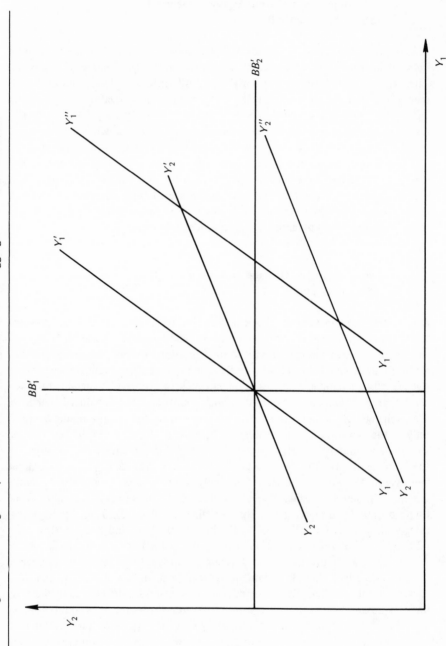

Figure 15-3.   Negatively Correlated Shocks Across Countries' Aggregate Demand Functions.

Table 15-1. Effects of Different Means of Financing Demand Shocks on Country Preferences for Exchange Rate Regimes.

Case	State of the World	Zero CAP Mobility Complete Sterilization	Non-zero (High) Capital Mobility Complete Sterilization	Zero Capital Mobility Incomplete Sterilization
I.	Increase in 2's demand for 1's exports financed by a fall in demand for 2's bonds	Conflict: 1 prefers flexible 2 prefers fixed	Conflict*	Conflict
II.	Increase in 2's demand for 1's exports financed by a fall in demand for 1's bonds by 2	Conflict: 1 prefers fixed 2 prefers flexible	Conflict	Conflict
III.	Increase in 2's demand for 1's exports financed by an equal decline in 2's demand for its own good, or on equal reduction in 1's demand for 2's good.	Harmony: both prefer flexible	Harmony: both prefer flexible	Harmony

*Here, as in Case II, there is conflict but preferences for regime depend on the relative degree of interest sensitivity of capital flow.

aggregate demand shocks, clearly the results tend to be closer to the case just considered than to those analyzed around Figure 15-1.

Given the cases and conditions considered, each country's choice of a preferred exchange rate regime may still be quite difficult on empirical grounds, let alone political, but is straightforward conceptually. If autonomous disturbances tend on average, weighted by number and size, to involve negatively correlated aggregate demand shocks in the two countries, flexible are preferable to fixed rates for both countries. Otherwise, one country will prefer flexible, the other fixed rates, with no a priori means of deciding on the optimal system for the world on grounds of automatic stabilization. Table 15-1 summarizes these results, as well as those discussed briefly below.

The policy results just derived regarding exchange rate regime hold in general and are not particularly dependent on the previous assumptions of interest- and income-insensitive capital flows, and complete sterilization of reserve flows. Relaxation of these assumptions does produce some interesting results. The flavor of these results is given below.[10] Table 15-1 summarizes some of the results.

In the above analysis, an increase in the demand for 1's exports financed by a fall in the demand for 2's bonds, caused an increase in Y_1 under fixed rates and under floating rates there was an *appreciation* that acted to reduce the increase in Y_1; but with income- and interest-sensitive capital flows such a shock can (but need not) lead to a *depreciation* for 1 and a further increase in Y_1. Further, the appropriate sterilization policy is quite dependent on the nature of shocks (*and their financing*) to which the system is subject.

The relative effect on stability of the two exchange rate regimes can be shown to depend greatly for either country on the *relative* degree of interest sensitivity of capital flows: *If the mobility of capital from one sort of bond to the other increases, given the average level of interest sensitivity, the country's preferred regime may well be reversed.*

It should be noted that the conflict over choice of regime demonstrated above when there is no capital mobility persists even in the case of high mobility. It is simply that the country preferring the fixed rate regime may now be different.

Adoption of the appropriate sterilization policies in the case of any particular shock can very much improve the performance of fixed rates. However, this result does not much improve the case for fixed rates. For example, in Figure 15-1 any shift that leaves two of the four curves in their initial positions can result in a return to the initial equilibrium with appropriate international sterilization policies. Thus, if shocks are *all* of this one sort, appropriate sterilization policies make fixed better than floating exchange rates for each country's stabilization. However, it is particularly important not to confuse the meaning of this latter point. If *all* shocks are of a particular and *predictable* sort it is as easy under flexible rates to adjust financial policies to offset them in response to incipient exchange rate changes as in response to minimal reserve flows.

The above discussion of how there might be conflict over choice of exchange rate regimes did not assume the predictability of each shock. On the contrary, the examples used assumed random shocks that could not be readily offset by discretionary policy and on average biased one country in favor and the other against flexible rates, because with every shock their interests on automatic stabilization grounds are opposed, save with negatively correlated aggregate demand shifts.[11]

Appropriate sterilization policies can reduce the costs of any fixed exchange rate regime. However, for any pattern of sterilization there are some patterns of shocks that lead the two countries to conflict over choice of regimes on automatic stabilization grounds.[12]

III: SUMMARY AND CONCLUSIONS

A simple graphical apparatus was developed to show the interactions of goods, money, and bond markets for two countries, incorporating usual assumptions about partial derivatives. This allows integrated consideration of IS, LM, and capital account shocks. Under very general conditions regarding capital mobility, aggregate demand shocks that are uncorrelated across countries will lead one country to prefer fixed and the other flexible rates on automatic stabilization grounds. The preferred regime for a country depends crucially on the compensating bond market shocks used to finance the shock to aggregate demand. These results contrast with more simplified single-country analyses, which compare the results of only export versus consumption function shocks, or depend crucially on the degree of capital mobility for qualitative results. We note that only when aggregate demand shocks are essentially negatively correlated across countries will nations agree on a preferred regime – floating rates.

These results indicate that agreement on exchange rate regimes will likely have to turn on more than self-interest grounds on this single issue of automatic stabilization. It has long been recognized there may be good reasons on these grounds for a country to peg to a larger neighbor. It seems from the above that the neighbors may have to seek a larger commonality of interests for such pegging to be agreeable all around.

NOTES TO CHAPTER 15

1. For an example of this argument, see Arthur Laffer, "Two Arguments for Fixed Exchange Rates," and Goffried Haberler's comment (and references) in Harry G. Johnson and Alexander K. Swoboda, eds., *The Economics of Common Currencies* (London, Allen Unwin, 1973): 25–39.

2. Much of the literature in this area considers only a single country and ignores all markets save that for the home-produced good– see Edward Tower and Thomas D. Willett, *The Theory of Optimum Currency Areas and Exchange Rate Flexibility: A More General Approach*, Princeton Study, 1976, esp. chapters V and VI. For analysis that considers only a single country but emphasizes its goods, money, and bond markets, see Franco Modigliani and Hossein Askari, "The International Transfer of Capital and the Propagation of Domestic Disturbances Under Alternative Payments Systems," Banca Nazionale del Lavoro *Quarterly Review* (December 1973): 295–310.

3. Russell S. Boyer, "Optimal Foreign Exchange Market Intervention," *Journal of Political Economy* (December 1978): 1045–56; Rudiger Dornbush, "Exchange Rate Rules and Macroeconomic Stability," MIT working paper, 1979; Walter Enders and Harvey Lapman, "Stability, Random Disturbances, and the Exchange Rate Regime," *Southern Economic Journal* (July 1979): 49–70; Stanley Fischer, "Stability and Exchange Rate Systems in a Monetarist Model of the Balance of Payments," in Robert Z. Aliber, ed., *The Political Economy of Monetary Reform* (Montclair, N.J.: Allanheld, Osman and Company, 1977), pp. 59–73; Jacob A. Frenkel, "International Reserves: Pegged Exchange Rates and Managed Float," in Karl Brunner and Allan Meltzer, eds., *Economic Policies in Open Economics*, vol. 9 of the Carnegie–Rochester Conference Series on Public Policy, a supplementary series to the *Journal of Monetary Economics* (July 1978): 111–40; Robert P. Flood, "Capital Mobility and the Choice of Exchange Rate System," *International Economic Review* 20, no. 2 (June 1979): 405–16; Elhanan Helpman and Assaf Razin, "Towards a Consistent Comparison of Alternative Exchange Rate Systems," *Canadian Journal of Eco-*

nomics XII, no. 3 (August 1979): 394–409; Dale W. Henderson, "Financial Policies in Open Economies," *American Economic Review* 69 (May 1979): 323–29; Ira Kaminow, "Economic Stability Under Fixed and Flexible Exchange Rates," *Journal of International Economics* 9 (1979): 277–85; Richard Marston, "Cross Country Effects of Stabilization, Reserve Currencies, and Foreign Exchange Intervention," *Journal of International Economics* 10 (1980): 63–78; Don Roper and Stephen J. Turnovsky, "Optimal Exchange Market Intervention in a Simple Stochastic Macro Model," *Canadian Journal of Economics* XIII, no. 2 (May 1980): 296–309; Nasser H. Saidi, "Fluctuating Exchange Rates and the International Transmission of Economic Disturbances," *Journal of Money, Credit and Banking* 12, no. 4 (November 1980): 575–91; Stephen J. Turnovsky, "The Relative Stability of Alternative Exchange Rate Systems in the Presence of Random Disturbances," *Journal of Money, Credit and Banking* (February 1976): 29–50; and Warren E. Weber, "Output Variability Under Monetary Policy and Exchange Rate Rules," *Journal of Political Economy* 89, no. 4 (1981): 733–51; plus the references cited in Notes of the above papers.

4. Franco Modigliani and Hossein Askari, "The International Transfer of Capital and the Propagation of Domestic Disturbances Under Alternative Payments Systems," (December 1973).

5. See Note 3.

6. See Edward Tower and Thomas D. Willett, *The Theory of Optimum Currency Areas and Exchange Rate Flexibility*; and Franco Modigliani and Hossein Askari, "The International Transfer of Capital and the Propagation of Domestic Disturbances Under Alternative Payments Systems."

7. The savings propensity assumption is implicit in Edward Tower and Thomas D. Willett, *The Theory of Optimum Currency Areas and Exchange Rate Flexibility*. Franco Modigliani and Hossein Askari, "The International Transfer of Capital and the Propagation of Domestic Disturbances Under Alternative Payments Systems," make the money demand function independent of the exchange rate. The excess demand for bonds functions are used here in place of the capital-flow function of much of the literature; this capital-flow function is generally assumed not to have the exchange rate as an argument. Note that this paper's assumption of constant goods prices is always used in the literature considered. This could, perhaps, be justified by the common assumption that sellers often meet demand changes with quantity rather than price changes.

8. The mathematics of the analysis are laid out in Appendix A.

9. See Appendix A.

10. Details are in an expanded version of this paper available from the author, at: Claremont Center for Economic Policy Studies, Claremont Graduate School, Claremont, Calif. 91711.

11. See Appendix A.

12. The shocks of concern in evaluating exchange rate regimes' automatic stabilization effects are clearly those that are *net* of all discretionary policies that are both desirable and institutionally feasible.

APPENDIX 15A

The partial derivatives of the system's functions are

$$\frac{\partial ExDY1}{\partial Y_1} < 0 \quad \text{(The marginal propensity to spend out of income is assumed less than unity.)}$$

$$\frac{\partial ExDY1}{\partial Y_2} > 0 \,; \; \frac{\partial ExDY1}{\partial i_1} < 0 \,; \; \frac{\partial ExDY1}{\partial E} < 0 \quad \text{(The Marshall–Lerner condition holds.)}$$

$$\frac{\partial ExDY2}{\partial Y_1} \,, \; \frac{\partial ExDY2}{\partial E} > 0 \,; \; \frac{\partial ExDY2}{\partial Y_2} \,, \; \frac{\partial ExDY2}{\partial i_2} < 0 \,;$$

$$\frac{\partial ExDM1}{\partial Y_1} > 0 \,, \; \frac{\partial ExDM1}{\partial i_1} < 0 \,; \; \frac{\partial ExDM2}{\partial Y_2} > 0 \,; \; \frac{\partial ExDM2}{\partial i_2} < 0 \,;$$

$$\frac{\partial ExDB1}{\partial Y_1} \,, \; \frac{\partial ExDB1}{\partial Y_2} > 0 \,; \; \frac{\partial ExDB1}{\partial i_1} \,, \; \frac{\partial ExDB2}{\partial i_2} > 0 \,.$$

(The value of the excess demand for 1's bonds rises with an increase in i_1, since 1's and 2's bonds are assumed to be gross substitutes and

$$\frac{\partial ExDY1}{\partial i_1} \,, \; \frac{\partial ExDM1}{\partial i_1} < 0 \,; \; \frac{\partial ExDY2}{\partial i_1} = \frac{\partial ExDM2}{\partial i_1} = 0) \,;$$

using the above partials and equation (15.7), it follows

$$\frac{\partial ExDY1}{\partial E} = \frac{-\partial ExDY2}{\partial E} \,; \; \frac{\partial ExDY1}{\partial Y_1} + \frac{\partial ExDY2}{\partial Y_1} < 0$$

and

$$\frac{\partial ExDY1}{\partial Y_2} + \frac{\partial ExDY2}{\partial Y_2} < 0 \,.$$

The graphical analysis can be rendered more precise. Rewrite the LM equations (15.3) and (15.4) as

$$i_1 = L_1 \left(Y_1, \overline{M}_1 + \alpha \Delta R \right) \,, \tag{15.3'}$$

$$i_2 = L_2 \left(Y_2, \overline{M}_2 - \alpha' \Delta R \right) \,, \tag{15.4'}$$

where

$$\frac{\partial L_1}{\partial Y_1} \,, \; \frac{\partial L_2}{\partial Y_2} > 0 \,; \; \frac{\partial L_1}{\partial M_1} \,, \; \frac{\partial L_2}{\partial M_2} < 0 \,.$$

Substitute (15.3′) into (15.1) to find a relationship between Y_1 and Y_2 for given values of E and ΔR, embodied in the curve $Y_1 Y_1$ in Figure 15–1; substitution of (15.4′) into (15.2) yields similar results for country 2 as in the curve $Y_2 Y_2$. Similar substitutions into (15.5) and (15.6)—this time substituting *both* (15.3′) and (15.4′) into each equation—yield the BB_1 and BB_2 curves.

The slope of $Y_1 Y_1$ is

$$\frac{dY_2}{dY_1}\bigg|_{Y_1 Y_1} = - \frac{\dfrac{\partial Y_1^d}{\partial Y_1} - 1 + \left(\dfrac{\partial Y_1^d}{\partial i_1} \dfrac{\partial L_1}{\partial Y_1}\right)}{\dfrac{\partial Y_1^d}{\partial Y_2}} > 0$$

and that of the $Y_2 Y_2$ curve is

$$\frac{dY_2}{dY_1}\bigg|_{Y_2 Y_2} = - \frac{\dfrac{\partial Y_2^d}{\partial Y_1}}{\left(\dfrac{\partial Y_2^d}{\partial Y_2} - 1\right) + \dfrac{\partial Y_2^d}{\partial i_2} \dfrac{\partial L_2}{\partial Y_2}} > 0 \; .$$

For the $Y_1 Y_1$ to be steeper than the $Y_2 Y_2$ curve requires

$$\frac{MPS_1 + MPM_1 - \dfrac{\partial Y_1^d}{\partial i_1} \dfrac{\partial L_1}{\partial Y_1}}{MPM_2} > \frac{MPM_1}{MPS_2 + MPM_2 - \dfrac{\partial Y_2}{\partial i_2} \dfrac{\partial L_2}{\partial Y_2}}$$

where MPS_j and MPM_j are the marginal propensities to save and import in country j. Clearly, under usual assumptions the numerator of the left-hand-side is greater than the right-hand-side's, while the right-hand-side denominator is larger than the left side's, so the inequality in fact must be valid.

The slope of BB_1 is

$$\frac{dY_2}{dY_1}\bigg|_{BB_1} = - \frac{\dfrac{\partial ExDB1}{\partial Y_1} + \dfrac{\partial ExDB1}{\partial i_1} \dfrac{\partial L_1}{\partial Y_1}}{\dfrac{\partial ExDB1}{\partial Y_2} \quad \dfrac{\partial ExDB1}{\partial i_2} \dfrac{\partial L_1}{\partial Y_2}}$$

and the slope of BB_2 is

$$\frac{dY_2}{dY_1}\bigg|_{BB_2} = - \frac{\dfrac{\partial ExDB2}{\partial Y_1} + \dfrac{\partial ExDB2}{\partial i_1} \dfrac{\partial L_1}{\partial Y_1}}{\dfrac{\partial ExDB2}{\partial Y_1} + \dfrac{\partial ExDB2}{\partial i_2} \dfrac{\partial L_2}{\partial Y_2}}$$

where positive slopes of the two BB curves follow from the derivatives assumed in Note 5 *and* the considerations in Note 8. Now, as the income and interest sensitivity of 2's demand for 1's bonds approaches zero, or $\dfrac{\partial ExDB1}{\partial Y_2}$ and $\dfrac{\partial ExDB2}{\partial i_2}$ approach zero, $\dfrac{dY_2}{dY_1}\bigg|_{BB_1}$ approaches infinity; and similarly income- and interest-sensitivity make $\dfrac{dY_2}{dY_1}\bigg|_{BB_2}$ approach zero or the BB_1 and BB_2 become vertical and horizontal respectively.

At another extreme, suppose the ratio $\dfrac{\partial ExDB1}{\partial i_1}\bigg/\dfrac{\partial ExDB1}{\partial i_2}$ remains constant but both terms grow very large to give greater and greater interest sensitivity for both countries. Then, increasing sensitivity need not change the (positive) slope of the BB_1 curve. Further, the BB_1 curve's slope may be steeper than the $Y_1 Y_1$ curve's or smaller than the $Y_2 Y_2$ curve's by simply increasing $\dfrac{\partial ExDB1}{\partial i_1}$ $\left(\text{and decreasing in algebraic value } \dfrac{\partial ExDB2}{\partial i_1}\right)$ while holding $\dfrac{dY_1^d}{di_1}$ and $\dfrac{dm_1}{di_1}$ constant. Increasing interest sensitivity of 2's demand for 2's bonds is shown by a less and less steep BB_1 curve. Similar statements hold mutatis mutandis for BB_2.

An increase in $\triangle R$ causes

$$\frac{dY_1}{d\triangle R}\bigg|_{Y_1 Y_1} = \frac{\dfrac{\partial ExDY_1}{\partial i_1}\dfrac{\partial L_1}{\partial M_1}\alpha}{\dfrac{\partial ExDY_1}{\partial Y_1}} \geq 0$$

as $\alpha \geq 0$,

$$\frac{dY_1}{d\triangle R}\bigg|_{BB_1} = -\frac{-(1-\alpha) + \dfrac{\partial ExDB1}{\partial i_1}\dfrac{\partial L_1}{\partial M_1}\alpha - \dfrac{\partial ExDB1}{\partial i_2}\dfrac{\partial L_2}{\partial M_2}\alpha'}{\dfrac{\partial ExDB1}{\partial Y_1} + \dfrac{\partial ExDB1}{\partial i_1}\dfrac{\partial L_1}{\partial Y_1}} \geq 0$$

under ordinary conditions;

$$\frac{dY_2}{d\triangle R}\bigg|_{Y_2 Y_2} = -\frac{-\dfrac{\partial ExDY_2}{\partial i_2}\cdot\dfrac{\partial L_2}{\partial M_2}\alpha'}{\dfrac{\partial ExDY2}{\partial Y_2}} \leq 0$$

as $\alpha > 0$, and

$$\frac{dY_2}{d\triangle R}\bigg|_{BB_2} = -\frac{(1-\alpha) + \dfrac{\partial ExDB2}{\partial i_1}\dfrac{\partial L_1}{\partial M_1}\alpha - \dfrac{\partial ExDB2}{\partial i_2}\dfrac{\partial L_2}{\partial M_2}\alpha'}{\dfrac{\partial ExDB2}{\partial Y_2} + \dfrac{\partial ExDB2}{\partial i_2}\dfrac{\partial L_2}{\partial Y_2}} < 0$$

under ordinary conditions. In words, reserve inflows into 1 shift the $Y_1 Y_1$ curve to the right unless they are sterilized in 1 by causing a monetary expansion that increases aggregate demand; they also shift the BB_1 curve to the right under partial, no, or complete sterilization in both countries through increasing the stock of bonds and/or lowering the interest rate by monetary expansion, thus requiring an increase in Y_1 to make demand again equal supply. These reserve flows are outflows from 2 that shift $Y_2 Y_2$ down unless completely sterilized, and shift BB_2 down under all normal conditions.

An increase in E is an appreciation from 1's viewpoint and (assuming the Marshall–Lerner condition holds) shifts $Y_1 Y_1$ to the left or,

$$\frac{dY_1}{dE}\bigg|_{Y_1 Y_1} = - \frac{\dfrac{\partial ExDY_1}{\partial E}}{\dfrac{\partial ExDY_1}{\partial Y_1}} < 0 \; ;$$

but this is a depreciation from 2's view point and shifts $Y_2 Y_2$ up, or

$$\frac{dY_2}{dE}\bigg|_{Y_2 Y_2} = - \frac{\dfrac{\partial ExDY_2}{\partial E}}{\dfrac{\partial ExDY_2}{\partial Y_2}} > 0 \; .$$

16 ESTIMATING THE INFLATIONARY EFFECTS OF EXCHANGE RATE CHANGES

Charles Pigott, John Rutledge,
and Thomas D. Willett

I. INTRODUCTION

The devaluations of the dollar in the early 1970s and the temporal association of the adoption of floating exchange rates with high rates of world inflation have generated considerable interest in the price level effects of exchange rate changes. Much of the early policy discussion of this issue, especially in Europe, used highly oversimplified models or scenarios to argue that the adoption of floating rates had made a major contribution to stimulating worldwide inflation through the generation of vicious circles of inflation and depreciation.

Subsequent debate established a better understanding of the nature of the relationships between exchange rate behavior and inflation. Of particular importance was the increased recognition that both exchange rates and inflation are endogenous variables so that the relationships between them over any particular periods will depend on the disturbances that have occurred and the policy reactions to these developments.[1] This is the same basic analytic point discussed in Chapter 3, which explains why there is no simple strong systematic relationship between interest rate and exchange rate changes.

There has also been increased recognition that just as under some circumstances exchange rate depreciation can worsen inflationary pressures, appreciation can at times reduce inflationary pressures. In the United States, concern with the inflationary consequences of the devaluation of the dollar in the early 1970s and the substantial depreciation in the later seventies has turned our attention to the contribution that the strong dollar of the 1980s may have made toward the reduction of inflation.

We have substantial reason to believe that the disinflationary effects of the recent dollar appreciation are far from trivial. The ratio of exports and imports to GNP has risen markedly over the past two decades; and even these ratios may substantially understate the domestic influence of international price developments, because many domestically produced and consumed goods and services are close substitutes for those that move in international trade.[2]

There has been considerable divergence of opinion, however, about just how strong these influences are, with some economists like Arthur Laffer, Robert Mundell, and Ronald McKinnon arguing that international influences are dominate, while most U.S. economists have argued that international effects will be considerably more modest. Such differences in view should be treated as propositions for empirical testing, and there have indeed been a number of published econometric estimates of the effects of changes in the external value of the dollar on U.S. prices. Unfortunately, however, we can have little confidence in these estimates except to give us a broad range of possible influence. The analysis of this paper strongly contradicts the rather widely held view that "the impact of import prices on domestic prices can thus be determined with considerable accuracy."[3]

The basic difficulty is that the models that have typically been used to make such estimates have made the same type of oversimplified assumptions about the exogeneity of exchange rate changes and regularity of policy responses that characterized the early stages of the vicious circle policy debate. It has not been sufficiently appreciated that the many qualifications that have been advanced concerning the simple vicious circle argument apply as well to econometric estimation of the price effects of exchange rate changes.

Our point is essentially a particular example of the Lucas critique of typical macroeconometric estimation.[4] In Sections II and III we discuss the standard approach to estimating the inflationary effects of exchange rate changes and its deficiencies from the standpoint of the Lucas and vicious circle critiques. Section IV presents empirical results that show that the critiques have considerable quantitative importance and that use of the standard approach gives rise to a wide range of estimates.

Our results give further support to views that these effects are neither trivial nor dominate the economy, but suggest that one cannot have great confidence in estimates that purport to show the impact of the recent appreciation of the dollar on the U.S. price level within one or two percentage points. The paper concludes with a brief discussion of directions for further research.

II. STANDARD WAGE PRICE BLOCK
FOR AN OPEN ECONOMY

Many researchers calculate the effects of exchange rate changes on domestic inflation using estimates from the simultaneous wage-price blocks of the major large-scale macroeconometric models.[5] The following three-equation prototype model characterizes the main features of these models extended to the open economy:

$$\dot{P} = a_{12}\dot{W} - a_{13}\dot{PROD} + a_{14}\dot{RENT} + a_{15}\dot{PRIMP} + f(U, U^*) + a_{10}, \quad (16.1)$$

$$\dot{W} = a_{21}\dot{P}^* + a_{22}\dot{PROD} + h(U, U^*) + a_{20}, \quad (16.2)$$

$$\dot{PRIMP} = \dot{XRATE} + \dot{FP}, \quad (16.3)$$

where P denotes the general price level, W the nominal wage rate, $PROD$ output per man hour, $RENT$ the required rental rate on capital, $PRIMP$ an index of import prices, U the unemployment rate, U^* the "natural" rate of unemployment, $\dot{P}^*$ the anticipated rate of price increase, $XRATE$ the exchange rate in units of domestic currency per unit of foreign currency, FP the foreign price level, and dotted variables denote percentage annual rates of change.

Equation (16.1) states that output prices respond to changes in factor costs (W, $RENT$), changes in productivity, changes in the price of imports, and to demand pressure or capacity utilization, represented by $f(U, U^*)$. This is designed to represent the notion that producers of domestic output set prices to cover full unit production cost plus a markup. Unit production cost is jointly determined by factor costs (W, $RENT$), by the prices of imports used as intermediate inputs, and by productivity ($PROD$). The markup that firms add to production costs varies with current market conditions. If the market is characterized by excess demand—that is, by a large book of orders relative to shipments, lack of excess capacity, and low unemployment rates—firms will increase their markup. Hence, the term $f(U, U^*)$ in equation (16.1).

Import prices enter the price equation since the general price index can be represented as a weighted average of the prices of domestically produced and consumed goods, and those of import goods, *and* because import goods are substitutable in both production and consumption with domestically produced goods. Import prices, productivity growth, the rental rate, the unemployment rate, the natural rate of unemployment, the exchange rate, and the foreign price level are assumed to be predetermined with respect to the wage price block— that is, it is supposed that there is not feedback from domestic prices and wages to these variables.

The wage equation is based on the idea that real wages are determined primarily by the growth of labor productivity, and by excess demand conditions in the labor market, $h(U, U^*)$. Nominal wage changes, then, are determined by these factors as well as by the expected inflation rate.

Equation (16.3) states that the rate of import price inflation is determined by both exchange rate changes and foreign inflation. This neglects changes in the costs of domestic resources used in acquiring and distributing import goods, and in importers' markup over cost, which are presumed to be of second-order significance to the inflation process.

Typical calculations of the effect of exchange rate changes on the domestic inflation rate distinguish the impact effect from the total effect. The impact effect measures the effect upon prices holding wages constant and is calculated by substituting (16.3) into (16.1) and taking the partial derivative of the resulting price equation $w.r.t.$ the rate of growth in the exchange rate:

$$\frac{\partial \dot{P}}{\partial \dot{XRATE}} = a_{15} . \tag{16.4}$$

Frequently, a_{15} is identified with the share of imports or of imports plus exports in GNP. More careful consideration suggests that a_{15} should exceed the share of imports in GNP to the degree that domestic goods are substitutable with imports.[6]

Calculations of the "total effect" also take into account the feedback effects of an initial price increase through its intermediate effects on wages. Calculations that allow for the simultaneous nature of the wage-price relation are derived by first solving the system (16.1) through (16.3) for the inflation rate:

$$\dot{P} = a_{12} h (U, U^*) + (a_{12} a_{22} - a_{13}) \dot{PROD} + a_{12} a_{21} \dot{P}^*$$
$$+ a_{15} (\dot{XRATE} + \dot{FP}) + a_{14} \dot{RENT} + f(U, U^*) . \tag{16.5}$$

Equation (16.5) can be interpreted as a short-run Phillips Curve, since it provides for situations in which the actual inflation rate differs from the rate that is expected by workers. Assuming that in the long run any given inflation rate becomes fully anticipated ($\dot{P} = \dot{P}^*$), and defining $g(U, U^*) = a_{12} h (U, U^*) + f(U, U^*)$, we can express the long-run Phillips Curve as:

$$\dot{P} = \frac{(a_{12} a_{22} - a_{13}) \dot{PROD} + g(U, U^*) + a_{14} \dot{RENT} + a_{15} (\dot{XRATE} + \dot{FP})}{1 - a_{12} a_{21}} . \tag{16.6}$$

The "total effect" of a change in the exchange rate on inflation is then calculated by evaluating the partial derivative of (16.6) $w.r.t.$ $XRATE$,

$$\frac{\partial \dot{P}}{\partial \dot{XRATE}} = \frac{a_{15}}{1 - a_{21} a_{12}} . \tag{16.7}$$

In (16.7), a_{21} is generally known as the wage/price link and a_{12} is the wage share of costs. If workers bargain implicitly for real rather than nominal wages—that is, when there is no money illusion—we would expect the value of a_{21} to be one. Since a_{12} is positive but less than one, the full effect will be greater than the impact effect.

Table 16-1. Estimates of the Inflationary Effects of Exchange Rate Changes.

Authors	Sample Period	Price Index	Impact Effect	Total Effect	Wage/Price Link
Kwack (1974)*	1959–71	CPI	0.15 (NA)	0.31	0.50 (NA)
Dornbusch/ Krugman (1976)	1955–75	CPI	0.14 (0.02)	0.42	0.67 (0.08)
Dornbusch (1978)	1965–77	CPI	0.15 (0.03)	0.26	0.43 (0.14)
	1965–77	GNP Deflator	0.15 (0.02)	0.25	0.40 (0.10)

*Kwack estimated the price equation after making the initial assumption $\dot{P} = \dot{P}^*$ and solving out the wage-change. He then used wage-price link estimates of previous authors to estimate the impact effect.

In order to obtain estimates of the parameters of this model, of course, a researcher must replace each of the conceptual variables in (16.2) through (16.3) with their empirical counterparts. Variations in the specification of these variables (especially the expected inflation variable) have led to literally hundreds of competing estimates for the parameters of open-economy Phillips Curve models of this type. Although it would be hopeless to attempt to catalog all of the differences in specification in these papers, we present in Table 16-1 a brief summary of the more important characteristics of several representative papers that present estimates for the United States.

As the estimates in Table 16-1 show, there has been considerable variation in the estimates of the effects of import price changes on domestic inflation that have been reported by different researchers. We will argue below that this instability is partially the result of a serious misspecification in the open-economy Phillips Curve models.

III. CAUSALITY AND THE DIFFICULTIES WITH THE STANDARD CALCULATIONS

The standard calculations of the effect of exchange rate changes upon prices outlined above are subject to two basic criticisms. Both arise from the failure to distinguish adequately between situations in which exchange rate changes are an exogenous cause of domestic price variations and those in which both are caused by some other factor. The first criticism concerns the way in which the wage-price block is used to calculate the impact of exchange rate changes and applies even when the true parameters of the block are known exactly; the criticism also applies with equal force to analogous calculations made for closed economies.

The second objection relates to the biases that are likely to arise in estimating the parameters of the wage-price block when the exchange rate is incorrectly assumed to be exogenous to that block. As the evidence presented in the next section suggests, estimates of the initial and final impact of exchange rate changes are likely to be unstable and (therefore) unreliable when the endogenous character of many exchange rate changes is not allowed for.

The standard computation of the full effect of exchange rates upon prices assumes implicitly that, aside from wages, all other relevant influences upon domestic inflation are held constant. Assume, for the moment, that the wage-price block represented by equations (16.1) through (16.3) and summarized in (16.6) is a correct description of the linkages among domestic prices, wages, and import prices. This means that when computing the full effect according to (16.7) we are assuming that productivity growth, the unemployment rate — actual and natural — the growth of capital's own rent, and the foreign inflation rate are constant — that is, are unaffected by exchange rate changes.

In general, a proper calculation of the full effect takes the relationship among the variables on the right hand side in (16.6) into account. This is done by taking the differential — not the partial derivative — of (16.6) and then dividing through by $dXRATE$ to obtain:

$$\frac{d\dot{P}}{dX\dot{R}ATE} = \frac{a_{12}\,a_{22} - a_{13}}{1 - a_{12}\,a_{21}}\,\frac{d\dot{PROD}}{dX\dot{R}ATE} + \frac{1}{1 - a_{12}\,a_{21}}\,\frac{dg\,(U,\,U^*)}{dX\dot{R}ATE}$$

$$+ \frac{a_{14}}{1 - a_{12}\,a_{21}}\,\frac{d\dot{RENT}}{dX\dot{R}ATE} + \frac{a_{15}}{1 - a_{12}\,a_{21}}$$

$$+ \frac{a_{15}}{1 - a_{12}\,a_{21}}\,\frac{d\dot{FP}}{dX\dot{R}ATE}\,. \qquad\qquad (16.7')$$

Equation (16.7') illustrates that $d\dot{P}/dX\dot{R}ATE$ will equal the standard estimate of the total effect given by the right-hand side of (16.7) only when all terms except the fourth term on the right-hand side of (16.7') equal zero. In other words, *the calculation given in (16.7) is a valid description of the inflationary effects of exchange rate changes only when PROD, U, U*, RENT, and FP are independent of exchange rate changes.*

Clearly, though, the ceteris paribus assumption required to make (16.6) valid is unrealistic. Even when an exchange rate change is exogenous to the *domestic* economy, it will arise from causes (such as portfolio shifts among national currencies or variations in terms of trade) that will often affect other variables in the wage-price block. For example, an exchange rate depreciation associated with a deterioration in the terms of trade may affect worker productivity and labor supply. Indeed, the standard calculation is particularly implausible in that it holds the actual unemployment rate constant. In reality, policymakers would be likely to follow much more complicated reaction functions which would be unlikely to leave unemployment unchanged. Essentially the constant unemployment rate assumption implies that the monetary and fiscal authorities would be highly accommodating in response to shocks to the economy.[7]

Thus, even if the standard wage-price block (16.1) – (16.3) is a true representation of the domestic inflationary process, the final impact of an exchange rate change on domestic prices will depend upon the origin of the former's variation and upon the monetary and fiscal policy responses of the authorities. (For further discussion see Sweeney and Willett 1976.) Hence, there is no single answer to the question of how much a given exchange rate change will affect domestic prices. The "standard" calculation (16.7) will be accurate only under fairly unrealistic circumstances. Furthermore, the extent to which exchange rate changes actually are a source of domestic inflation in any given period depends crucially upon the sources of the disturbances, in particular upon the frequency and severity of autonomous exchange rate changes—that is—those *not* caused by domestically generated inflationary pressures.[8] Of itself, the wage-price blocks, however skillfully used, provide no information about the sources or the importance of such autonomous exchange rate changes; indeed, to do so is likely to require an explicit model of exchange rate determination, as will be discussed further in the conclusions.

A very similar point applies to the estimation of the linkages of the wage-price block as well; when the endogenous nature of many observed exchange rate changes is *not* taken into account in such estimation, the estimated coefficient will reflect the factors producing exchange rate changes and the policy-response patterns prevailing during the sample period. One should expect the estimated coefficients to remain stable over a given period only if there has been little change in the pattern of disturbances and in macro policymakers' reaction functions.

Failure to account for exchange rate changes that are endogenous can lead to biased estimates of the wage-price block. When the endogeneity of exchange rates is not properly accounted for, the estimated relation between exchange rates and domestic prices will reflect their *average* association—that is, correlation (controlling for the other predetermined variables of the wage-price block), over the sample period. The estimates of the parameters of the wage-price block then will reflect those periods when exchange rate changes were endogenous (say, induced by domestic macroeconomic policies) as well as those when exchange rate movements were exogenous to the domestic economy. For this reason, calculations of impact and full effects derived from such estimates are likely to be misleading—even when the exchange rate changes can be assumed to be exogenous.

Consider the following simple illustration. Suppose that variables such as rent, productivity, unemployment, and foreign import prices are ignored and that wages change proportionately with prices so real wages are constant. Then the wage-price block (16.1) through (16.3) can be reduced to a relation between domestic price changes and exchange rate changes.[9] Assume that the equilibrium rate of inflation, $\dot{P}$, determined by the relevant (for this purpose unspecified) complete econometric model can be represented by the following reduced form equation:

$$\dot{P} = \pi_{10} + \pi_{11} z_1 + \pi_{12} z_2 + - \pi_{1k} z_k \qquad (16.8)$$

where the π's represent the coefficients of the (k) exogenous variables (z_1 through z_k; these include the random disturbances) that jointly determine inflation in the reduced form equation. Similarly, there is a reduced form equation for exchange rate changes:

$$X\dot{R}ATE = \pi_{20} + \pi_{21} z_1 + - \pi_{2k} z_k . \qquad (16.9)$$

Now in this case, the estimated (full) impact of exchange rates on prices will simply reflect their correlation as determined by the reduced forms *and* the behavior of the exogenous variables, $z_1 - z_k$. More precisely, the ordinary least-squares regression coefficient of $\dot{P}$ on $X\dot{R}ATE$ will be the correlation of the two times the ratio of the standard deviation of the former to the latter. Each of these elements will depend upon the behavior of the exogenous variables as well as upon the reduced form coefficients, π. That is, letting $d\dot{P}/dX\dot{R}ATE$ stand for the ordinary least-squares coefficient of $\dot{P}$ on $X\dot{R}ATE$ in this simple case, π can be written as

$$\frac{d\dot{P}}{dX\dot{R}ATE} = \left[\sum_{j=1}^{k} \sum_{i=1}^{k} \pi_{1j} \pi_{2i} \rho_{ij} \sigma_i \sigma_j \right] / \left[\sum_{j=1}^{k} \sum_{i=1}^{k} \pi_{2i} \pi_{2j} \rho_{ij} \sigma_i \sigma_j \right]$$

$$(16.10)$$

where ρ_{ij} is the correlation of z_i and z_j and σ_i is the standard deviation of z_i (the numerator is the covariance of $\dot{P}$ and $X\dot{R}ATE$, or their correlation times the product of their standard deviations; the denominator is simply the variance of $X\dot{R}ATE$).

Thus, the statistical relation between $\dot{P}$ and $X\dot{R}ATE$, which in this simple case would be used to measure the full impact of exchange rates upon prices, depends not only upon the reduced form coefficients, π, but also on the pattern of behavior of the exogenous variables, as measured by their correlations and standard deviations. Estimates of (16.10) calculated over different time periods may then be expected to vary — even if the π do not change — because the pattern of changes in the exogenous variables is not likely to remain stable. Hence, when the endogenaity of exchange rate changes is not accounted for, measures of the full impact of exchange rates upon prices will actually reflect their correlation (in more realistic cases, controlled for other variables), and for this reason we would expect such estimates to be highly unstable and not robust to changes in the sample period.

For example, let the rate of domestic money growth be represented by z_1 and the rate of real government spending growth be represented by z_2. Then a sample period that is dominated by major swings in monetary policy (i.e., σ_1 large and $\sigma_2 - \sigma_k = o$, such as we might expect in U.K. and Italian data during the late sixties) will yield an estimate of (16.10) which is approximately π_{11}/π_{21}. The same calculation made over a different sample period that is dominated by large swings in government spending—that is, σ_2 large and σ_1, $\sigma_3 - \sigma_k = o$—would yield an estimate of (16.10) that is approximately π_{12}/π_{22}. In general, there is no presumption that these ratios of reduced form multipliers should be equal.[10]

Finally, let z_k represent truly exogenous factors influencing the currencies in which investors prefer to hold their assets. A sample period that is dominated by exogenous shifts in asset preferences ($\sigma_1 - \sigma_{k-1} = 0$; σ_k large) would yield an estimate of (16.10) that was approximately equal to π_{1k}/π_{2k}. The latter experiment comes closest to yielding a true estimate of the inflationary effects of exchange rate change since the disturbances generating both price and exchange rate change originate in the foreign exchange market. The problem is that the multiplier that we would like to measure (π_{1k}/π_{2k}) is buried within (16.10), and standard procedures have no way of extracting this multiplier from the "generalized" multiplier (16.10) that is produced by the standard calculations.

Of course, in more realistic cases, the other variables of the wage-price block such as productivity, unemployment, and so forth that are ignored in the above illustration will normally be considered in calculating the impact of exchange rates on prices. This will complicate the calculations underlying the basic argument without altering its basic implication. In particular, the full impact of exchange rate changes on prices (obtained by applying ordinary least squares to the wage-price block without accounting for the endogenaity of exchange rate changes) will still reflect the pattern of behavior of the exogenous variables, although in a somewhat more complex fashion than in (16.10).

Thus, the argument makes it clear why short-run patterns of price and exchange rate movements tend to vary across countries as well as from one historical episode to another for a particular country. It also illustrates why we expect to find unstable estimates of both the impact effect (16.4) and the total effect (16.7) in standard open-economy Phillips Curve models.[11]

IV. EVIDENCE ON INSTABILITY OF STANDARD ESTIMATES FOR THE UNITED STATES

It would not be feasible to report evidence on the stability of each of the many variations in the general model presented above that have appeared in the liter-

ature. Instead, we will make our point by examining the stability of the following simple empirical specification of the model represented by equations (16.1)
through (16.3) that, as we noted above, is representative of many open economy
Phillips Curve equations.

$$\dot{P}_T = b_1 + b_2 \dot{W}_T + b_3 \, PR\dot{I}MP_T \, , \tag{16.11}$$

$$\dot{W} = b_4 + b_5 \, U_T^{-1} + b_6 \, \dot{P}_{T-1} \, . \tag{16.12}$$

(Here, the lagged price change $\dot{P}_{T-1}$ is used as a proxy for expected inflation in
the wage equation.)

By substituting the right-hand side of (16.12) into (16.11) we can represent
the block-reduced form for inflation as

$$\dot{P}_T = a_1 + a_2 \, U_T^{-1} + a_3 \, PR\dot{I}MP_T + a_4 \, \dot{P}_{T-1} \, , \tag{16.13}$$

where $a_1 = (b_1 + b_2 \, b_4)$, $a_2 = b_2 \, b_5$, $a_3 = b_3$, and $a_4 = b_2 \, b_6$.

In this simple model we would express the impact effect of an increase in import prices as a_3 while the total effect is represented by $a_3 / (1 - a_4)$.

If the arguments of the preceding two sections are correct, the parameter
estimates of (16.13) should be biased and inconsistent and should be unstable—
that is, their estimated values should depend on the variance-covariance structure of the exogenous variables in the "true" macro model. In this section we
present evidence showing the instability of the parameters of (16.13).

Table 16-2 presents estimates of the price equation (16.13) obtained by
alternative choices of sample period using quarterly data. Inflation is measured
as the (annualized) four-quarter-moving-average of quarterly changes in the GNP
price deflator.

In the first row of Table 16-2, we have restricted the sample period to Q1/
65-Q4/77. Although not significant, the unemployment parameter is consistent
with a standard negatively sloped Phillips Curve. The estimated $PR\dot{I}MP_T$ coefficient is significantly greater than zero and suggests that a 1 percent depreciation
of the dollar, if fully passed through into increased import prices, will raise
domestic inflation by eight basis points in the short run and by thirty-three
basis points in the long run.[12]

The second row of Table 16-2 presents estimates of the price equation for
the longer sample period Q1/50-Q2/78. For the longer period the intercept is
positive, and the unemployment coefficient has the "wrong" sign. The impact
effect of a 1 percent depreciation is slightly higher at ten basis points: The full
effect is now thirty-seven basis points.

The remaining rows of Table 16-2 present price equation estimates obtained
by splitting the longer Q1/50-Q3/78 sample period at various points. Rows (3)
and (4) split the sample period at Q3/71, when the price freeze was imposed.

Table 16-2. Parameter Estimates of Equation (16.15) $\dot{P}_T = a_1 + a_2 U_T^{-1} + a_3 PR\dot{I}MP_T + a_4 \dot{P}_{T-1}$, where $\dot{P} =$ annualized *four-quarter-moving-average* of quarterly percentage changes in the GNP deflator.

Sample Period	$\hat{a}_1$	$\hat{a}_2$	$\hat{a}_3$	$\hat{a}_4$	$\dfrac{\hat{a}_3}{1-\hat{a}_4}$	$\bar{R}^2$	SSE	DW	Number of Observations
Q1/65–Q4/77	-0.108 (-0.123)	4.093 (1.427)	0.079 (5.014)	0.761 (8.489)	0.331	0.829	44.86	1.900	52
Q1/50–Q2/78	0.915 (1.495)	-1.365 (-0.559)	0.095 (4.458)	0.743 (9.206)	0.370	0.712	268.17	1.791	114
Q1/50–Q2/71	1.060 (1.504)	-1.704 (-0.502)	0.130 (3.051)	0.703 (4.586)	0.438	0.522	219.19	1.892	86
Q3/71–Q2/78	-2.988 (-1.027)	18.83 (1.251)	0.038 (0.998)	0.944 (5.331)	0.679	0.739	42.47	1.250	28
Q1/50–Q4/64	1.249 (1.481)	-1.199 (-0.281)	0.171 (3.258)	0.451 (1.939)	0.311	0.447	187.60	2.100	60
Q1/65–Q2/78	-0.197 (-0.192)	3.827 (1.147)	0.069 (3.765)	0.825 (8.000)	0.394	0.782	63.43	1.476	54
Q1/50–Q4/59	1.913 (1.516)	-2.486 (-0.446)	0.185 (2.873)	0.358 (1.255)	0.288	0.433	169.35	2.169	40
Q1/60–Q4/69	0.244 (0.232)	-2.758 (-0.365)	-0.008 (-0.089)	1.203 (4.193)	0.039	0.744	25.41	2.002	40
Q1/70–Q2/78	-0.996 (-0.490)	7.893 (0.832)	0.061 (2.191)	0.860 (5.781)	0.436	0.729	48.19	1.351	34

T-statistics are given in parentheses below their corresponding coefficients.

Rows (5) and (6) split the sample period at Q1/65 – before the Vietnam War. Rows (7), (8), and (9) split the sample period into decades at Q1/60 and Q1/70. The variation in results is striking. The intercept varies from a low of -2.988 percent to a high of 1.913 percent – nearly a 5 percent shift in the intercept of the Phillips Curve. The unemployment coefficient is negative – the Phillips Curve has the wrong slope – in five out of nine cases, with estimates varying from -2.578 to 18.83. The impact effect of import price changes varies between -1 basis points and eighteen basis points, and shows the wrong sign during the 1960s. The full effect of import prices varies from four basis points during the 1960s to sixty-eight basis points in the postfreeze period. One of the estimated price equations implies unstable dynamic adjustment ($a_4 = 1.203$). The adjusted R^2 remains high, and the Durbin–Watson statistic (although not strictly appropriate in this situation due to the presence of the lagged dependent variable in the estimating equation) remains reasonably close to two through all this shifting and sign-changing.

Table 16-3 presents similar estimates replacing the GNP deflator with the annualized four-quarter-moving-average of consumer price changes as the measure of inflation. The results are similar. The intercept varies between -4.527 and 0.376. The unemployment coefficient varies from 0.968 to 29.788 and is never significantly greater than zero. The impact effect of a 1 percent depreciation varies from 0.0014 (less than one-seventh of one basis point) to twenty basis points. The full effect of a 1 percent depreciation of the dollar varies from three basis points to fifty-three basis points.

Table 16-4 replicates the estimates from Table 16-2 for the price deflator but measures the price variables as quarter-to-quarter changes, rather than as four-quarter-moving-averages. The estimates show great fluctuation in the intercept (-3.358 to 2.431). The unemployment coefficient has the wrong sign in three of nine cases and is significantly positive only once. The impact effect of a 1 percent change in import prices varies from four basis points to twenty-two basis points. The full effect varies from four basis points to eighteen basis points. The lagged inflation term has the wrong sign in three cases, paradoxically suggesting that the full effects in these cases are less than the impact effects.

Table 16-5 similarly replicates estimates from Table 16-3 for the consumer price index, now measuring inflation as the quarterly change in the index. The estimates of Table 16-5 exhibit the same instability of intercept and unemployment coefficients that we found in Tables 16-2 through 16-5. The impact effect varies from three basis points during the 1960s to fourteen basis points during the pre-Vietnam period. The full effect fluctuates from three basis points to twenty-two basis points. It is perhaps surprising that this range is only marginally higher than for the comparable GNP deflator estimates even though import prices enter directly into the CPI, but not the deflator.

Taken as a whole, these estimates suggest that there may be substantial biases and instabilities in the standard calculations, although because of the ordinary

Table 16-3. Parameter Estimates of Equation (16.15) $\dot{P} = a_1 + a_2 U_T^{-1} + a_3 PR\dot{I}MP_T + a_4 \dot{P}_{T-1}$; where $\dot{P}$ = annualized *four-quarter-moving-average* of quarterly percentage changes in the consumer price index.

Sample Period	$\hat{a}_1$	$\hat{a}_2$	$\hat{a}_3$	$\hat{a}_4$	$\dfrac{\hat{a}_3}{1-\hat{a}_4}$	$\bar{R}^2$	SSE	DW	Number of Observations
Q1/65–Q4/77	-0.561 (-0.644)	5.794 (1.932)	0.085 (4.622)	0.774 (8.934)	0.376	0.852	52.08	1.690	52
Q1/50–Q2/78	0.203 (0.348)	1.442 (0.594)	0.118 (5.640)	0.732 (10.740)	0.440	0.772	265.46	1.564	114
Q1/50–Q2/71	-0.051 (-0.076)	2.770 (0.895)	0.183 (5.200)	0.653 (6.350)	0.527	0.645	199.22	1.673	86
Q3/71–Q2/78	-4.527 (-1.332)	29.788 (1.658)	0.0135 (0.269)	0.968 (4.977)	0.422	0.766	47.29	1.354	28
Q1/50–Q4/64	0.297 (0.367)	1.128 (0.296)	0.197 (4.861)	0.562 (3.920)	0.450	0.584	171.44	1.766	60
Q1/65–Q2/78	-0.541 (-0.548)	5.366 (1.579)	0.075 (3.621)	0.820 (8.427)	0.417	0.814	69.95	1.468	54
Q1/50–Q4/59	0.376 (0.307)	0.968 (0.186)	0.202 (4.067)	0.552 (3.194)	0.451	0.584	157.18	1.702	40
Q1/60–Q4/69	-0.926 (-0.991)	5.320 (0.892)	0.0014 (0.016)	0.955 (4.427)	0.031	0.778	25.67	2.085	40
Q1/70–Q2/78	-1.006 (-0.475)	9.228 (0.899)	0.068 (2.042)	0.812 (5.456)	0.362	0.757	55.48	1.416	40

T-statistics are given in parentheses below their corresponding coefficients.

Table 16-4. Parameter Estimates of Equation (16.15) $\dot{P}_T = a_1 + a_2 U_T^{-1} + a_3 PR\dot{I}MP_T + a_4 \dot{P}_{T-1}$, where $\dot{P}$ = annualized *quarter-to-quarter* percentage change in the GNP deflator.

Sample Period	$\hat{a}_1$	$\hat{a}_2$	$\hat{a}_3$	$\hat{a}_4$	$\dfrac{\hat{a}_3}{1-\hat{a}_4}$	$\bar{R}^2$	SSE	DW	Number of Observations
Q1/65–Q4/77	2.009 (1.870)	−1.604 (−0.425)	0.056 (3.231)	0.608 (6.184)	0.143	0.661	88.94	2.512	52
Q1/50–Q3/78	2.431 (3.146)	−3.530 (−1.099)	0.094 (4.259)	0.443 (5.449)	0.169	0.496	473.50	2.388	115
Q1/50–Q2/71	1.056 (1.240)	5.594 (1.454)	0.169 (4.442)	0.056 (0.470)	0.179	0.301	320.20	2.029	86
Q3/71–Q3/78	0.768 (0.276)	6.817 (0.429)	0.039 (1.164)	0.647 (4.390)	0.110	0.527	77.33	2.268	29
Q1/50–Q4/64	1.014 (1.106)	6.249 (1.470)	0.219 (5.252)	−0.229 (−1.602)	0.178	0.348	221.25	1.984	60
Q1/65–Q3/78	2.422 (2.107)	−2.788 (−0.684)	0.055 (2.966)	0.589 (5.804)	0.134	0.617	112.17	2.343	55
Q1/50–Q4/59	1.825 (1.358)	3.849 (0.689)	0.229 (4.556)	−0.258 (−1.490)	0.182	0.361	190.78	1.956	40
Q1/60–Q4/69	−3.358 (−3.619)	27.64 (5.060)	0.041 (0.701)	−0.044 (−0.260)	0.039	0.618	37.93	1.927	40
Q1/70–Q3/78	1.481 (0.704)	2.565 (0.286)	0.044 (1.718)	0.627 (4.708)	0.118	0.528	84.20	2.311	35

T-statistics are given in parentheses below their corresponding coefficients.

Table 16-5. Parameter Estimates of Equation (16.15) $\dot{P}_T = a_1 + a_2 U_T^{-1} + a_3 PR\dot{I}MP_T + a_4 \dot{P}_{T-1}$, where $\dot{P}$ = annualized *quarter-to-quarter* percentage change in the consumer price index.

Sample Period	$\hat{a}_1$	$\hat{a}_2$	$\hat{a}_3$	$\hat{a}_4$	$\dfrac{\hat{a}_3}{1-\hat{a}_4}$	$\bar{R}^2$	SSE	DW	Number of Observations
Q1/65–Q4/77	1.212 (1.196)	0.476 (0.128)	0.067 (3.715)	0.659 (7.404)	0.196	0.747	88.87	2.309	52
Q1/50–Q2/78	1.306 (1.780)	-0.909 (-0.290)	0.093 (4.328)	0.581 (8.117)	0.222	0.617	447.03	2.227	114
Q1/50–Q2/71	-0.062 (-0.070)	6.170 (1.563)	0.115 (3.184)	0.380 (3.695)	0.185	0.398	337.83	2.201	86
Q3/71–Q2/78	1.382 (0.511)	2.050 (0.131)	0.064 (1.882)	0.647 (4.670)	0.181	0.659	68.99	1.628	28
Q1/50–Q4/64	0.018 (0.018)	5.343 (1.152)	0.143 (3.505)	0.237 (1.874)	0.187	0.349	268.66	2.164	60
Q1/65–Q2/78	1.578 (1.450)	-0.811 (-0.202)	0.065 (3.302)	0.664 (6.881)	0.193	0.708	109.98	1.971	54
Q1/50–Q4/59	0.189 (0.122)	4.585 (0.717)	0.143 (2.806)	0.262 (1.671)	0.194	0.343	247.78	2.160	40
Q1/60–Q4/69	-3.503 (-3.596)	25.225 (4.559)	0.027 (0.452)	0.158 (0.970)	0.032	0.656	39.90	1.937	40
Q1/70–Q2/78	1.460 (0.711)	1.382 (0.127)	0.063 (2.306)	0.642 (5.012)	0.176	0.640	82.19	1.875	34

T-statistics are given in parentheses below their corresponding coefficients.

(and often substantial) sampling variation encountered in much empirical work, the evidence cannot be taken as conclusive. At the least, the results illustrate the great uncertainty about the magnitude of the effects of exchange rates upon domestic prices.

V. CONCLUDING REMARKS

Our short empirical exercise found a range of impact effects on U.S. prices running from negative values to 2.3 percentage points for a 10 percent change in the dollar. With estimated wage-price interactions taken into account, the resulting range ran from 0.3 to 6.8 percentage points. While it is possible that the "true" coefficients for some types of disturbances could be even outside of this range, we consider it unlikely. Our guess would be that a sustained 10 percent change in the real exchange rate of the dollar would be likely to lead to changes in the U.S. price level on the order of, say, 1.5 to 3.5 percent, while a nominal change that merely reflected differential rates of inflation would have little independent influence on domestic prices.

Our major point, however, is that in general, while such effects will frequently be important, we are quite far from having good estimates of what these effects are likely to be under many circumstances. To develop better estimates, one will need to develop more complete models of wage, price, and exchange rate determination that emphasize the role of expectations and underlying policy behavior.[13] As recent work has clearly indicated, this is no easy task and could never realistically be expected to achieve highly precise estimates. Still such efforts may be able to reduce the range of uncertainty and thus in our judgment are worth the effort.

NOTES TO CHAPTER 16

1. For discussion and references to the vicious circle debate see Thomas D. Willett, *Floating Exchange Rates and International Monetary Reform* (Washington, D.C.: American Enterprise Institute, 1977), ch. 2; and Thomas D. Willett and Matthias Wolf, "The Vicious Circle Debate: Some Conceptual Distinctions," *Kyklos* 2 (1983): 231–48.

2. For discussions of these questions see Morris Goldstein, "Comment" on "The Price Effects of Exchange Rate Changes," by Peter Isard, in Peter B. Clark, Dennis E. Logue, and Richard J. Sweeney, eds., *The Effects of Exchange Rate Adjustments* (Washington, D.C.: U.S. Treasury Department, 1974), pp. 402–5.

3. Rudiger Dornbusch, "Monetary Policy Under Exchange Rate Flexibility," in *Managed Exchange Rate Flexibility* (Boston: Federal Reserve Bank of Boston, 1978), p. 115.

4. Robert E. Lucas, "Econometric Policy Evaluation: A Critique," in Karl Brunner and Allen H. Meltzer, eds., *The Phillips Curve and Labor Markets*, supplement to *Journal of Monetary Economics* (Amsterdam: North-Holland, 1976): 19–46.

5. Models of this type are discussed in John Rutledge, "The Unemployment-Inflation Tradeoff: A Review Article," (Claremont, Calif.: Claremont Working Papers, 1975). Although Phillips considered import prices in his classic paper, A. W. Phillips, "The Relation Between Unemployment and the Rate of Change of Money Wages in the United Kingdom, 1867–1957," *Economica* 25 (November 1958): 283–99, the first and formal open-economy Phillips Curve model was estimated by L. A. Dicks–Mireaux, "The Interrelationship Between Cost and Price Changes, 1946–1959, A Study of Inflation in Post War Britain," *Oxford Economic Papers*, vol. 13 (1961), pp. 267–92. Since then dozens of variations on this theme have been made. Out of these, Richard G. Lipsey and James M. Parker, "Two Equation Prototype Model," in their "Income Policy: A Reappraisal," *Economica* 37: 146 (May 1970): 115–38, and James Tobin's "Standard Wage Price Block," in his "The Wage Price Mechanism: Overview of the Conference," *The Econometrics of Price Determination* (Washington, D.C.: The Federal Reserve System Board of Governors, 1972), stand out as representative analytical models. The extention of these models to open economies is more recent but increasingly popular. For examples of this approach, see Rudiger Dornbusch and Paul Kurgman, "Flexible Exchange Rates in the Short Run," *Brookings Papers on Economic Activity*, No. 3 (1976), 537–81; Rudiger Dornbusch, "Monetary Policy Under Exchange Rate Flexibility"; Morris Goldstein, "Have Flexible Exchange Rates Made Macroeconomic Policy More Difficult? A Survey of Issues and Evidence," presented at the Conference on Macroeconomics Under Flexible Exchange Rates, Madrid, Spain (September 1979), Princeton Special Paper in International Economics, 1980; Sung Kwack, "The Effects of Foreign Inflation on Domestic Prices and the Relative Price Advantage of Exchange Rate Changes," in Peter B. Clark, Dennis E. Logue, and Richard J. Sweeney, eds., *The Effects of Exchange Rate Adjustments*, Joel L. Prabken, "The Exchange Rates and Domestic Inflation," Federal Reserve Bank of New York, *Quarterly Review* 4: 2 (Summer, 1979): 49–55; Robert Solomon, "Exchange Rates and Inflation," Brookings Institution 1980 (Mimeo.); and Erich Spitaller, "A Model of Inflation and its Performance in Seven Main Industrial Countries, 1958–1976," *IMF Staff Papers* 25: 2 (June 1978): 254–77. A review of estimates on the inflationary impact of exchange rate changes can be found in Peter Hooper and Barbara R. Lowrey, "Impact of the Dollar Depreciation on the U.S. Price Level: An Analytical Survey of Empirical Estimates," *International Finance Discussion Papers* 128 (January 1979).

6. The coefficients on the import price variable are usually assumed to reflect the share of tradable goods in the aggregate price index. The tradable goods sector will be larger than the volume of goods actually traded, of course, so that the use of the Import/GNP ratio would understate the

impact of a change in import price on the aggregate price level. In balance of payments models we tend to use a two-fold tradable, nontradable goods distinction with infinite cross price elasticities among all tradable goods and zero direct cross-price elasticities between these and nontradable goods. In fact, of course, goods and even services fall across a continuum of cross-price elasticities and treating all categories which have a tradable component as if they were pure tradable goods would overstate the impact effect of exchange rate changes just as looking only at the actual share of imports would understate it. a_{15} will also be influenced by the degree of "pass through" from exchange rate changes to domestic currency prices of exports and imports. This will in general be lower for exogenous exchange rate changes, the larger the economy in question. The observed relationship between exchange rate changes and export and import prices will be influenced by the cause of exchange rate changes along the same line as the discussion of impact effect on domestic prices in the text. To abstract from this problem and to allow estimation over a longer period in our empirical work we have followed the convention of using import prices directly in our regression. For recent studies and surveys of the earlier literature on pass through estimates, see Morris Goldstein, "Have Flexible Exchange Rates Made Macroeconomic Policy More Difficult?"; Peter Hooper and Barbara Lowrey, "Impact of the Dollar Depreciation on the U.S. Price Level: An Analytical Survey of Empirical Estimates"; W. Robinson, T. R. Webb and M. A. Townsend, "The Influences of Exchange Rate Changes on Prices: A Study of Eighteen Industrial Countries," *Economica* 46 (February 1979): 27–50; and Robert Solomon, "Exchange Rates and Inflation," Brookings Institution 1980. (Mimeo.) For examples of the use of input–output tables to attempt to estimate the size of the tradable goods sector, see R. Berner, Peter B. Clark, Jared Enzler, and Barbara R. Lowrey, "International Sources of Domestic Inflation," Joint Economic Committee, Studies in Price Stability and Economic Growth, 94th Congress, 1st Session, paper no. 3 (August 1975); Philip Cagan, "Imported Inflation 1973–74 and the Accommodation Issue," *Journal of Money, Credit and Banking* 12: 1 (February 1980): 1–16; Willson Nordhaus and John Shoven, "Inflation 1973: The Year of Infamy," *Challenge* 17 (May–June 1974): 14–22. The alternative channels through which a change in import price can influence the domestic price and wage determination process are presented and discussed in Deardorff and Stern's study of international linkages: Allen V. Deardorff and Robert M. Stern, "Modeling the Effects of Foreign Price Determination: Some Econometric Evidence and Implications for Theoretical Analysis," Banca Nazionale del Lavoro *Quarterly Review* 127 (December 1978): 333–53. Note that import prices are direct components of the CPI and WPI, but not of the GNP deflator, which is also often used in these types of estimates.

7. For further discussion see Richard J. Sweeney and Thomas D. Willett, "The Inflationary Impact of Exchange Rate Changes: Some Theoretical Considerations," in Peter B. Clark, Dennis E. Logue, and Richard J. Swee-

ney, eds., *The Effects of Exchange Rate Adjustments* (Washington, D.C., U.S. Treasury, 1976), pp. 45–61.

8. We are not the first writers to raise this issue, of course. Haberler's classic criticism of the vicious circle explanation of the German hyperinflation pointed out that it is improper to consider exchange rates to be completely exogenous to the domestic inflation process; see Gottfried Haberler, *The Theory of International Trade*, (London: W. Hodge and Co., 1936). This issue was also pointed out by William Poole and others in the discussion following Rudiger Dornbusch and Paul Krugman, "Flexible Exchange Rates in the Short Run;" Carlos Rodriquez, "A Stylized Model of the Devaluation-Inflation Spiral," *IMF Staff Papers* 25: 1 (March 1978); and in our earlier discussions in Thomas D. Willett, *Floating Exchange Rates and International Monetary Reform* (Washington, D.C.: American Enterprise Institute, 1977; and Charles Pigott, John Rutledge and Thomas D. Willett, "Some Difficulties in Estimating the Inflationary Impact of Exchange Rate Changes" (Mimeo.), presented at the Western Economic Association Meetings, June 1978. The importance of distinguishing between exogenous and endogenous components of exchange rate adjustments in empirical estimates is also indicated in Michael Bruno, "Exchange Rates, Import Costs, and Wage-Price Dynamics," *Journal of Political Economy* 86; 3 (June 1978): 379–404; Peter Hooper and Barbara Lowrey, "Impact of the Dollar Depreciation of the U.S. Price Level: An Analytical Survey of Empirical Estimates," *International Finance Discussion Papers* 128 (January 1979). Despite the number of authors who have clearly been aware of this difficulty, it has continued to be ignored in most papers.

Some attention has been given to applying Granger–Sims-type causality tests to the relationships between inflation and exchange rates. See, for example, Jacob A. Frenkel, "Purchasing Power Parity: Doctrinal Perspective and Evidence from the 1920s," *Journal of International Economics* 8: 2 (May 1978): 169–91, but we have considerable doubts about the interpretation of such tests when both variables are endogenous to a more complete structural model. Procedures which establish "cause" and "effect" based on the temporal pattern of their covariation cannot adequately consider the influence of omitted third factors. This argument has been well-known at least since Haberler's brilliant discussion of price and exchange rate dynamics during hyperinflation. Haberler argued that the statistical observation that exchange rate change precedes price change during hyperinflation does not imply causality, in the normal use of the term, because exchange rates respond relatively quickly to changes in inflation expectations; see Gottfried Haberler, *The Theory of International Trade*. See also the similar arguments by John F. O. Bilson, "The Vicious Circle Hypothesis," *IMF Staff Papers* 26: 1 (March 1979): 1–37. On the general economic meaning of Granger–Sims-type causality testing, see the recent papers by Rodney J. Jacobs, Edward Leamer, and Michael Ward, "Difficulties with Testing for Causality," *Economic Inquiry* (July 1979): 401–13; and

Arnold Zellner, "Causality and Econometrics," in *Three Aspects of Policy and Policymaking: Knowledge, Data and Institutions*, a supplementary series to the *Journal of Monetary Economics* 10 (1979): 9–54. For an interesting recent analysis that makes use of extensions of the Granger–Sims approach to more variables so that money can also be included see Masahiro Kawai, "Exchange Rate-Price Causality in the Recent Floating Period" in David Bigman and Teizo Taya, eds., *The Functioning of Floating Exchange Rates* (Cambridge, Mass.: Ballinger, 1980), pp. 197–220. Kawai finds that including money as a third variable significantly affected his empirical results in a number of instances.

9. The model will now be:

$$(i') \quad \dot{P} = a_{12}\,\dot{W} + a_{15}\,PR\dot{I}MP = \dot{P} = a_{12}\dot{P} + a_{15}\,XR\dot{A}TE$$

since $\dot{W} = \dot{P}$ in this simple example, then,

$$(i'') \quad \dot{P} = (a_{15}/1 - a_{12})\,XR\dot{A}TE \ .$$

In the above illustration, it is supposed that it is this latter relation that is estimated. In more realistic cases, of course, other variables will appear on the right side of (i'').

10. In fact, careful consideration suggests that π_{11}/π_{12} and π_{12}/π_{22} should be opposite in sign since both increased money growth and increased government spending will raise inflation, while increased money growth depreciates the exchange rate but increased government spending (assuming it raises the budget deficit) by raising the domestic interest rate may lead to exchange rate appreciation if capital mobility is sufficiently great.

11. The problem of the stability of coefficients in open-economy models was emphasized by Morris Goldstein, "Comment," in Peter Clark, Dennis E. Logue, and Richard Sweeney, eds., *The Effects of Exchange Rate Adjustments*, although he focused particularly on the coefficient of prices on wages, while we emphasize the instability of the import price coefficients as well. See also Morris Goldstein, "The Trade-Off Between Inflation and Unemployment: A Survey of the Econometric Evidence for Selected Countries," *IMF Staff Papers* (November 1972): 647–98; and Morris Goldstein, "The Effect of Exchange Rate Changes on Wages and Prices in the United Kingdom: An Empirical Study," *IMF Staff Papers* 21 (November 1974): 694–739. Other biases in the estimates of equations 16.4 and 16.7 may arise from deficiencies in the specification of standard Phillips Curve models. These include the specification and frequent instability of policy reaction functions, possibly incorrect specifications of expectations, including particularly the use of simple adaptive expectations models, and the assumption that there is a stable relation between price markups over cost and excess demand. For detailed discussion of these and other problems, see John Rutledge, "Neoclassical Model of Wage and Price Dynamics," in The Proceedings of the 1977 West Coast Academic/Federal Reserve Economic Research Seminar (San Francisco, Federal Reserve Bank of San Francisco), pp. 97–128.

12. The relationship between exchange rate and import price changes will, of course, vary depending on what causes the exchange rate change, just as will the relationships between exchange rates and domestic inflation.

13. The exchange rate modelling project of the Federal Reserve Board is an important effort in this direction. See, for example, Guy Stevens, et al., *The U.S. Economy in an Interdependent World: A Multicountry Model* (Washington, D.C.: Board of Governors of the Federal Reserve System, 1984).

17 DOLLAR APPRECIATION AND THE REAGAN DISINFLATION

J. Harold McClure, Jr.

From the double-digit levels of inflation in 1980, the consumer price growth rate has dropped below 5 percent in 1983. The very deep recession is partly responsible, but if one accepts the conventional wisdom of previously estimated Phillips Curves, even the massive amounts of excess supply can explain only two to three points of the disinflation. More generous estimates of the effectiveness of demand restraint might suggest a four-point decline.[1] One possible explanation suggested by critics of Keynesian econometric models is that historically estimated Phillips Curves understate the effectiveness of a vigorously pursued tight monetary program. For example, the Lucas critique (1976) argues that as perceived policymaking rules change, the economic structure—including the slope of the short-run Phillips Curve—may shift. A perceived real commitment by the new administration to ending inflation might speed the process of disinflation. For example, Cagan-Fellner (1984) argue that a standard wage-unemployment equation would overforecast the amount of inflation from 1981 onwards.[2]

Another possibility is that inclusion of import price behavior in an open-economy Phillips model can help explain the rapid disinflation without appeal to a Lucas critique argument. Part of the high inflation in 1979-80 was due to rising import prices and dollar devaluation. Likewise, the fall in inflation was accentuated by dollar appreciation, which gave negative import price inflation.

To assess the relative roles of excess supply and import prices, an open-economy Phillips model was estimated from 1961 to 1980, and simulated from 1981 to mid-1983. Ending the estimation period in 1980 allows a crude check for the Lucas critique: If the true Phillips slope did become steeper, then the simulation model should overforecast inflation. The actual data on consumer price inflation, import price changes, and excess supply is given in Table 17-1.

Table 17-1. Measures of Inflation and Excess Supply: 1981-83.

	Consumer Price Inflation	Import Price Inflation	Capacity Utilization	Unemployment Rate
1981/1	8.20	5.16	80.6	7.4
2	6.76	0.00	80.8	7.37
3	7.49	-12.19	80.3	7.4
4	6.74	-2.35	75.9	8.3
1982/1	5.02	-8.20	72.9	8.8
2	3.77	-11.64	71.6	9.4
3	6.48	11.99	71.0	9.97
4	4.06	-4.68	69.0	10.67
1983/1	2.11	-18.82	70.7	10.37
2	4.95	9.19	73.7	10.1

Source: All data are from Citibase. Unemployment figures are the average of that quarter's monthly unemployment rate. The inflation numbers are calculated as $(P/P(-1)-1) \cdot 400$ where P represents the consumer price deflator and the import price deflator.

The model rests on two relationships. The first is the Phillips Curve notion that domestic inflation $(\hat{P}_d)$ depends on excess supply or the "Gap" and the past history of inflation as given by a four-quarter lag of consumer price inflation (π):[3]

$$\hat{P}_d = f(Gap) + \sum_{i=1}^{4} b_i \, \pi_{t-i} \tag{17.1}$$

where $\sum_{i=1}^{4} b_i = 1$ and $f' < 0$.

Consumer price inflation is a weighted average of $\hat{P}_d$ and import price inflation $(\hat{P}_m)$:

$$\pi = (1-a) \cdot \hat{P}_d + a \cdot \hat{P}_m \; . \tag{17.2}$$

The weight for import prices (a) can range from the import-to-GNP ratio to the tradables-to-GNP ratio depending upon one's assessment of the substitutability among tradable goods. The reduced form of this system is:

$$\pi_t = (1-a) \cdot f'(Gap) + a \cdot \hat{P}_m + \sum_{i=1}^{4} C_i \, \pi_{t-1} \tag{17.3}$$

where $\Sigma C_i = 1-a$.

This model was estimated using two proxies for excess supply: the capacity utilization rate and the unemployment rate. Table 17-2 presents the results of both versions. The excess supply coefficients are as large, or slightly larger, than previous work had obtained.[4] The estimated import price coefficients (a is be-

Table 17-2. Inflation Equations 1961–80.

Constant	Excess* Supply	Import Price Inflation	π_{-1}	π_{-2}	π_{-3}	π_{-4}	R^2/DW
(a) −7.99	0.0994	0.0611	0.413	0.037	0.399	0.034	0.877
(−2.76)	(2.96)	(3.83)	(3.48)	(0.32)	(3.43)	(0.30)	1.81
(b) 1.27	−0.159	0.0663	0.473	0.039	0.379	−0.04	0.865
(2.17)	(−1.34)	(4.01)	(3.88)	(0.32)	(3.12)	(−0.34)	1.78

*Equation (a) uses capacity utilization as excess supply; Equation (b) uses unemployment. Lagged inflation is labelled π_{-i} where i = the number of quarters. The numbers in parentheses are t-statistics.

tween 0.06 and 0.07) were lower than most of those previously estimated. Thus, a typical estimate from previous studies ($a = 0.15$) was also used as a medium value.[5] Since the hypothesis is that these effects are important, the analysis was limited to low and medium estimates. Choosing a higher value for the import price weight would only strengthen this paper's contention.

Three types of simulations are reported in Table 17-3: the predicted inflation using ex post data for excess supply and import price inflation, a simulation using the value of π for $\hat{P}_m$, and a simulation using the consumer price inflation of industrial nations for $\hat{P}_m$. Even with the low value of a, both the capacity utilization and unemployment versions overstate the amount of disinflation. If Reaganomics steepened the Phillips trade-off, we find no evidence of it.

The second set of simulations implicitly imposes a crawling peg type of exchange rate management that tries to keep the real exchange rate constant. If the Federal Reserve had wished to do this, it would have had to allow some nominal appreciation as foreign prices rose relative to domestic prices. Note that this simulation gives inflation predictions of one and a half to two points higher than the actual data version, using the estimated value of a. For the high value of a, this difference is from three to seven points.

The other set of simulations takes import price inflation to equal the foreign inflation rate, which is a means to explore the implications of a fixed *nominal* exchange rate when foreign inflation is higher than domestic inflation. Using the estimated value of a, the predicted values of inflation lie two to three points above the simulations using actual data. With $a = 0.15$, this difference becomes four to eight points.

These simulations suggest that, contrary to the Lucas critique arguments, without dollar appreciation the recession would not have lowered inflation as rapidly as in the recent experience. It is the strength of the dollar that offers the major explanation of the speed of disinflation. The dollar's appreciation may have been the result of the mix of easy fiscal policy and tight monetary policy. Models that omit this channel or vector autoregressive models may falsely indicate a structural shift. A model of the demand-inflation process that incorpo-

Table 17-3. Actual and Simulated Rates of U.S. Inflation 1981-83.

A. *Capacity Utilization Equation Simulations*

Quarter	Actual Inflation	Actual $\hat{P}_m$ Low a	Actual $\hat{P}_m$ High a	$\hat{P}_m = \hat{P}_c$ Low a	$\hat{P}_m = \hat{P}_c$ High a	$\hat{P}_m = \hat{P}*$ Low a	$\hat{P}_m = \hat{P}*$ High a
81/1	8.20	8.78	9.23	8.97	9.69	9.07	9.96
2	6.76	8.14	8.32	8.63	9.52	8.89	10.16
3	7.49	6.96	5.97	8.38	9.43	8.58	9.94
4	6.74	6.41	5.98	7.64	9.00	7.84	9.49
82/1	5.02	5.21	4.35	6.78	8.21	7.04	8.84
2	3.77	3.87	2.07	6.08	7.50	6.54	8.62
3	6.48	4.39	4.47	5.57	7.36	5.85	8.06
4	4.06	2.84	2.03	4.61	6.38	4.87	7.01
83/1	2.11	0.95	-1.81	3.94	5.53	4.31	6.43
2	4.95	2.28	1.90	3.87	5.79	4.22	6.66

B. *Unemployment Equation Simulations*

Quarter	Actual Inflation	Actual $\hat{P}_m$ Low a	Actual $\hat{P}_m$ High a	$\hat{P}_m = \hat{P}_c$ Low a	$\hat{P}_m = \hat{P}_c$ High a	$\hat{P}_m = \hat{P}*$ Low a	$\hat{P}_m = \hat{P}*$ High a
81/1	8.20	8.44	8.88	8.64	9.33	8.76	9.60
2	6.76	7.66	7.87	8.21	9.10	8.50	9.76
3	7.49	6.38	5.47	7.95	9.03	8.19	9.60
4	6.74	5.94	5.49	7.38	8.75	7.61	9.29
82/1	5.02	4.95	4.08	6.77	8.20	7.06	8.86
2	3.77	3.69	1.94	6.20	7.62	6.70	8.75
3	6.48	4.41	4.42	5.79	7.54	6.12	8.29
4	4.06	3.13	2.36	5.09	6.81	5.39	7.46
83/1	2.11	1.23	-1.33	4.48	6.01	4.87	6.90
2	4.95	2.50	2.11	4.26	6.07	4.63	6.91

rates both a Phillips curve and an endogenous exchange rate channel, such as those suggested by Gordon (1982) and McClure (1984), could explain the rapid disinflation without any appeal to a shift in the economic structure.

NOTES TO CHAPTER 17

1. See, for example, Okun (1978) and Gordon and King (1982).
2. Vroman (1983) also argues that the Phillips Curve steepened in recent years, citing the rapid deceleration of wages in 1982 and early 1983. Studies by Englander-Los (1983) and Blanchard (1984), however, find that there is no evidence of a significant shift in standard Phillips curves, although the latter's one period ahead forecasts overestimate the amount of inflation from late 1981 onwards. Blanchard also argues that the public's perception of the

policy regime did shift, but not in October 1979 – the advent of Volkerism – but rather, in 1981. Taylor (1984) also argues that both the policy regime and the inflation–unemployment relation has shifted, but his vector auto-regression model as well as the one estimated by Gordon–King cannot distinguish between the demand-excess supply effect and the demand-exchange rate channel. Finally, Perry (1983) finds only weak evidence that wage equations overforecast inflation, while the Gordon–King equations actually underforecast inflation.

3. Use of a longer lag does not substantially alter the equation. The lagged inflation coefficients beyond four quarters all have very low t-statistics.

4. This simple model displays some of the same characteristics as a more elaborate model estimated by Gordon (1982). His excess supply coefficient was also higher than Phillips models without import price effects. Demand affects inflation through unemployment and exchange rates in both models. Finally, his finding that explicit use of a wage equation actually worsens the forecasting performance as compared with a reduced form of the wage-price block corresponds to my finding that unemployment is positively correlated with wage inflation. Had I stimulated a model with equations (17.1) and (17.2) using wage inflation for $\hat{P}_d$, it would have predicted acceleration of inflation, whereas estimation of equation (17.3) more reasonably suggested that excess supply lowers inflation.

5. For references to this literature and discussion of the difficulties of estimating these coefficients, see the preceding paper by Pigott, Rutledge, and Willett.

REFERENCES

Blanchard, Oliver J. 1984. "The Lucas Critique and the Volker Disinflation," *American Economic Review* 74, no. 2 (May): 211–15.

Cagan, Phillip and William Fellner. 1984. "The Cost of Disinflation. Credibility and the Deceleration of Wages 1982–1983," in *Essays in Contemporary Economic Problems – Disinflation*, edited by William Fellner. Washington, D.C.: American Enterprise Institute for Public Policy Research.

Englander, A. Steven, and Cornelius A. Los. 1983. "The Stability of the Phillips Curve and its Implications for the 1980s." Federal Reserve Bank of New York *Research Paper*, No. 8303 (February).

Gordon, Robert J. 1982. "Inflation, Flexible Exchange Rates, and the Natural Rate of Unemployment," in *Workers, Jobs, and Inflation*, edited by Martin J. Bailey. Washington, D.C.: Brookings Institute.

Gordon, Robert J., and Stephen R. King. 1982. "The Output Cost of Disinflation in Traditional and Vector Autoregressive Models." *Brookings Papers on Economic Activity* (1): 205–42.

Lucas, Robert E. 1976. "Econometric Policy Evaluation: A Critique," in *The Phillips Curve and Labor Markets*, edited by Karl Brunner and Allan H. Meltzer. Carnegie–Rochester Conference Series on Public Policy, Vol. 1 (1976): 19–46.

McClure, J. Harold, Jr. 1984. "Rational and Static Expectations in an Open Economy Model," *Claremont Working Papers*, Claremont Center for Economic Policy Studies.

Okun, Arthur M. 1978. "Efficient Disinflationary Policies," *American Economic Review* 68, no. 2 (May): 348–52.

Perry, George L. 1983. "What Have We Learned About Disinflation?" *Brookings Papers on Economic Activity* (2): 587–602.

Taylor, John B. 1984. "Recent Changes in Macro Policy and its Effects: Some Time–Series Evidence," *American Economic Review* 74, no. 2 (May): 206–10.

Pigott, Charles, John Rutledge, and Thomas D. Willett. 1984. "Estimating the Inflationary Effects of Exchange Rate Changes." Chapter 16 in this volume.

Vroman, Wayne. 1983. *Wage Inflation: Prospects for Deceleration.* Washington, D.C.: Urban Institute Press.

18 THE DEFICIT AND THE DOLLAR

Thomas D. Willett

As was discussed in Chapter 13, once highly oversimplified views are discarded, there is considerable uncertainty about the design of desirable strategies for international macroeconomic policy coordination. Even apart from problems of international cooperation, it is often too difficult to identify shocks in a sufficiently precise and timely manner to make implementation of national or internationally coordinated policy fine-tuning technically feasible. In the early and mid-1980s, however, there has been no such informational difficulty involved with the "shock" of huge current and projected future U.S. budget deficits. From the perspective of coordination issues, in this situation a strong case can be made that an optimal (or desirable) policy strategy would reflect a commonality rather than a conflict of economic interests between the United States and our trading partners.[1] The high U.S. interest rates caused by tight money and easy fiscal policy have been a major cause of the great strength of the dollar in the foreign exchange markets in the early 1980s. It seems ironic that fiscal irresponsibility can lead to a stronger value of the currency, but in a world of high capital mobility this is just what happens as long as the monetary authorities are expected to maintain a non-accommodative stance so that the deficit is not monetized. The resulting tight financial conditions attract international capital flows and cause appreciation of the currency.[2]

I am indebted to Marc Bremer, Harold McClure and Richard Sweeney for helpful comments on earlier versions of this paper.

273

I. COSTS AND BENEFITS OF THE STRONG DOLLAR

This was not an entirely unwelcomed set of developments. There is widespread agreement that a substantial strengthening of the dollar from its lows in the late 1970s was highly desirable from both U.S. and international perspectives. The dollar continues to occupy a place of considerable importance in the post-Bretton Woods international monetary system and it is generally accepted that restoration of confidence in the dollar and some strengthening of its foreign exchange value were necessary conditions for a return to greater global monetary stability. The strong dollar also made an important contribution to speeding up the disinflationary process in the United States, as was shown in Chapter 17. To some extent the frequent complaints from abroad about the complications that the strong dollar has created for foreign macroeconomic and balance of payments policies were the inevitable consequence of wanting to have one's cake and eat it too. From foreign perspectives, U.S. policy is typically seen as being too hot or too cold and is seldom just right. Complaints are virtually assured about adverse inflationary effects abroad when the dollar is strong and adverse employment effects when the dollar is weak. The corresponding positive employment effects in the first case and disinflationary effects in the second are seldom given equal billing. Just as a good bit of the gains from restoring monetary stability in the U.S. will be shared abroad, it is not unreasonable that some of the costs of this process be shared as well.

However, as was discussed in Chapters 1 and 2, a very good case can be made that there has been considerable overkill in the magnitude of the dollar's rise and that from a normative economic standpoint a softening of the dollar would be desirable from both U.S. and international perspectives. This should reduce European complaints as well as those from U.S. export and import competing industries that have suffered a substantial competitive disadvantage from the strength of the dollar. With substantial international capital mobility, it is the U.S. traded goods sector and foreign economies which are bearing much of the brunt of the "crowding out" effects of the huge U.S. budget deficits. From a U.S. standpoint, given the size of the budget deficits, it is desirable that these effects be spread out widely over the U.S. and world economies, rather than being concentrated narrowly on the domestic investment and housing sectors.

Whether this would be desirable for other countries as well would depend heavily on the magnitude of the effects and on the state of their own domestic economies, as discussed in the literature on optimal stabilization policy in open economies (see Chapter 15). To some extent the U.S. monetary fiscal mix of the early 1980s could be seen as a useful way of reducing the normal deflationary effects of the U.S. recession on foreign economies via the Keynesian international trade balance mechanism. By stimulating trade surplus abroad through the strong dollar, the strength of the Keynesian linkages would be reduced from their levels under fixed rates (although at the expense of increased transmission through other channels).

Where a major conflict between U.S. and foreign economic interests emerges is in the question of second-best policy. A strong case can be made that the best policy strategy from both U.S. and foreign economic interests is to bring the budget deficit under control. This, in turn, would be expected to soften the international value of the dollar, although the magnitude of this effect is open to considerable uncertainty. If the deficit is not substantially reduced, however, then aggregate U.S. economic interests would likely be served by a broader spreading of the effects of the deficit than would foreign economic interests. Such foreign concerns should be considered, in that case, as an additional argument for reducing the U.S. budget deficits. As will be discussed below, such international arguments for bringing the U.S. budget deficit under control are reinforced by the possibility that the prolonged continuation of huge U.S. deficits might not be continuously financed by the smooth inflow of foreign capital as predicted by the currently popular exchange rate models based on assumptions of perfect international capital mobility.

II. THE IMPORTANCE OF HOW THE DOLLAR IS LOWERED

How a fall in the dollar is brought about is of crucial importance, however. Our studies find little support for the views of those critics who see the foreign exchange markets as being commonly dominated by irrationality and who predict that once the dollar begins to fall, whenever that may come, it will almost inevitably turn into a disorderly plunge. On the other hand, we have had more than one instance of official efforts to talk or force down a rate leading to a substantial loss of confidence and consequent disorderly plunge. The plunges of the Canadian dollar in 1962 and the U.S. dollar in 1977 are cases in point. Efforts to force down the dollar through massive official intervention and/or the adoption of highly expansionary monetary policy could well run this danger (as well as that of directly rekindling domestic inflationary expectations).

The appropriate way to lower the dollar is to bring the budget deficit under control. There is of course a currently popular view in Washington among supply siders, rational expectations theorists, and political operatives, which argues that budget deficits don't influence interest rates because the private sector foresees the corresponding change in their future tax liabilities and adopts offsetting behavior. Thus an increase in public dissaving will be offset by an increase in private saving. The popular empirical argument that supports this view, based on the absence of a strong positive correlation between budget deficits and interest rates, is specious. The actual correlation for the United States for much of the post-war period is negative, but this is because deficits and interest rate movements have both been heavily influenced by business cycle fluctuations, with interest rates typically being low and deficits high during recessions and vice versa during booms. When the state of the economy is taken into account then significant positive effects of active budget deficits can be found, with a typical estimate finding that a $100 billion full employment budget deficit would raise U.S. interest rates by 100 basis points or more.[3]

There is greater substance to the more technical literature on the discounting of the public debt. While the empirical results are quite mixed, it does not seem unreasonable to interpret them as being broadly consistent with the view that such private sector adjustments are significantly greater than zero and significantly less than completely offsetting.[4] In other words, these and many other considerations influence the quantitative magnitude of interest rate and exchange rate effects, but do not undercut the basic argument. (They do help to highlight, however, the importance on resource allocation and growth grounds of focusing on both the level of government expenditures and the deficit, rather than on the latter alone.)

On domestic allocation grounds it is difficult to differ with the supply-side, rational expectations argument (which was made by Milton Friedman long before either of these schools became popular), that the level of government expenditures is probably more important than how they are financed between taxes and debt. From an international perspective, however, it may be that this order of importance should be reversed. In any event, international considerations certainly provide additional arguments for reducing the size of the deficit. This would improve the U.S. trade position and reduce (at least somewhat) domestic protectionist pressures and at the same time reduce European complaints. It would also ease the magnitude of the developing countries' international debt burden that has been substantially increased by the strength of the dollar and high U.S. interest rates. (These of course have been far from the only reasons for the current international debt "crisis," however.)[5]

The U.S. budget deficits unfortunately provide a good example not only of the potential economic benefits at times from international policy cooperation but also of the frequent political difficulties involved in efforts at international cooperation or coordination. While there appears to be a consensus among a quite high majority of economists about the desirability of reducing the U.S. budget deficits, the political feasibility of securing substantial reductions remains open to considerable doubt.[6]

III. DANGERS OF NOT BRINGING DOWN THE DEFICIT

As was discussed above, from a purely national aggregate efficiency standpoint (although not from that of the interests of many U.S. industries), if the deficit cannot be brought under control, then continuation of a basic policy of laissez faire toward the exchange rate of the dollar is probably the wisest second-best strategy for the United States. Such a continuation of the status quo would not itself be without substantial risks, however. International capital mobility is certainly high, but it may not be nearly as high as is frequently assumed in the currently popular asset market models of exchange rates.[7] Between the views of predominant market irrationality adopted by many floating rate critics and the perfect rational market views contained in many exchange rate models may lie a real world of foreign exchange market participants who on average have "reasonable" if not rational expectations, but who often face capital constraints, have somewhat limited time horizons, and react strongly to perceived increases in risk and uncertainty.

Concerns expressed by some economists that these considerations cause severe problems of short-term exchange rate instability under floating rates because of insufficient stabilizing speculation do not appear to have been borne out except for occasional periods of disorderly market conditions. While many exchange traders clearly have a very short time horizon, many other market participants have had long enough time horizons to keep short-run perverse trade adjustments (J-curve effects) from being a major cause of exchange rate instability.[8] But while many participants have time horizons of more than a few months, for most financial transactors this effective horizon may often be a few years rather than a few decades.[9] There is some evidence that many international lenders have suffered in the past from the hubris that if things turned difficult in the borrowing country, they'd be sharp enough to get out before many costs had accumulated.[10] But such ability to get out before "the market falls much" cannot by definition be available to the average investor.

It could be that a nontrivial portion of the recent foreign financial investment in the United States has been based on expectations that the Fed would "hang tough" for at least some time, coupled with the expectation that if accommodation were restored in the future and expectations of inflation rose substantially again, they could pull out rather quickly.[11] Under such a condition of different effective average time horizons between the international and domestic sectors, much of the current level of high long-term nominal interest rates could be due to worries by domestic investors about a future resurgence of inflation, without this yet acting as a strong discouragement to international investors. If recent capital inflows have been heavily influenced by effective expectations horizons of only a few years and/or the supply of capital flows proves to be considerably less than perfectly elastic, then continuing large U.S. budget deficits and/or increased future propensities for monetary accommodation could lead to a substantial drying up or reversal of large capital inflows. This could generate a disruptive plunge of the dollar.[12]

Such a scenario is of course not a certainty. We still know far too little about the effective time horizons, capital constaints, and decisionmaking processes of different types of international transactors.[13] But by the same token, we do not have good reason to be confident that this is not a serious prospect. While from the standpoint of economic research we should welcome a direct test, I would gladly forego this opportunity in the interests of international stability and national economic welfare.

NOTES TO CHAPTER 18

1. As will be discussed below, this conclusion will not necessarily hold from the perspectives of extreme supply-side economics. For discussion of distinctions among different types of supply-side economics and references to the literature, see McClure and Willett (1983).
2. See Chapter 13, and the discussion of exchange rate analysis in Chapter 2. This interpretation of the strength of the dollar is now quite common. See, for example, Arndt (1984), Blanchard and Dornbusch (1984), Krugman (1983), and Laney (1984). However, it is not consistent with all of the new portfolio approach models in which an increase in dollar denominated debt can be seen as a cause of dollar depreciation. See, for example, the recent survey by Frankel (1983) and the discussion in Isard (1983), where initial expectations of a *reduction* in budget deficits under President Reagan is analyzed as a cause of dollar appreciation.

    In traditional models, the exchange rate effects depend on the strength of international capital mobility. With only moderate mobility, depreciation would be predicted as the initial trade balance effect of expansion and would exceed the capital account effects. Recent simulations by the Federal Reserve Board reflecting intermediate views of the degree of international capital mobility have suggested that the exchange rate effects of the budget deficits may be a good bit smaller than many recent discussions have implied. Using the MPS model a modest depreciation effect was found while with their new multicountry model a moderate appreciation was found. See, for example, Cohen and Clark (1984), and Stevens, et al. (1984). Full analysis of the international effects of fiscal deficits requires also distinguishing between current and projected future deficits, and temporary and permanent deficits. For recent analysis along these lines, see Frenkel and Razin (1984). The distinction between full employment and recession induced deficits will be discussed below.
3. See, for example, Makin (1983).
4. For recent empirical studies and references to the technical literature on this topic, see Kormendi (1983), Plosser (1982), and Reid (1984).
5. See, for example, Dale and Mattione (1984).
6. For further discussion of policy coordination issues and the political and economic difficulties of implementation, see the papers and discussion in part four of Dreyer, Haberler, and Willett (1978) and part six of Dreyer, Haberler and Willett (1982).
7. While direct empirical studies of the degree of capital mobility have fallen somewhat out of fashion, the earlier literature on this subject typically

found that international capital mobility between countries was generally significant, but considerably less than infinite for many types of capital flows. See, for example, Branson (1968) and Farrell (1976), and the results of the Federal Reserve Board research discussed in note 2. The studies which find substantial ability of national monetary authorities to sterilize the money supply effects of international capital flows also imply considerably less than infinite capital mobility, as do studies which find significant positive correlations between national savings and investment behavior. On the former type of studies see, for example, Obstfeld (1981) and Laney and Willett (1982) and the references they cite; and on the latter, see Feldstein and Horioka (1980), Feldstein (1983), and von Furstenberg (1983). Such arguments that international capital mobility is not infinite do not, of course, argue that there isn't a good deal of international capital market integration and that between some types of markets, for example the Euro currency markets, it may be virtually complete. See, for example, Herring and Marston (1976) and Logue, Salant, and Sweeney (1976). For a useful discussion of the relationships between perfect capital mobility and perfect asset substitutability, see Frankel (1983).

8. For discussion of the insufficient stabilizing speculation hypothesis, see McKinnon (1976), (1979) and (1984), and for a critical analysis of its general empirical importance see Willett (1977, pp. 38–40). While the empirical results on exchange market efficiency presented by Sweeney in this volume do not suggest that insufficient stabilizing speculation has been a major cause of large exchange rate fluctuations, his results are consistent with the view that exchange markets are somewhat thin and do not fully offset leaning against the wind intervention strategies by many central banks which attempt to slow down exchange rate movements.

9. Note that while the time horizon of direct investors may be several decades, that for many of the associated international financial transactions by the same corporation may be much shorter. For an interesting recent discussion of time horizons of different types of market participants see Armington (1984). While for some purposes some decision makers will undoubtedly have a discrete time horizon in mind, the effects that we loosely ascribe to limited time horizons may be the results of rational risk averse actions by decisionmakers who view many types of uncertainty as being an increasing function of time. For further discussion, see Willett (1976).

10. See Guttentag and Herring (1984).

11. Consistent with this view, it appears that most of the recent capital inflows in the United States have been short-term rather than long-term. See Kubarych (1984). Note that many of the effects of the budget deficits on international capital flows may be indirect. They lead to general financial market tightness which reduces capital outflows and increases inflows, much of which may not go directly into government securities.

The apparent heavy concentration of capital flows on the short end of the spectrum raises doubts about the recent analysis in the CEA Annual Report (1984) which argues that the spot rate of the dollar is above its long run equilibrium by roughly 30 percent, based on the assumption that an expected 3 percent a year depreciation for ten years is needed to compensate for an estimated 3 percent real interest rate differential on ten year bonds. For further discussion on this compensating mechanism, which assumes perfect capital mobility, see Isard (1983) and Chapters 2 and 3 in this volume.

12.   The foreign exchange market has certainly not been entirely free of expressions of such concern. See, for example, Cross (1984).

13.   This obviously should be an important area for research.

REFERENCES

Armington, Paul S. and Catherine Wolford. 1984. "A Model-Based Analysis of Dollar Fluctuations," *Brookings Discussion Papers in International Economics.* Washington, D.C.: The Brookings Institution (January).

Arndt, Sven W. 1984. "The External Effects of U.S. Disinflation," in *Essays in Contemporary Economic Problems: Disinflation*, edited by William Fellner. Washington, D.C.: American Enterprise Institute for Public Policy Research.

Blanchard, O. and Rudiger Dornbusch. 1984. "U.S. Deficits, the Dollar and Europe," *Banca Nazionale del Lavoro Quarterly Review*, No. 148 (March): 89–113.

Branson, William H. 1968. *Financial Capital Flows in the U.S. Balance of Payments.* Amsterdam: North–Holland.

Cohen, Darrell and Peter B. Clark. 1984. "The Effects of Fiscal Policy on the U.S. Economy." Board of Governors of the Federal Reserve System. *Staff Papers*, No. 136 (January).

Council of Economic Advisors. 1984. *Annual Report, Economic Report of the President.* Washington, D.C.: Government Printing Office.

Cross, Sam Y. 1984. "Treasury and Federal Reserve Foreign Exchange Operations." Federal Reserve Bank of New York *Quarterly Review* 9, no. 2 (Summer): 64–66.

Dale, Richard S. and Richard P. Mattione. 1983. *Managing Global Debt.* Washington, D.C.: The Brookings Institution.

Dreyer, Jacob S., Gottfried Haberler, and Thomas D. Willett, eds. 1978. *Exchange Rate Flexibility.* Washington, D.C.: American Enterprise Institute for Public Policy Research.

_____. *The International Monetary System.* 1982. Washington, D.C.: American Enterprise Institute for Public Policy Research.

Farrell, Victoria S. 1983. "Capital Mobility and the Efficacy of Fiscal Policy Under Alternative Exchange Rate Systems," in *Eurocurrencies and the International Monetary System*, edited by Carl H. Stern, John H. Makin, and Dennis E. Logue. Washington, D.C.: American Enterprise Institute for Public Policy Research.

Feldstein, Martin. 1983. "Domestic Savings and International Capital Flows," *European Economic Review* 21, no. 112 (March/April): 129–51.

Feldstein, Martin, and C. Horioka. 1980. "Domestic Savings and International Capital Flows," *The Economic Journal* 90, no. 2 (June): 314–29.

Frankel, Jeffrey A. 1983. "Monetary and Portfolio-Balance Models of Exchange Rate Determination," in *Economic Interdependence and Flexible Exchange Rates*, edited by Jagdeep S. Bhandari and Bluford H. Putnam. Cambridge and London: MIT Press.

Frenkel, Jacob A., ed. 1983. *Exchange Rates and International Macroeconomics.* Chicago and London: University of Chicago Press for the National Bureau of Economic Research.

Frenkel, Jacob A., and Assaf Razin. 1984. "Fiscal Policies, Debt, and International Economic Interdependence." National Bureau of Economic Research *Working Paper* No. 1266 (January).

Guttenberg, Jack M. and Richard J. Herring. 1984. "Commercial Bank Lending to Developing Countries: From Overlending to Underlending to Structural Reform." *Brookings Discussion Papers in International Economics*, No. 16 Washington, D.C.: The Brookings Institution (June).

Herring, Richard J. and Richard C. Marston. 1976. "Forward Market and Interest Rates in the Currency and National Money Markets," in *Eurocurrencies and the International Monetary System*, edited by Carl H. Stern, John H. Makin and Dennis E. Logue. Washington, D.C.: American Enterprise Institute for Public Policy Research.

Isard, Peter. 1983. "An Accounting Framework and Some Issues for Modeling How Exchange Rates Respond to the News," in *Exchange Rates and International Macroeconomics*, edited by Jacob A. Frenkel. Chicago and London: University of Chicago Press.

Kormendi, Roger C. 1983. "Government Debt, Government Spending and Private Sector Behavior." *American Economic Review* 73, no. 5 (December 1983): 994–1010.

Krugman, Paul R. 1983. "International Aspects of U.S. Monetary and Fiscal Policy," in *The Federal Reserve Bank of Boston Conference Series*, No. 27 (October): 112–33.

Kubarych, Roger M. 1984. "Financing the U.S. Current Account Deficit," Federal Reserve Board of New York *Quarterly Review* 9, no. 2 (Summer): 24–31.

Logue, Dennis E., Michael A. Salant, and Richard J. Sweeney. 1976. "International Integration of Financial Markets: Survey Synthesis, and Results," in *Eurocurrencies and the International Monetary System*, edited by Carl H. Stern, John H. Makin, and Dennis E. Logue. Washington, D.C.: American Enterprise Institute for Public Policy Research.

Laney, Leroy O. 1984. "The Strong Dollar, The Current Account, and Federal Deficits: Cause and Effect." Federal Reserve Board of Dallas *Economic Review* (January): 1–14.

Laney, Leroy O., and Thomas D. Willett. 1982. "The International Liquidity Explosion and Global Monetary Expansion: 1970–72." *Journal of International Money and Finance* (August): 141–52.

Makin, John H. 1983. "Real Interest, Money Surprises, Anticipated Inflation and Fiscal Deficits." *The Review of Economics and Statistics* 65, no. 3 (August): 374–84.

McClure, J. Harold, Jr., and Thomas D. Willett. 1983. "Understanding the Supply Siders," in *Reaganomics: A Mid-Term Report*, edited by William Craig

Stubblebine and Thomas D. Willet. San Francisco: Institute for Contemporary Studies.

McKinnon, Ronald I. 1976. "Floating Exchange Rates 1973–74: The Emperor's New Clothes," in *Institutional Arrangements and the Inflation Problem*, edited by Karl Brunner and Allen H. Meltzer. Carnegie–Rochester Conference Series on Public Policy, vol. 3, pp. 79–114.

_____. 1984. "The J-Curve, Stabilizing Speculation, and Capital Constraints on Foreign Exchange Dealers," in *Floating Exchange Rates and the State of World Payments*, edited by David Bigman and Teizo Taya. Cambridge, Mass.: Ballinger Publishing Co.

_____. 1979. *Money in International Exchange: The Convertible Currency System*. New York: Oxford University Press.

Obstfeld, Maurice. 1982. "Can We Sterilize: Theory and Evidence." *American Economic Review* 72, no. 2 (May 1982): 45–50.

Plosser, Charles I. 1982. "Government Financing Decision and Asset Returns." *Journal of Monetary Economics* 9, no. 3 (May): 325–52.

Reid, Bradford G. 1984. "The Ricardian Equivalence Hypothesis: Additional Empirical Tests." University of Alberta. (Unpublished manuscript.)

Stevens, Guy V.G., *et al.* 1984. *The U.S. Economy in an Interdependent World: A Multi-Country Model*. Washington, D.C.: Board of Governors of the Federal Reserve System.

von Furstenberg, George M. 1983. "Domestic Determinants of the Current Account Balance of the United States," *Quarterly Journal of Economics* 98, no. 3 (August): 401–25.

Willett, Thomas D. 1976. "A Comment on Oil Prices, Terms of Trade and Transfers: Static and Dynamic Aspects," in *The International Monetary System and the Developing Countries*, edited by Danny M. Leipziger. Washington, D.C.: Agency for International Development.

_____, *Floating Exchange Rates and International Monetary Reform*. 1977. Washington, D.C.: American Enterprise Institute for Public Policy Research.

INDEX

ABOUT THE CONTRIBUTORS

Marc Bremer is a Ph.D. candidate at The Claremont Graduate School. A graduate of California State University, Los Angeles, and the London School of Economics, he is specializing in international and financial analysis.

Aïda Der Hovanessian is an international economist with Chemical Bank. She recently received her Ph.D. in finance from The Claremont Graduate School.

Dean DeRosa is an international economist with the U.S. Treasury. A specialist in quantitative analysis, he received his Ph.D. from the University of Oregon.

Susan Feigenbaum is Assistant Professor of Economics at Claremont McKenna College. Holder of a Ph.D. from the University of Wisconsin, she specializes in the areas of applied quantitative analysis and public economics. Her work has appeared in journals such as *Economic Inquiry, Public Finance Quarterly*, and *National Tax Journal*.

Paul Flacco is Assistant Professor of Economics at The American University. A former faculty member at Claremont McKenna College, he received his Ph.D. from the University of Oregon. A specialist on the effects of uncertainty, he has recently published articles in *Contemporary Policy Issues* and the *Southern Economic Journal*.

Joachim Harnack is an economist with the International Monetary Fund. A recent recipient of the Ph.D. from The Claremont Graduate School, he is cur-

291

rently conducting research on the effects of pegged versus flexible exchange rates in macroeconomic stability.

Waseem Khan is an international economist with First Interstate Bank. Author of several articles on the monetary approach to exchange rates and international financial developments, he received his Ph.D. from The Claremont Graduate School.

J. Harold McClure is Assistant Professor of Economics at The Claremont Graduate School. A recent recipient of the Ph.D. from Vanderbilt University, he has been conducting research in the areas of supply side economics, international finance, and exchange rate behavior.

Charles Pigott is a senior economist with the international section of the research department of the Federal Reserve Bank of San Francisco. A former member of the international research staff at the U.S. Treasury, he received his Ph.D. from M.I.T. He has published a number of articles on various aspects of international monetary economics.

Christopher Radcliffe is an economist with the General Dynamics Corporation and a Ph.D. candidate at The Claremont Graduate School. A specialist in international and defense issues, he has had papers appear in the *American Economic Review* and *Southern Economic Journal.*

John Rutledge is President of the Claremont Economics Institute. A former member of the faculties at Tulane University and Claremont McKenna College, and the office of international monetary research at the U.S. Treasury, he received his Ph.D. from the University of Virginia. He is currently specializing in economic forecasting.

Peter A. Sharp is Assistant Professor of Finance at California State University, Sacramento. A recent recipient of the Ph.D. from The Claremont Graduate School, he is conducting research on domestic and international financial issues.

Gary Smeal is an international economist at Chemical Bank. A former member of the international research staff at the U.S. Treasury, he did his graduate work at the University of Pennsylvania and specializes in international quantitative analysis.

Jerry G. Thursby is Associate Professor of Economics at Ohio State University. A specialist in econometric analysis, he received his Ph.D. from the University of North Carolina. He has published in the *Journal of the American Statistical Association, Review of Economics* and *Statistics and International Economic Review.*

Marie Thursby is Associate Professor of Economics at Ohio State University. A former consultant to the office of international monetary research at the U.S. Treasury, she received her Ph.D. from the University of North Carolina. A specialist in international trade issues, her articles have appeared in such journals as *Contemporary Policy Issues, Journal of International Economics* and *Review of Economics and Statistics.*

Arthur D. Warga is Visiting Associate Professor of Finance at Columbia University. A former faculty member at The Claremont Graduate School, he received his Ph.D. from the University of Michigan. He is author of a number of papers in domestic and international finance.

ABOUT THE EDITORS

Sven W. Arndt is Resident Scholar in International Economics and Director of the International Trade Project at the American Enterprise Institute, and is currently Professor of Economics at the University of California, Santa Cruz. He has taught at several universities including Stanford University, UCLA, The Institute for Advanced Studies, Vienna, and the University of Mannheim, West Germany. He was formerly Director of the Office of Monetary Research at the U.S. Treasury Department. He is the editor of *The Political Economy of Austria* and his articles have appeared in the *American Economic Review, Econometrica, Journal of Political Economy* and *Kredit und Kapital.*

Richard J. Sweeney is Charles M. Stone Professor of Monetary Theory at Claremont McKenna College. He is also editor of the journal, *Economic Inquiry*, published by the Western Economics Association. He has his Ph.D. from Princeton and his B.A. from U.C.L.A. He has taught at U.C.L.A., Texas A&M, the University of Virginia, and the Tuck School of Business at Dartmouth College, and spent four years at the U.S. Treasury Department. His major fields are finance and monetary economics, with special emphasis on international issues in these areas. He works on both theoretical and empirical problems, as well as devoting considerable time to public policy questions. He is the author or editor of seven books, and has more than fifty published journal articles, chapters and special papers. He is currently finishing the book, *Wealth Effects and Monetary Theory* and is working on papers examining arbitrage pricing models, evaluating the burden of the debt, and improving ability to use forward exchange rates to forecast spot exchange rate movements.

Thomas D. Willett, an adjunct scholar of the American Enterprise Institute, is Director of The Claremont Center for Economic Policy Studies and Horton Professor of Economics at The Claremont Graduate School and Claremont McKenna College. He has written widely in the areas of economic policy, political economy, and international economics. A former Deputy Assistant Secretary of the Treasury for International Research and Planning, he has also taught at Cornell and Harvard Universities and served on the staff of the Council of Economic Advisers. He received his B.A. from the College of William and Mary, and Ph.D. from the University of Virginia.